# Hey! You're Reading in the Wrong Direction!

## This is the end of this graphic novel!

To properly enjoy this VIZ graphic novel, please turn it around and begin reading from right to left. Unlike English, Japanese is read right to left, so Japanese comics are read in reverse order from the way English comics are typically read.

This book has been printed in the original Japanese format in order to preserve the orientation of the original artwork. Have fun with it!

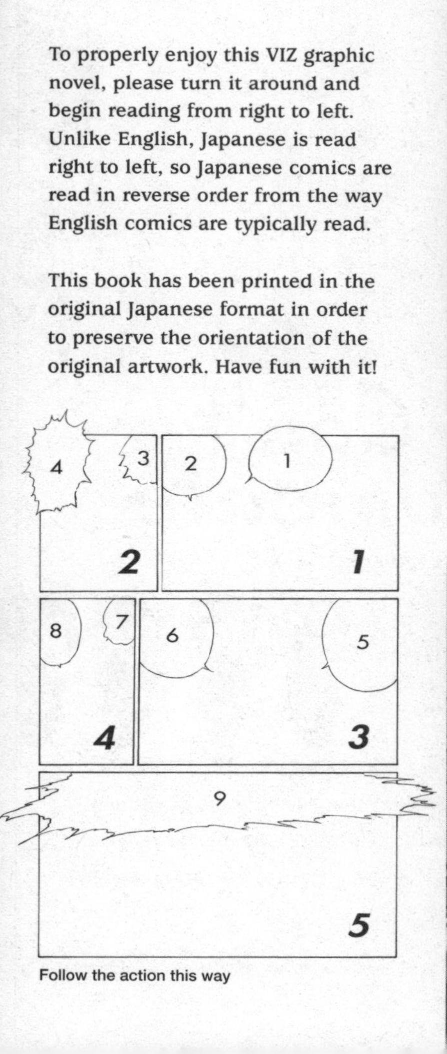
1
2
3
4
1
2
5
6
7
8
3
4
9
5

Follow the action this way

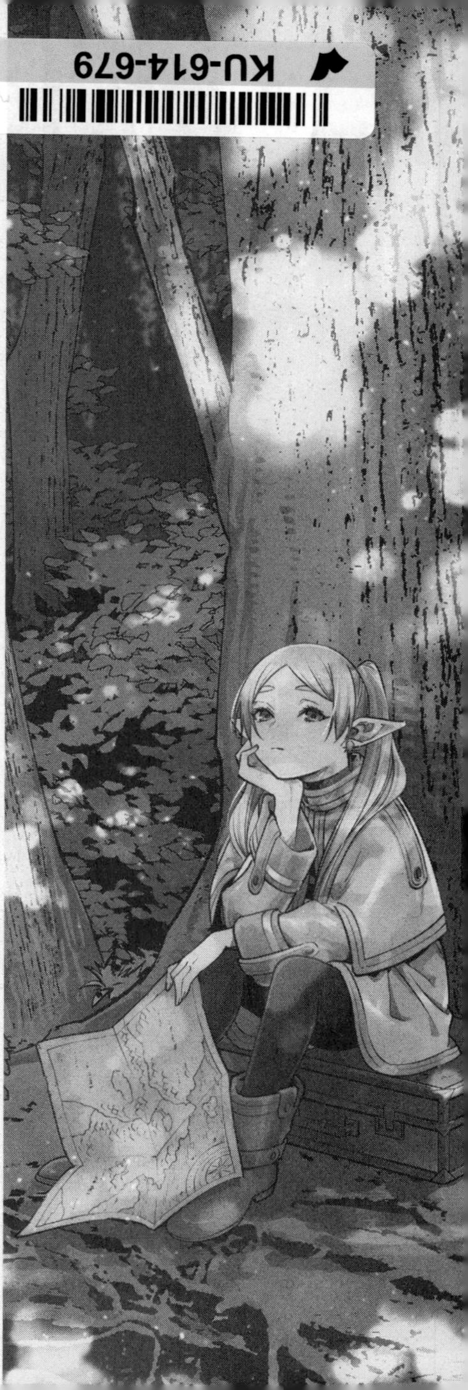

# Komi Can't Communicate

*Story & Art by Tomohito Oda*

## The journey to a hundred friends begins with a single conversation.

Socially anxious high school student Shoko Komi's greatest dream is to make some friends, but everyone at school mistakes her crippling social anxiety for cool reserve. With the whole student body keeping its distance and Komi unable to utter a single word, friendship might be forever beyond her reach.

# Frieren
## Beyond Journey's End

1

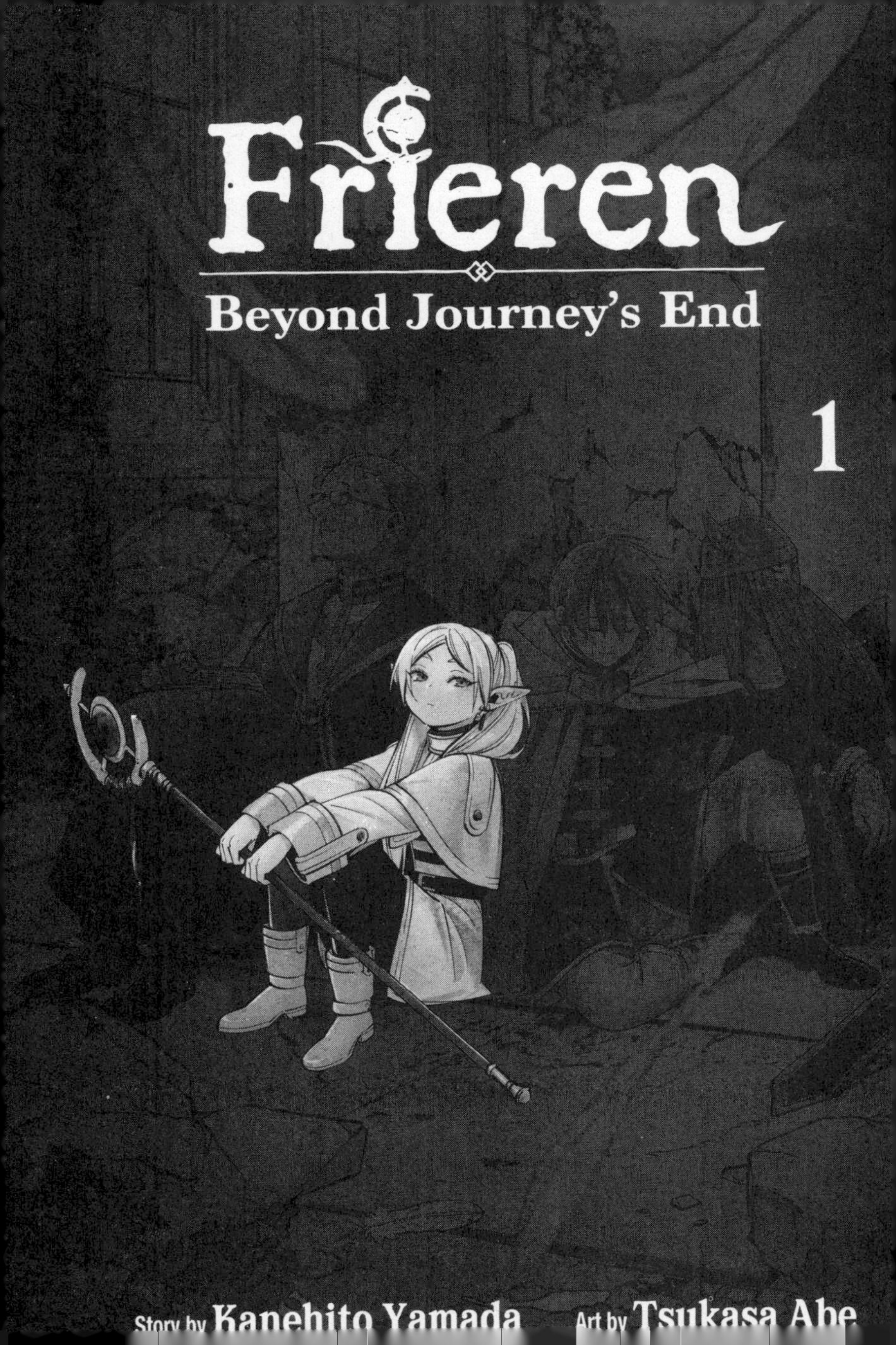

Story by Kanehito Yamada Art by Tsukasa Abe

# CONTENTS

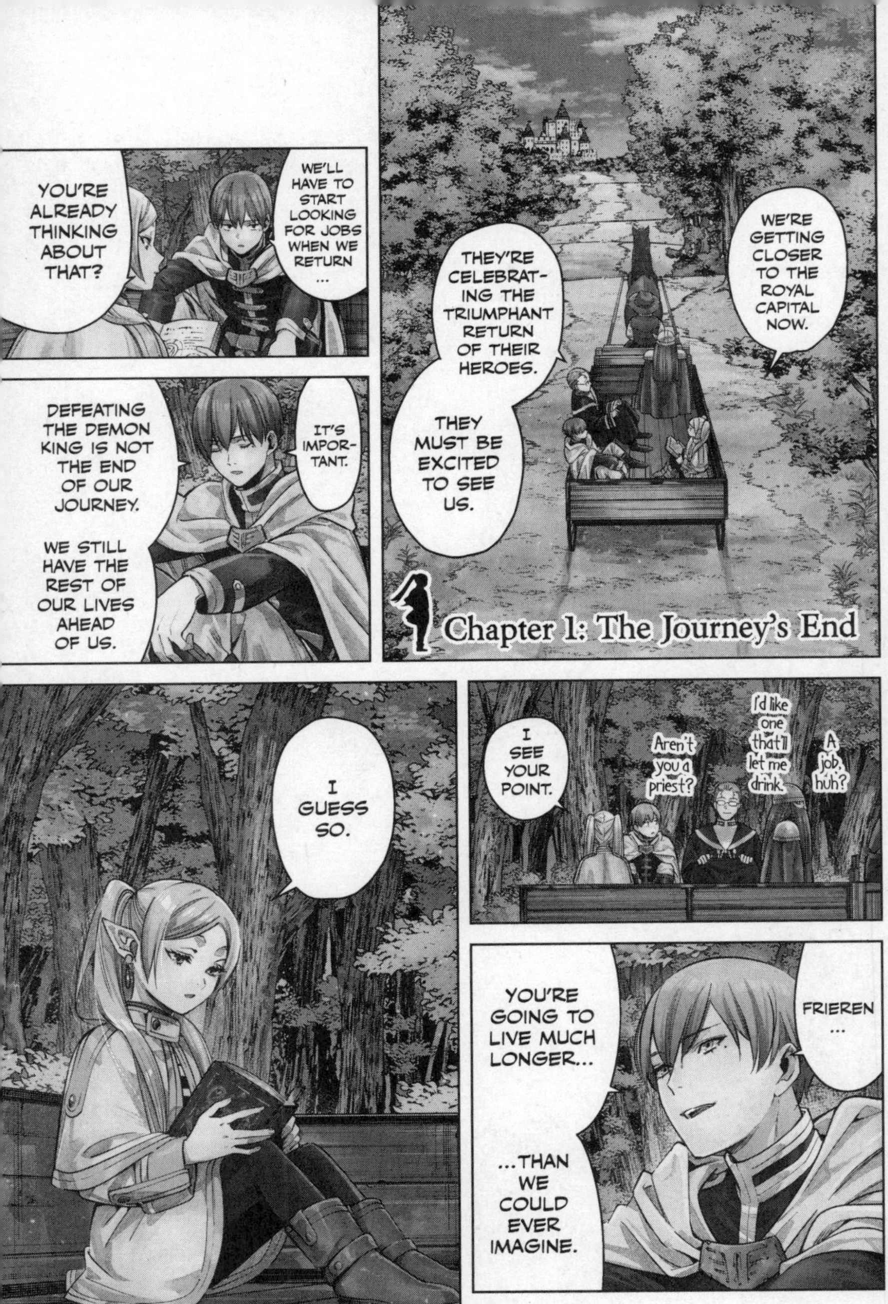
WE'RE GETTING CLOSER TO THE ROYAL CAPITAL NOW.
THEY'RE CELEBRATING THE TRIUMPHANT RETURN OF THEIR HEROES.
THEY MUST BE EXCITED TO SEE US.
Chapter 1: The Journey's End
WE'LL HAVE TO START LOOKING FOR JOBS WHEN WE RETURN...
YOU'RE ALREADY THINKING ABOUT THAT?
IT'S IMPORTANT.
DEFEATING THE DEMON KING IS NOT THE END OF OUR JOURNEY.
WE STILL HAVE THE REST OF OUR LIVES AHEAD OF US.
A job, huh?
I'd like one that'll let me drink.
Aren't you a priest?
I SEE YOUR POINT.
FRIEREN...
YOU'RE GOING TO LIVE MUCH LONGER...
...THAN WE COULD EVER IMAGINE.
I GUESS SO.

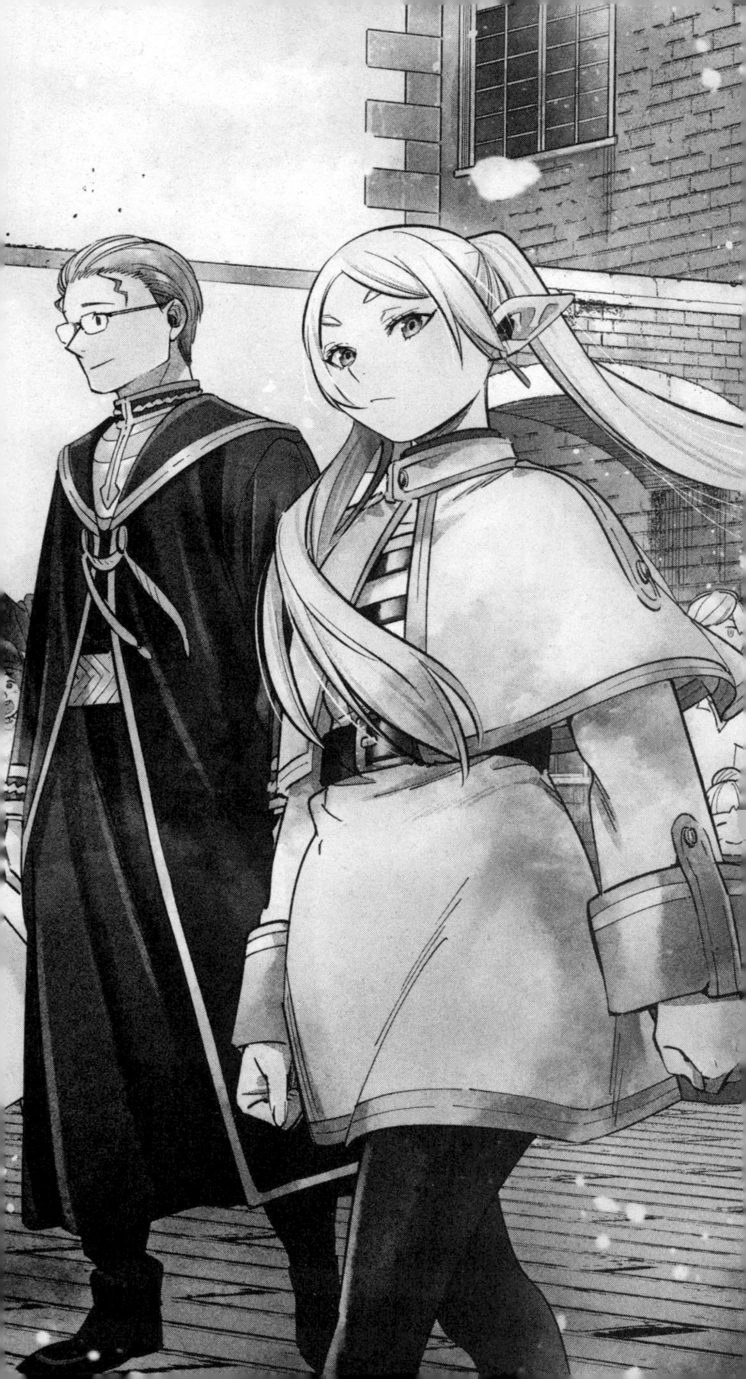

# Chapter 1: The Journey's End

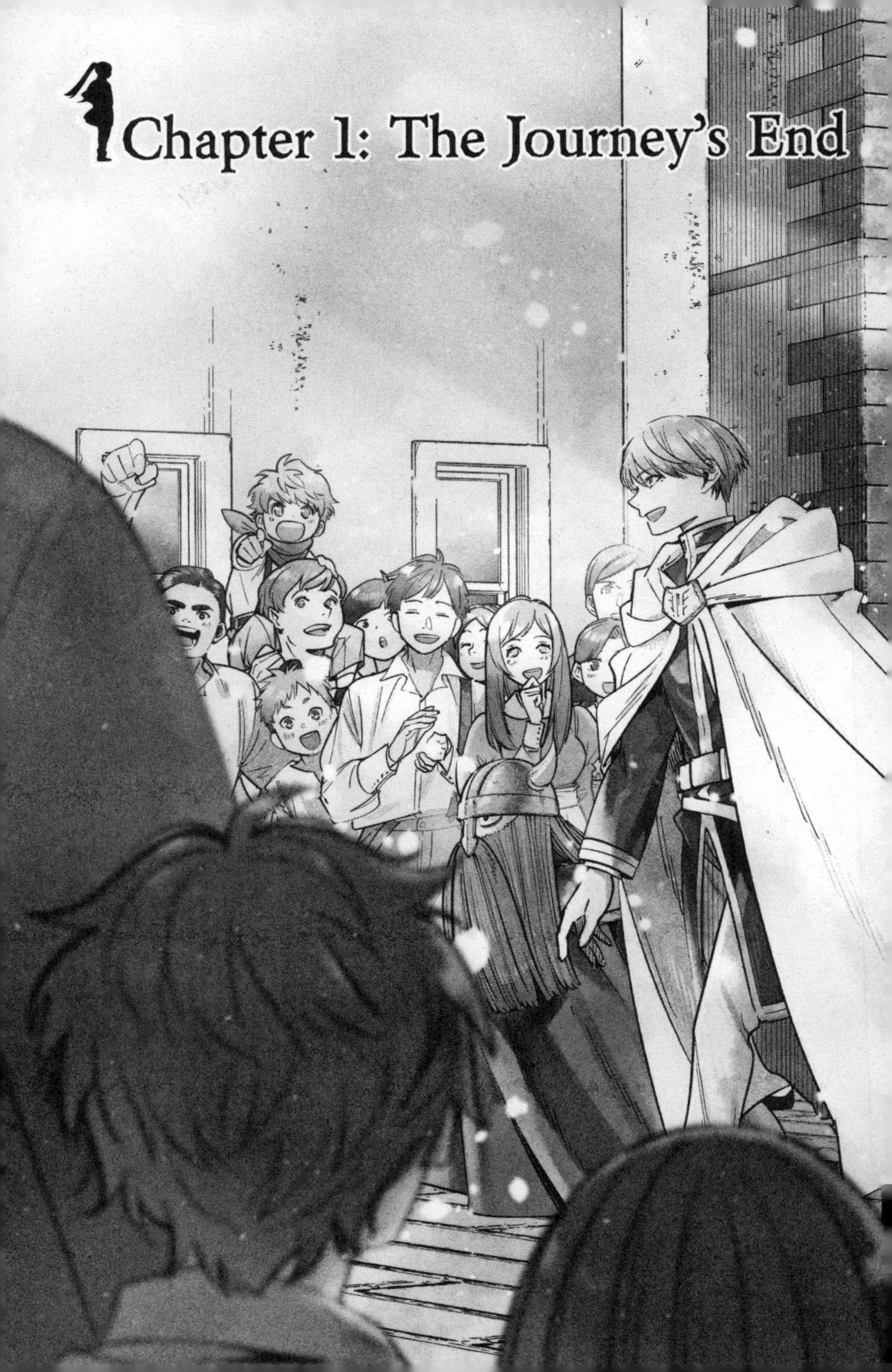

Frieren

Beyond Journey's End

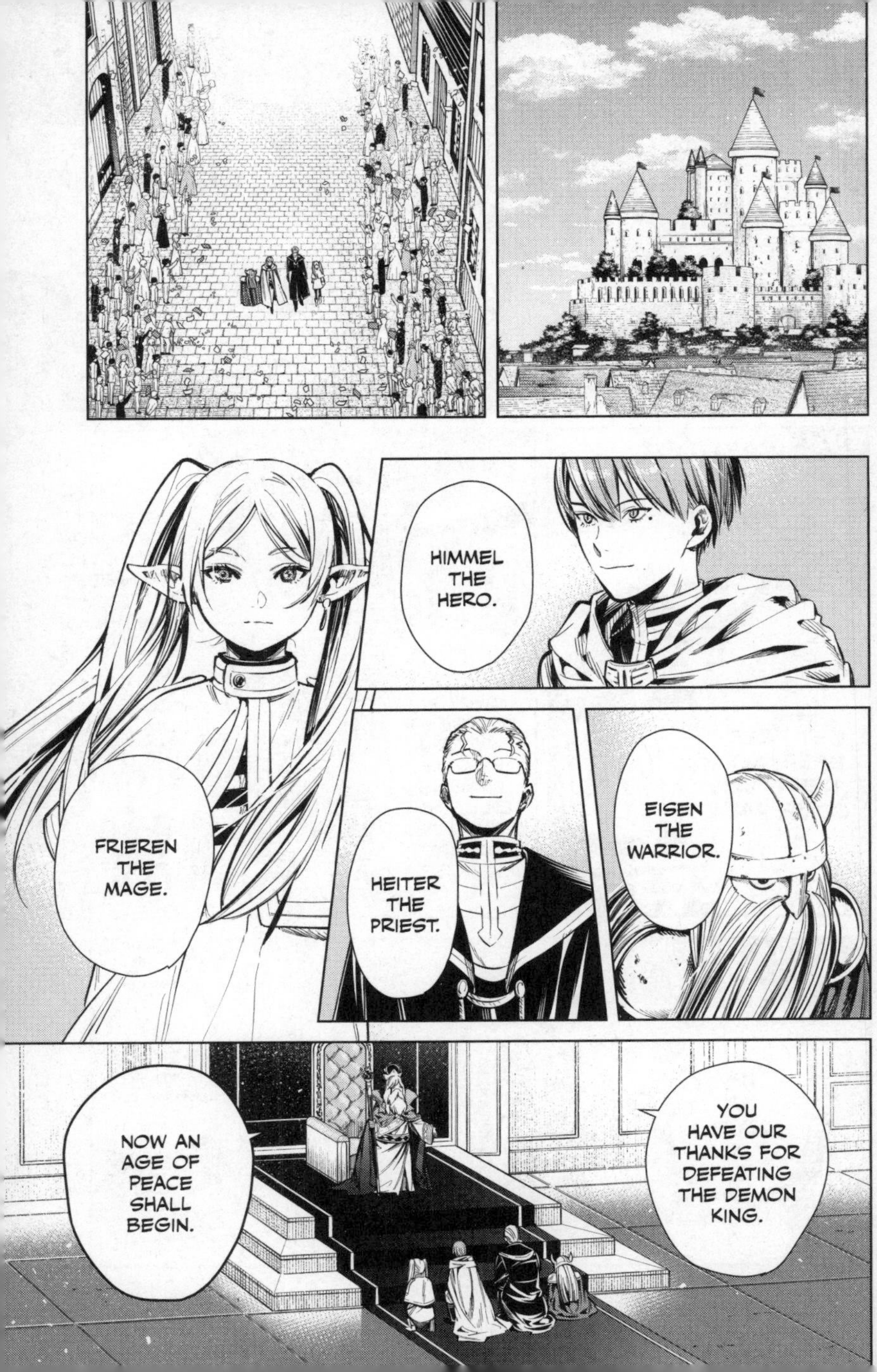
HIMMEL THE HERO.
EISEN THE WARRIOR.
HEITER THE PRIEST.
FRIEREN THE MAGE.
YOU HAVE OUR THANKS FOR DEFEATING THE DEMON KING.
NOW AN AGE OF PEACE SHALL BEGIN.

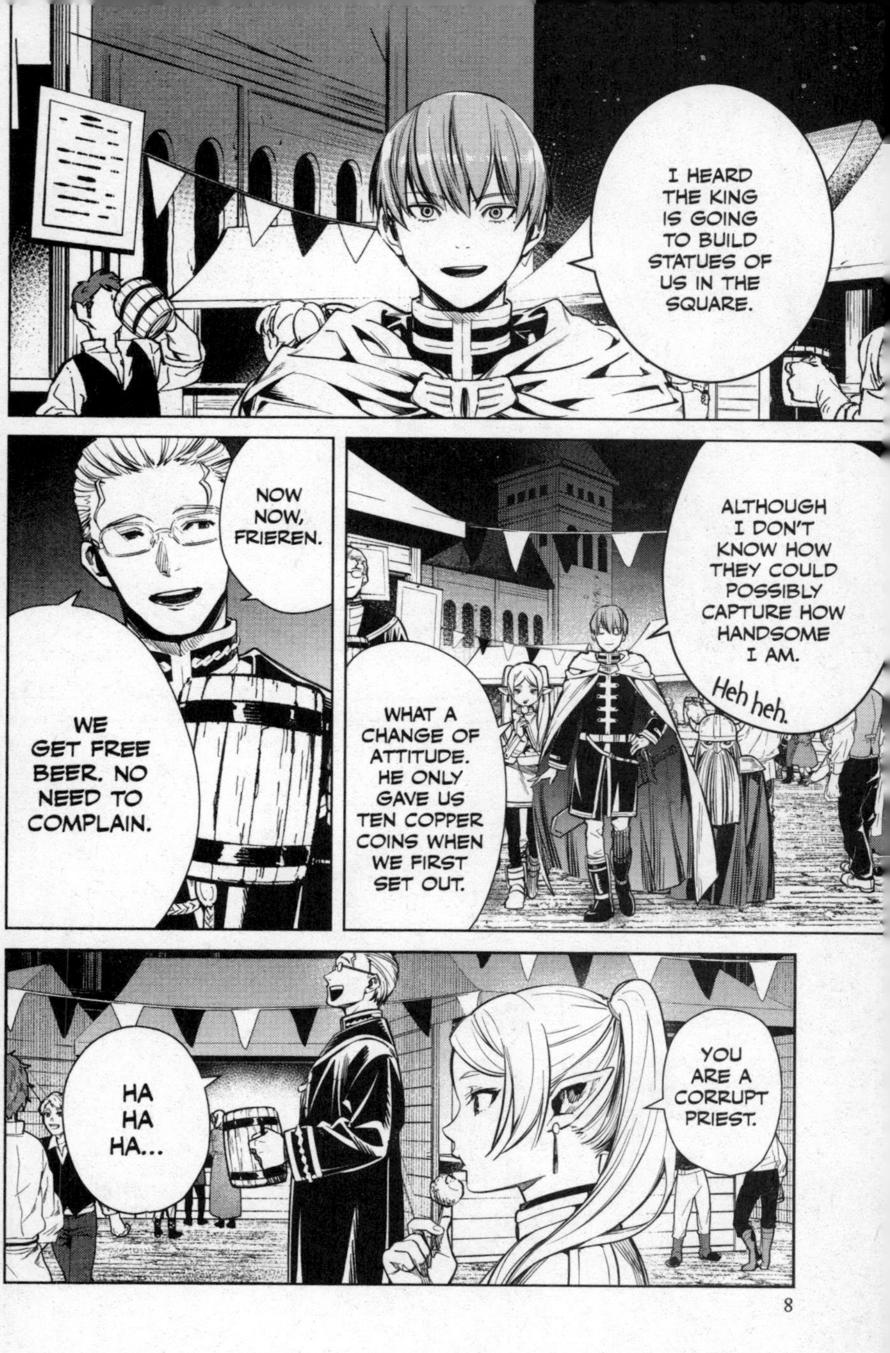
I HEARD THE KING IS GOING TO BUILD STATUES OF US IN THE SQUARE.
ALTHOUGH I DON'T KNOW HOW THEY COULD POSSIBLY CAPTURE HOW HANDSOME I AM.
Heh heh.
WHAT A CHANGE OF ATTITUDE. HE ONLY GAVE US TEN COPPER COINS WHEN WE FIRST SET OUT.
NOW NOW, FRIEREN.
WE GET FREE BEER. NO NEED TO COMPLAIN.
YOU ARE A CORRUPT PRIEST.
HA HA HA...

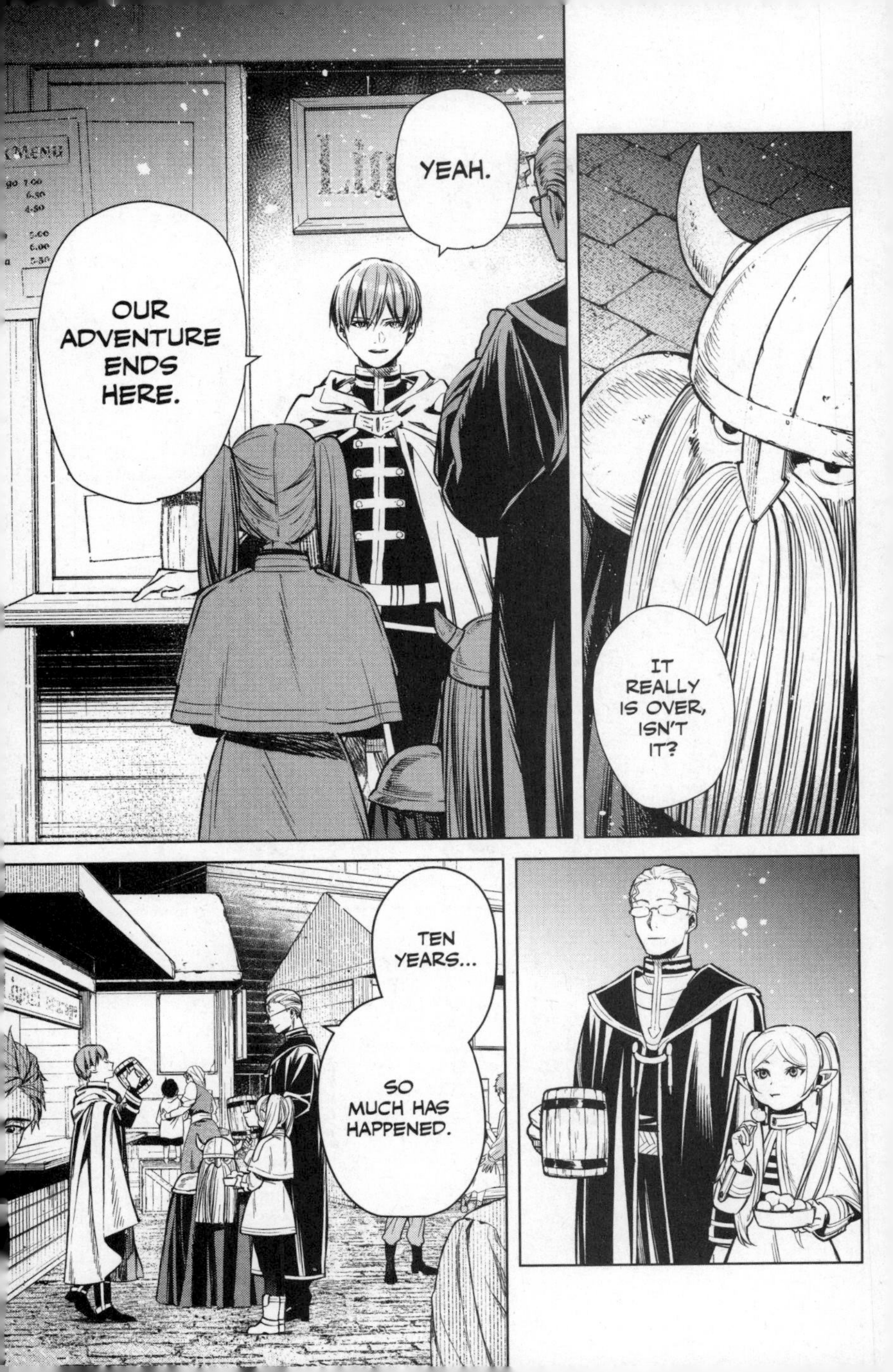
IT REALLY IS OVER, ISN'T IT?
YEAH.
OUR ADVENTURE ENDS HERE.
TEN YEARS...
SO MUCH HAS HAPPENED.

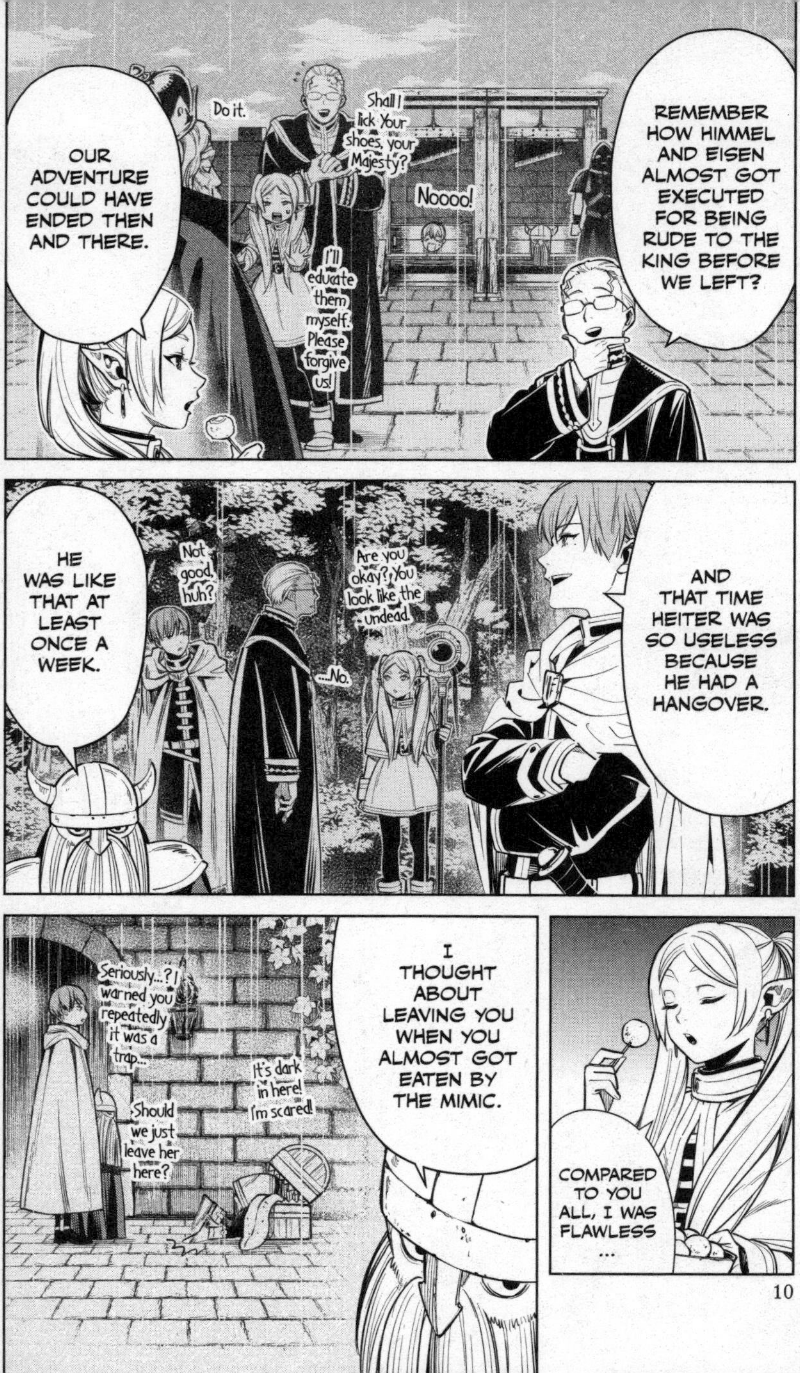
REMEMBER HOW HIMMEL AND EISEN ALMOST GOT EXECUTED FOR BEING RUDE TO THE KING BEFORE WE LEFT?
Shall I lick Your shoes, your Majesty?
Do it.
Noooo!
I'll educate them myself. Please forgive us!
OUR ADVENTURE COULD HAVE ENDED THEN AND THERE.
AND THAT TIME HEITER WAS SO USELESS BECAUSE HE HAD A HANGOVER.
Are you okay? You look like the undead.
Not good, huh?
...No.
HE WAS LIKE THAT AT LEAST ONCE A WEEK.
COMPARED TO YOU ALL, I WAS FLAWLESS ...
I THOUGHT ABOUT LEAVING YOU WHEN YOU ALMOST GOT EATEN BY THE MIMIC.
It's dark in here! I'm scared!
Seriously...?! I warned you repeatedly it was a trap...
Should we just leave her here?

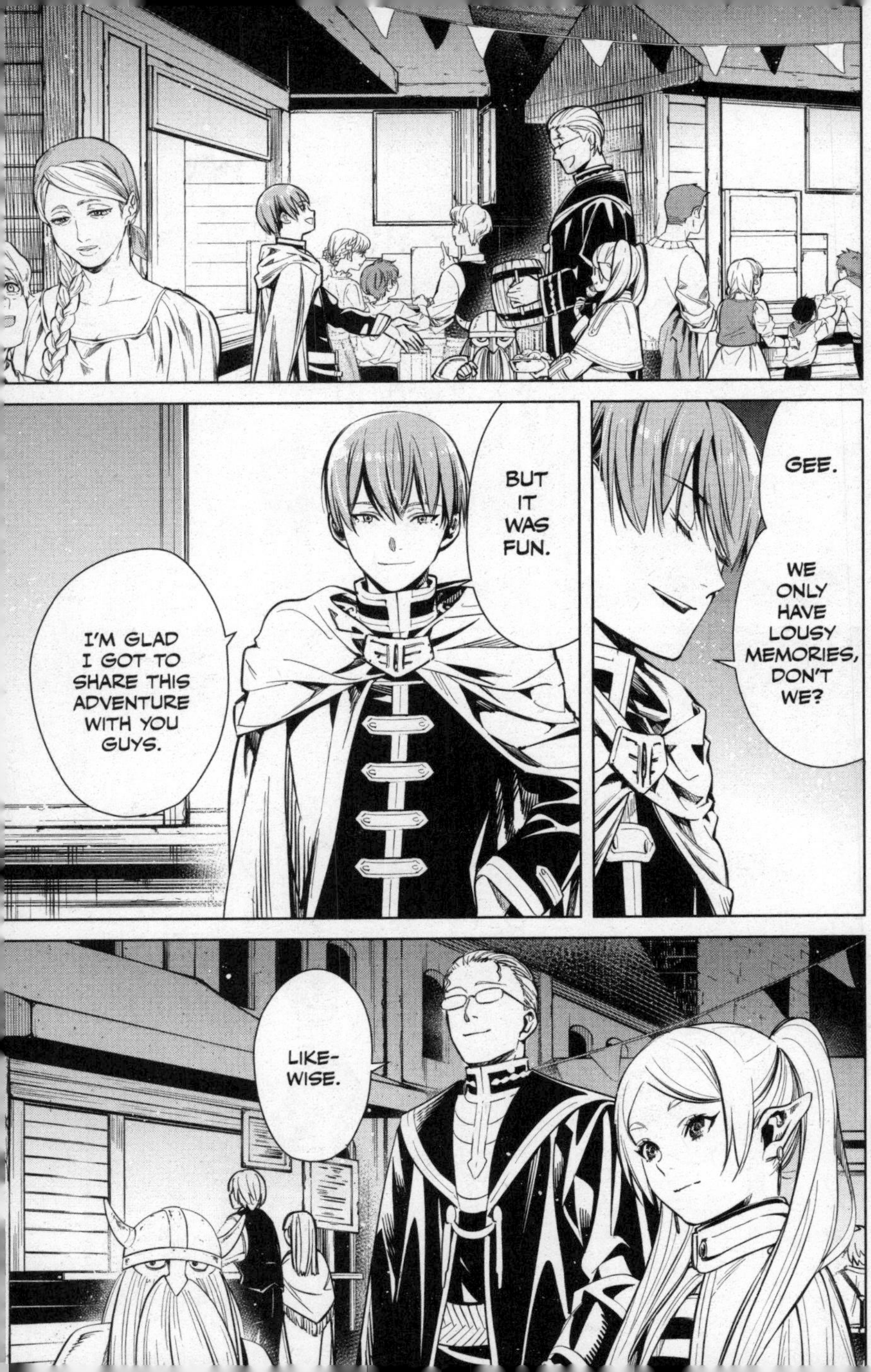
GEE.
WE ONLY HAVE LOUSY MEMORIES, DON'T WE?
BUT IT WAS FUN.
I'M GLAD I GOT TO SHARE THIS ADVENTURE WITH YOU GUYS.
LIKE-WISE.

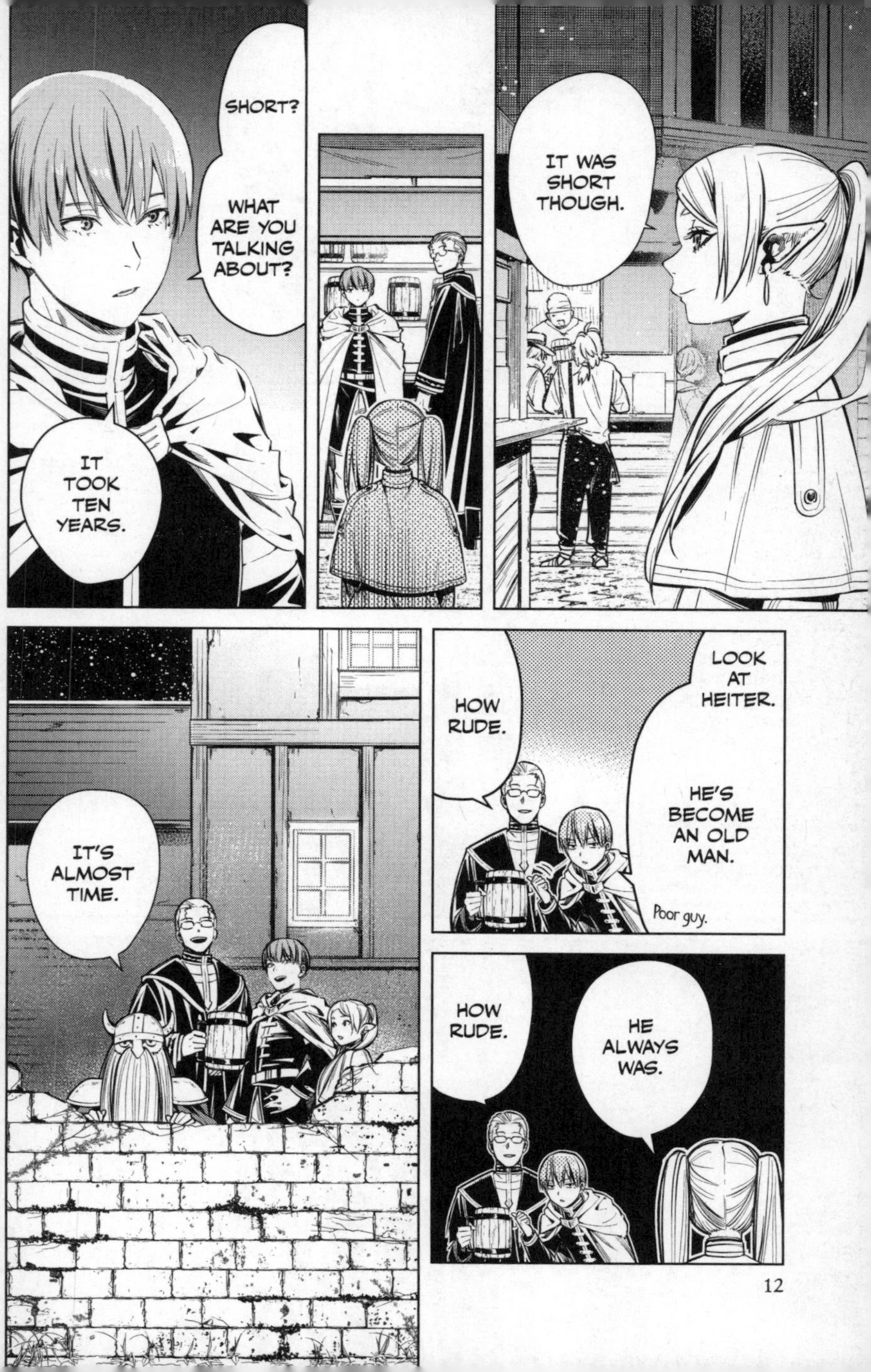
IT WAS SHORT THOUGH.
SHORT?
WHAT ARE YOU TALKING ABOUT?
IT TOOK TEN YEARS.
LOOK AT HEITER.
HE'S BECOME AN OLD MAN.
Poor guy.
HOW RUDE.
HE ALWAYS WAS.
HOW RUDE.
IT'S ALMOST TIME.

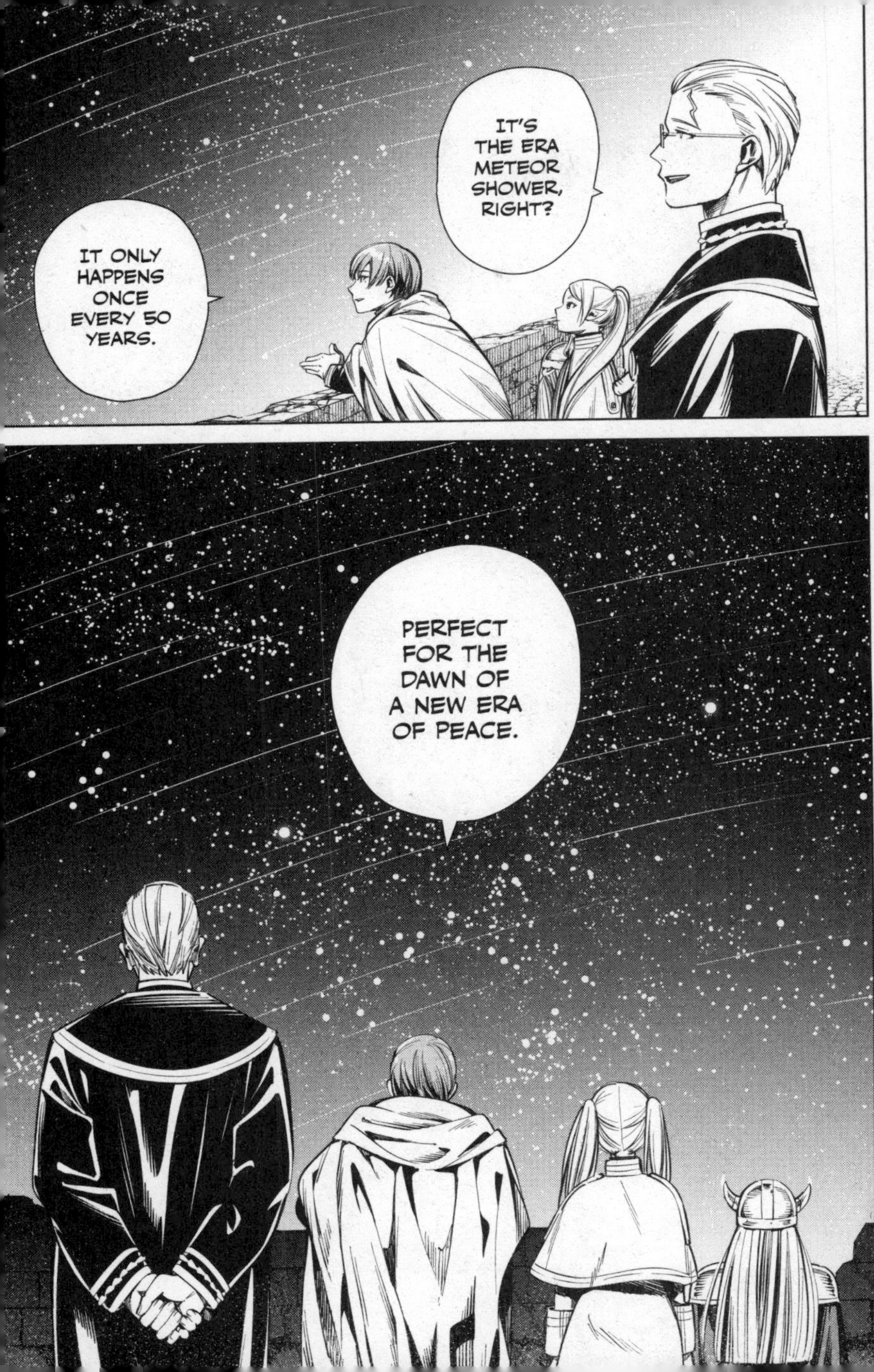
IT'S THE ERA METEOR SHOWER, RIGHT?
IT ONLY HAPPENS ONCE EVERY 50 YEARS.
PERFECT FOR THE DAWN OF A NEW ERA OF PEACE.

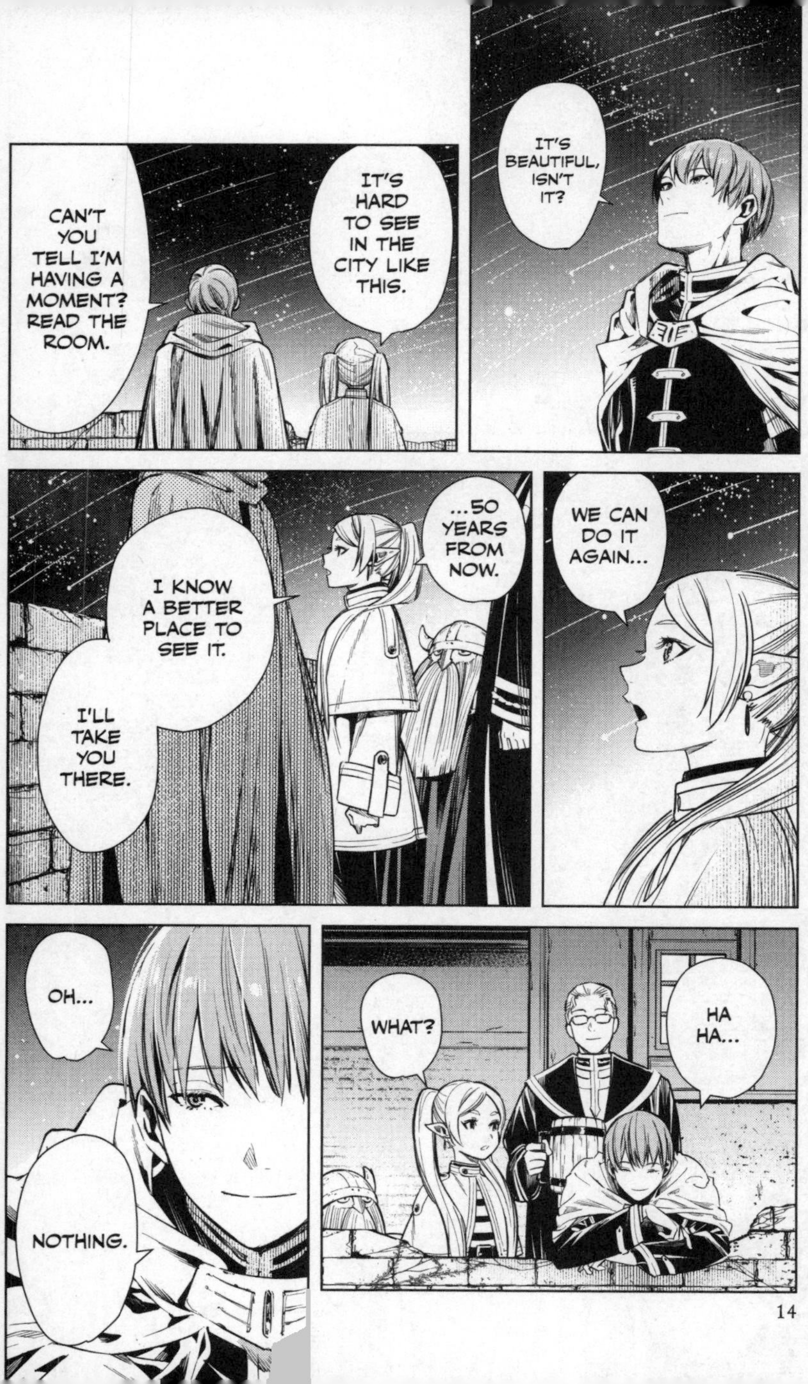
IT'S BEAUTIFUL, ISN'T IT?
IT'S HARD TO SEE IN THE CITY LIKE THIS.
CAN'T YOU TELL I'M HAVING A MOMENT? READ THE ROOM.
WE CAN DO IT AGAIN...
...50 YEARS FROM NOW.
I KNOW A BETTER PLACE TO SEE IT.
I'LL TAKE YOU THERE.
HA HA...
WHAT?
OH...
NOTHING.

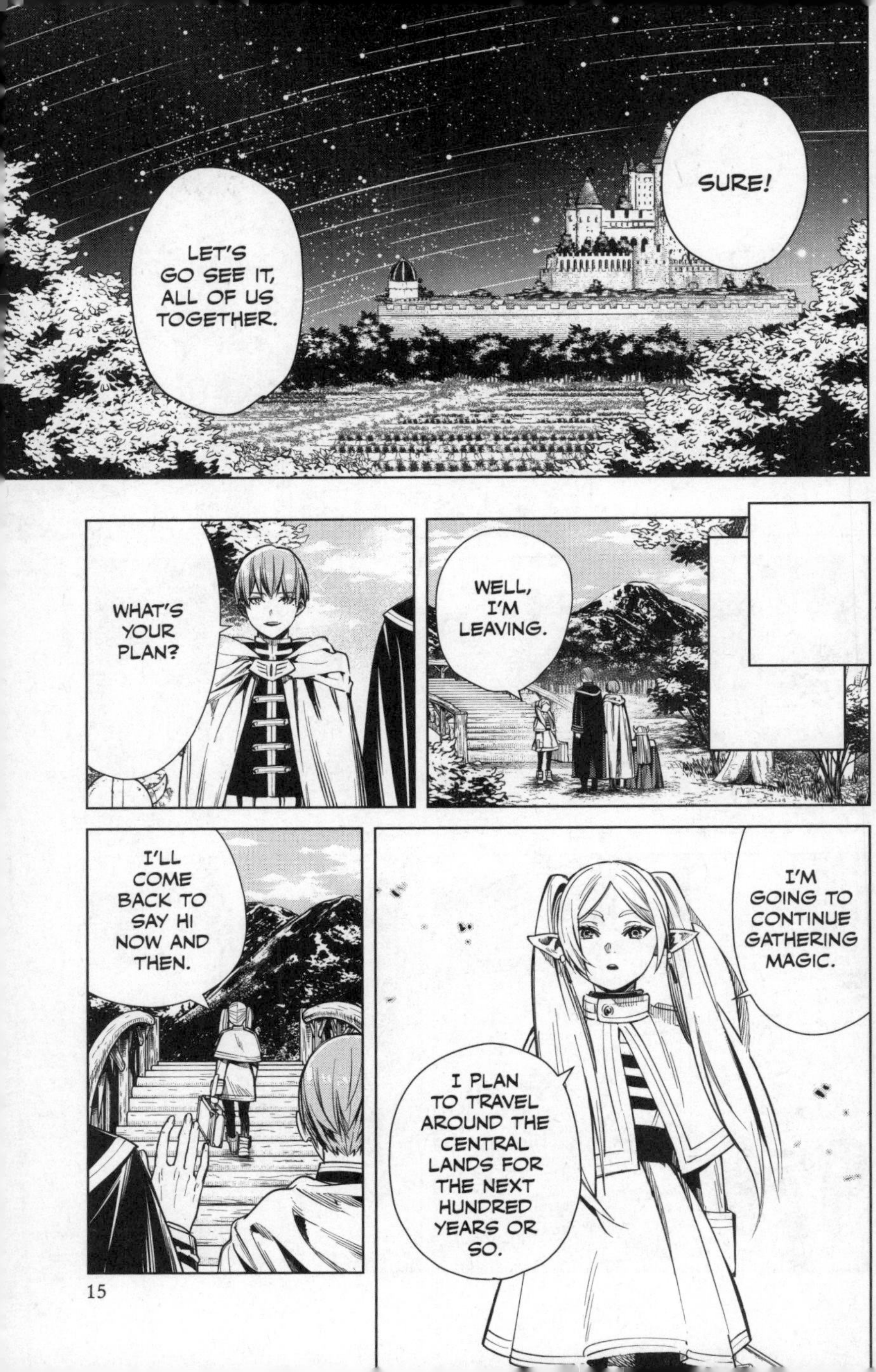
SURE!
LET'S GO SEE IT, ALL OF US TOGETHER.
WELL, I'M LEAVING.
WHAT'S YOUR PLAN?
I'M GOING TO CONTINUE GATHERING MAGIC.
I PLAN TO TRAVEL AROUND THE CENTRAL LANDS FOR THE NEXT HUNDRED YEARS OR SO.
I'LL COME BACK TO SAY HI NOW AND THEN.

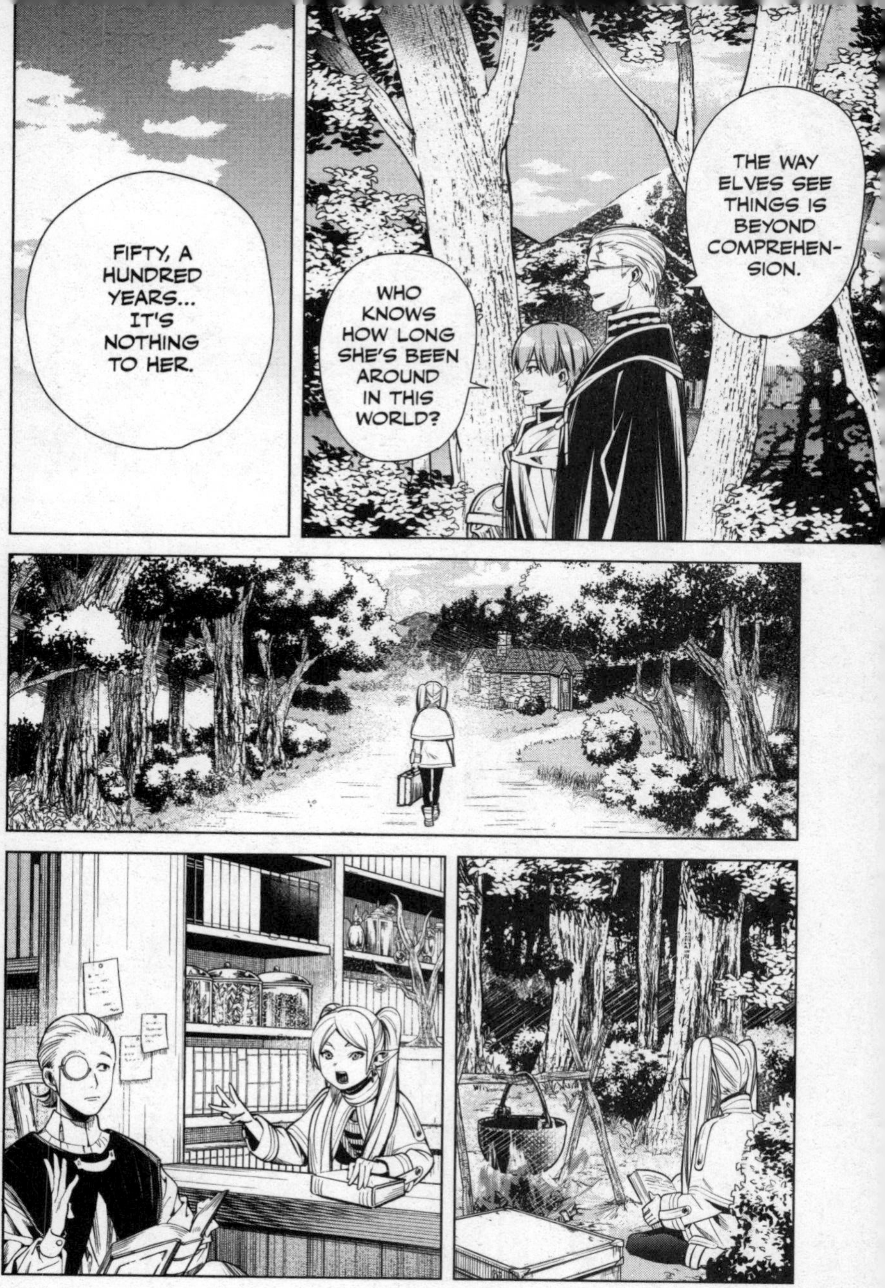
THE WAY ELVES SEE THINGS IS BEYOND COMPREHENSION.
WHO KNOWS HOW LONG SHE'S BEEN AROUND IN THIS WORLD?
FIFTY, A HUNDRED YEARS... IT'S NOTHING TO HER.

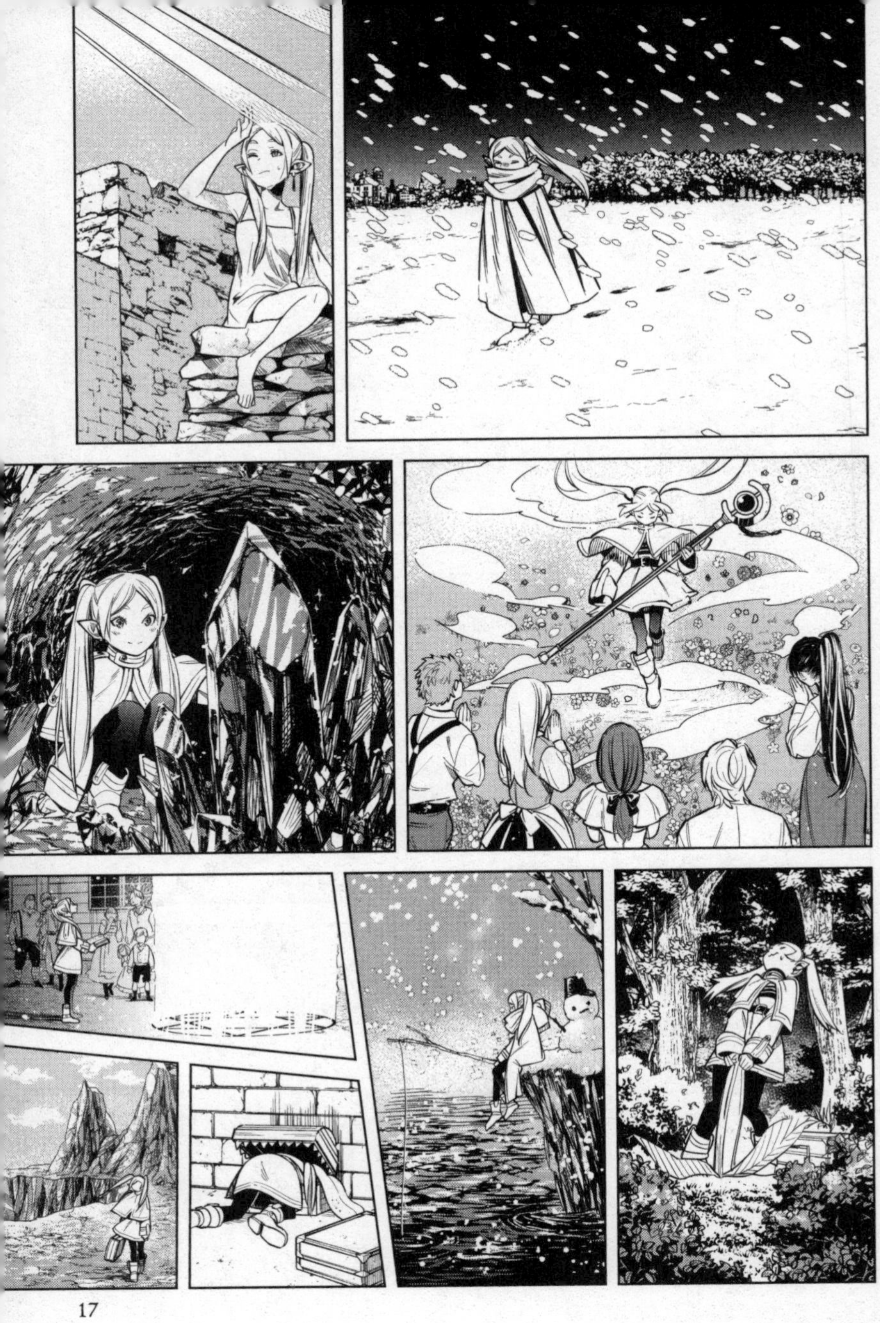

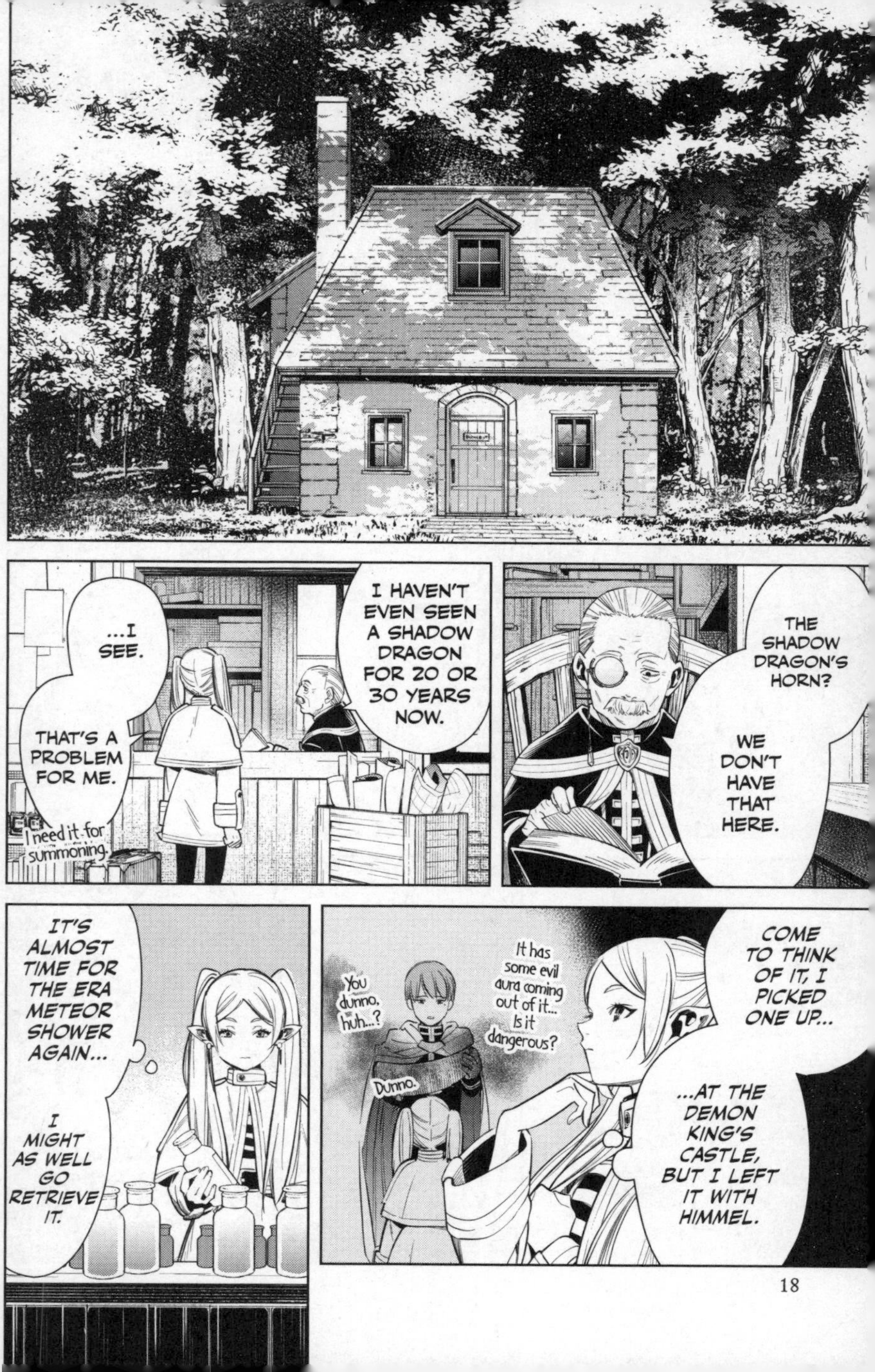
THE SHADOW DRAGON'S HORN?
WE DON'T HAVE THAT HERE.
I HAVEN'T EVEN SEEN A SHADOW DRAGON FOR 20 OR 30 YEARS NOW.
...I SEE.
THAT'S A PROBLEM FOR ME.
I need it for summoning.
COME TO THINK OF IT, I PICKED ONE UP...
...AT THE DEMON KING'S CASTLE, BUT I LEFT IT WITH HIMMEL.
It has some evil aura coming out of it... Is it dangerous?
You dunno, huh...?
Dunno.
IT'S ALMOST TIME FOR THE ERA METEOR SHOWER AGAIN...
I MIGHT AS WELL GO RETRIEVE IT.

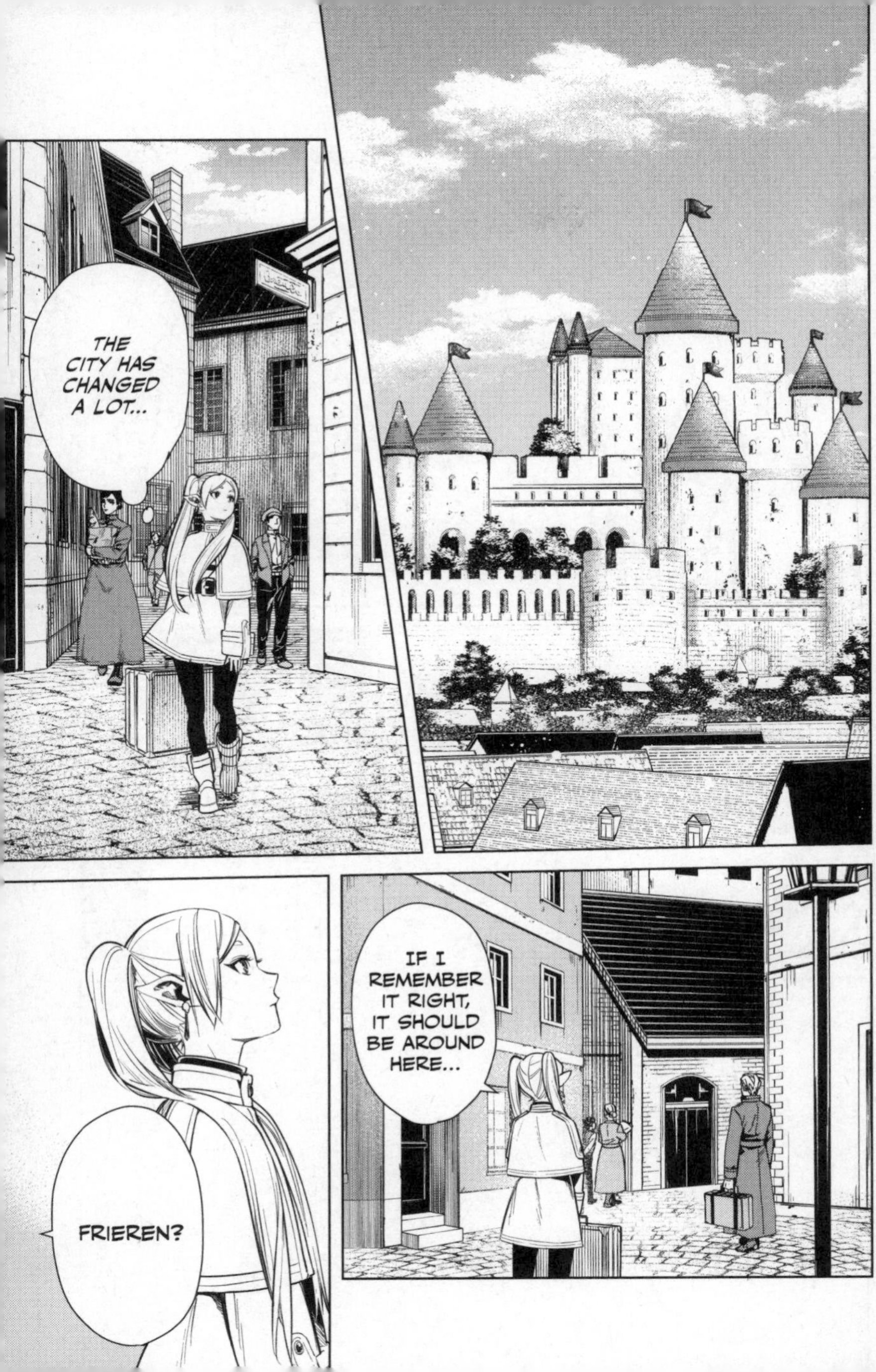
THE CITY HAS CHANGED A LOT...
IF I REMEMBER IT RIGHT, IT SHOULD BE AROUND HERE...
FRIEREN?

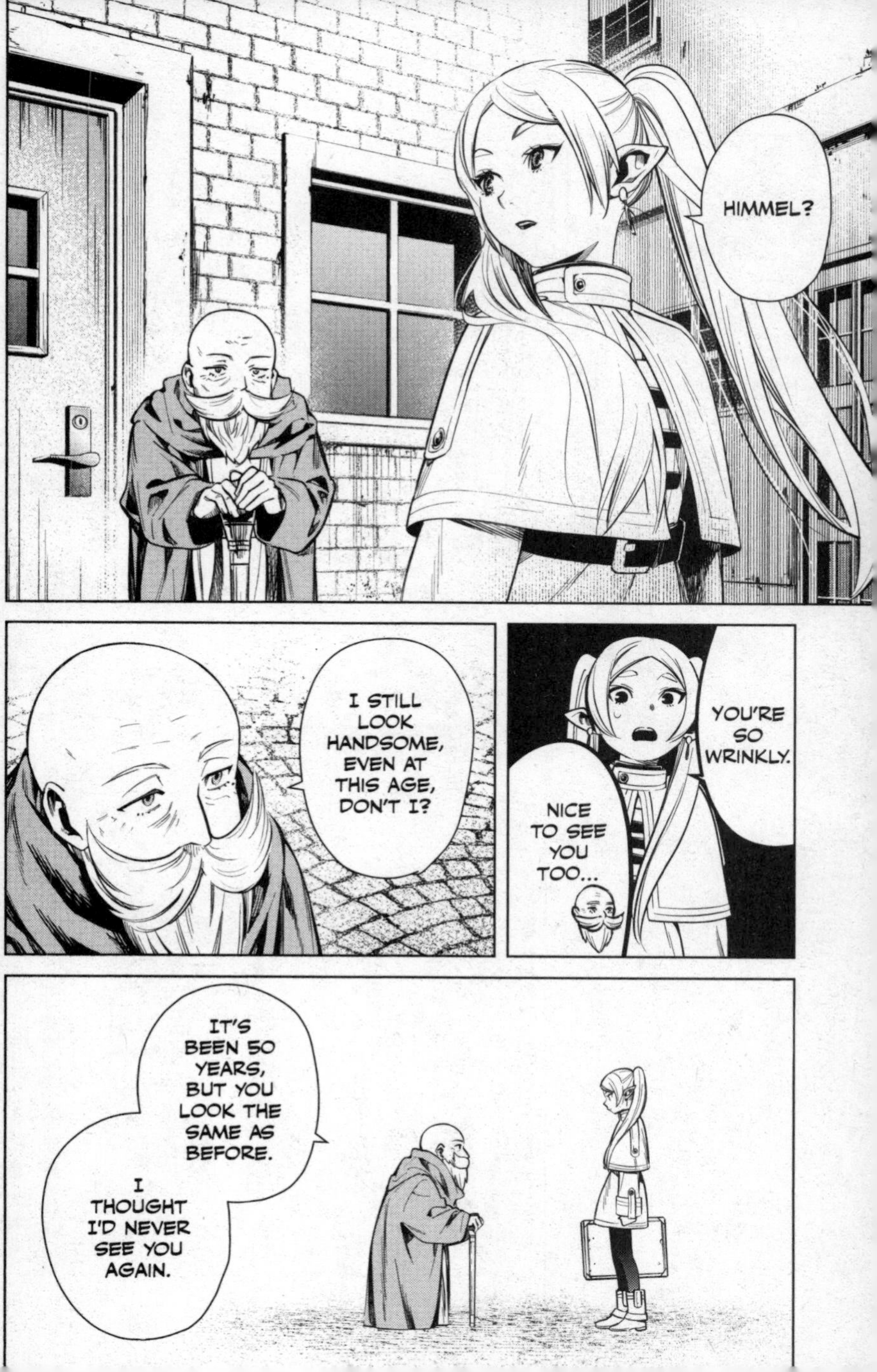
HIMMEL?
YOU'RE SO WRINKLY.
NICE TO SEE YOU TOO...
I STILL LOOK HANDSOME, EVEN AT THIS AGE, DON'T I?
IT'S BEEN 50 YEARS, BUT YOU LOOK THE SAME AS BEFORE.
I THOUGHT I'D NEVER SEE YOU AGAIN.

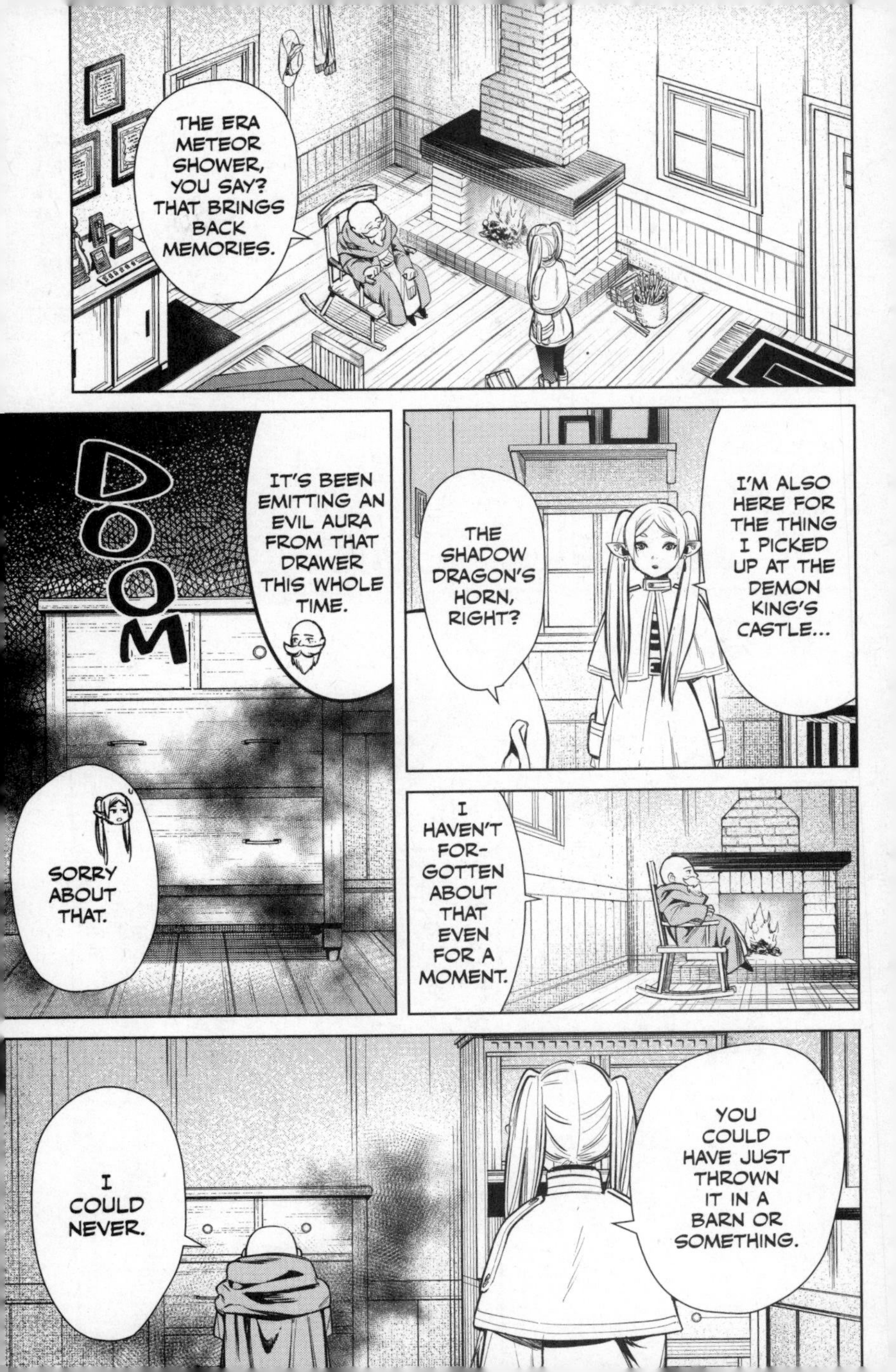
THE ERA METEOR SHOWER, YOU SAY? THAT BRINGS BACK MEMORIES.
I'M ALSO HERE FOR THE THING I PICKED UP AT THE DEMON KING'S CASTLE...
THE SHADOW DRAGON'S HORN, RIGHT?
I HAVEN'T FOR-GOTTEN ABOUT THAT EVEN FOR A MOMENT.
IT'S BEEN EMITTING AN EVIL AURA FROM THAT DRAWER THIS WHOLE TIME.
DOOM
SORRY ABOUT THAT.
YOU COULD HAVE JUST THROWN IT IN A BARN OR SOMETHING.
I COULD NEVER.

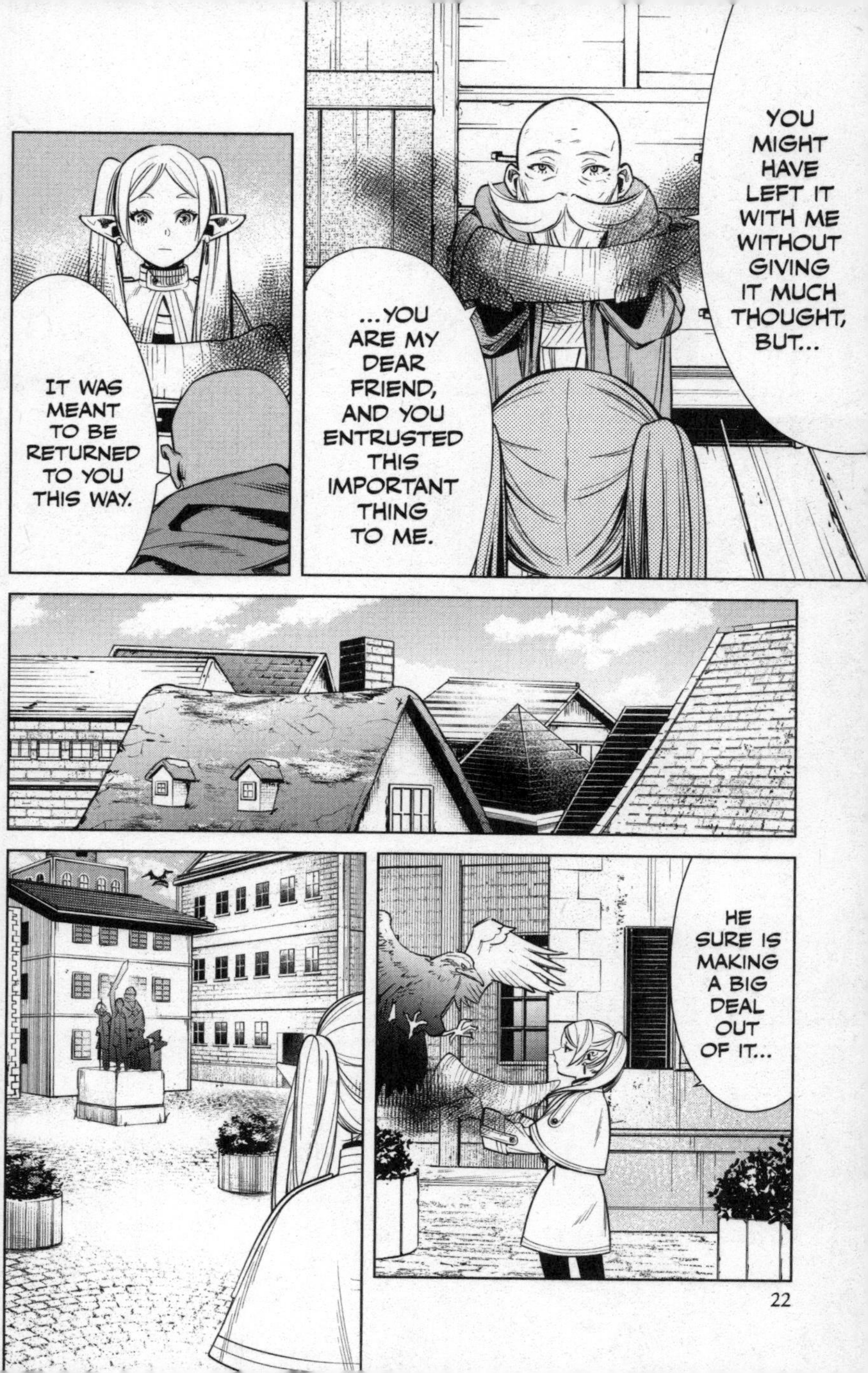
YOU MIGHT HAVE LEFT IT WITH ME WITHOUT GIVING IT MUCH THOUGHT, BUT...
...YOU ARE MY DEAR FRIEND, AND YOU ENTRUSTED THIS IMPORTANT THING TO ME.
IT WAS MEANT TO BE RETURNED TO YOU THIS WAY.
HE SURE IS MAKING A BIG DEAL OUT OF IT...

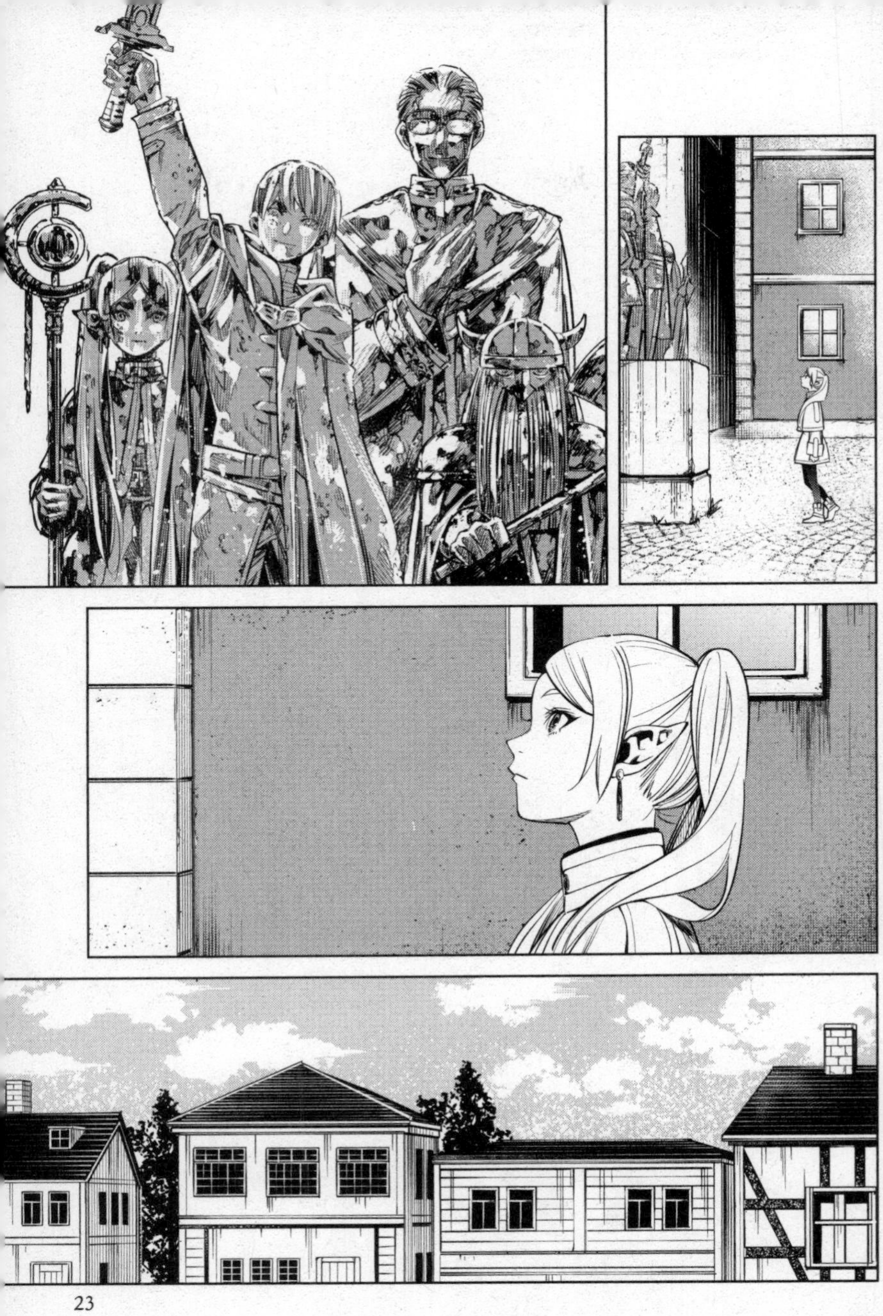

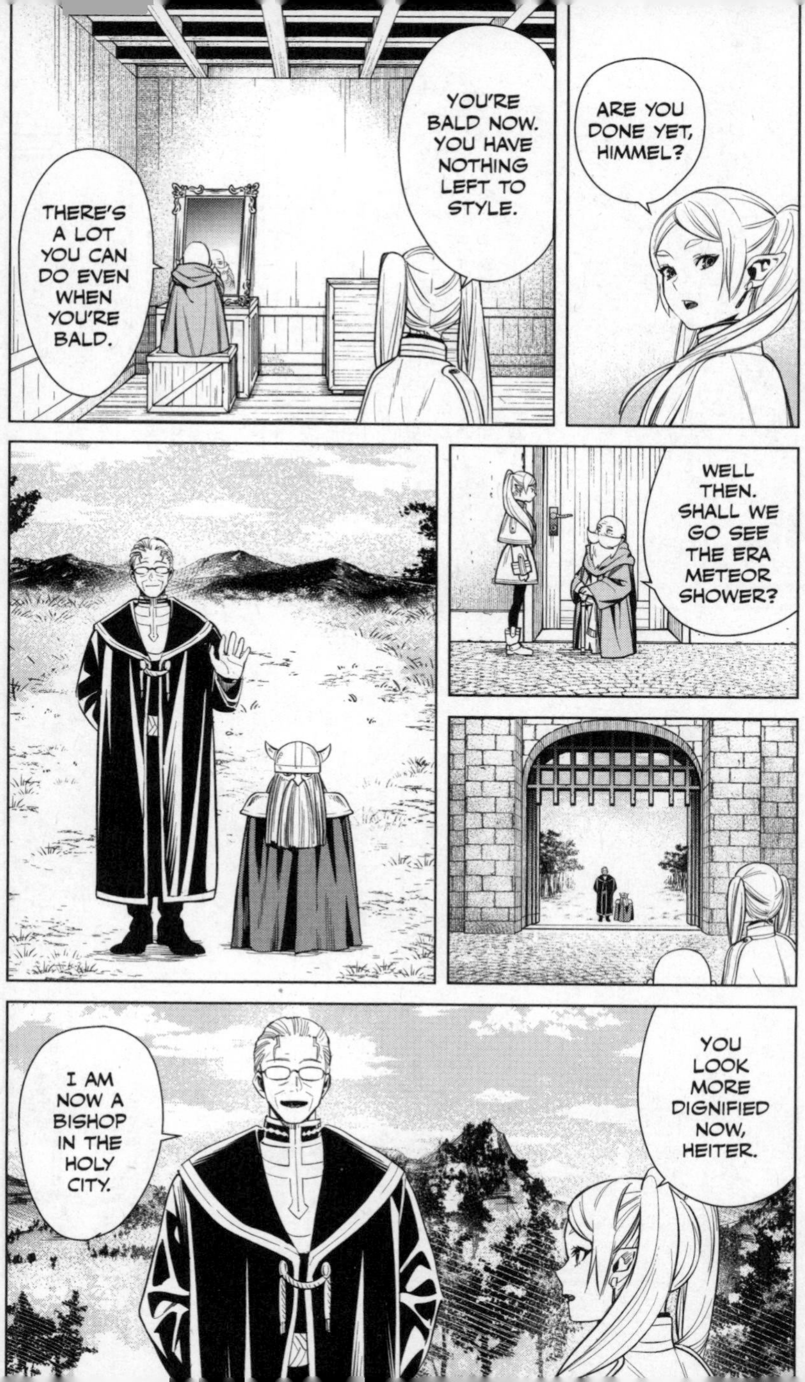
ARE YOU DONE YET, HIMMEL?
YOU'RE BALD NOW. YOU HAVE NOTHING LEFT TO STYLE.
THERE'S A LOT YOU CAN DO EVEN WHEN YOU'RE BALD.
WELL THEN. SHALL WE GO SEE THE ERA METEOR SHOWER?
YOU LOOK MORE DIGNIFIED NOW, HEITER.
I AM NOW A BISHOP IN THE HOLY CITY.

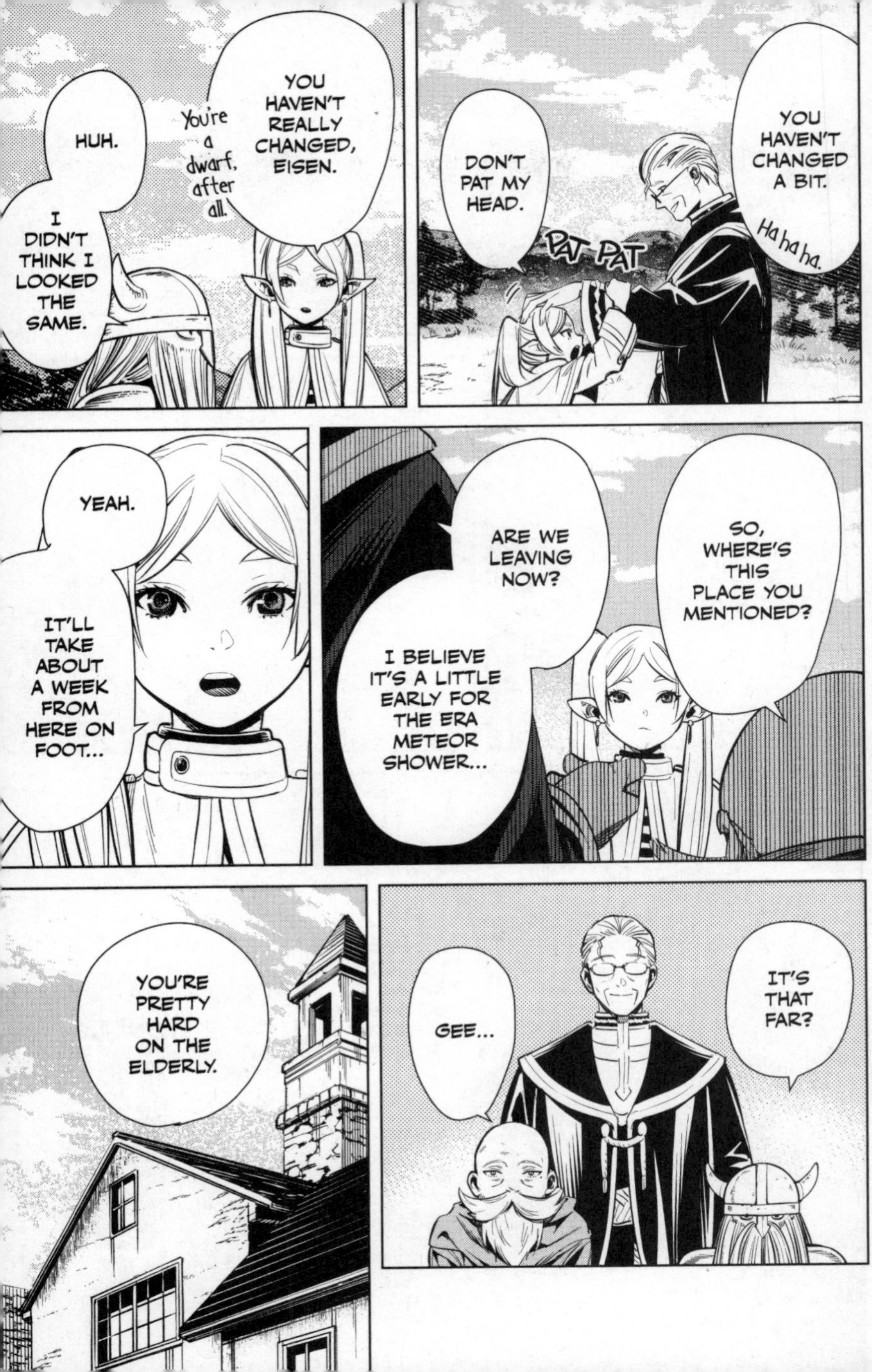
YOU HAVEN'T CHANGED A BIT.
Ha ha ha.
PAT PAT
DON'T PAT MY HEAD.
YOU HAVEN'T REALLY CHANGED, EISEN.
You're a dwarf, after all.
HUH.
I DIDN'T THINK I LOOKED THE SAME.
SO, WHERE'S THIS PLACE YOU MENTIONED?
ARE WE LEAVING NOW?
I BELIEVE IT'S A LITTLE EARLY FOR THE ERA METEOR SHOWER...
YEAH.
IT'LL TAKE ABOUT A WEEK FROM HERE ON FOOT...
IT'S THAT FAR?
GEE...
YOU'RE PRETTY HARD ON THE ELDERLY.

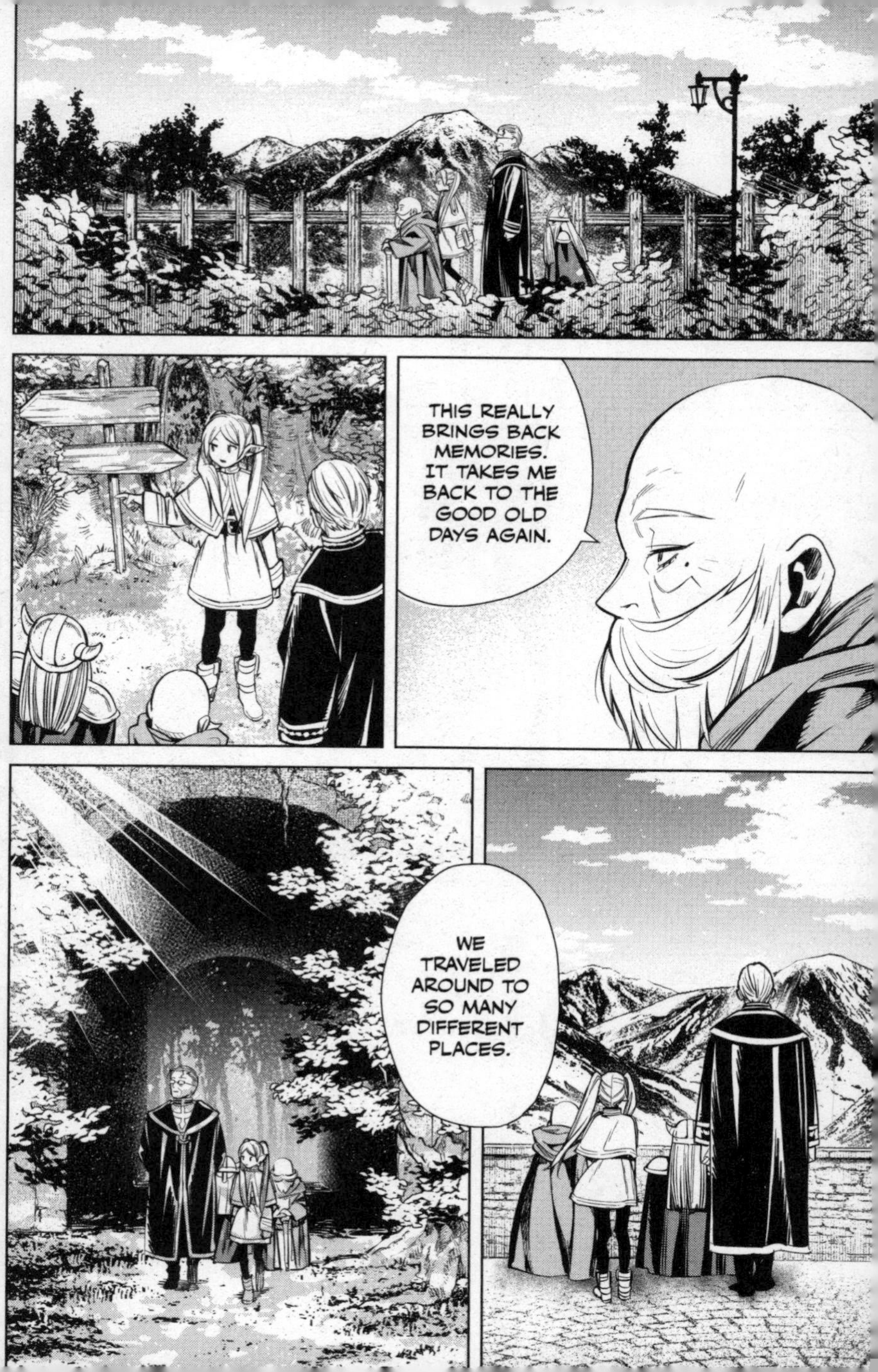
THIS REALLY BRINGS BACK MEMORIES. IT TAKES ME BACK TO THE GOOD OLD DAYS AGAIN.
WE TRAVELED AROUND TO SO MANY DIFFERENT PLACES.

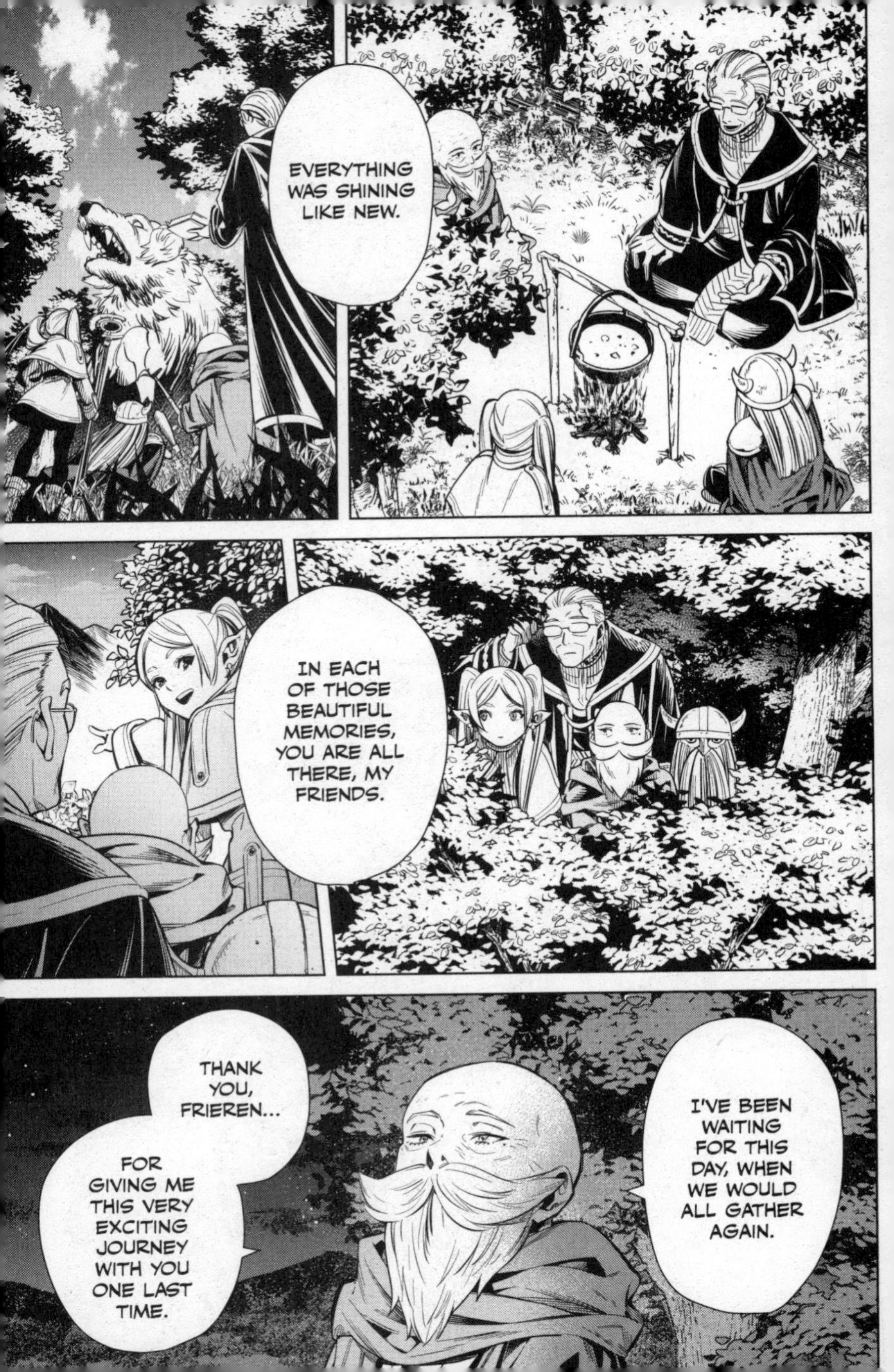
EVERYTHING WAS SHINING LIKE NEW.
IN EACH OF THOSE BEAUTIFUL MEMORIES, YOU ARE ALL THERE, MY FRIENDS.
I'VE BEEN WAITING FOR THIS DAY, WHEN WE WOULD ALL GATHER AGAIN.
THANK YOU, FRIEREN...
FOR GIVING ME THIS VERY EXCITING JOURNEY WITH YOU ONE LAST TIME.

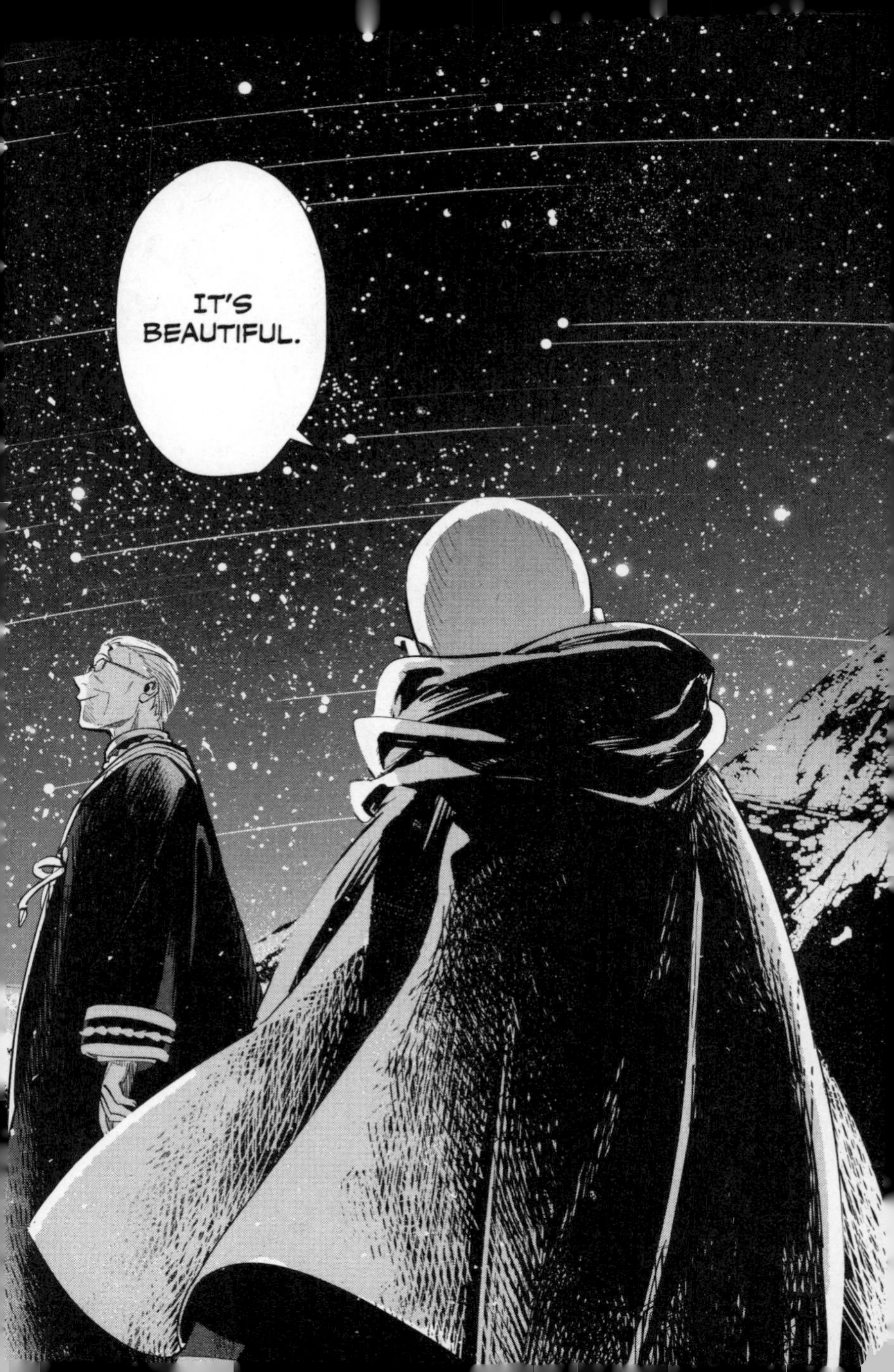
IT'S BEAUTIFUL.

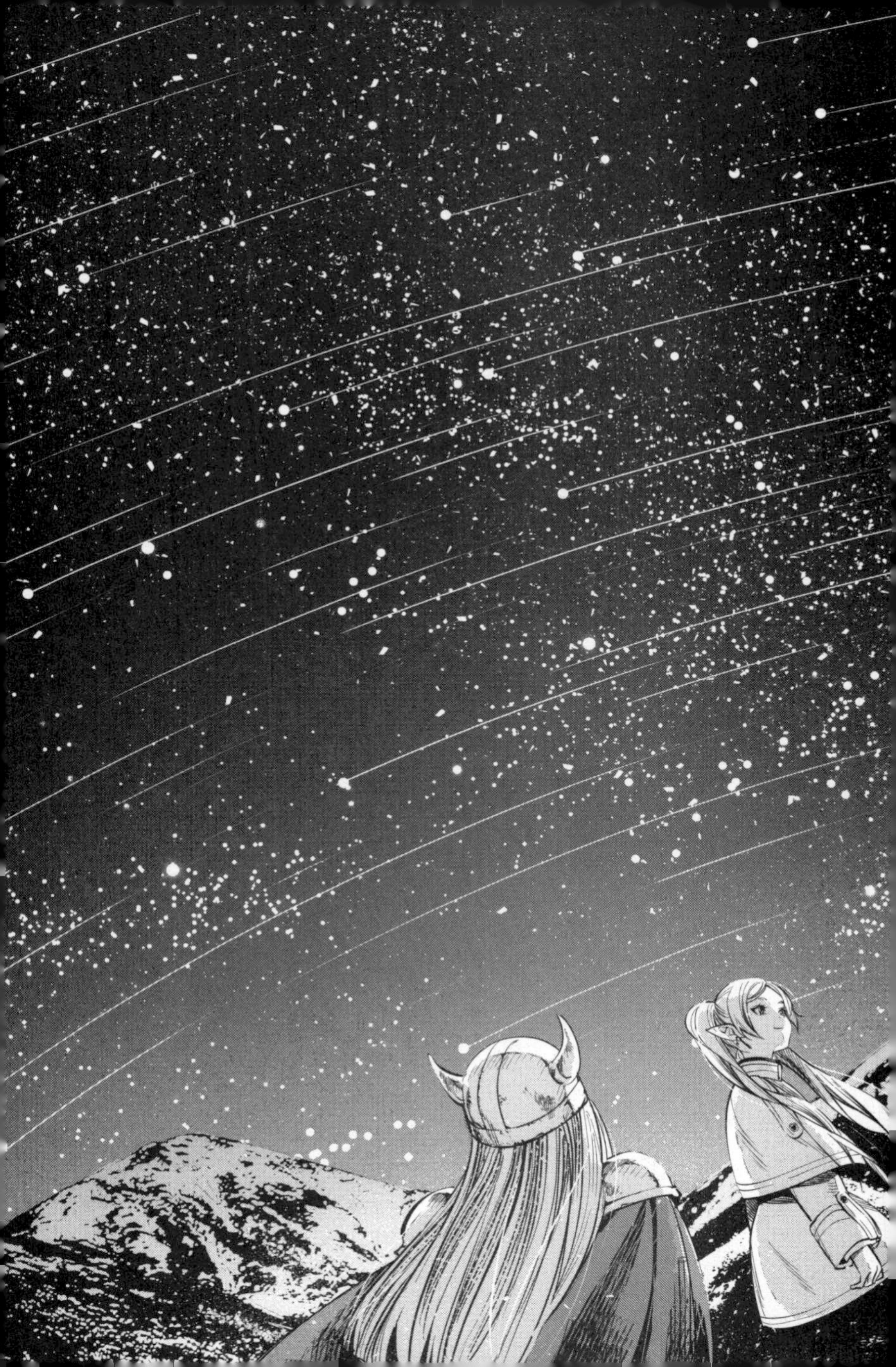

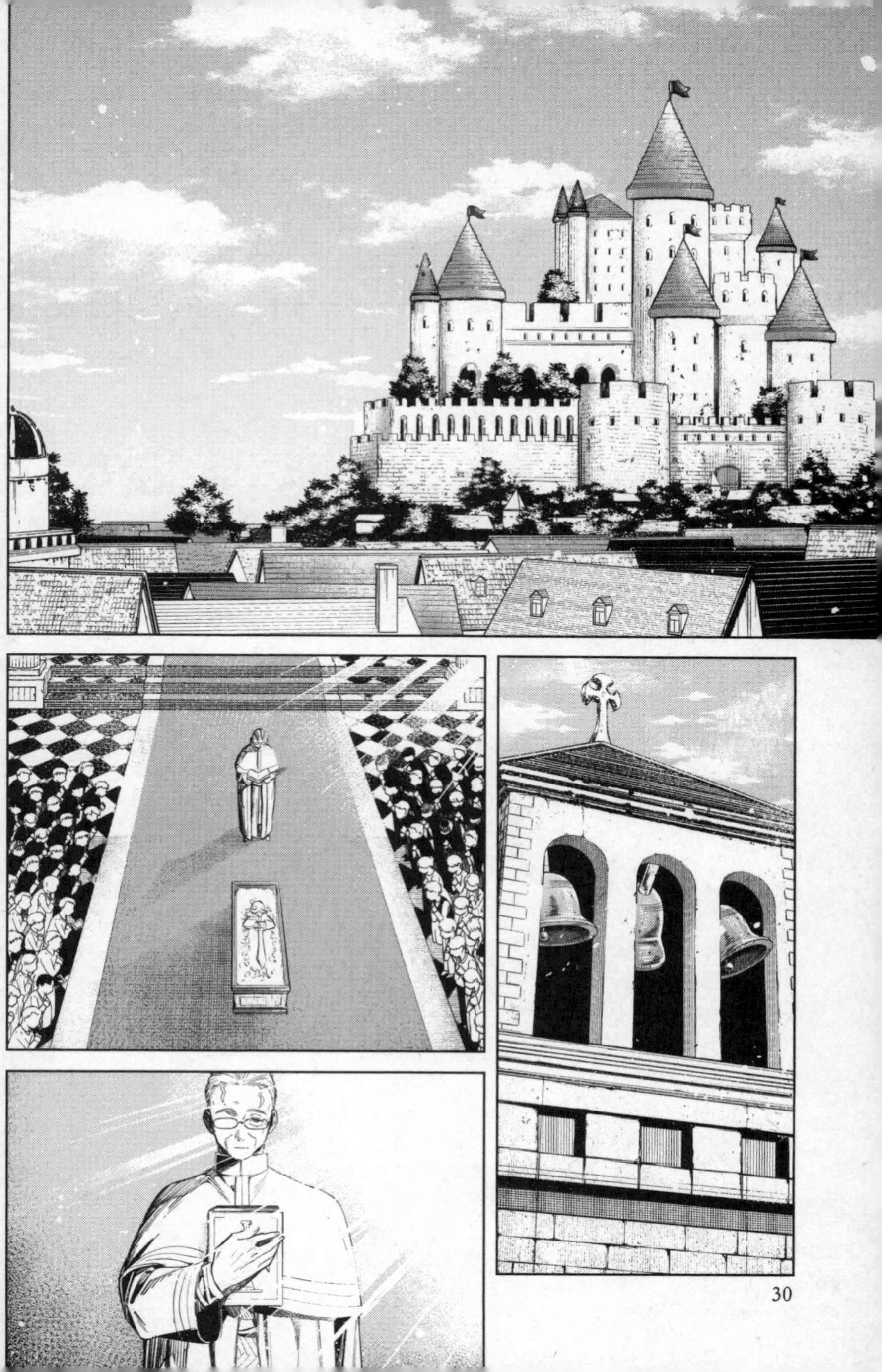

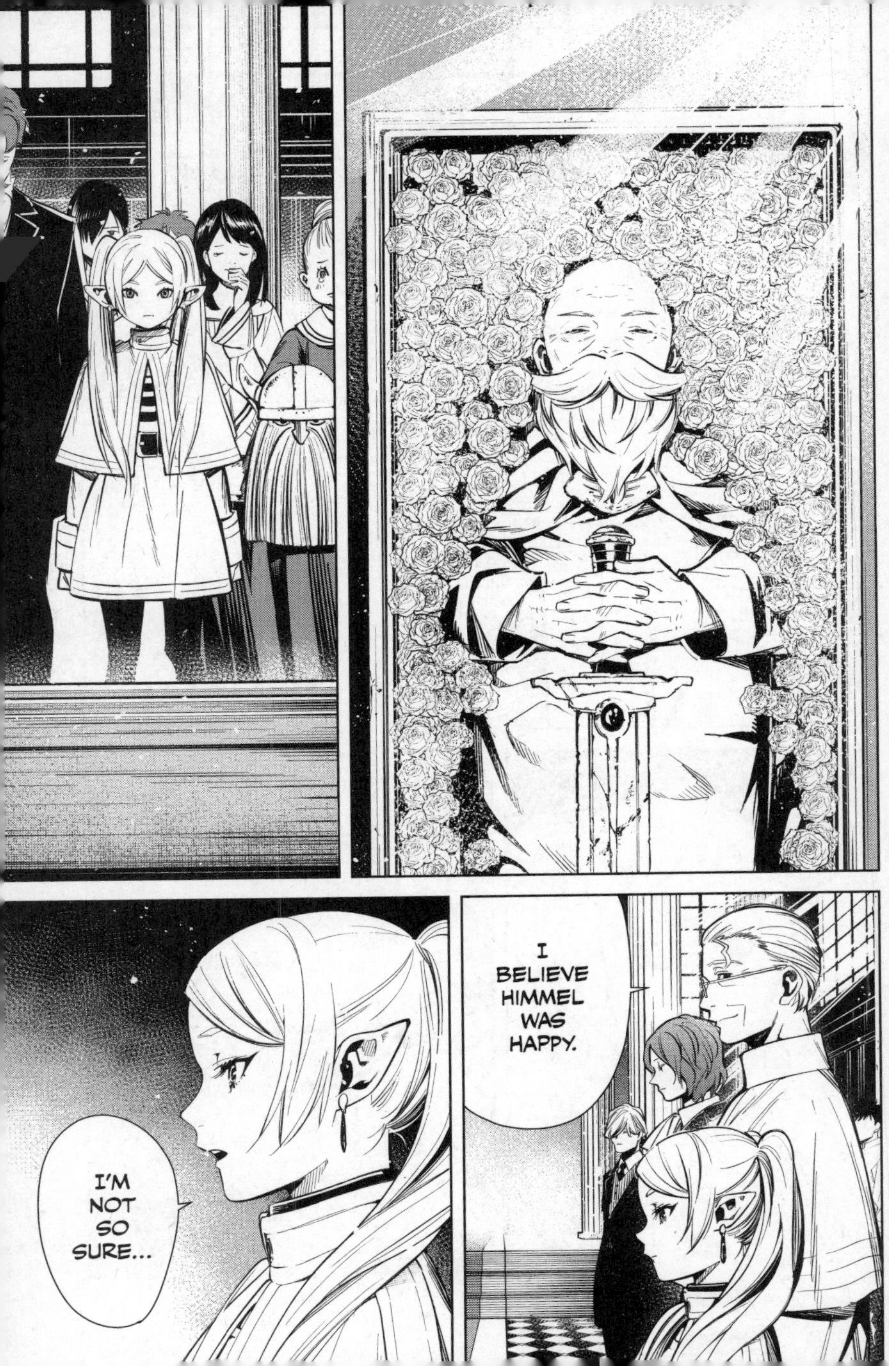
I BELIEVE HIMMEL WAS HAPPY.
I'M NOT SO SURE...

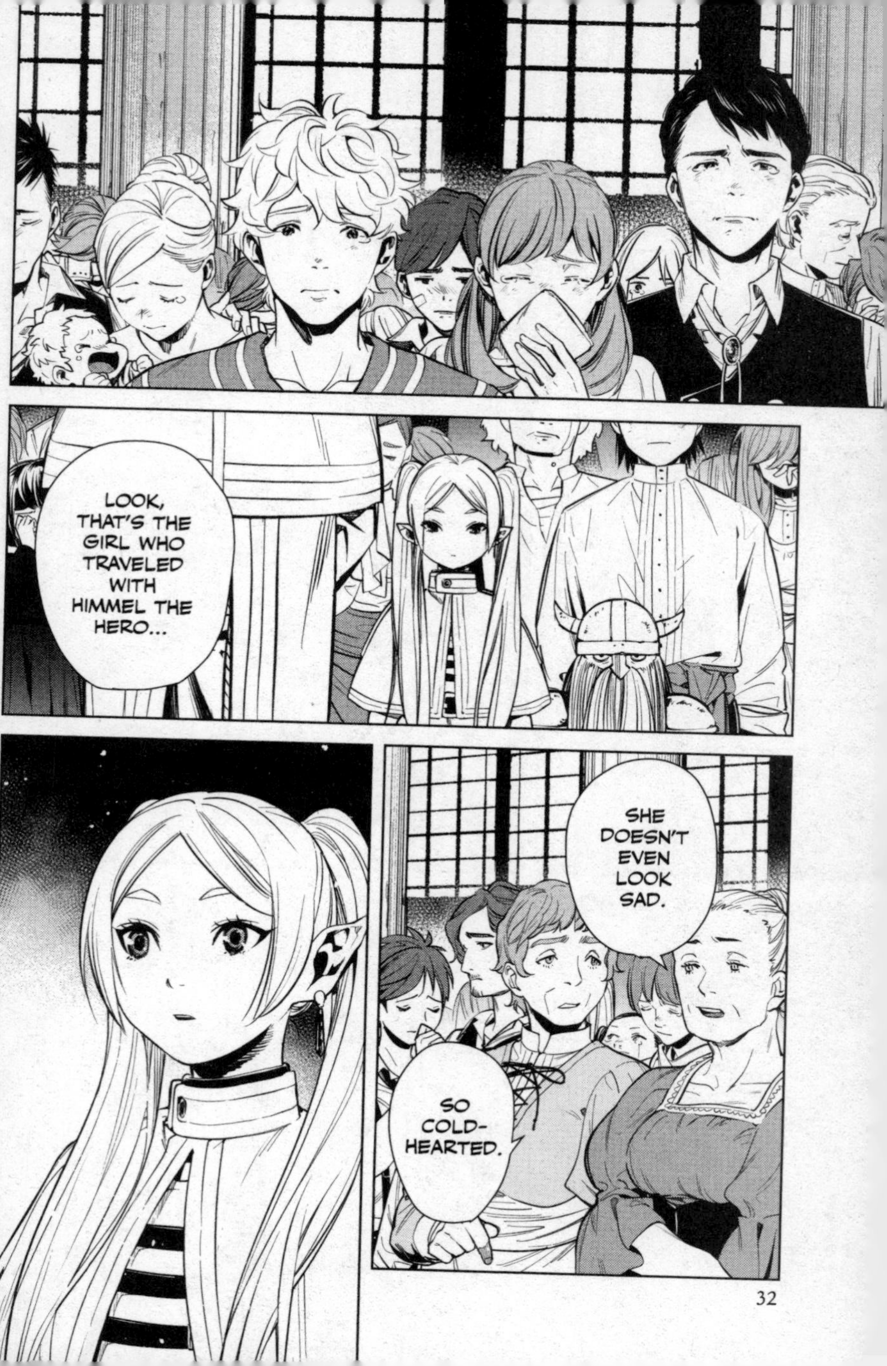
LOOK, THAT'S THE GIRL WHO TRAVELED WITH HIMMEL THE HERO...
SHE DOESN'T EVEN LOOK SAD.
SO COLD-HEARTED.

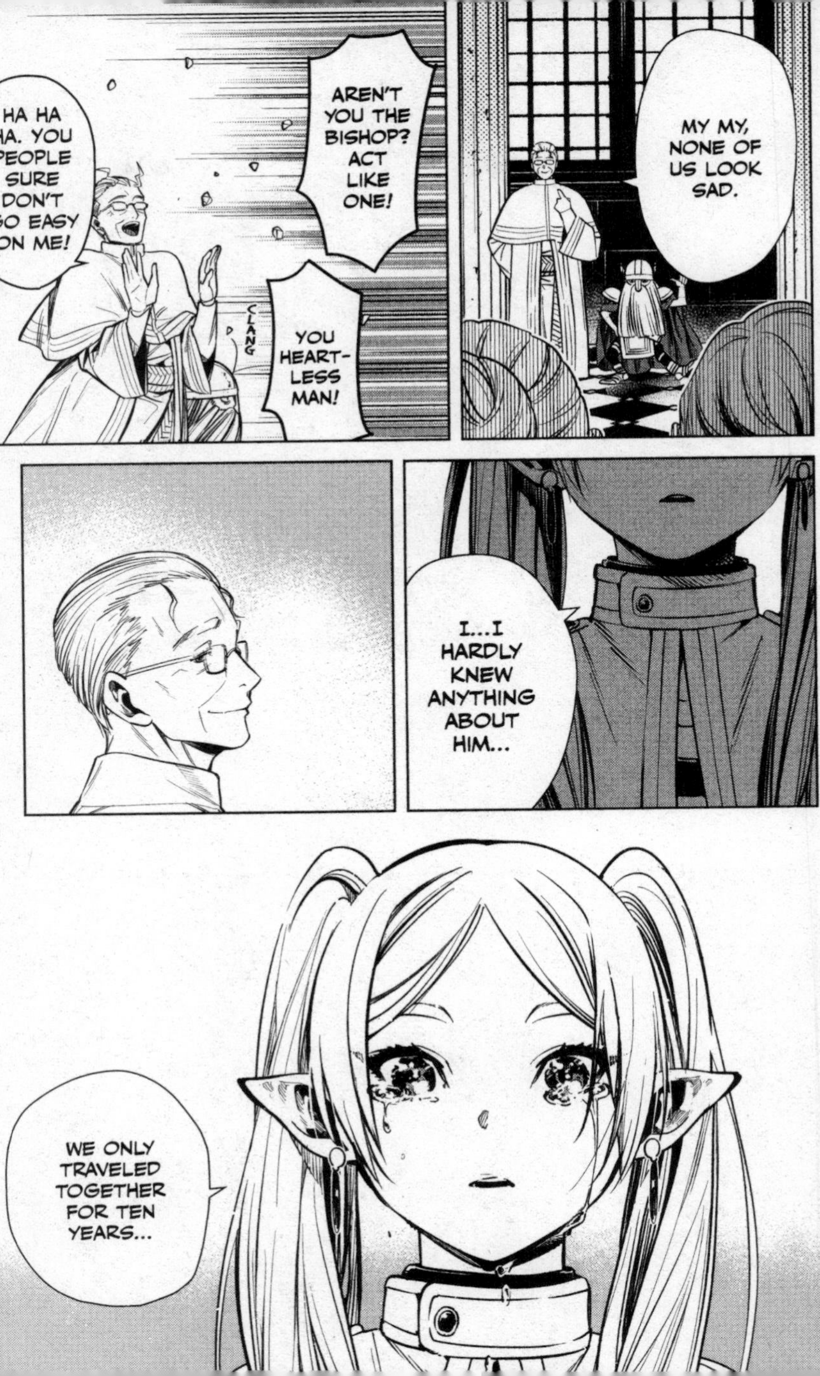
MY MY, NONE OF US LOOK SAD.
AREN'T YOU THE BISHOP? ACT LIKE ONE!
YOU HEART-LESS MAN!
CLANG
HA HA HA. YOU PEOPLE SURE DON'T GO EASY ON ME!
I...I HARDLY KNEW ANYTHING ABOUT HIM...
WE ONLY TRAVELED TOGETHER FOR TEN YEARS...

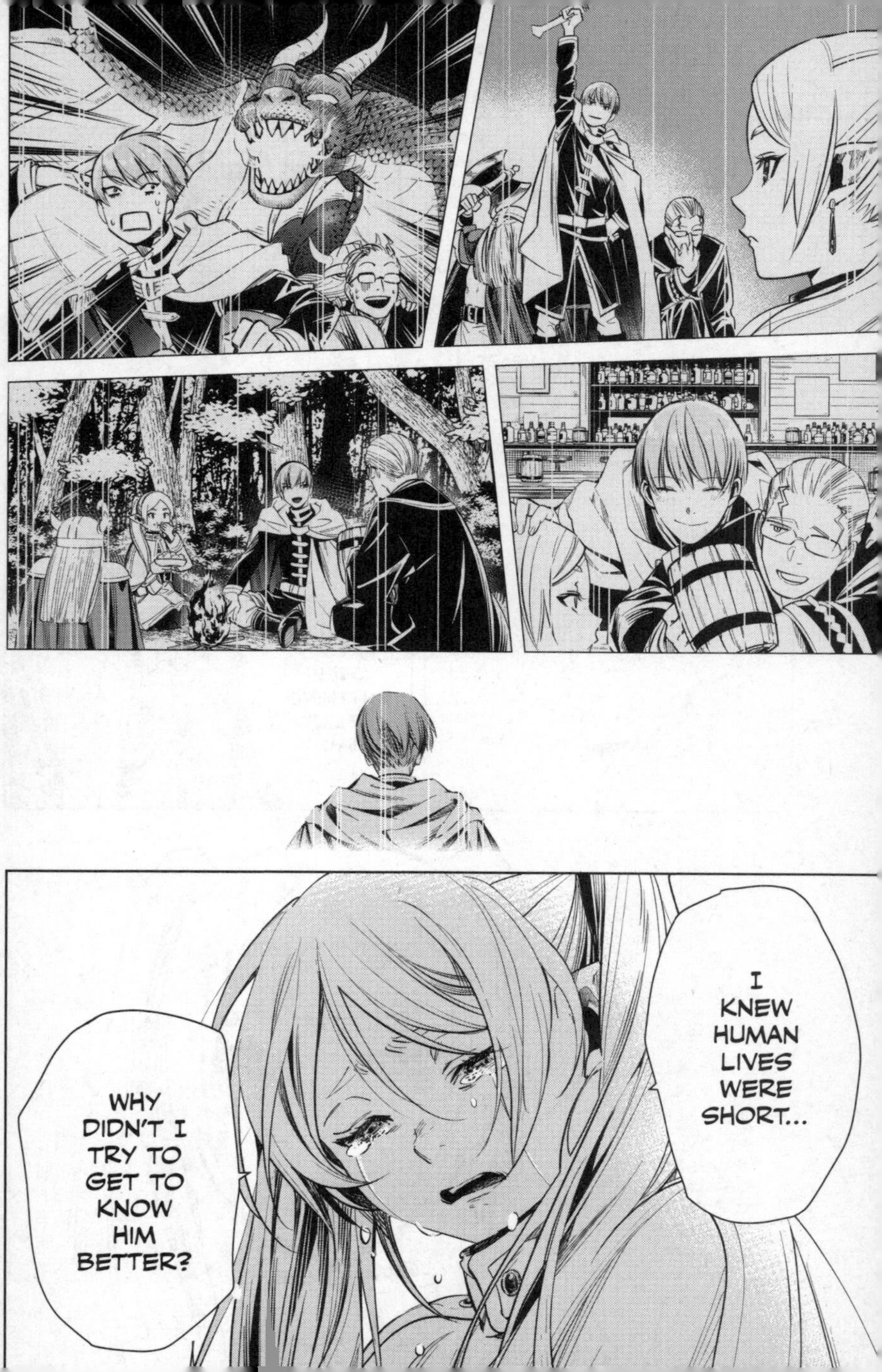
I KNEW HUMAN LIVES WERE SHORT...
WHY DIDN'T I TRY TO GET TO KNOW HIM BETTER?

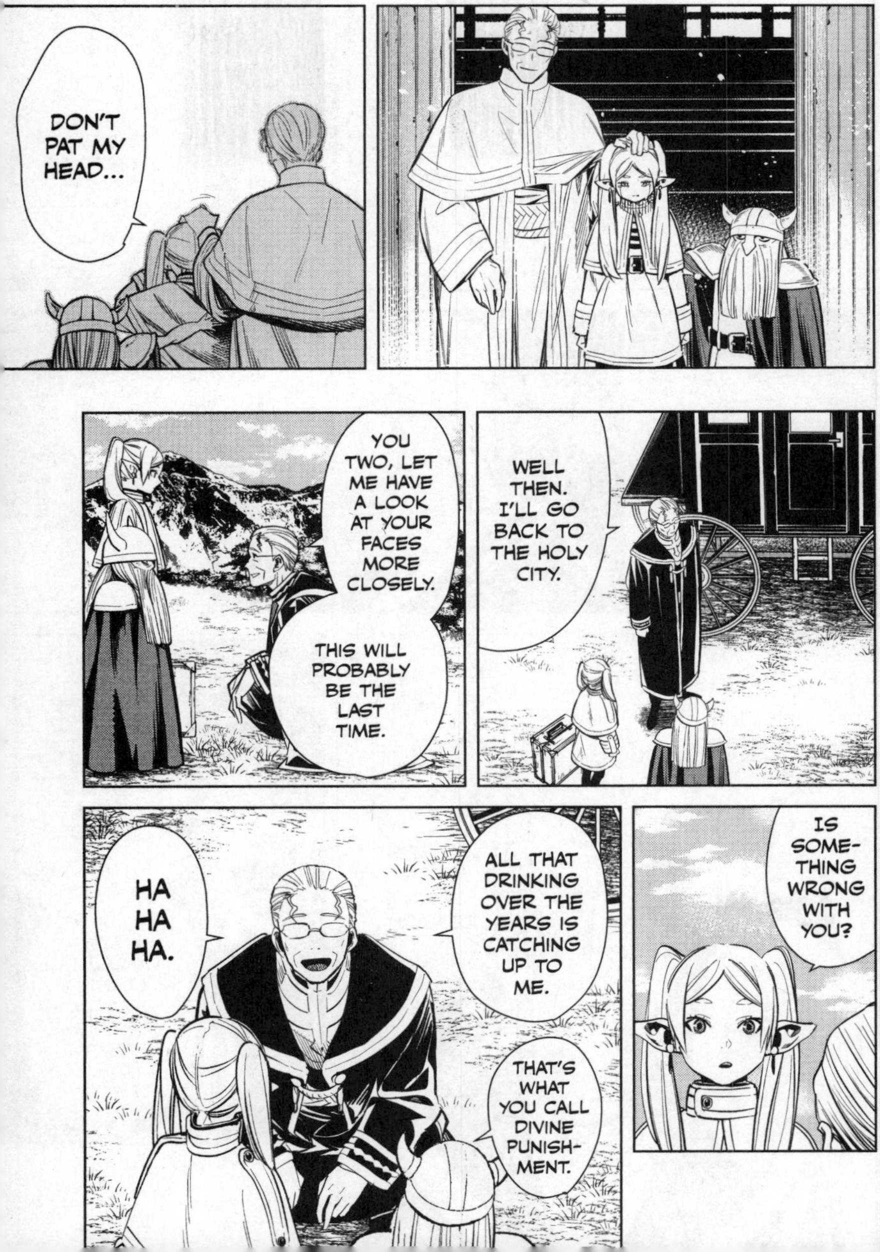
DON'T PAT MY HEAD...
WELL THEN. I'LL GO BACK TO THE HOLY CITY.
YOU TWO, LET ME HAVE A LOOK AT YOUR FACES MORE CLOSELY.
THIS WILL PROBABLY BE THE LAST TIME.
IS SOMETHING WRONG WITH YOU?
ALL THAT DRINKING OVER THE YEARS IS CATCHING UP TO ME.
HA HA HA.
THAT'S WHAT YOU CALL DIVINE PUNISHMENT.

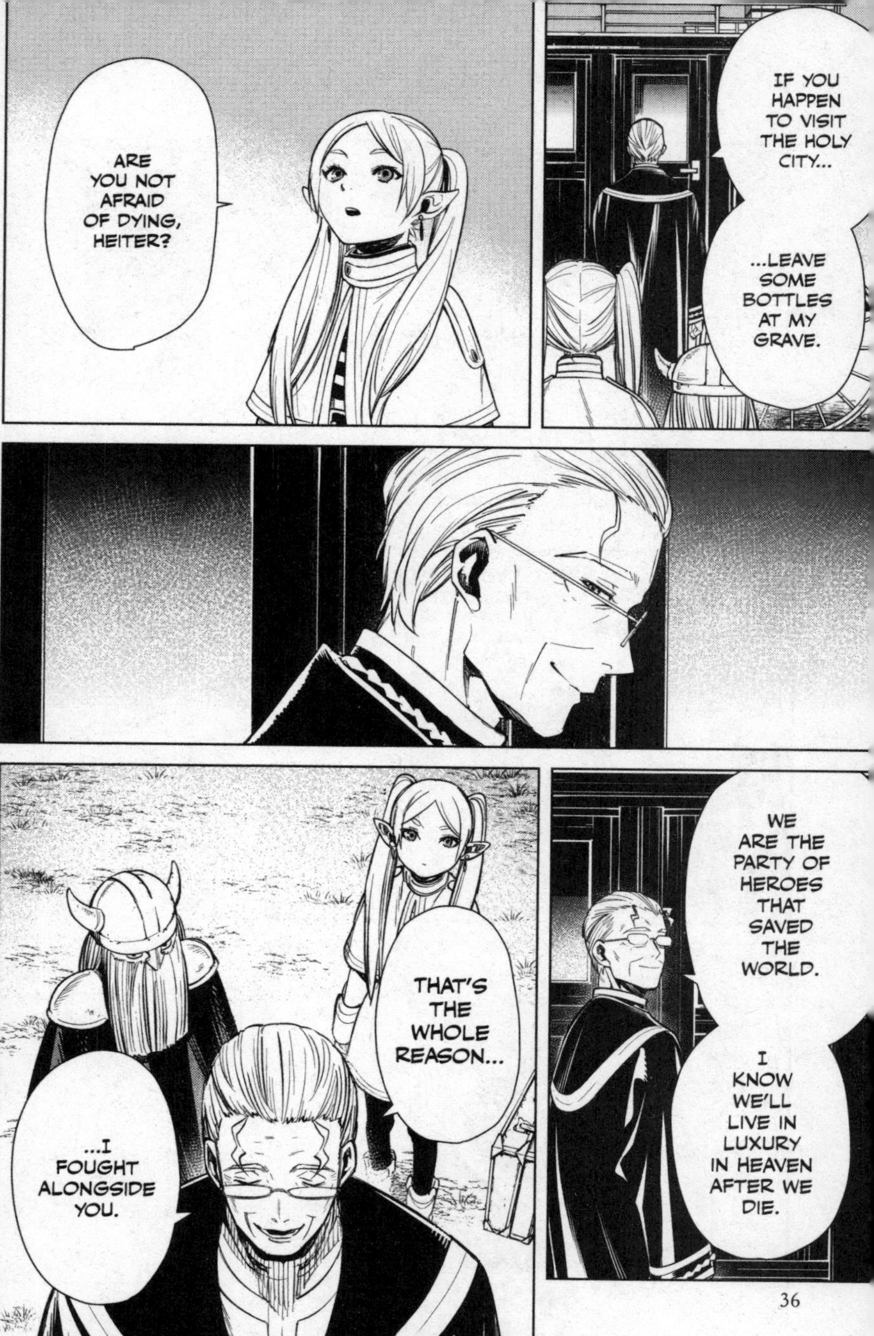
IF YOU HAPPEN TO VISIT THE HOLY CITY...
...LEAVE SOME BOTTLES AT MY GRAVE.
ARE YOU NOT AFRAID OF DYING, HEITER?
WE ARE THE PARTY OF HEROES THAT SAVED THE WORLD.
I KNOW WE'LL LIVE IN LUXURY IN HEAVEN AFTER WE DIE.
THAT'S THE WHOLE REASON...
...I FOUGHT ALONGSIDE YOU.

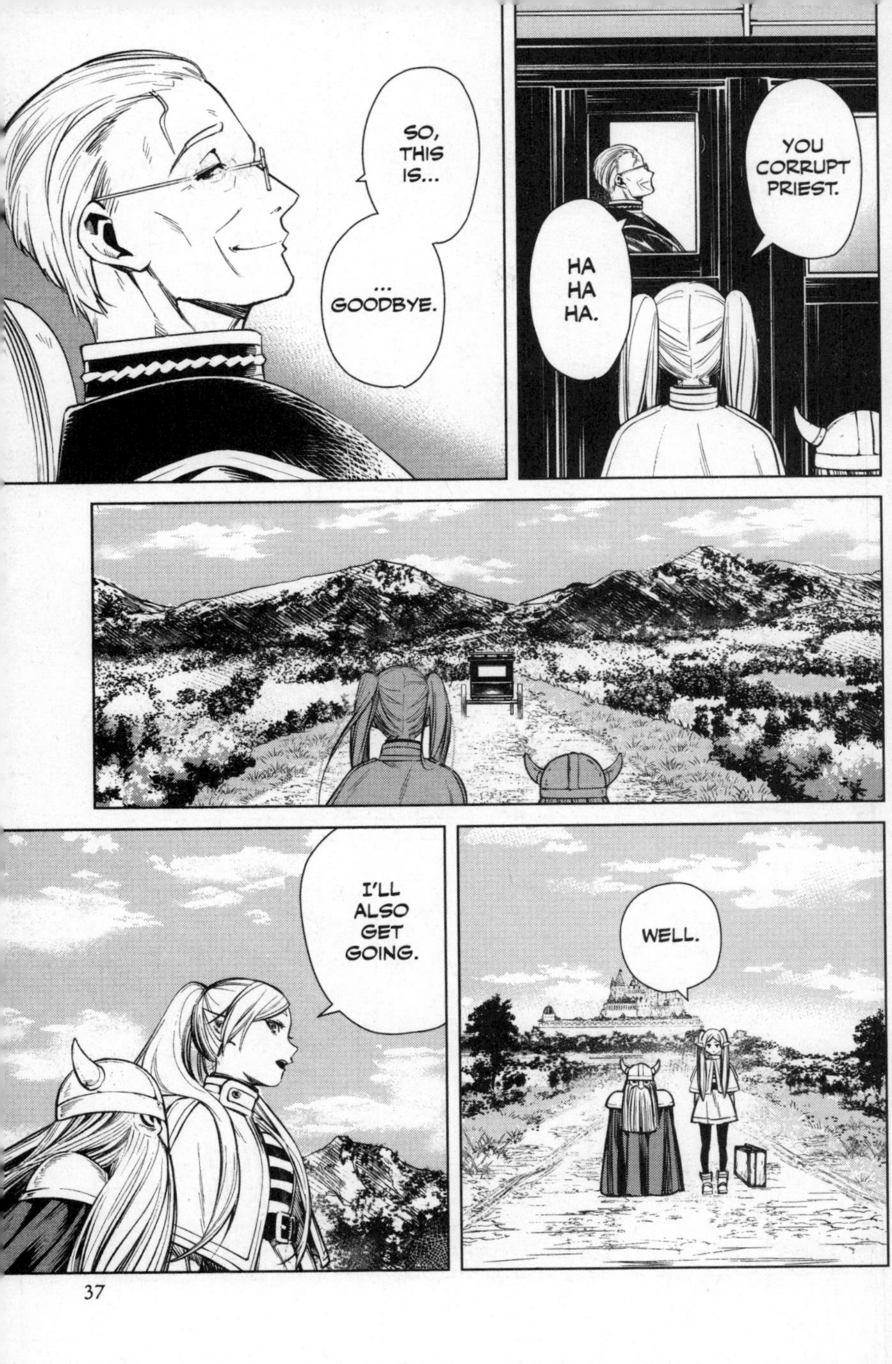
YOU CORRUPT PRIEST.
HA HA HA.
SO, THIS IS...
... GOODBYE.
WELL.
I'LL ALSO GET GOING.

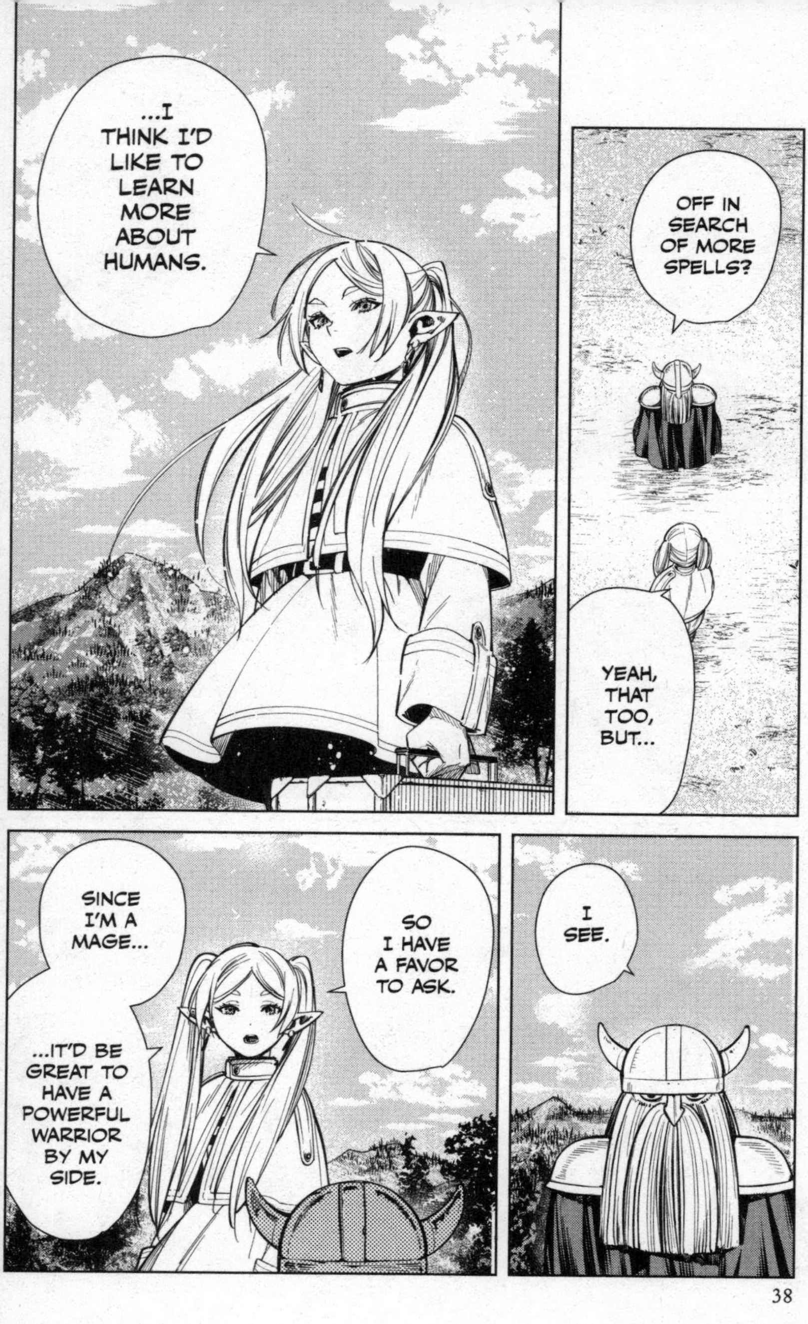
OFF IN SEARCH OF MORE SPELLS?
YEAH, THAT TOO, BUT...
...I THINK I'D LIKE TO LEARN MORE ABOUT HUMANS.
I SEE.
SO I HAVE A FAVOR TO ASK.
SINCE I'M A MAGE...
...IT'D BE GREAT TO HAVE A POWERFUL WARRIOR BY MY SIDE.

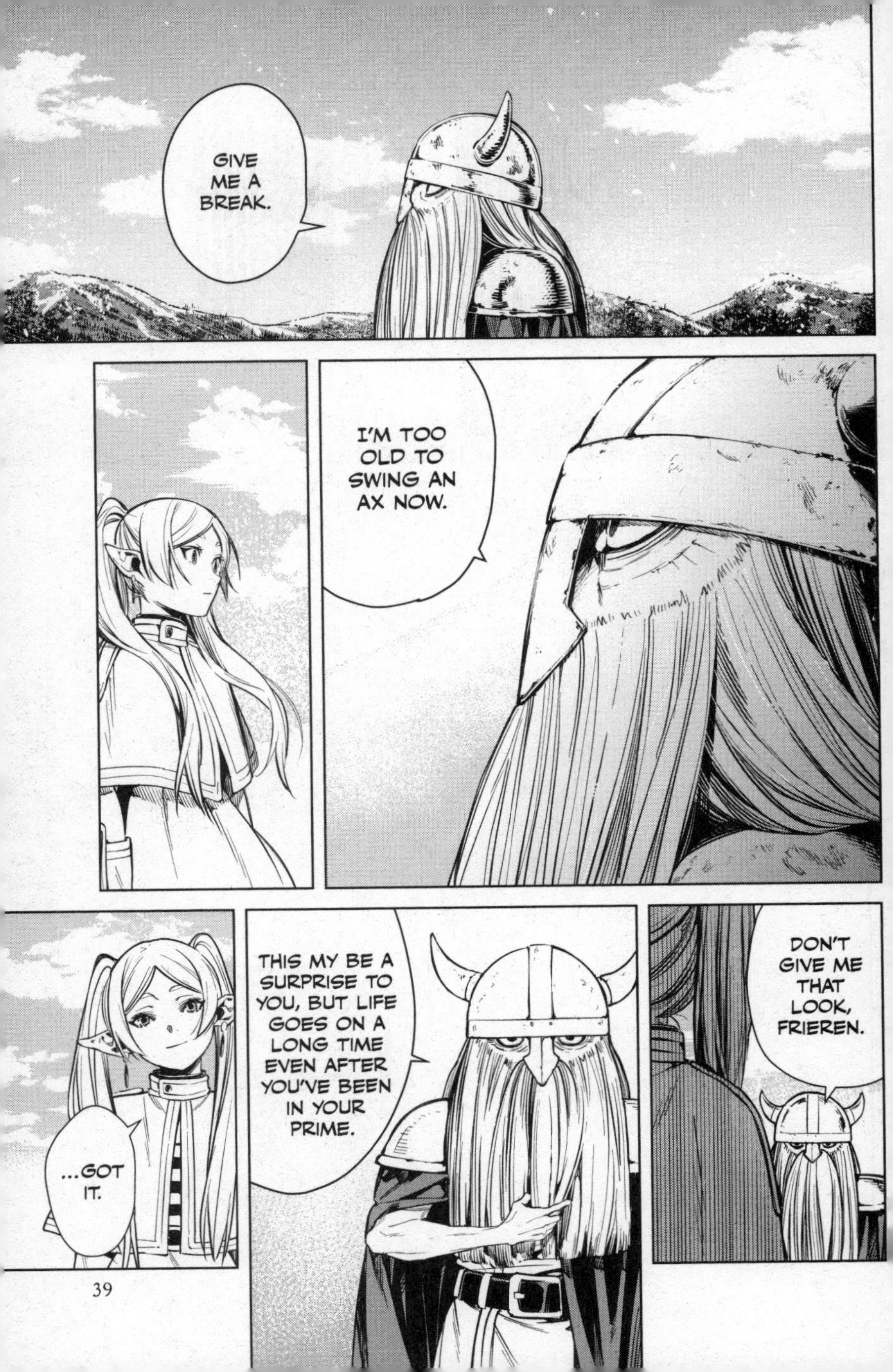
GIVE ME A BREAK.
I'M TOO OLD TO SWING AN AX NOW.
DON'T GIVE ME THAT LOOK, FRIEREN.
THIS MY BE A SURPRISE TO YOU, BUT LIFE GOES ON A LONG TIME EVEN AFTER YOU'VE BEEN IN YOUR PRIME.
...GOT IT.

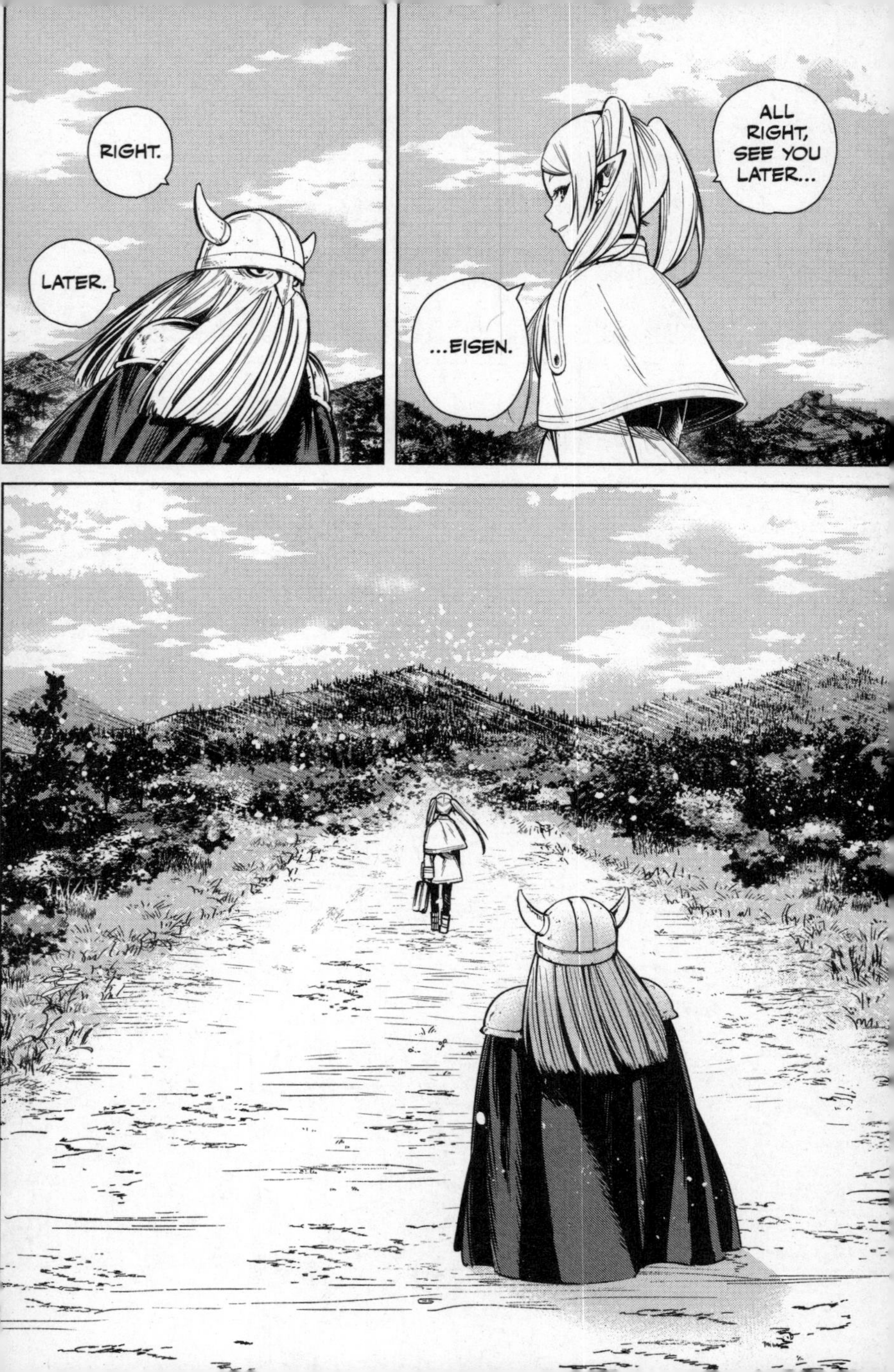
ALL RIGHT, SEE YOU LATER...
...EISEN.
RIGHT.
LATER.

# Chapter 2: The Priest's Lie

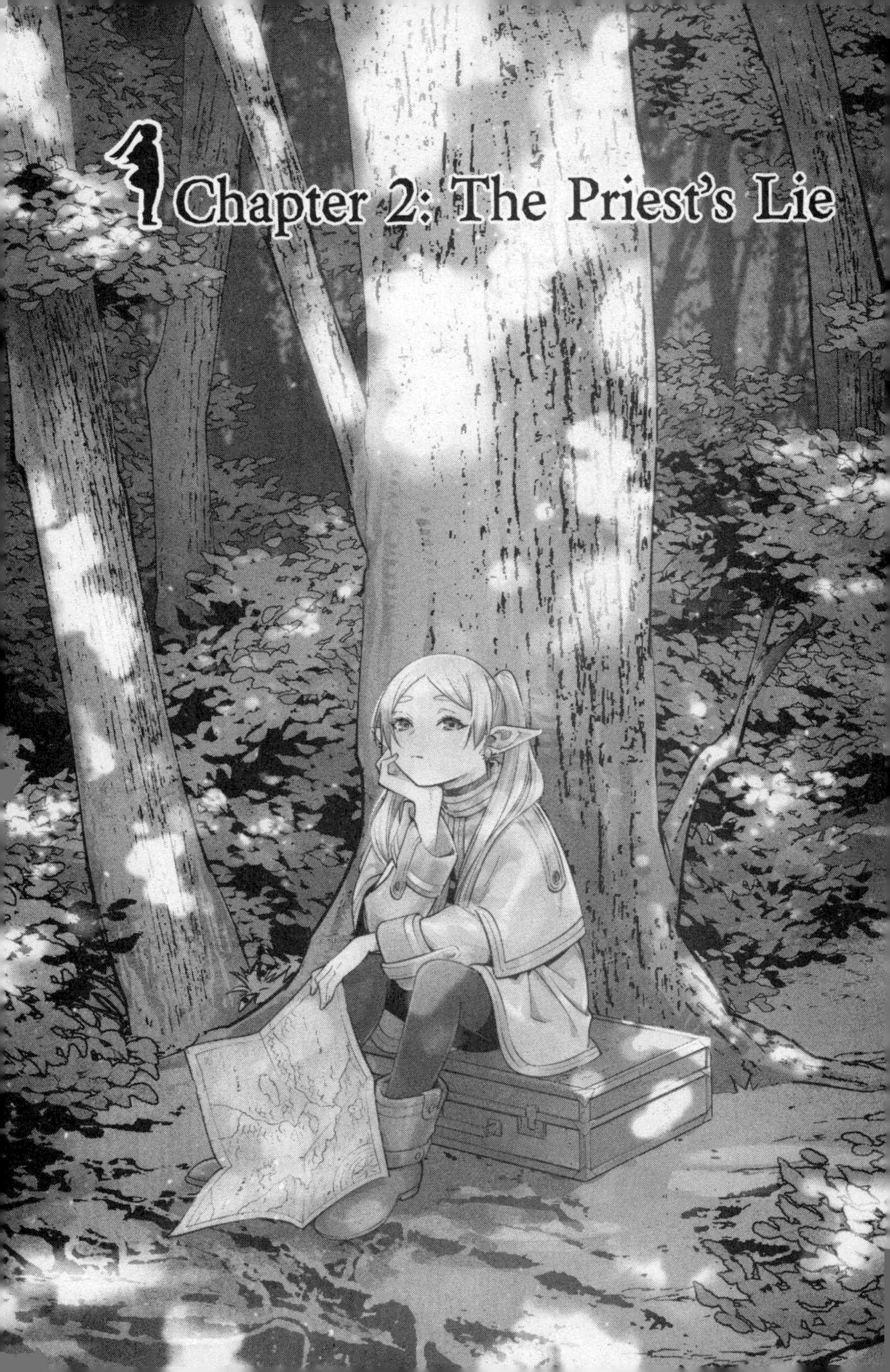

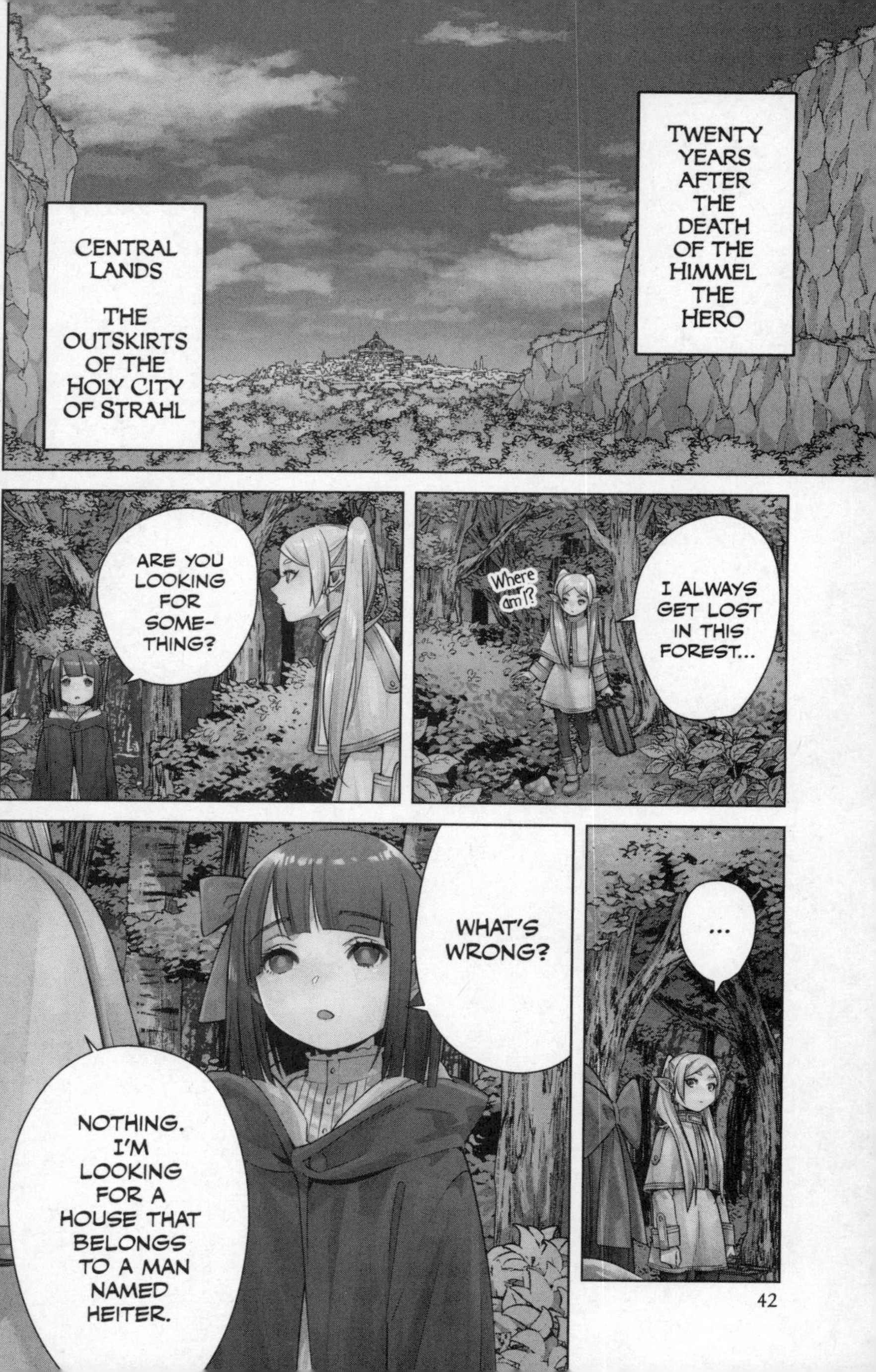
TWENTY YEARS AFTER THE DEATH OF THE HIMMEL THE HERO
CENTRAL LANDS
THE OUTSKIRTS OF THE HOLY CITY OF STRAHL
Where am I?
I ALWAYS GET LOST IN THIS FOREST...
ARE YOU LOOKING FOR SOME-THING?
...
WHAT'S WRONG?
NOTHING. I'M LOOKING FOR A HOUSE THAT BELONGS TO A MAN NAMED HEITER.

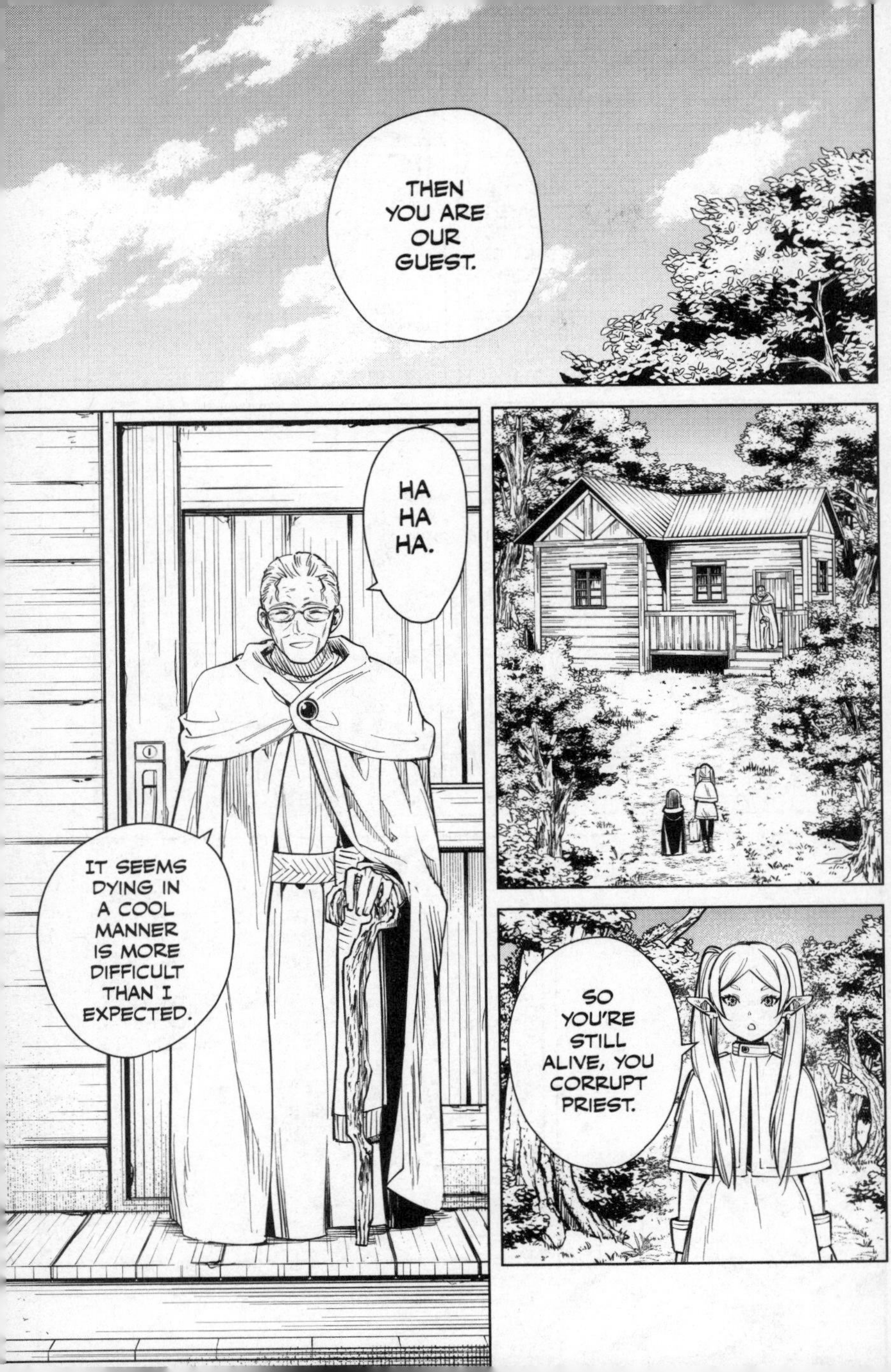
THEN YOU ARE OUR GUEST.
SO YOU'RE STILL ALIVE, YOU CORRUPT PRIEST.
HA HA HA.
IT SEEMS DYING IN A COOL MANNER IS MORE DIFFICULT THAN I EXPECTED.

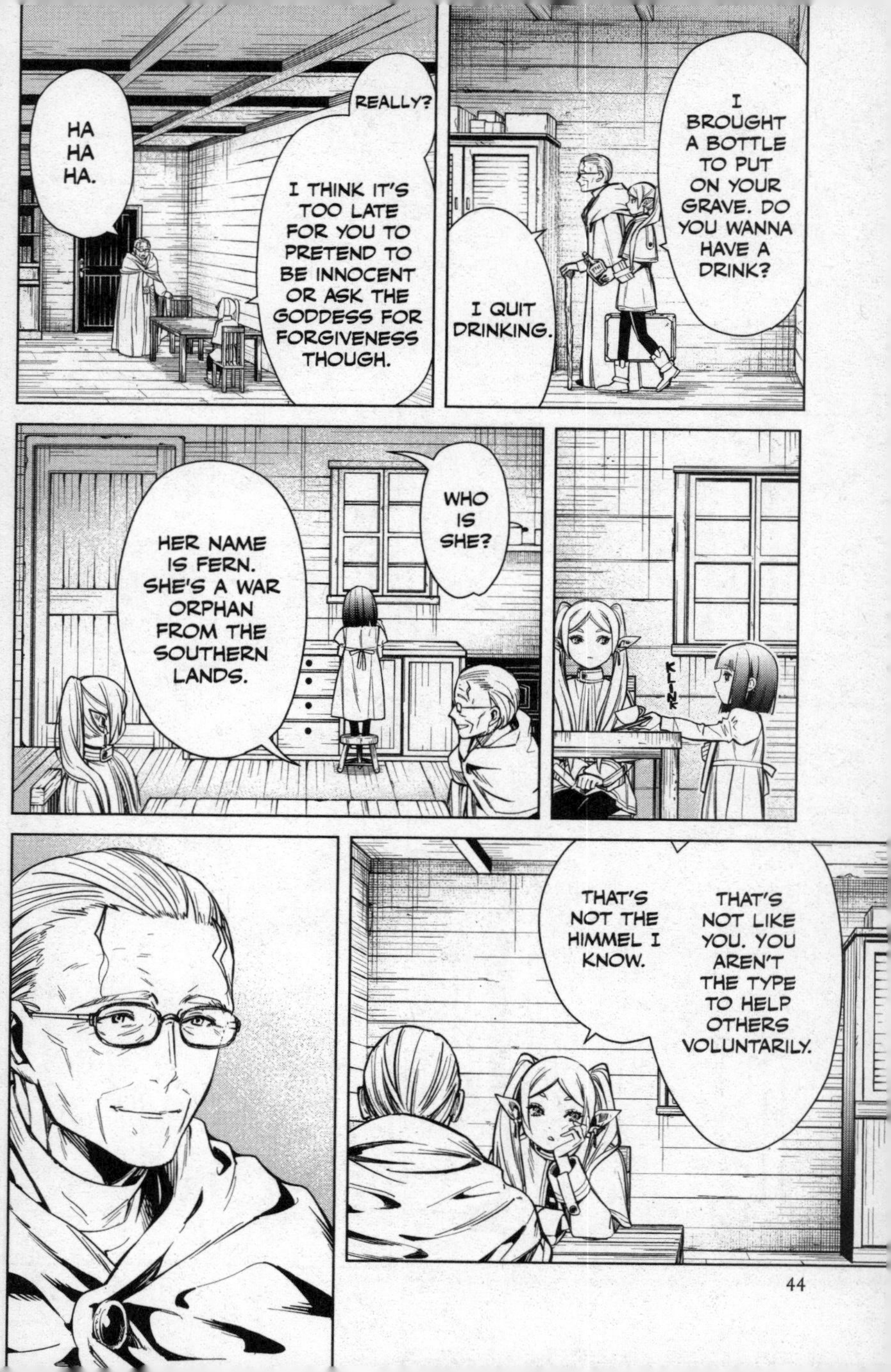

I BROUGHT A BOTTLE TO PUT ON YOUR GRAVE. DO YOU WANNA HAVE A DRINK?
I QUIT DRINKING.
REALLY?
I THINK IT'S TOO LATE FOR YOU TO PRETEND TO BE INNOCENT OR ASK THE GODDESS FOR FORGIVENESS THOUGH.
HA HA HA.
KLINK
WHO IS SHE?
HER NAME IS FERN. SHE'S A WAR ORPHAN FROM THE SOUTHERN LANDS.
THAT'S NOT LIKE YOU. YOU AREN'T THE TYPE TO HELP OTHERS VOLUNTARILY.
THAT'S NOT THE HIMMEL I KNOW.

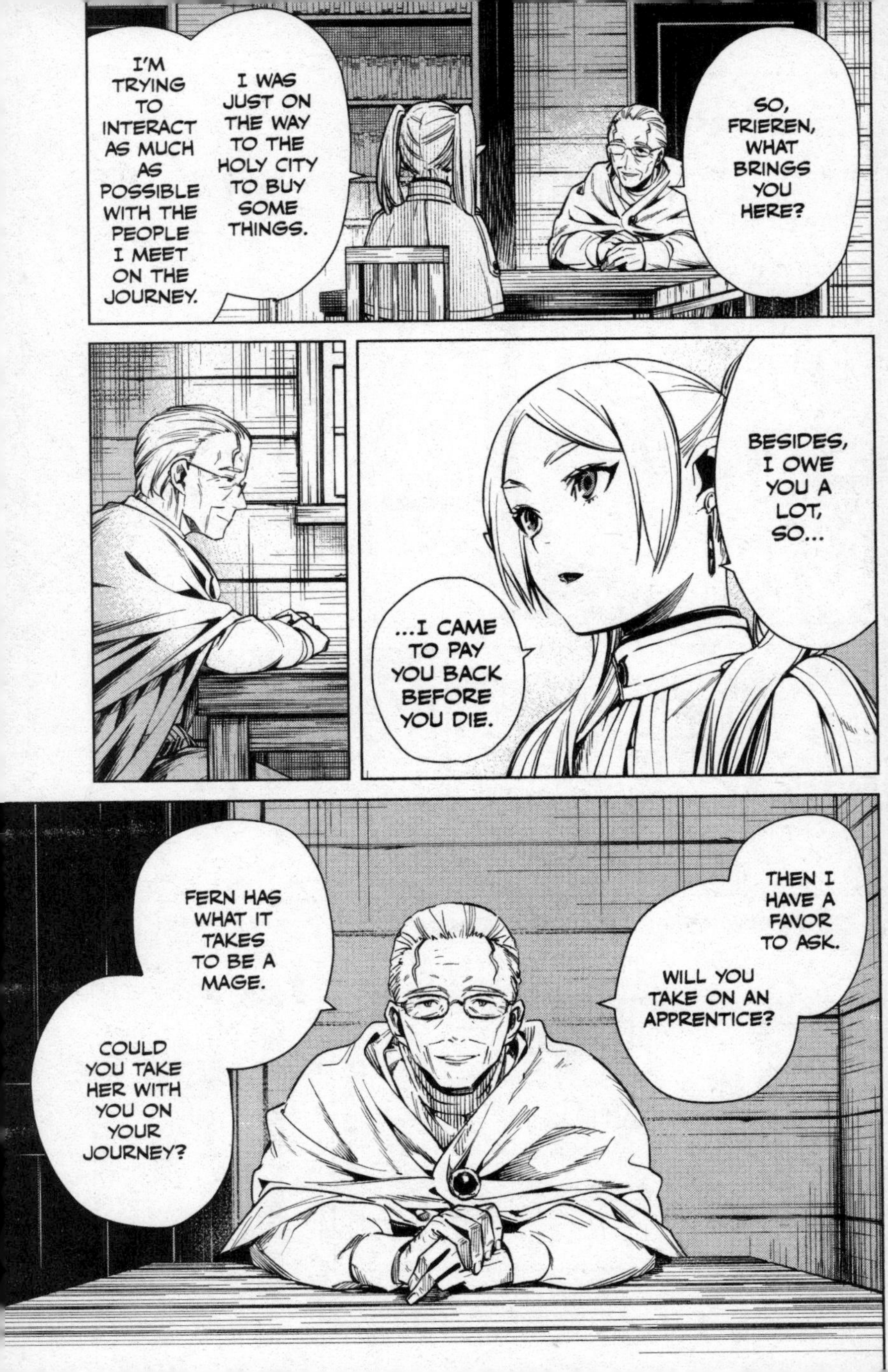
SO, FRIEREN, WHAT BRINGS YOU HERE?
I WAS JUST ON THE WAY TO THE HOLY CITY TO BUY SOME THINGS.
I'M TRYING TO INTERACT AS MUCH AS POSSIBLE WITH THE PEOPLE I MEET ON THE JOURNEY.
BESIDES, I OWE YOU A LOT, SO...
...I CAME TO PAY YOU BACK BEFORE YOU DIE.
THEN I HAVE A FAVOR TO ASK.
WILL YOU TAKE ON AN APPRENTICE?
FERN HAS WHAT IT TAKES TO BE A MAGE.
COULD YOU TAKE HER WITH YOU ON YOUR JOURNEY?

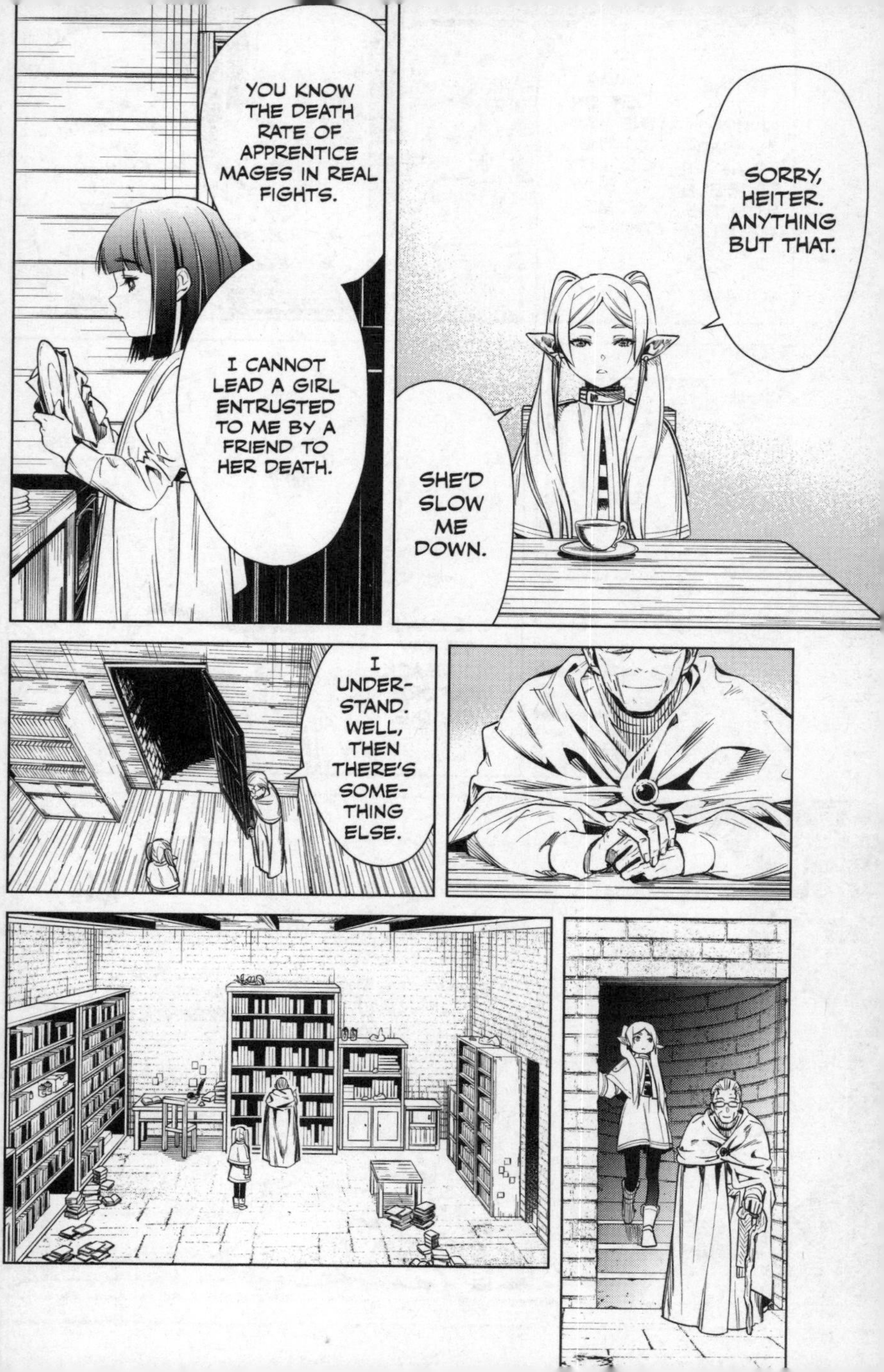
SORRY, HEITER. ANYTHING BUT THAT.
SHE'D SLOW ME DOWN.
YOU KNOW THE DEATH RATE OF APPRENTICE MAGES IN REAL FIGHTS.
I CANNOT LEAD A GIRL ENTRUSTED TO ME BY A FRIEND TO HER DEATH.
I UNDER-STAND. WELL, THEN THERE'S SOME-THING ELSE.

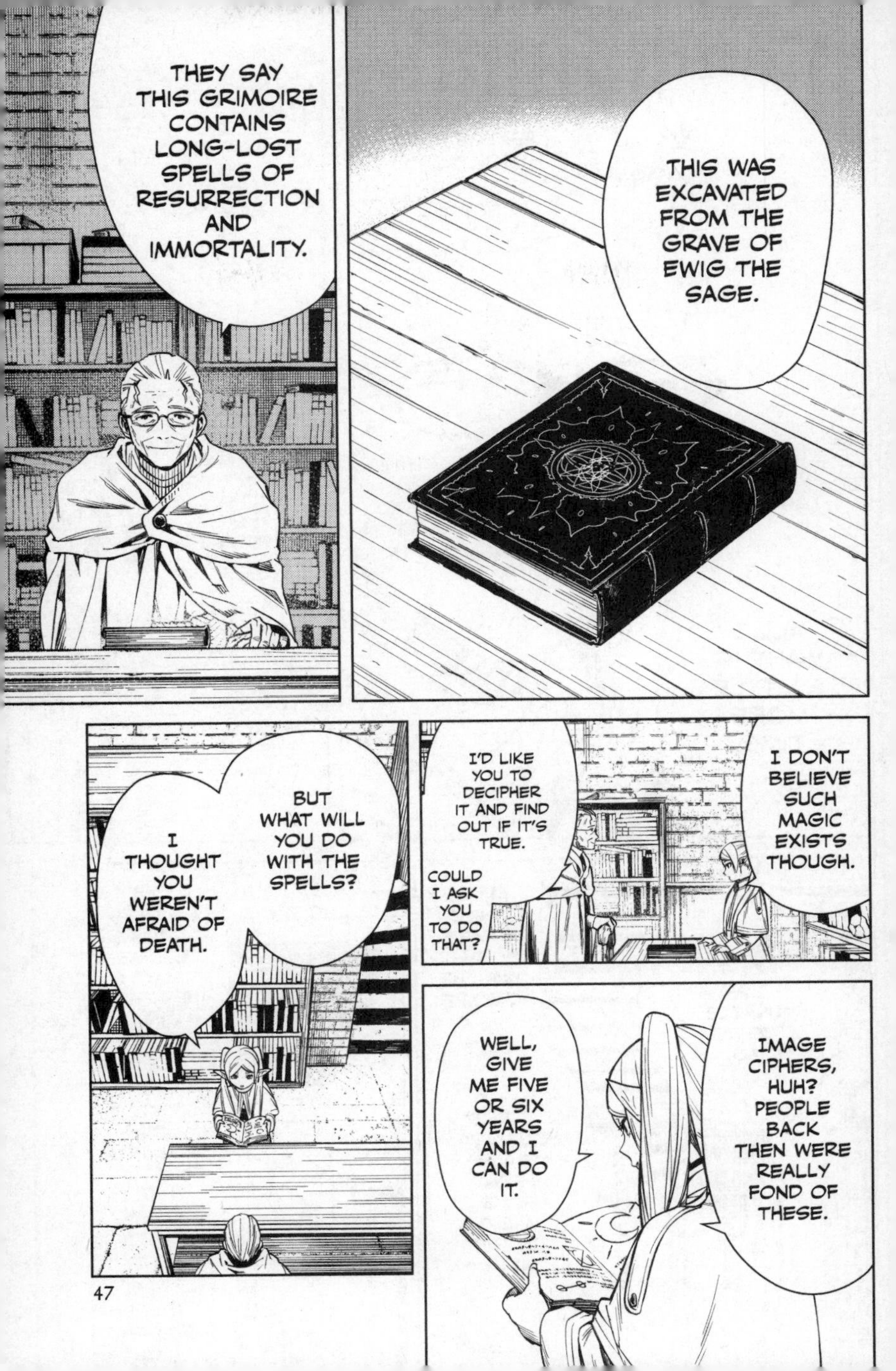
THIS WAS EXCAVATED FROM THE GRAVE OF EWIG THE SAGE.
THEY SAY THIS GRIMOIRE CONTAINS LONG-LOST SPELLS OF RESURRECTION AND IMMORTALITY.
I DON'T BELIEVE SUCH MAGIC EXISTS THOUGH.
I'D LIKE YOU TO DECIPHER IT AND FIND OUT IF IT'S TRUE.
COULD I ASK YOU TO DO THAT?
IMAGE CIPHERS, HUH? PEOPLE BACK THEN WERE REALLY FOND OF THESE.
WELL, GIVE ME FIVE OR SIX YEARS AND I CAN DO IT.
BUT WHAT WILL YOU DO WITH THE SPELLS?
I THOUGHT YOU WEREN'T AFRAID OF DEATH.

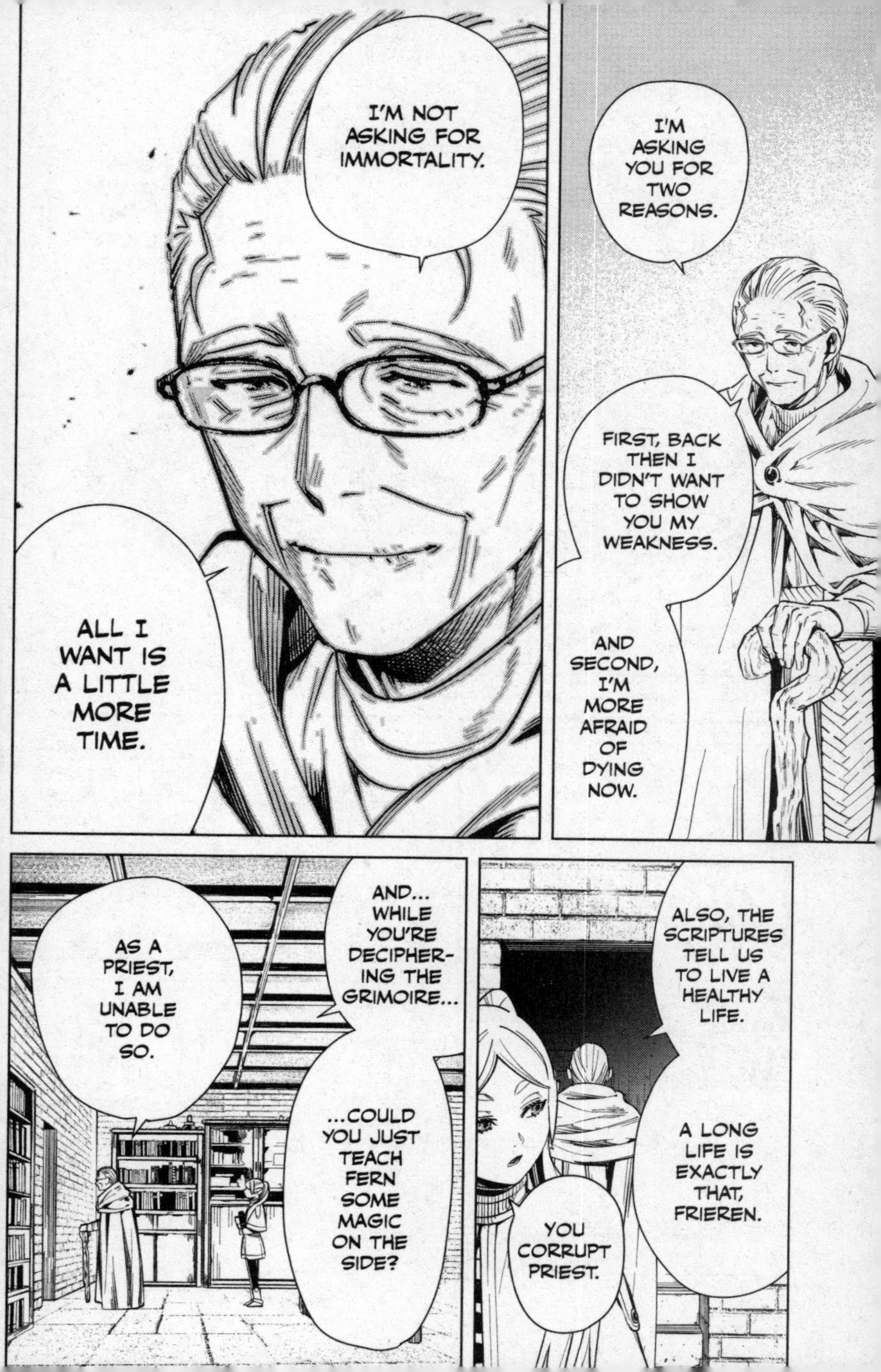
I'M ASKING YOU FOR TWO REASONS.
FIRST, BACK THEN I DIDN'T WANT TO SHOW YOU MY WEAKNESS.
AND SECOND, I'M MORE AFRAID OF DYING NOW.
I'M NOT ASKING FOR IMMORTALITY.
ALL I WANT IS A LITTLE MORE TIME.
ALSO, THE SCRIPTURES TELL US TO LIVE A HEALTHY LIFE.
A LONG LIFE IS EXACTLY THAT, FRIEREN.
YOU CORRUPT PRIEST.
AS A PRIEST, I AM UNABLE TO DO SO.
AND... WHILE YOU'RE DECIPHER-ING THE GRIMOIRE...
...COULD YOU JUST TEACH FERN SOME MAGIC ON THE SIDE?

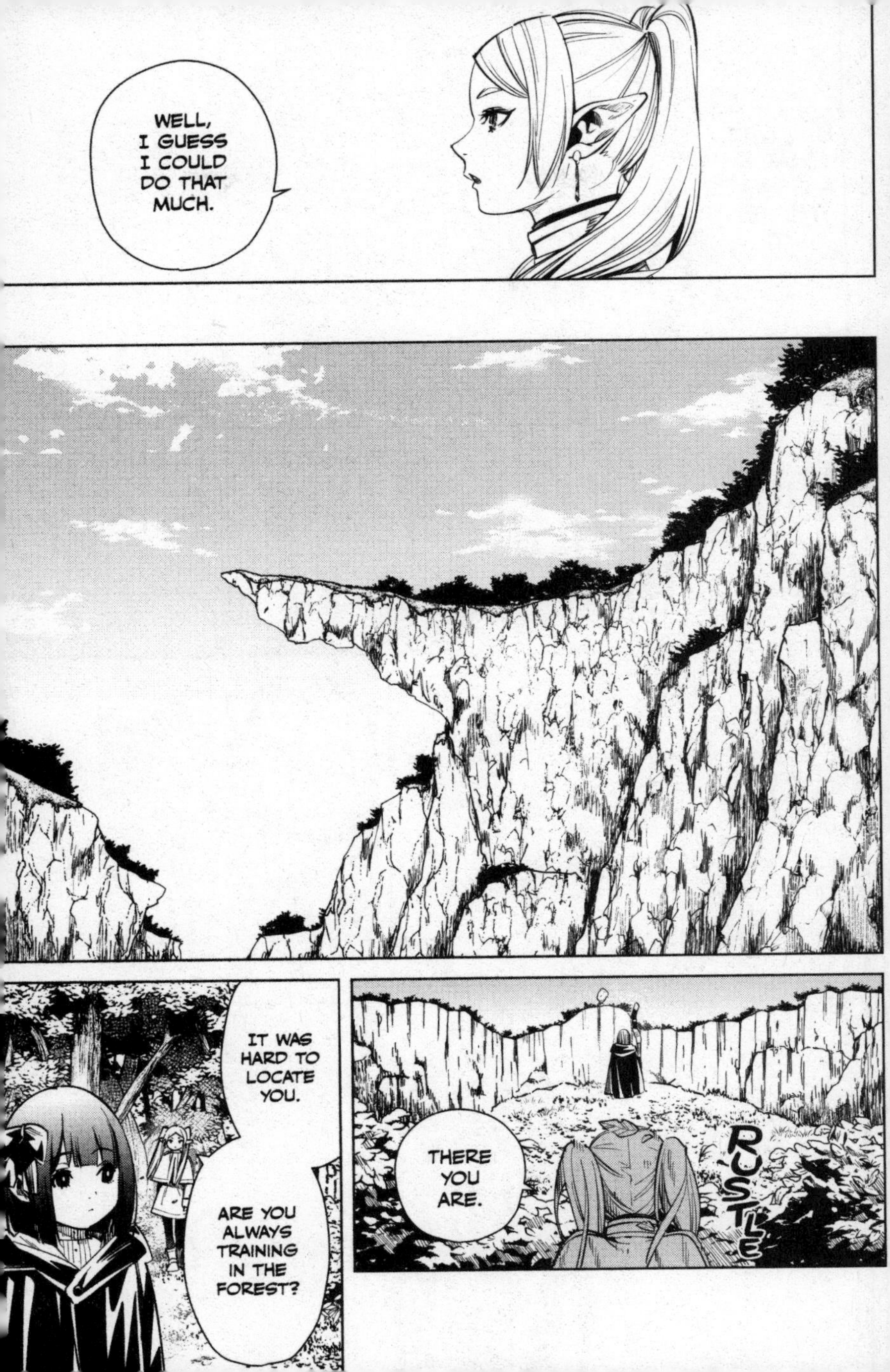
WELL, I GUESS I COULD DO THAT MUCH.
RUSTLE
THERE YOU ARE.
IT WAS HARD TO LOCATE YOU.
ARE YOU ALWAYS TRAINING IN THE FOREST?

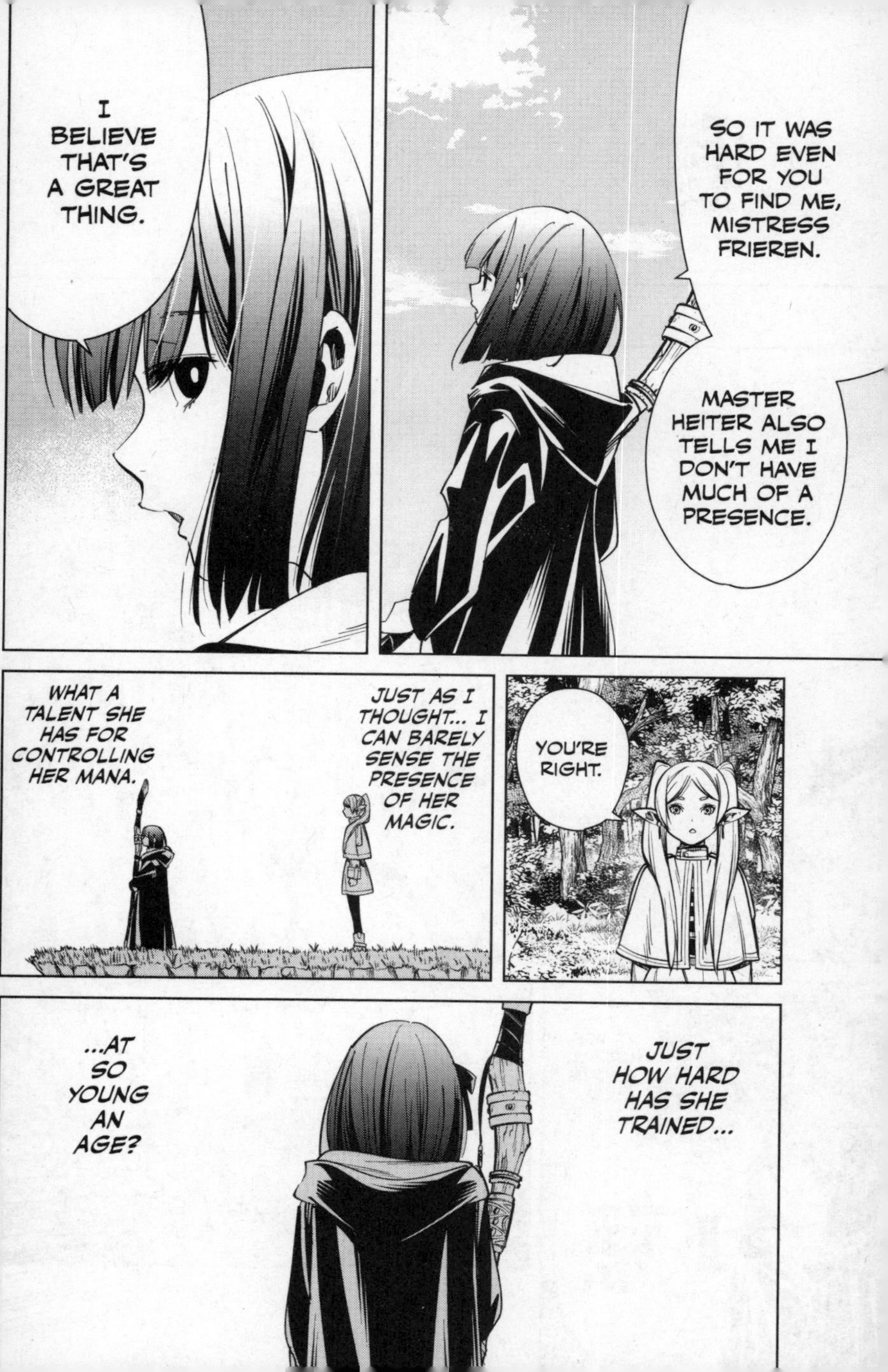
SO IT WAS HARD EVEN FOR YOU TO FIND ME, MISTRESS FRIEREN.
MASTER HEITER ALSO TELLS ME I DON'T HAVE MUCH OF A PRESENCE.
I BELIEVE THAT'S A GREAT THING.
YOU'RE RIGHT.
JUST AS I THOUGHT... I CAN BARELY SENSE THE PRESENCE OF HER MAGIC.
WHAT A TALENT SHE HAS FOR CONTROLLING HER MANA.
JUST HOW HARD HAS SHE TRAINED...
...AT SO YOUNG AN AGE?

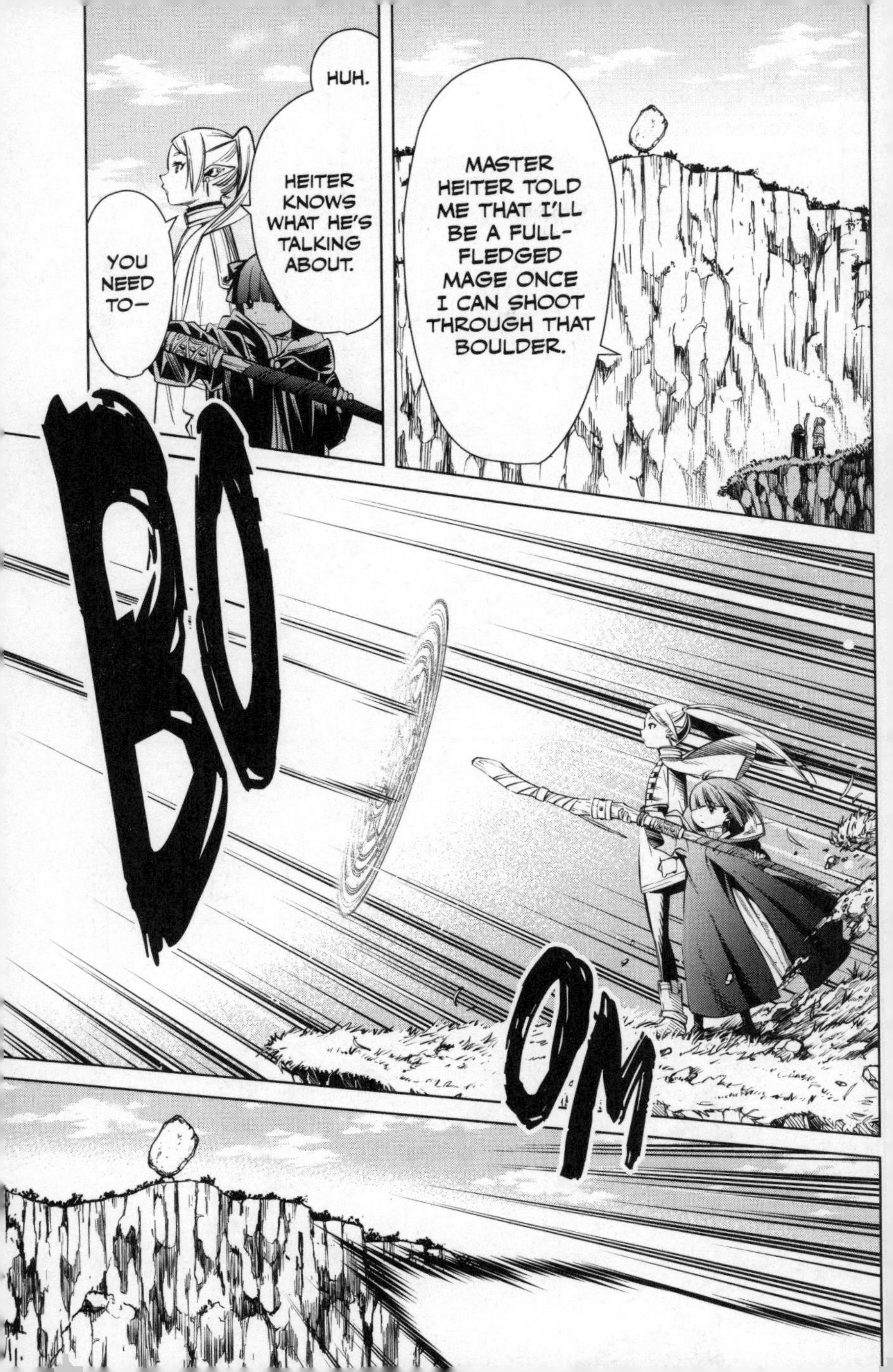
MASTER HEITER TOLD ME THAT I'LL BE A FULL-FLEDGED MAGE ONCE I CAN SHOOT THROUGH THAT BOULDER.
HUH.
HEITER KNOWS WHAT HE'S TALKING ABOUT.
YOU NEED TO—
BOOM

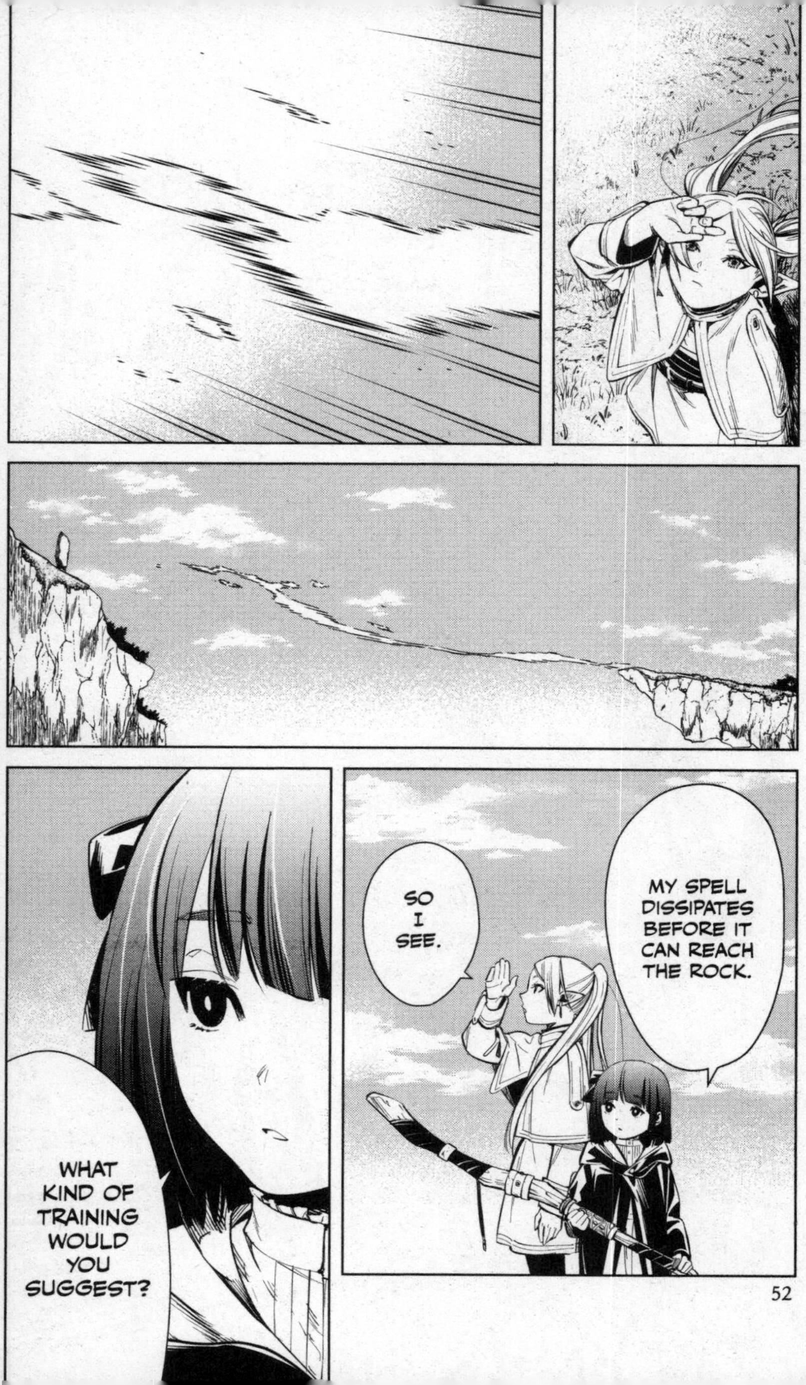
MY SPELL DISSIPATES BEFORE IT CAN REACH THE ROCK.
SO I SEE.
WHAT KIND OF TRAINING WOULD YOU SUGGEST?

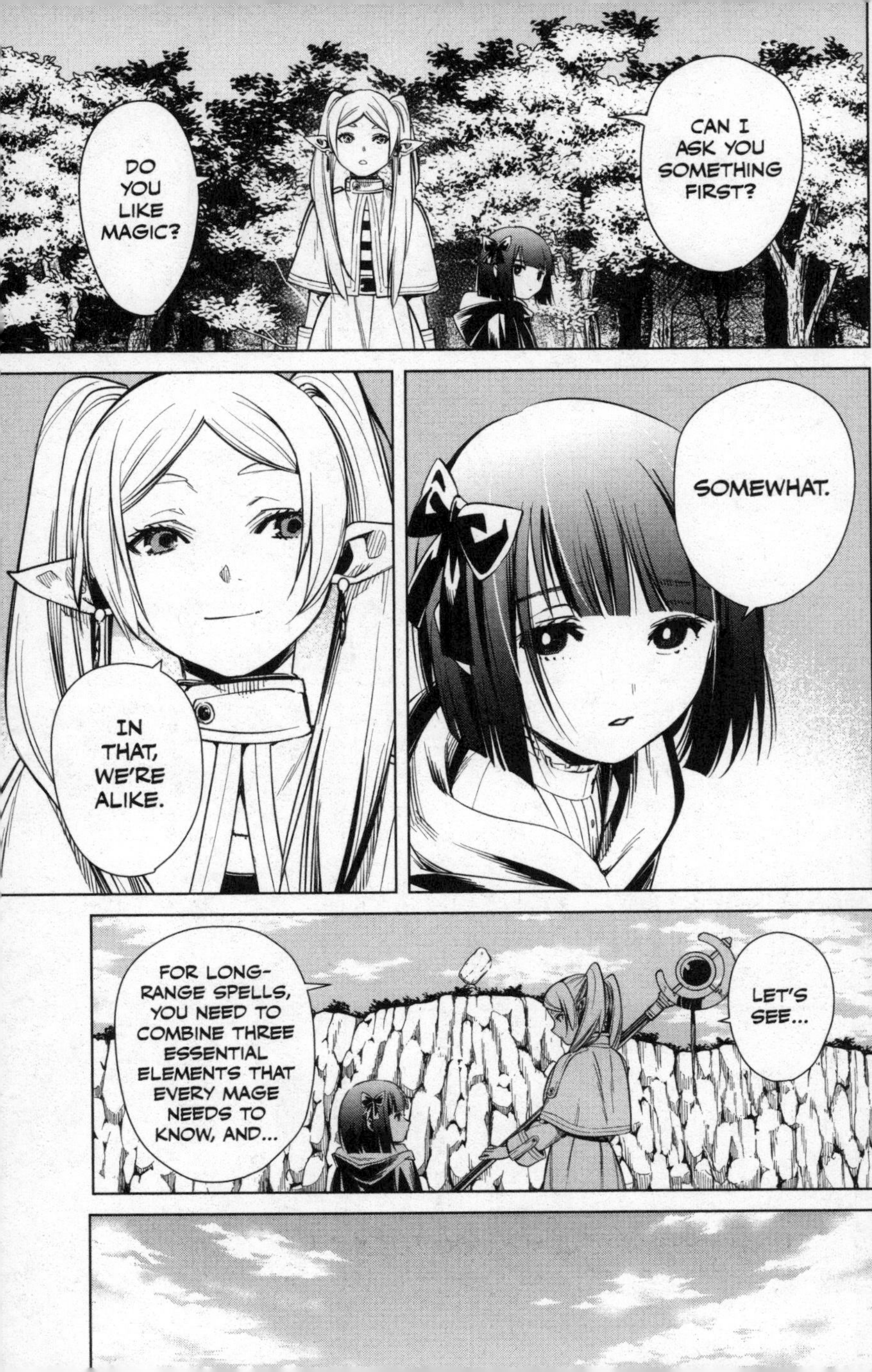
CAN I ASK YOU SOMETHING FIRST?
DO YOU LIKE MAGIC?
SOMEWHAT.
IN THAT, WE'RE ALIKE.
LET'S SEE...
FOR LONG-RANGE SPELLS, YOU NEED TO COMBINE THREE ESSENTIAL ELEMENTS THAT EVERY MAGE NEEDS TO KNOW, AND...

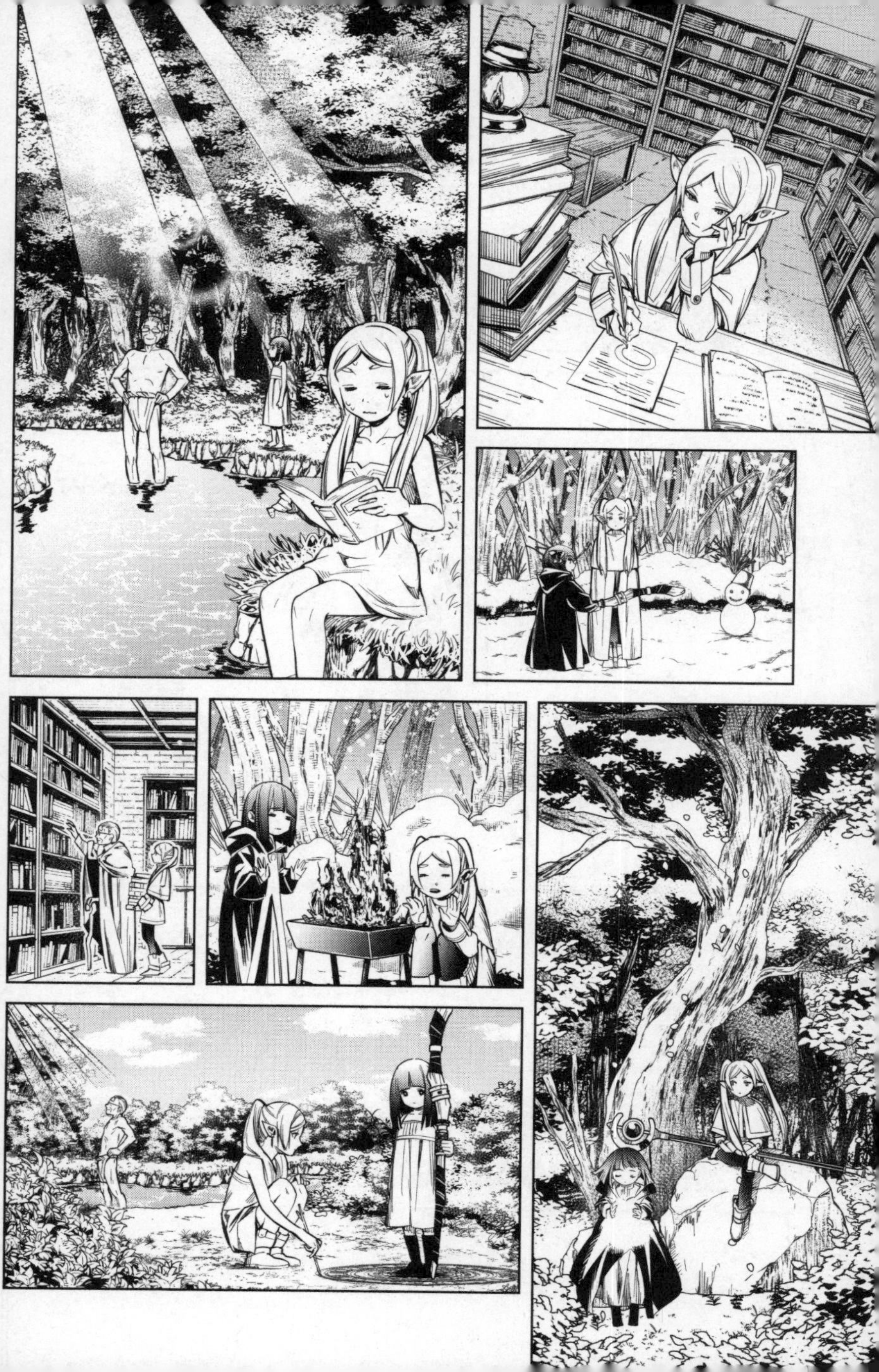

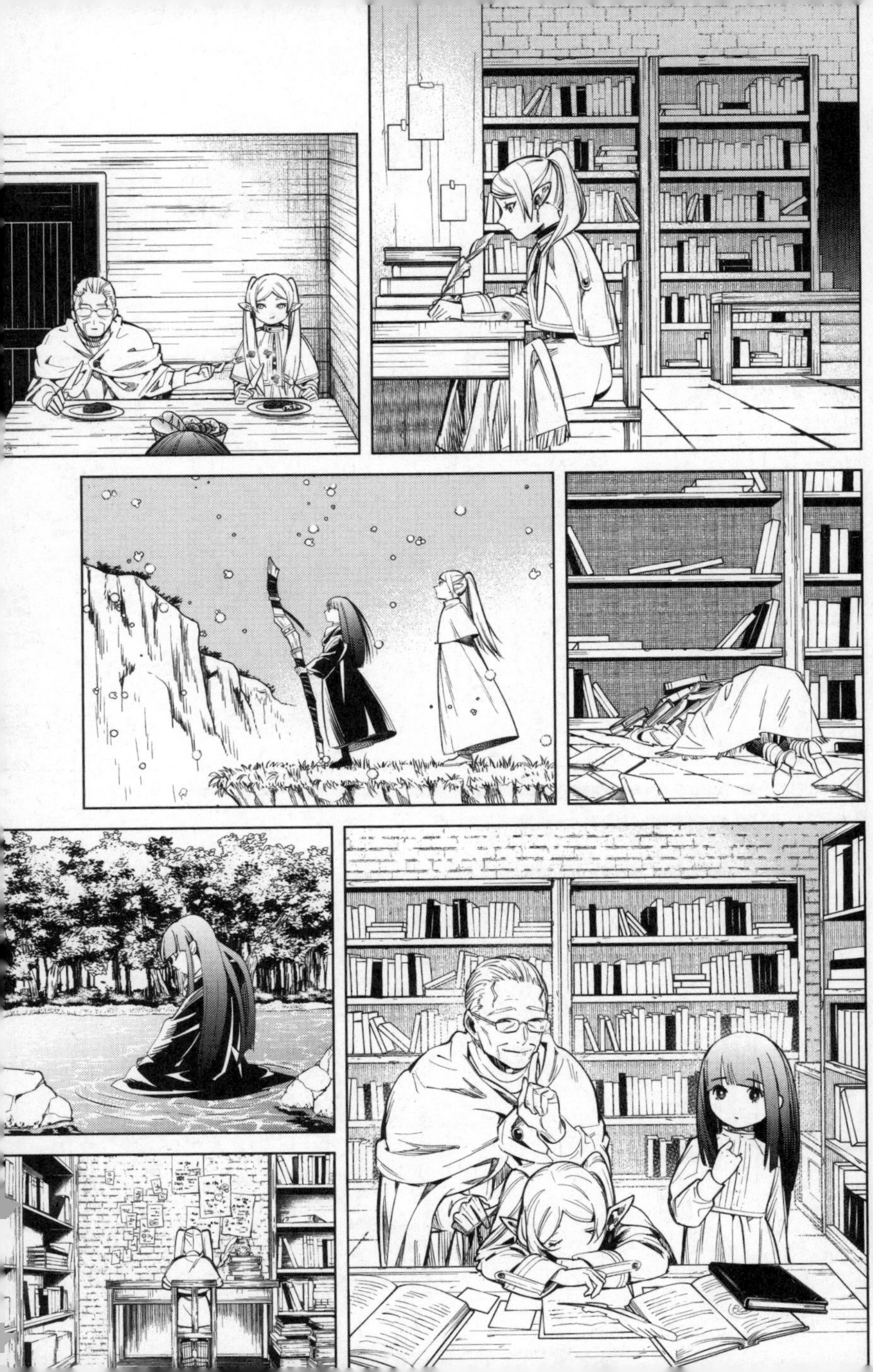

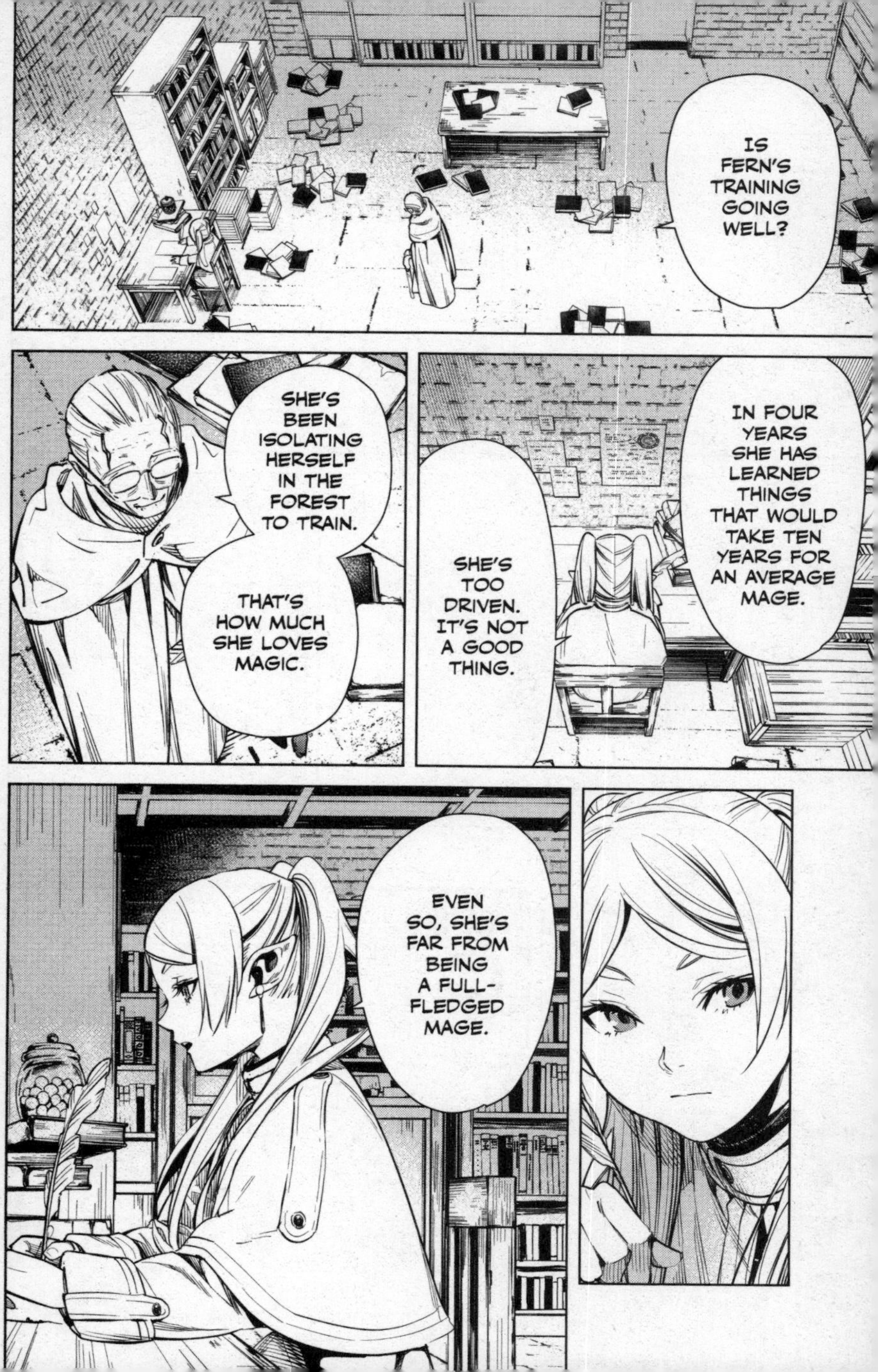
IS FERN'S TRAINING GOING WELL?
IN FOUR YEARS SHE HAS LEARNED THINGS THAT WOULD TAKE TEN YEARS FOR AN AVERAGE MAGE.
SHE'S TOO DRIVEN. IT'S NOT A GOOD THING.
SHE'S BEEN ISOLATING HERSELF IN THE FOREST TO TRAIN.
THAT'S HOW MUCH SHE LOVES MAGIC.
EVEN SO, SHE'S FAR FROM BEING A FULL-FLEDGED MAGE.

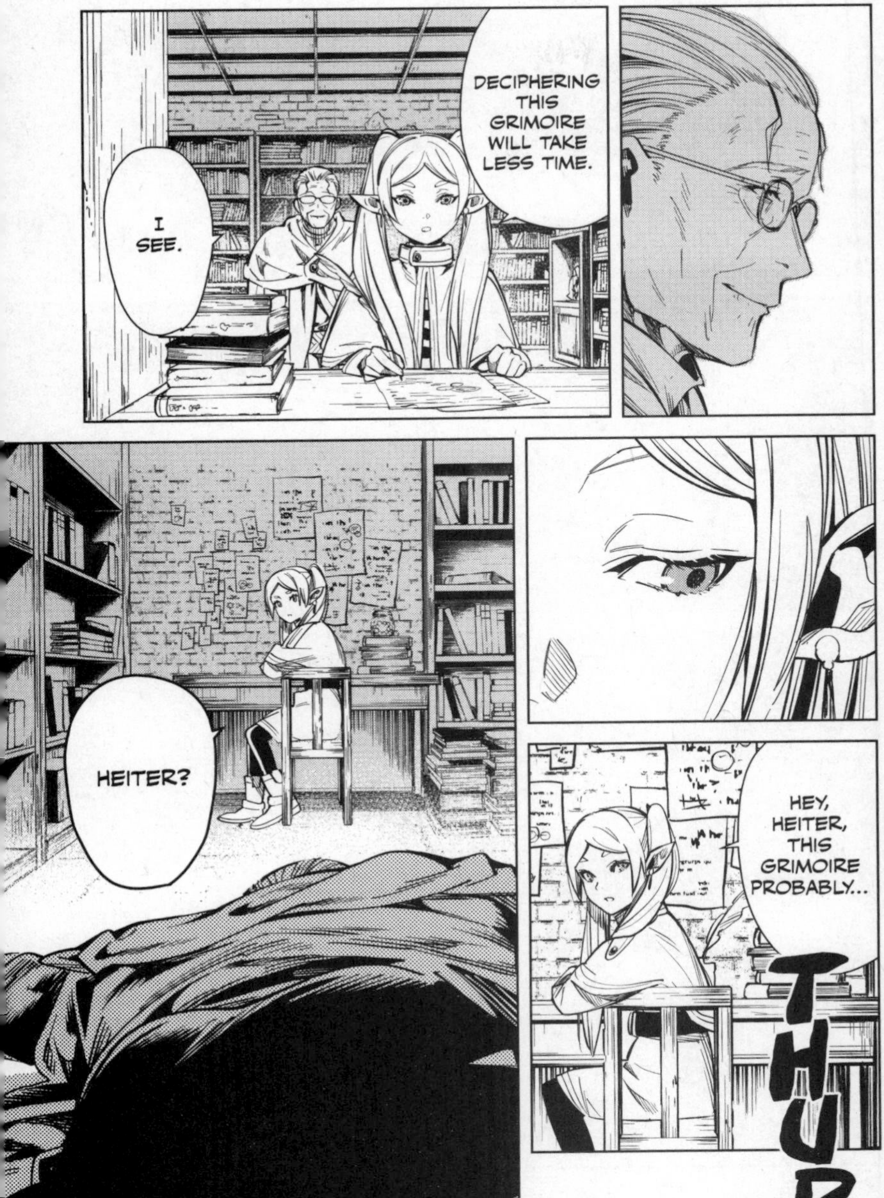
DECIPHERING THIS GRIMOIRE WILL TAKE LESS TIME.
I SEE.
HEY, HEITER, THIS GRIMOIRE PROBABLY...
THUD
HEITER?

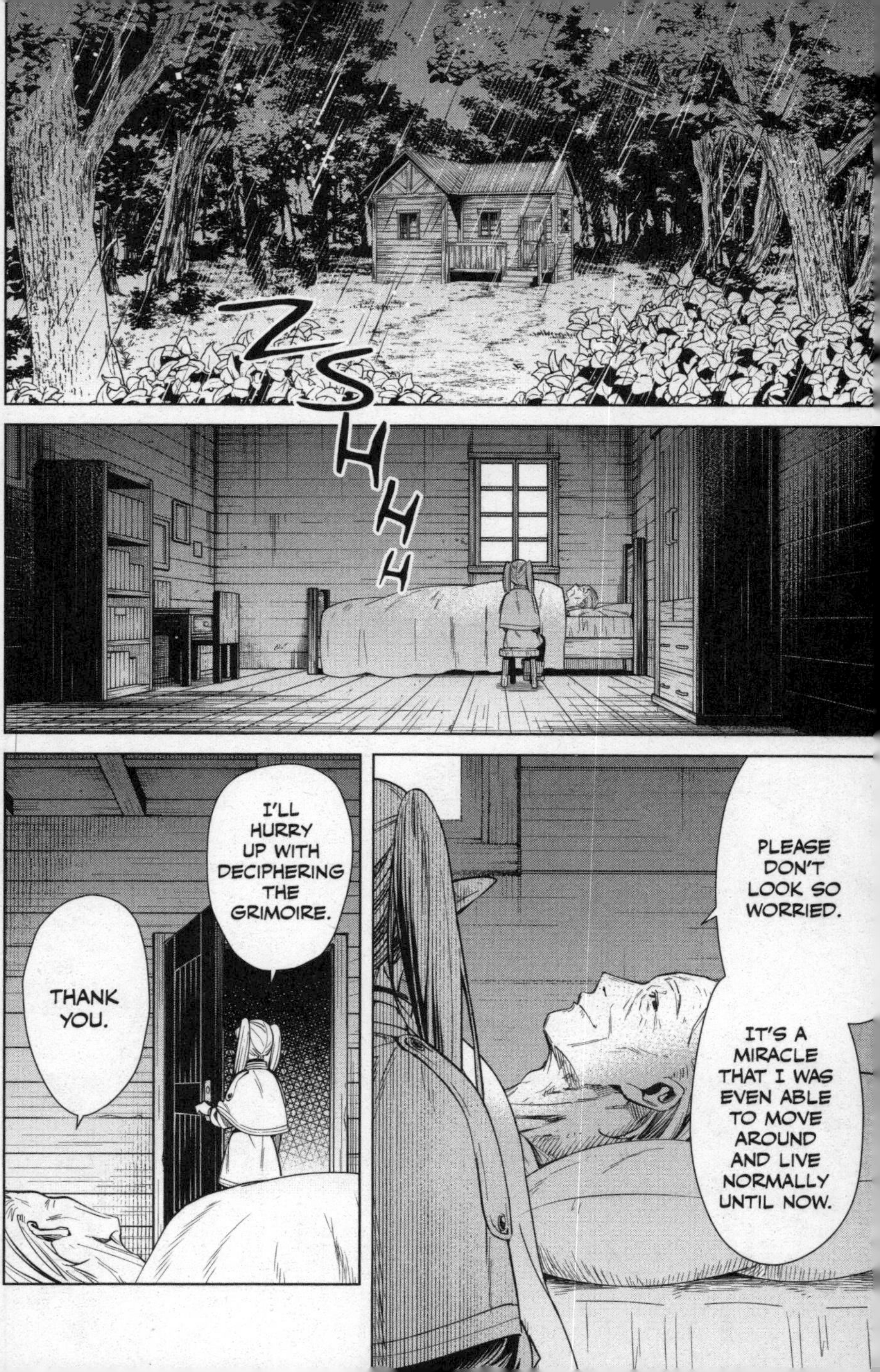
ZSHHHH
PLEASE DON'T LOOK SO WORRIED.
IT'S A MIRACLE THAT I WAS EVEN ABLE TO MOVE AROUND AND LIVE NORMALLY UNTIL NOW.
I'LL HURRY UP WITH DECIPHERING THE GRIMOIRE.
THANK YOU.

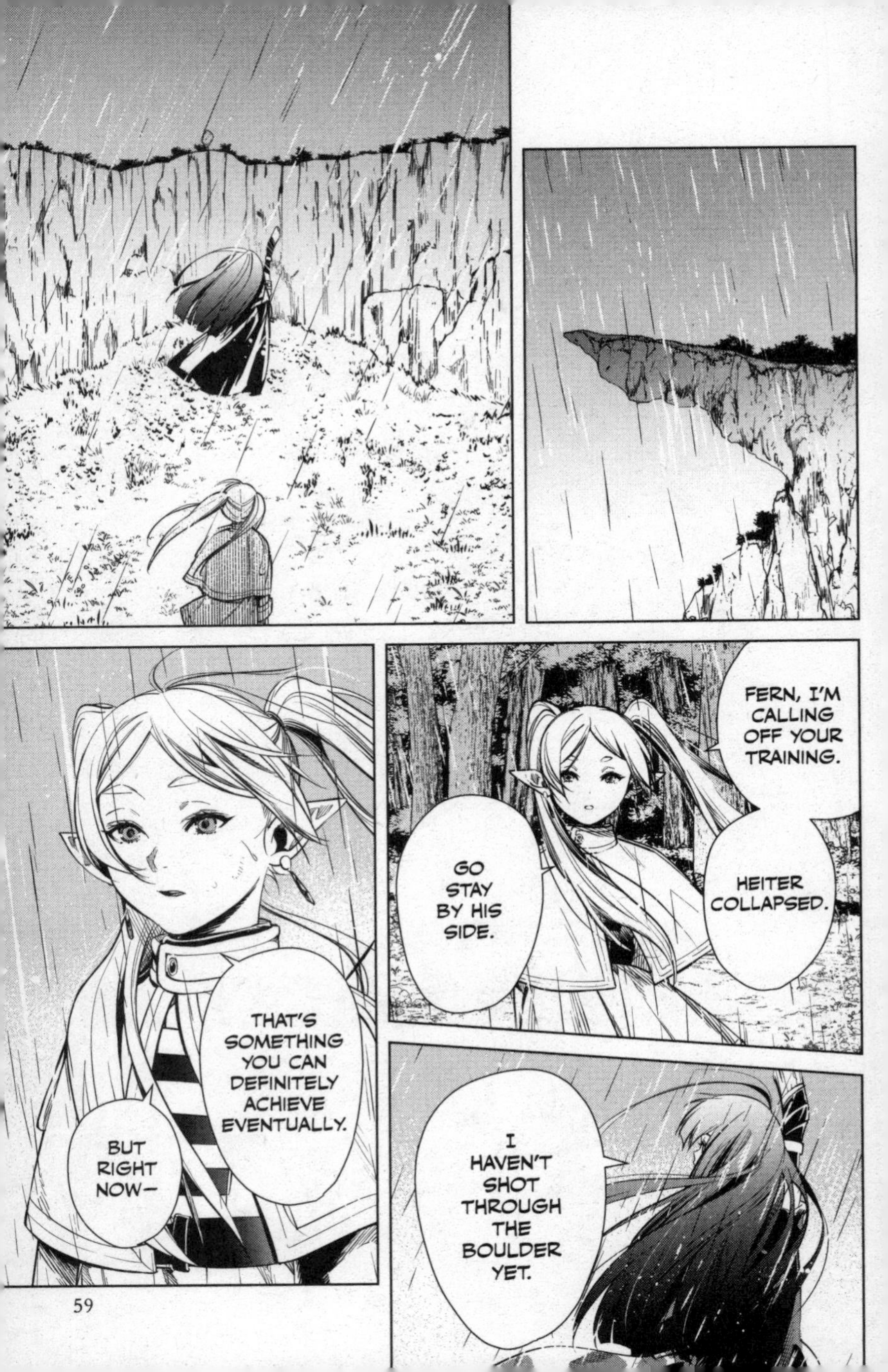
FERN, I'M CALLING OFF YOUR TRAINING.
HEITER COLLAPSED.
GO STAY BY HIS SIDE.
I HAVEN'T SHOT THROUGH THE BOULDER YET.
THAT'S SOMETHING YOU CAN DEFINITELY ACHIEVE EVENTUALLY.
BUT RIGHT NOW—

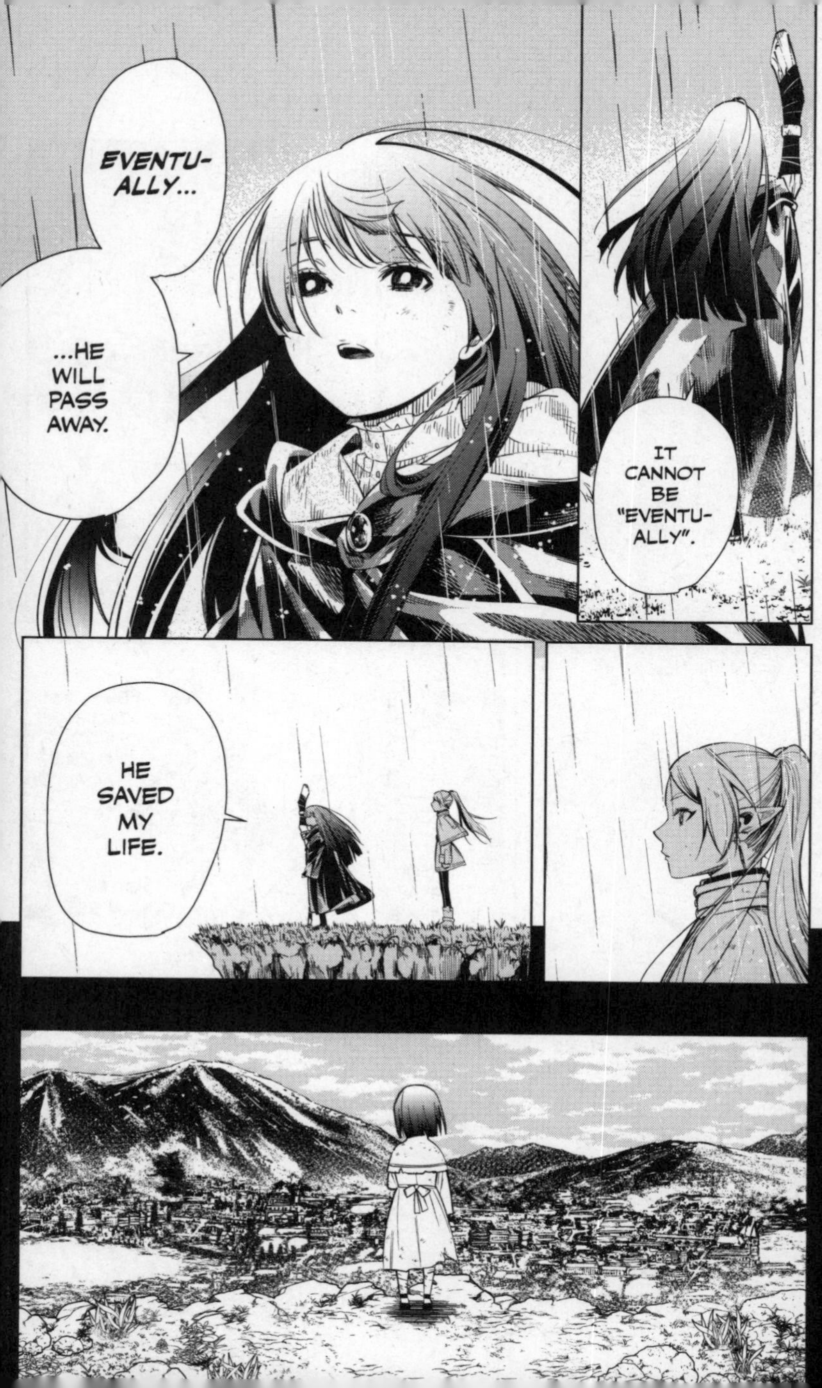
IT CANNOT BE "EVENTU-ALLY".
EVENTU-ALLY...
...HE WILL PASS AWAY.
HE SAVED MY LIFE.

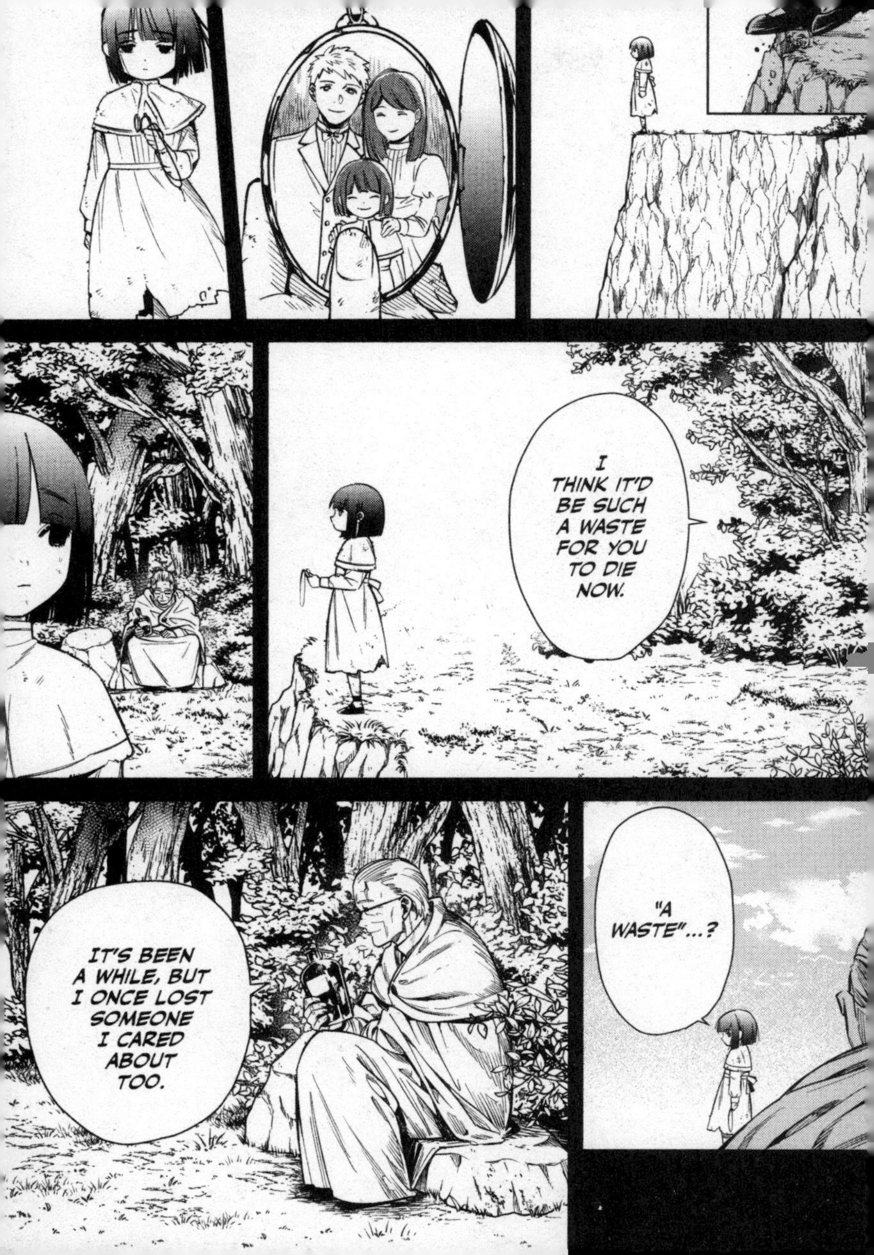
I THINK IT'D BE SUCH A WASTE FOR YOU TO DIE NOW.
"A WASTE"...?
IT'S BEEN A WHILE, BUT I ONCE LOST SOMEONE I CARED ABOUT TOO.

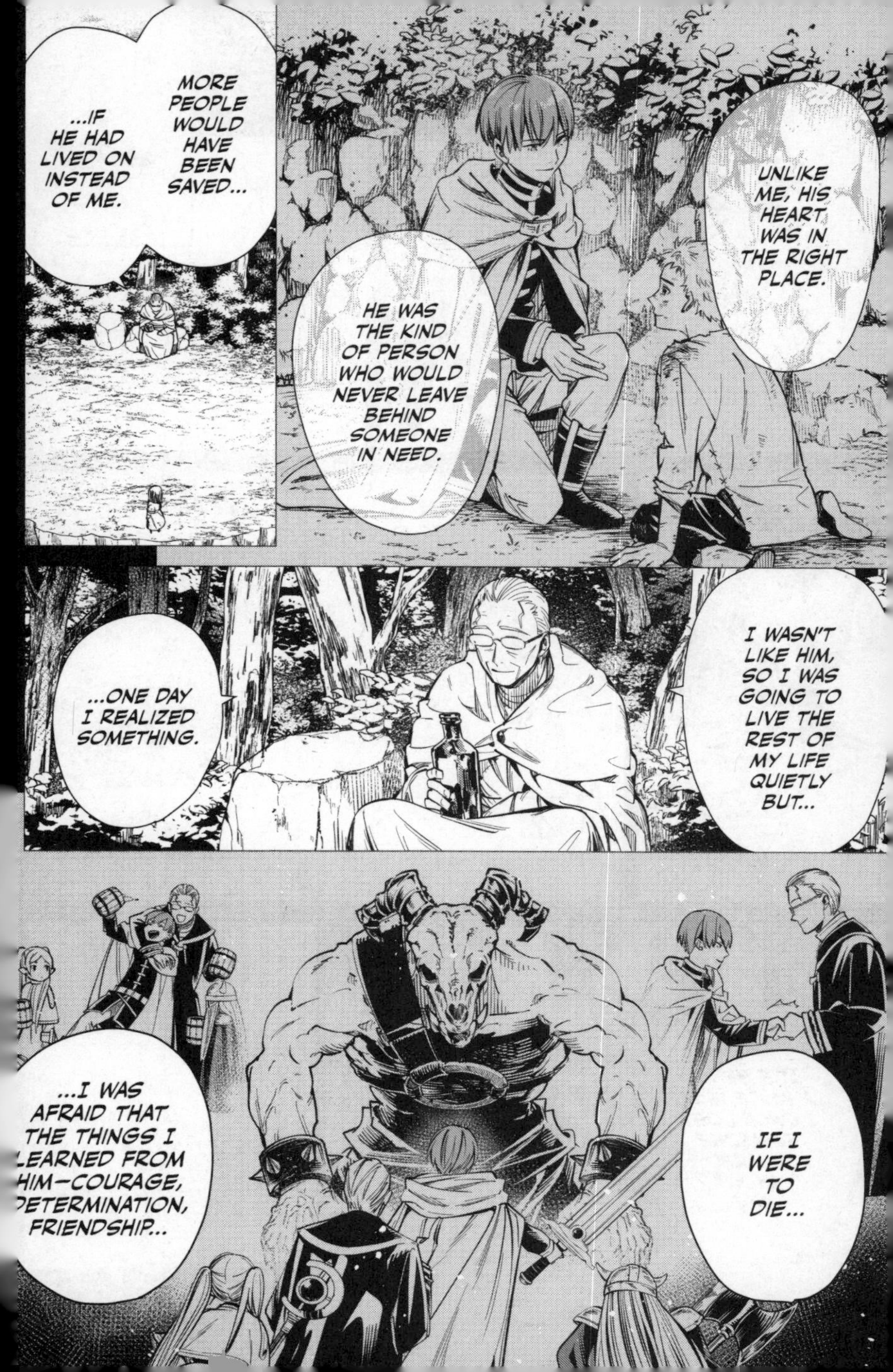
UNLIKE ME, HIS HEART WAS IN THE RIGHT PLACE.
HE WAS THE KIND OF PERSON WHO WOULD NEVER LEAVE BEHIND SOMEONE IN NEED.
MORE PEOPLE WOULD HAVE BEEN SAVED...
...IF HE HAD LIVED ON INSTEAD OF ME.
I WASN'T LIKE HIM, SO I WAS GOING TO LIVE THE REST OF MY LIFE QUIETLY BUT...
...ONE DAY I REALIZED SOMETHING.
IF I WERE TO DIE...
...I WAS AFRAID THAT THE THINGS I LEARNED FROM HIM—COURAGE, DETERMINATION, FRIENDSHIP...

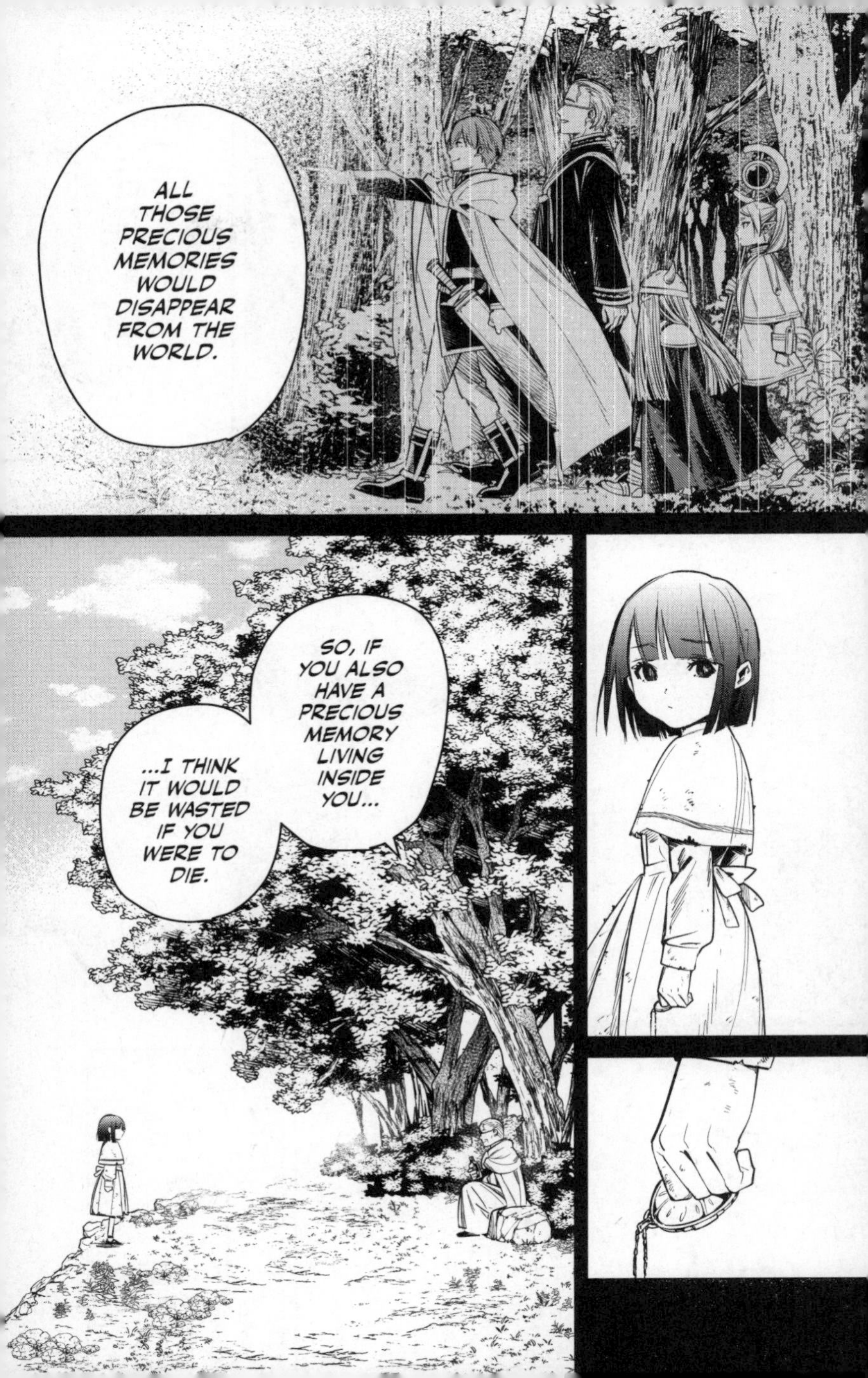
ALL THOSE PRECIOUS MEMORIES WOULD DISAPPEAR FROM THE WORLD.
SO, IF YOU ALSO HAVE A PRECIOUS MEMORY LIVING INSIDE YOU...
...I THINK IT WOULD BE WASTED IF YOU WERE TO DIE.

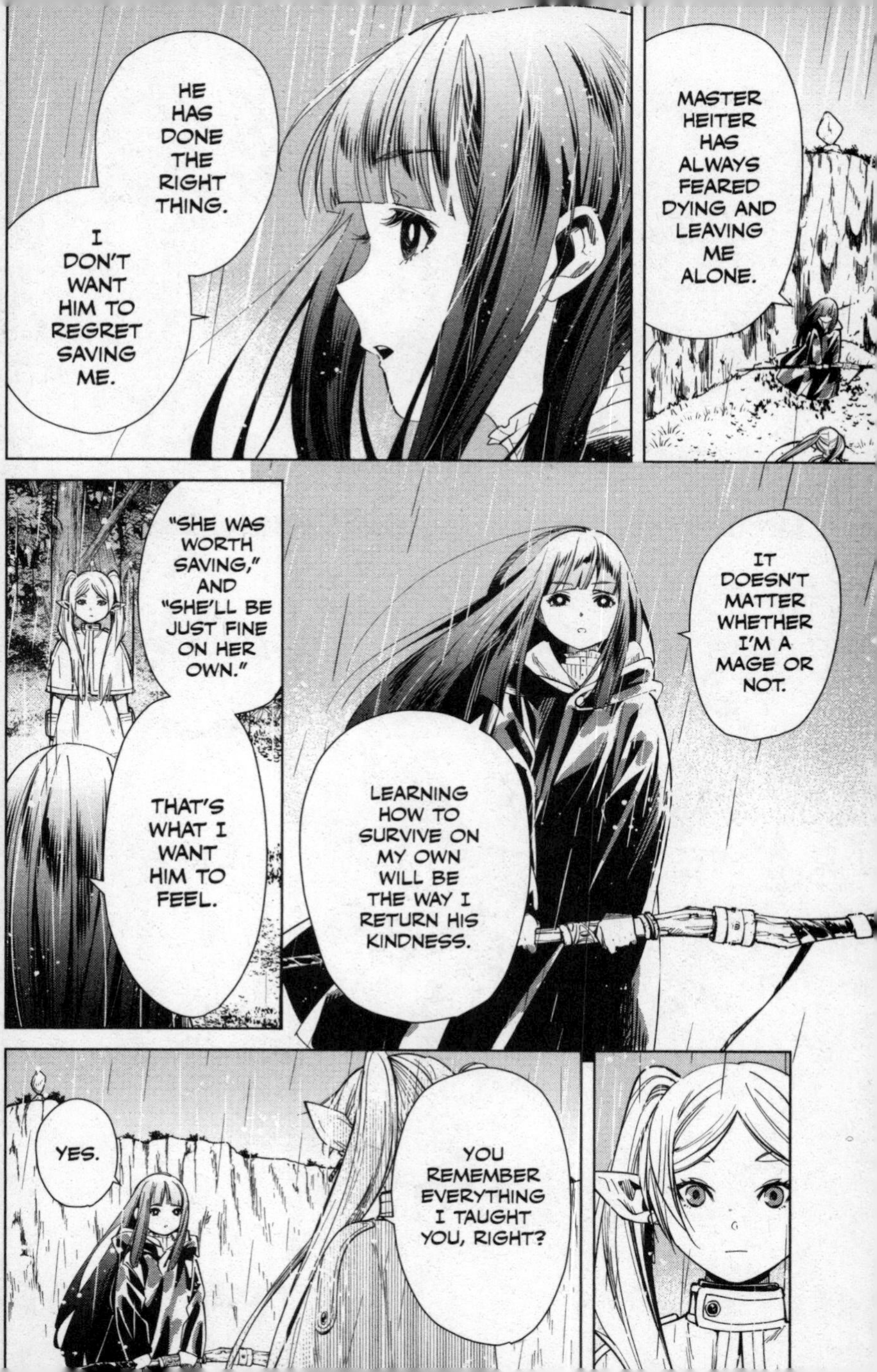
MASTER HEITER HAS ALWAYS FEARED DYING AND LEAVING ME ALONE.
HE HAS DONE THE RIGHT THING.
I DON'T WANT HIM TO REGRET SAVING ME.
IT DOESN'T MATTER WHETHER I'M A MAGE OR NOT.
LEARNING HOW TO SURVIVE ON MY OWN WILL BE THE WAY I RETURN HIS KINDNESS.
"SHE WAS WORTH SAVING," AND "SHE'LL BE JUST FINE ON HER OWN."
THAT'S WHAT I WANT HIM TO FEEL.
YOU REMEMBER EVERYTHING I TAUGHT YOU, RIGHT?
YES.

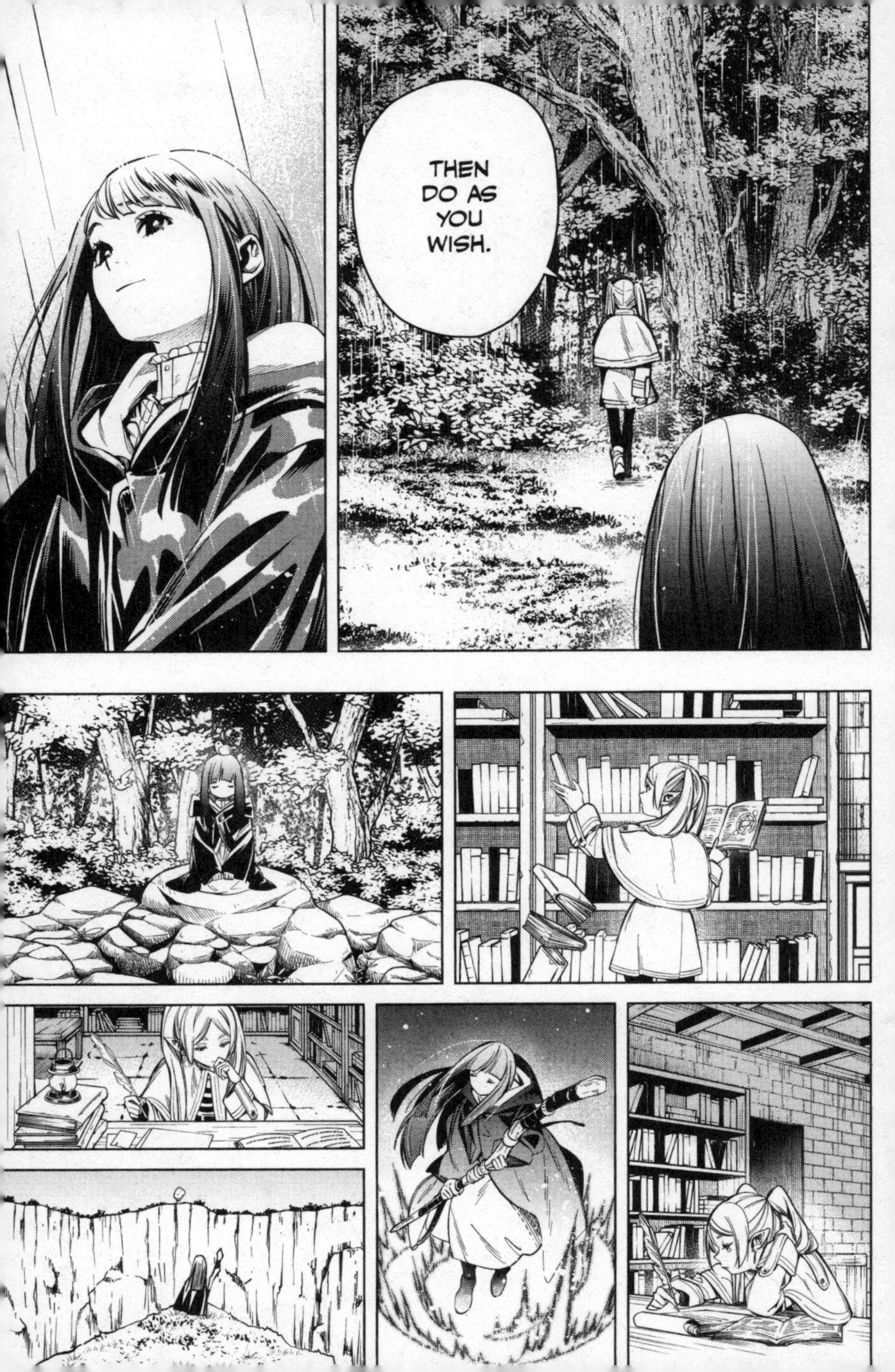
THEN DO AS YOU WISH.

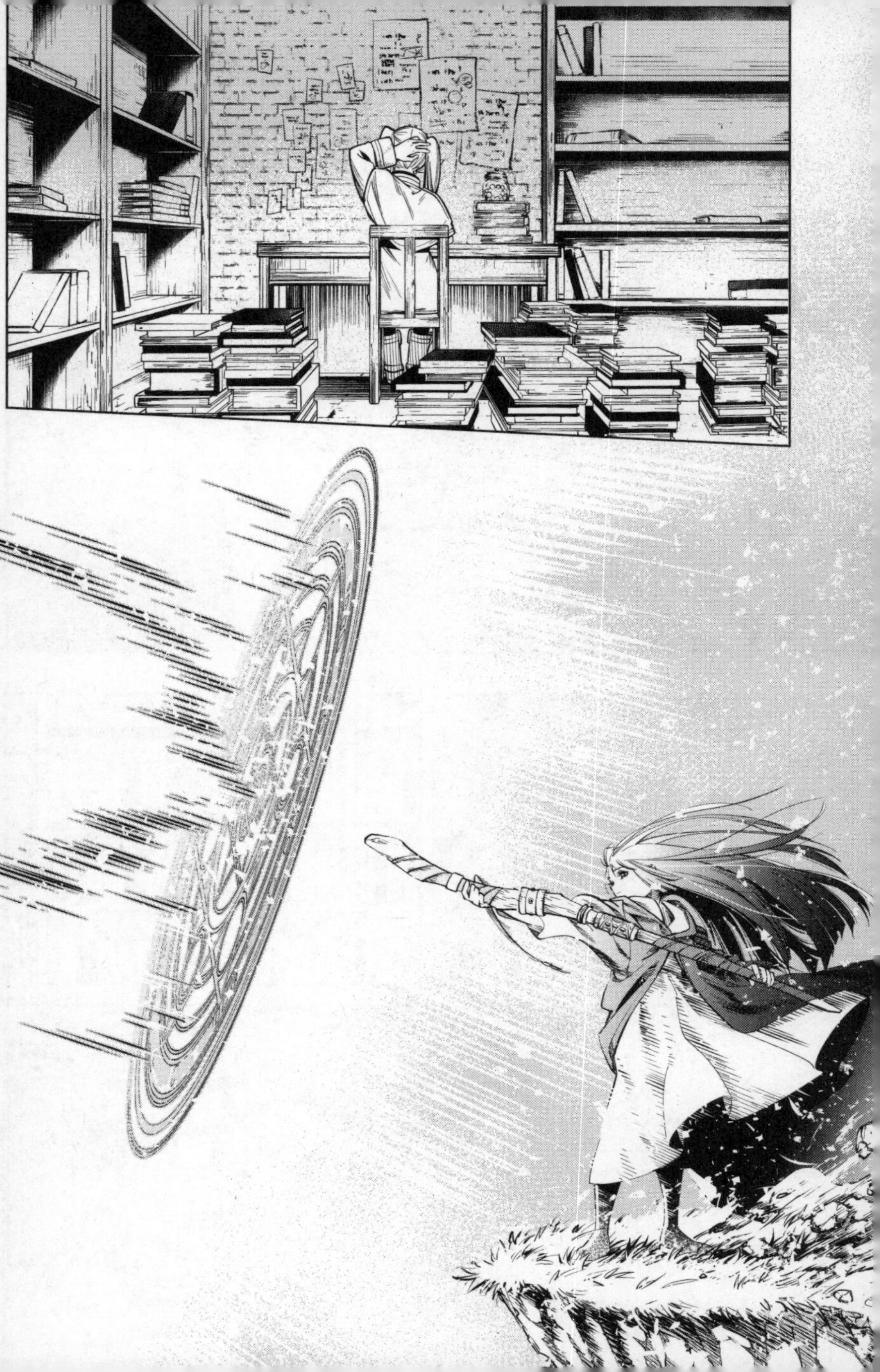

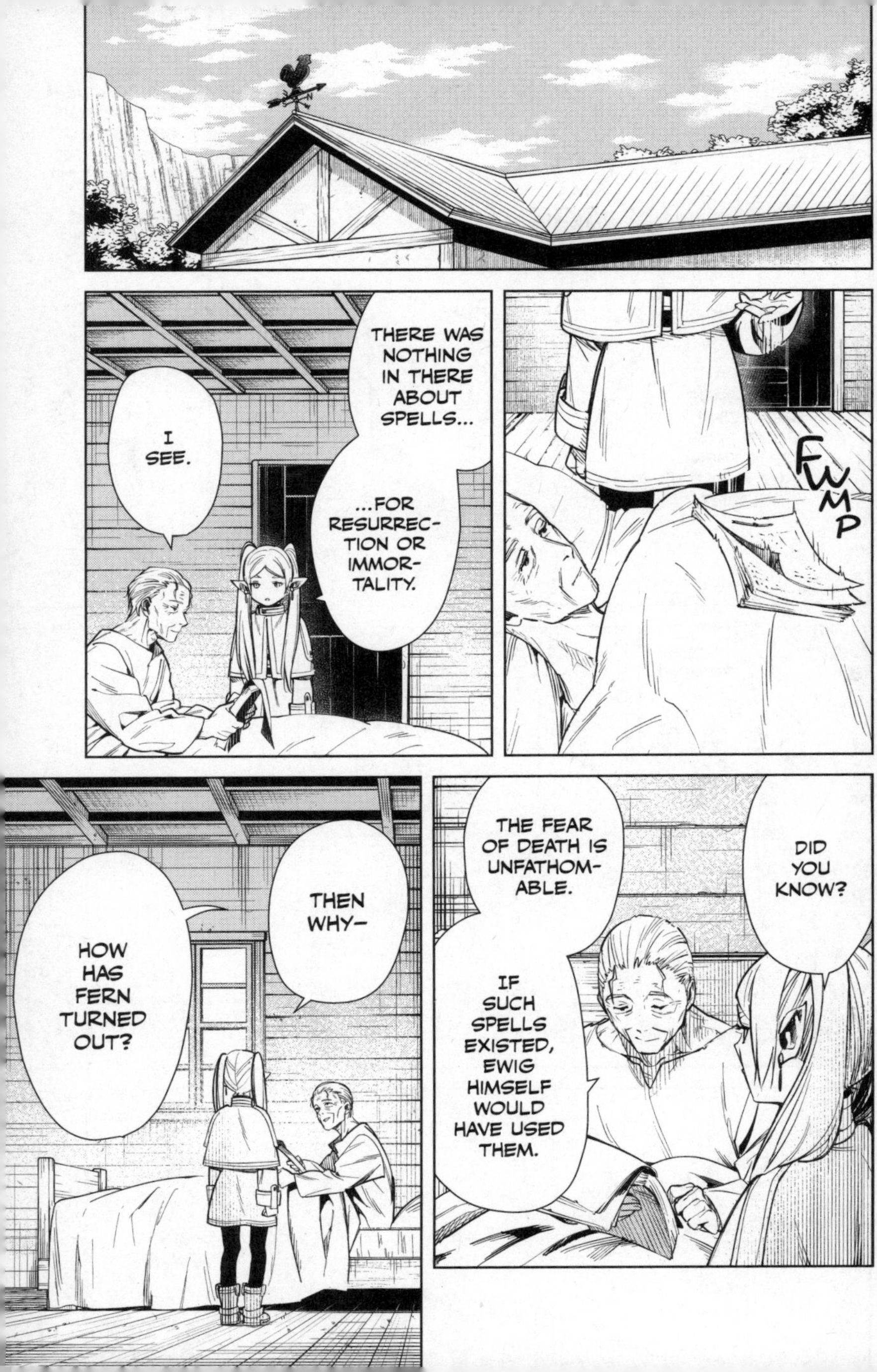
FWMP
THERE WAS NOTHING IN THERE ABOUT SPELLS...
...FOR RESURRECTION OR IMMORTALITY.
I SEE.
DID YOU KNOW?
THE FEAR OF DEATH IS UNFATHOMABLE.
IF SUCH SPELLS EXISTED, EWIG HIMSELF WOULD HAVE USED THEM.
THEN WHY—
HOW HAS FERN TURNED OUT?

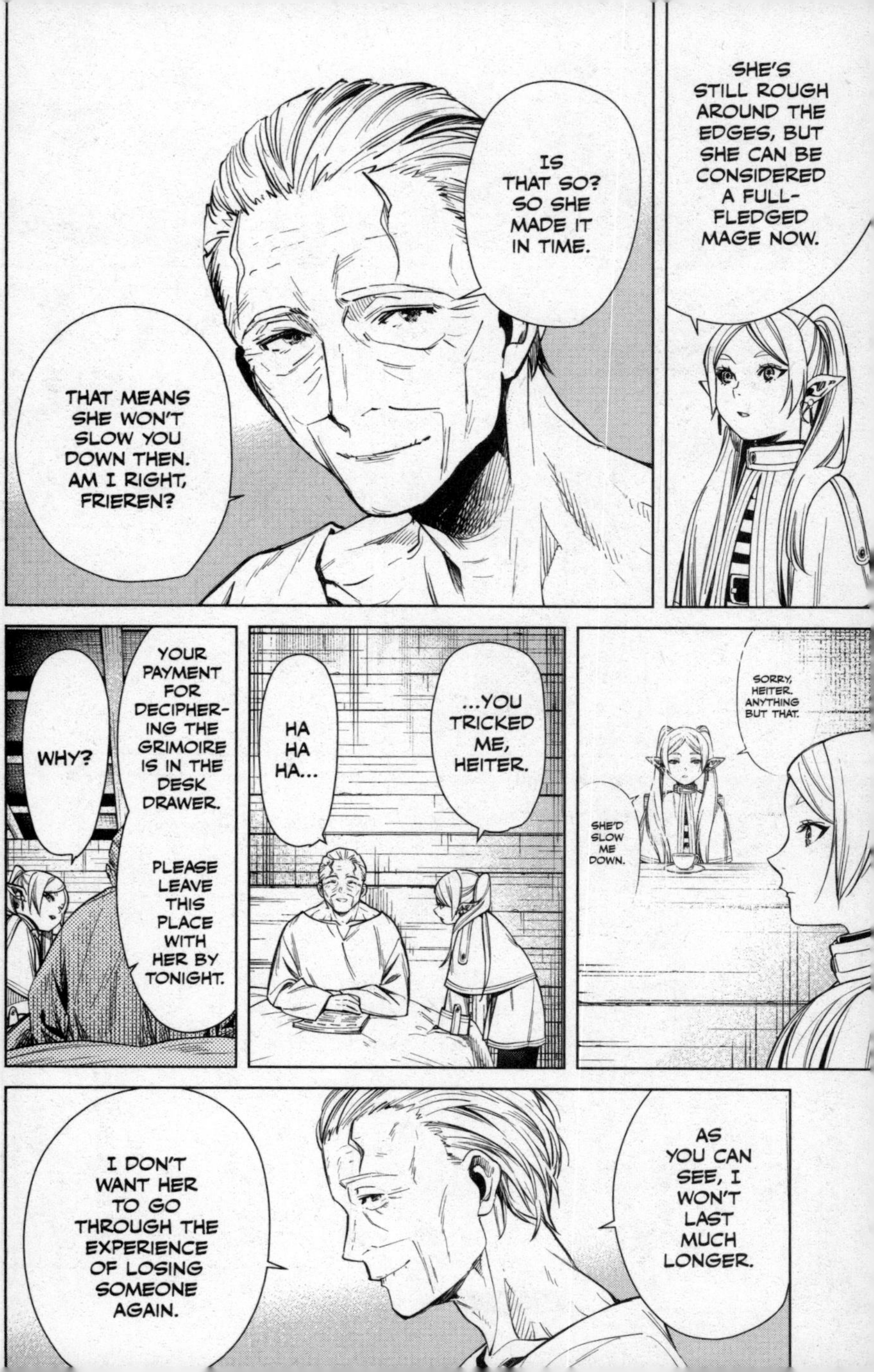
SHE'S STILL ROUGH AROUND THE EDGES, BUT SHE CAN BE CONSIDERED A FULL-FLEDGED MAGE NOW.
IS THAT SO? SO SHE MADE IT IN TIME.
THAT MEANS SHE WON'T SLOW YOU DOWN THEN. AM I RIGHT, FRIEREN?
SORRY, HEITER. ANYTHING BUT THAT.
SHE'D SLOW ME DOWN.
...YOU TRICKED ME, HEITER.
HA HA HA...
YOUR PAYMENT FOR DECIPHERING THE GRIMOIRE IS IN THE DESK DRAWER.
WHY?
PLEASE LEAVE THIS PLACE WITH HER BY TONIGHT.
AS YOU CAN SEE, I WON'T LAST MUCH LONGER.
I DON'T WANT HER TO GO THROUGH THE EXPERIENCE OF LOSING SOMEONE AGAIN.

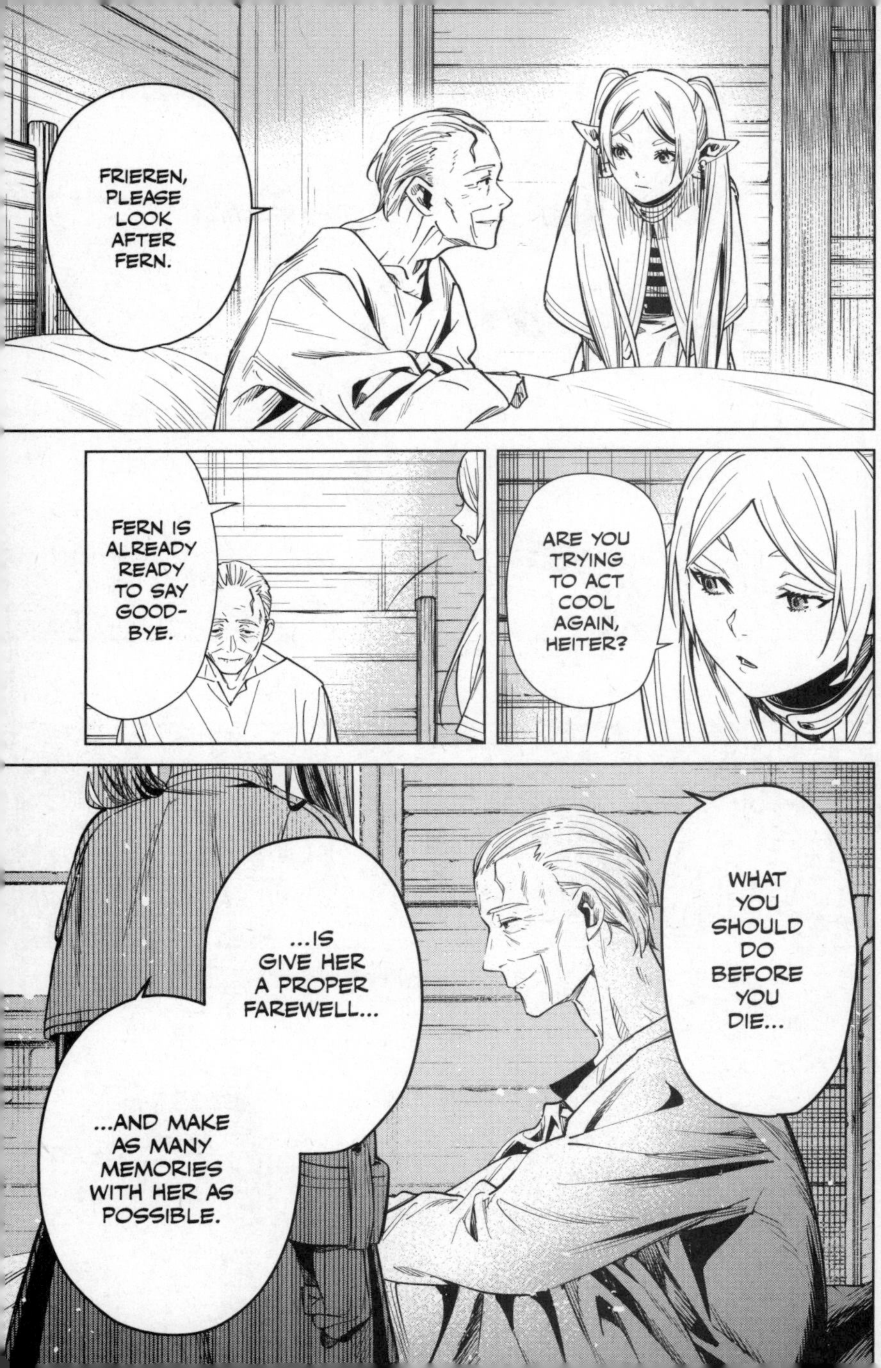
FRIEREN, PLEASE LOOK AFTER FERN.
ARE YOU TRYING TO ACT COOL AGAIN, HEITER?
FERN IS ALREADY READY TO SAY GOOD-BYE.
WHAT YOU SHOULD DO BEFORE YOU DIE...
...IS GIVE HER A PROPER FAREWELL...
...AND MAKE AS MANY MEMORIES WITH HER AS POSSIBLE.

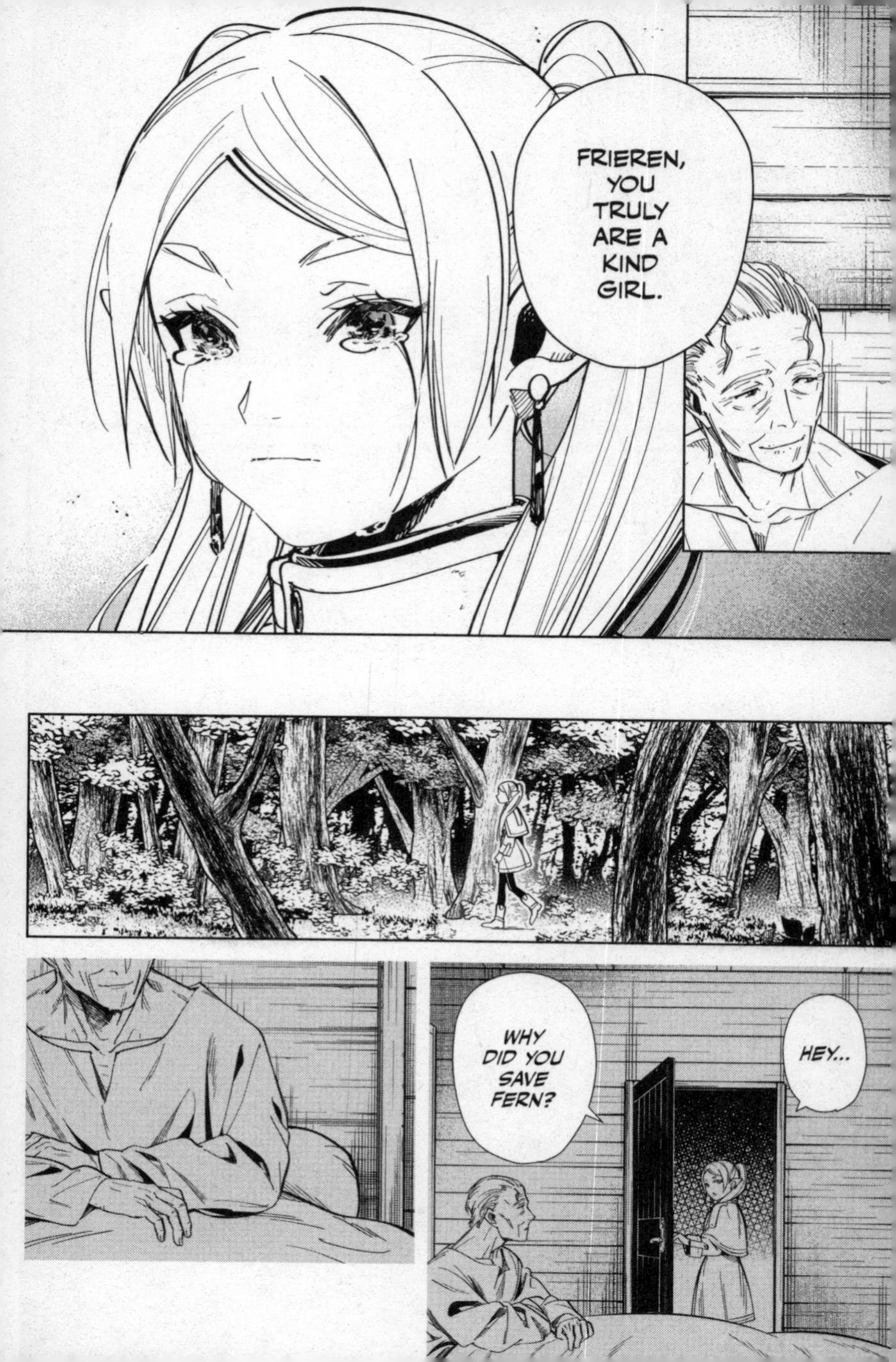
FRIEREN, YOU TRULY ARE A KIND GIRL.
HEY...
WHY DID YOU SAVE FERN?

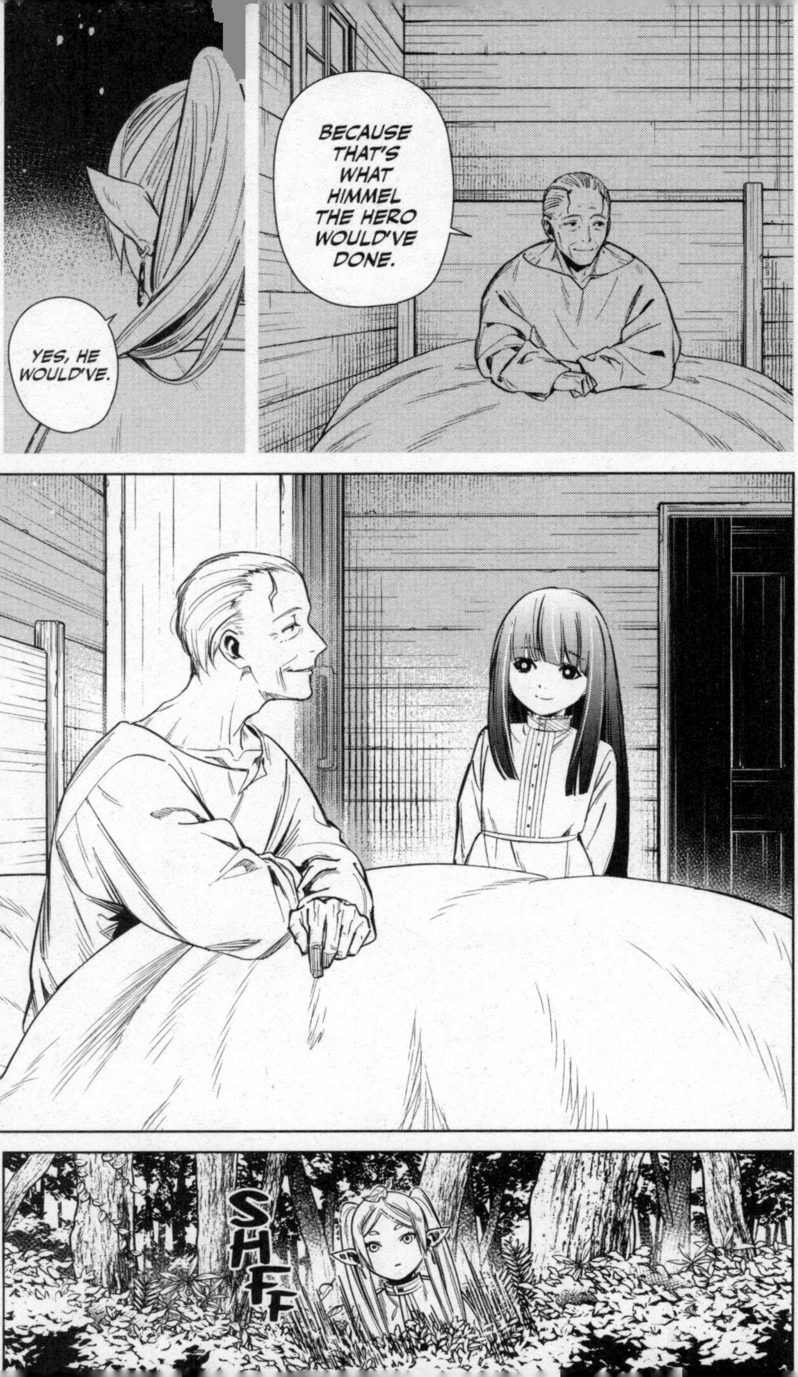
BECAUSE THAT'S WHAT HIMMEL THE HERO WOULD'VE DONE.
YES, HE WOULD'VE.
SHFF

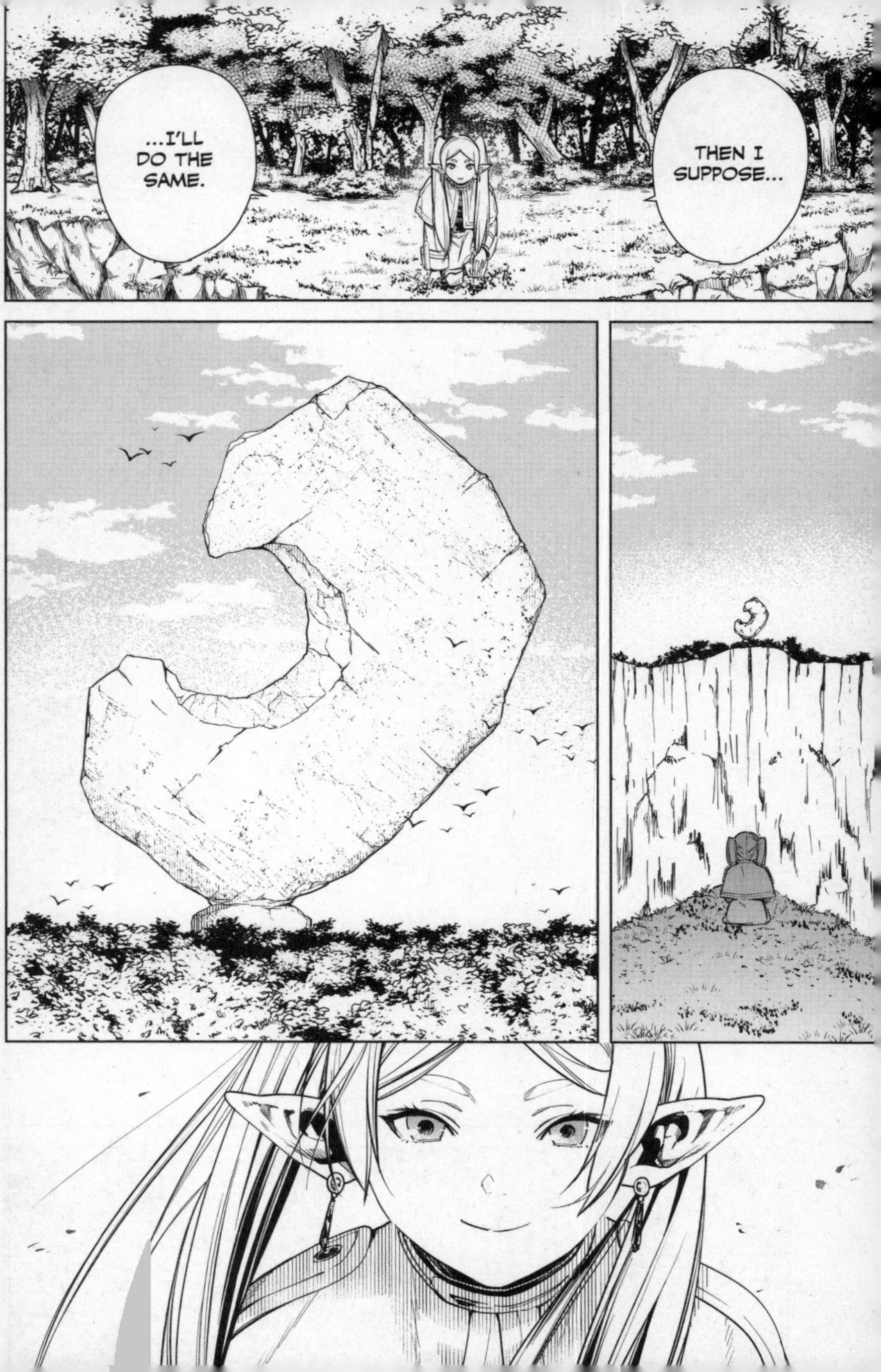
THEN I SUPPOSE...
...I'LL DO THE SAME.

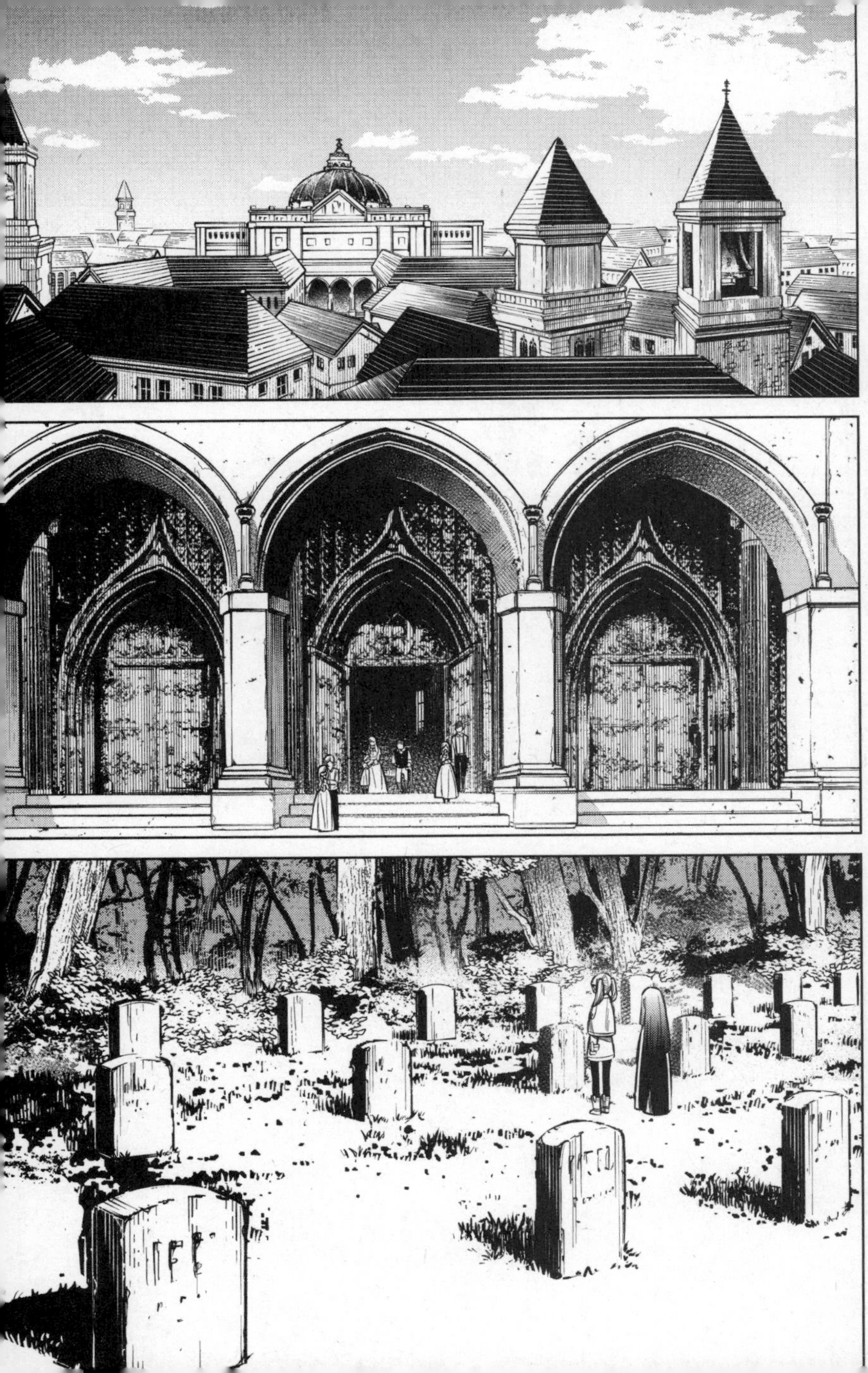

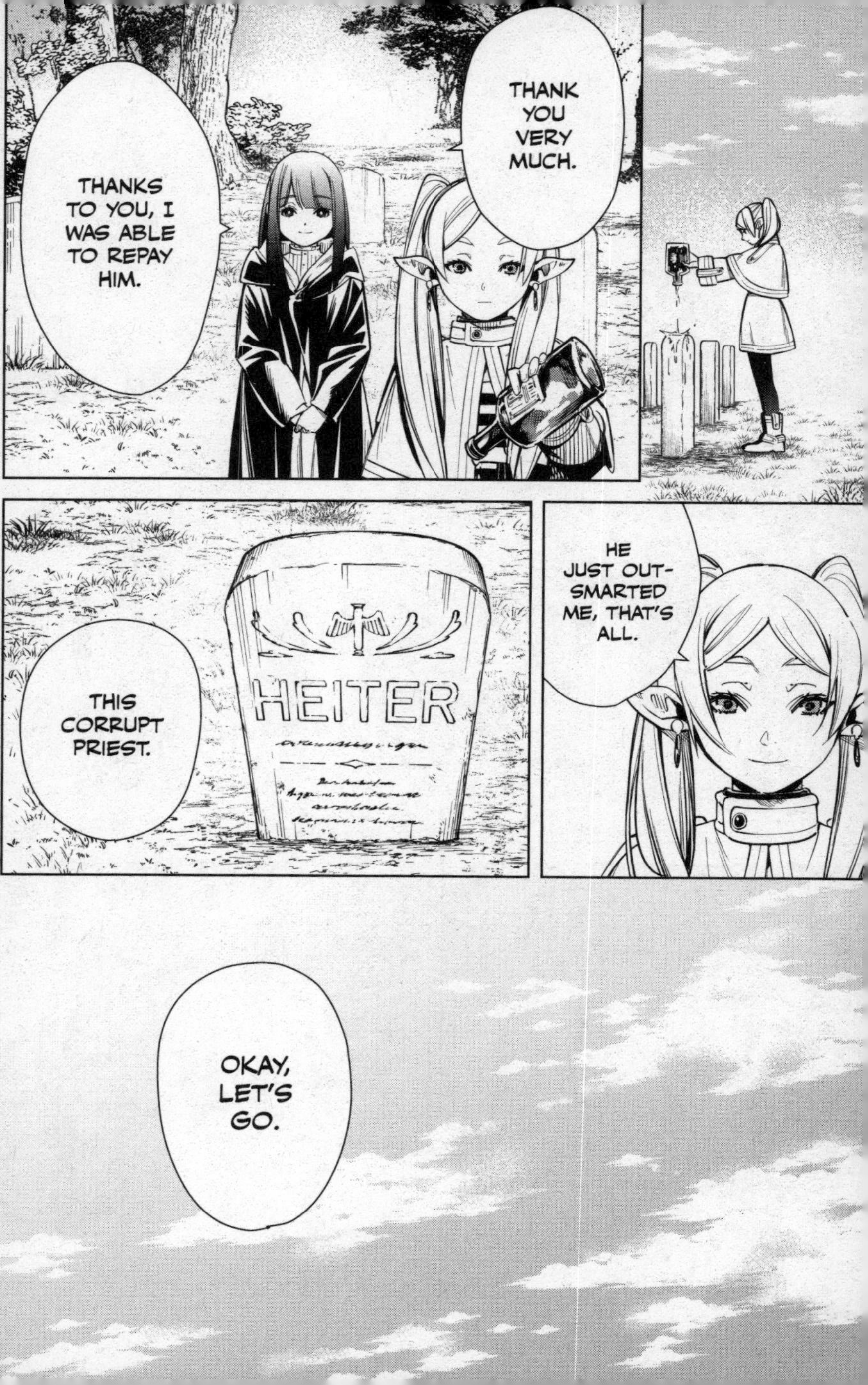
THANK YOU VERY MUCH.
THANKS TO YOU, I WAS ABLE TO REPAY HIM.
HE JUST OUT-SMARTED ME, THAT'S ALL.
HEITER
THIS CORRUPT PRIEST.
OKAY, LET'S GO.

Frieren

Beyond Journey's End

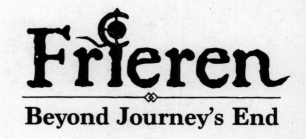

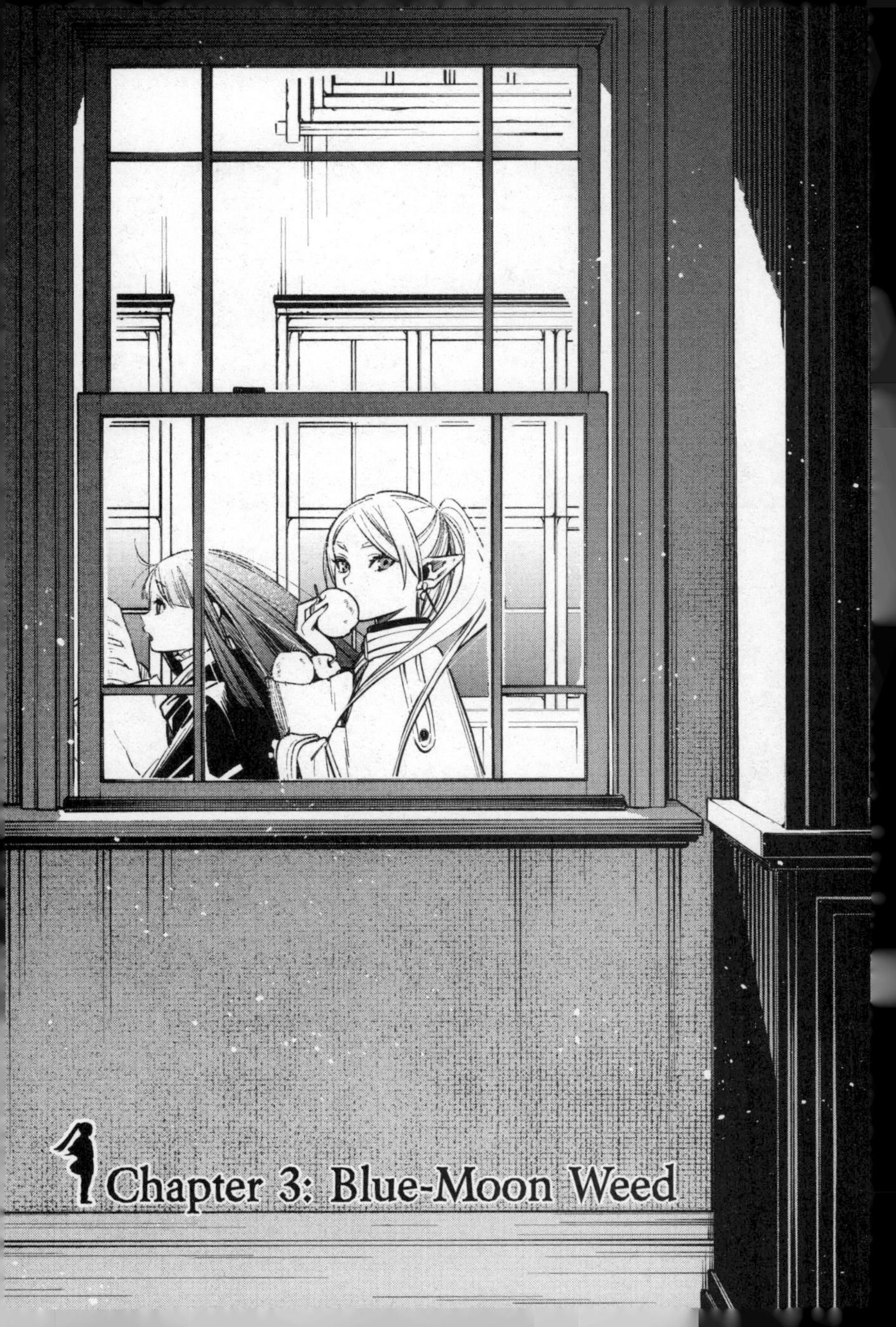
Chapter 3: Blue-Moon Weed

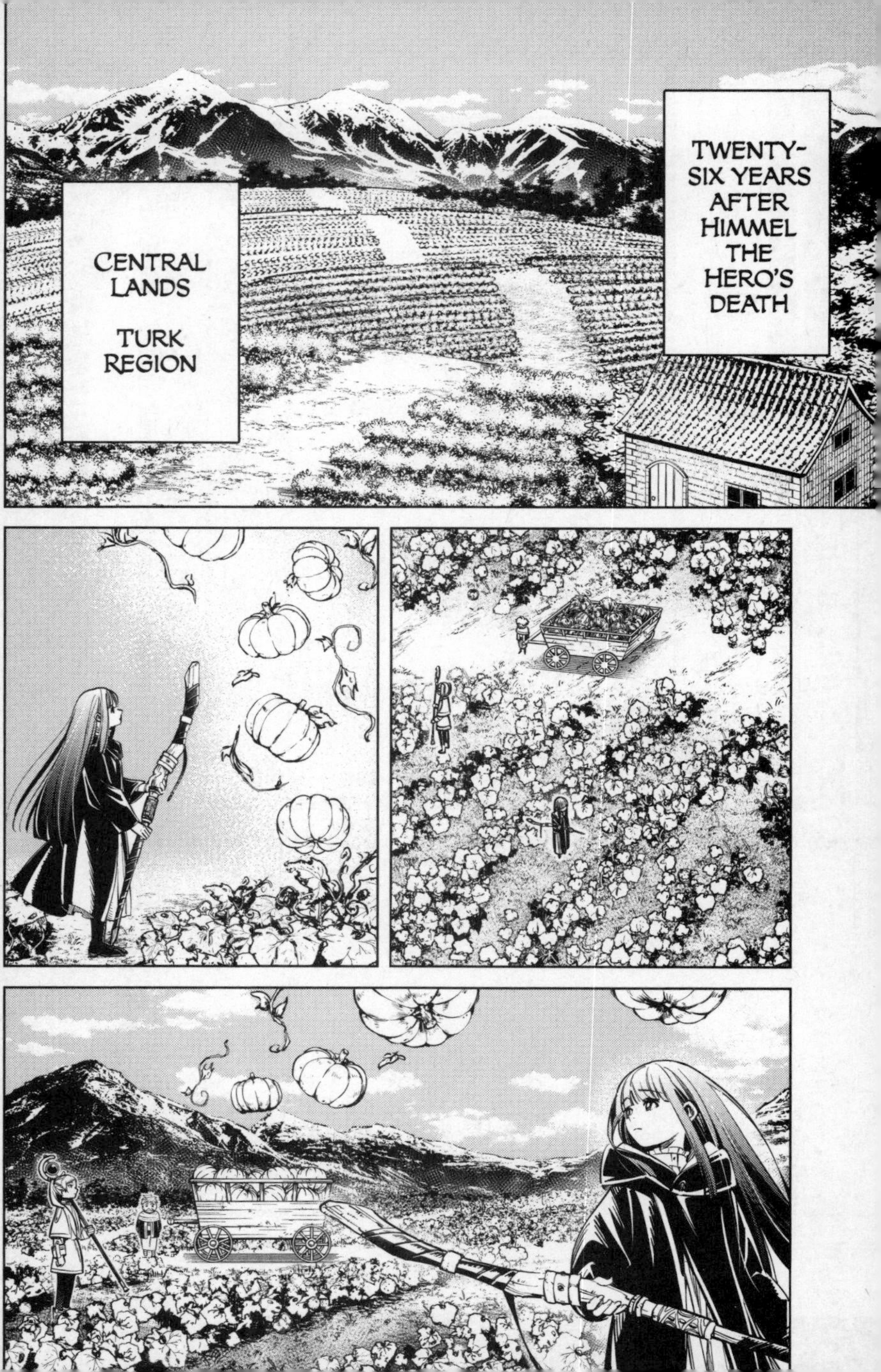
TWENTY-SIX YEARS AFTER HIMMEL THE HERO'S DEATH
CENTRAL LANDS
TURK REGION

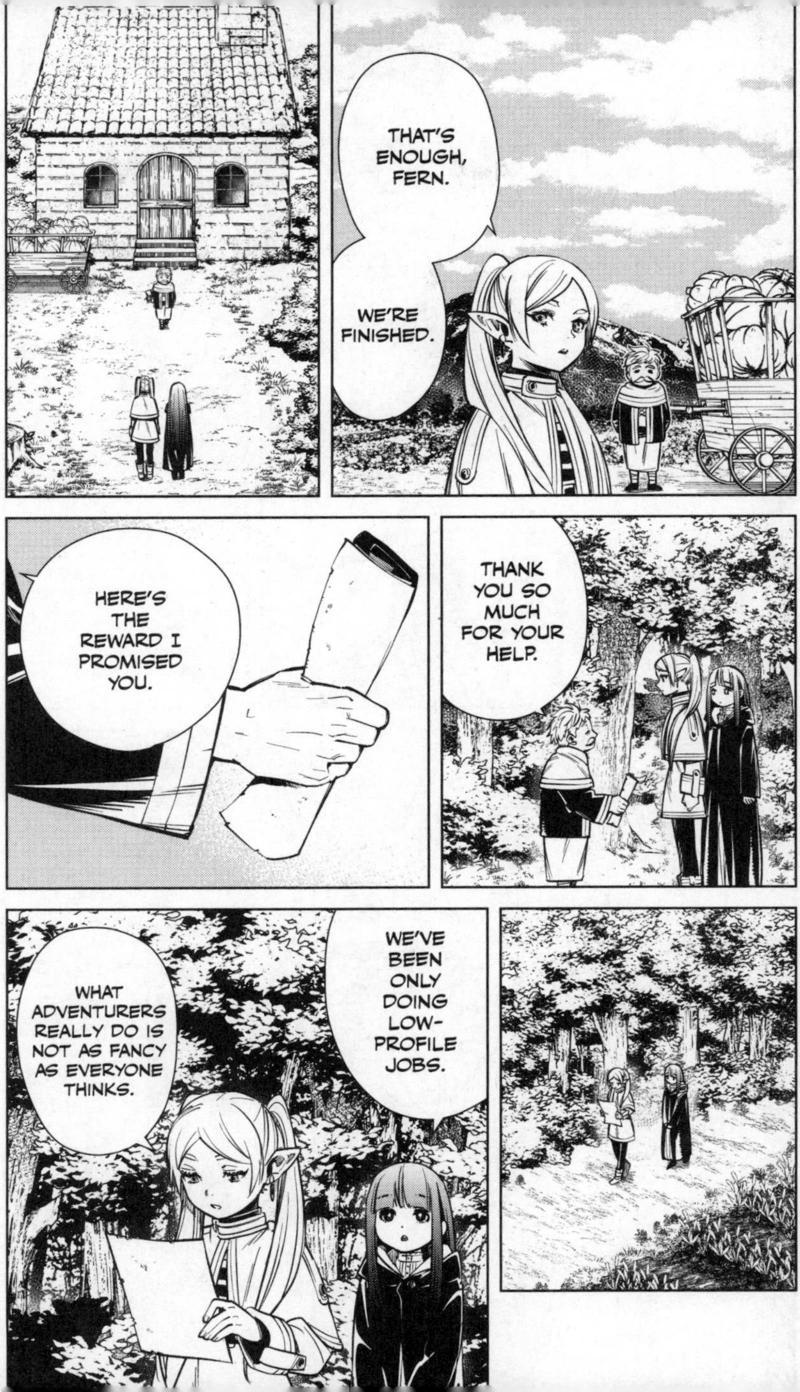

THAT'S ENOUGH, FERN.
WE'RE FINISHED.
THANK YOU SO MUCH FOR YOUR HELP.
HERE'S THE REWARD I PROMISED YOU.
WE'VE BEEN ONLY DOING LOW-PROFILE JOBS.
WHAT ADVENTURERS REALLY DO IS NOT AS FANCY AS EVERYONE THINKS.

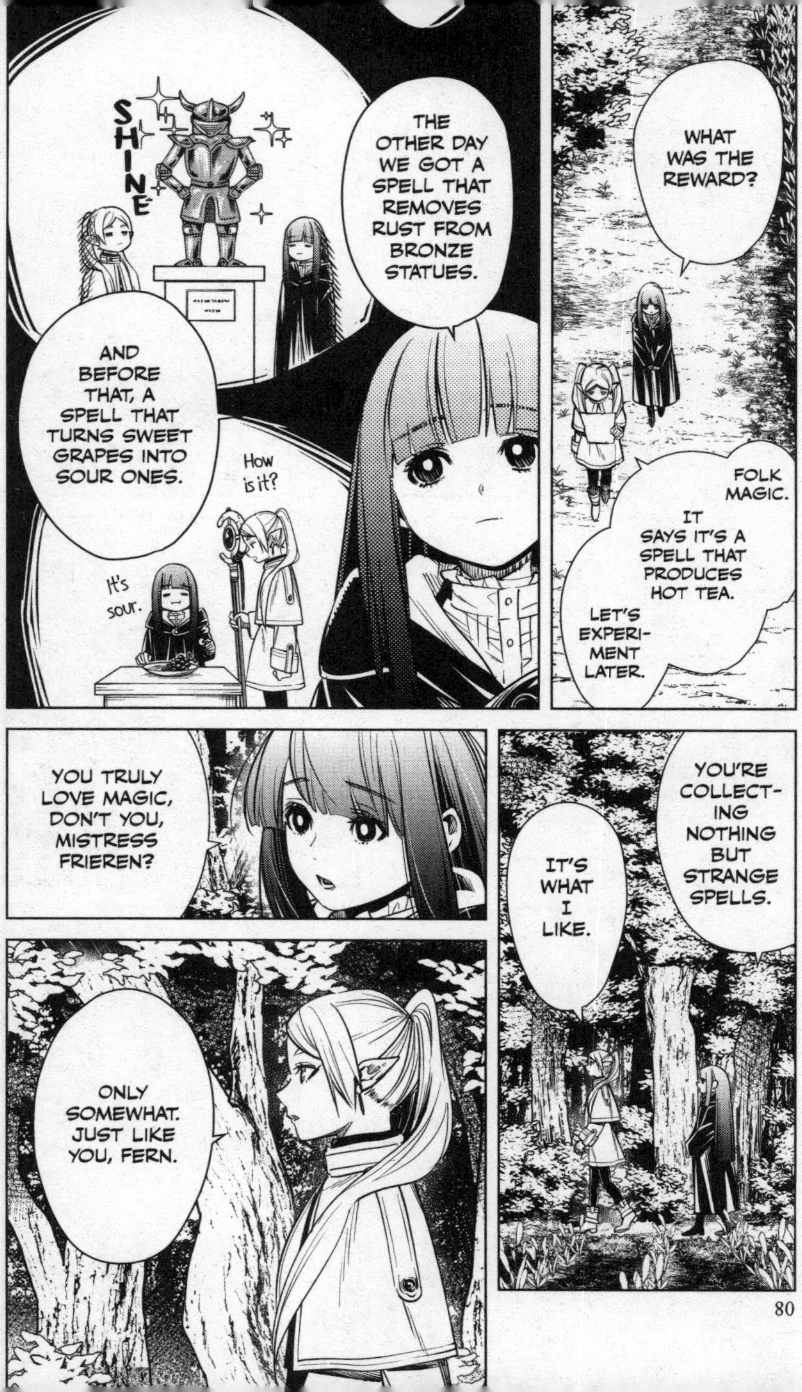
WHAT WAS THE REWARD?
FOLK MAGIC.
IT SAYS IT'S A SPELL THAT PRODUCES HOT TEA.
LET'S EXPERIMENT LATER.
THE OTHER DAY WE GOT A SPELL THAT REMOVES RUST FROM BRONZE STATUES.
SHINE
AND BEFORE THAT, A SPELL THAT TURNS SWEET GRAPES INTO SOUR ONES.
How is it?
It's sour.
YOU'RE COLLECT-ING NOTHING BUT STRANGE SPELLS.
IT'S WHAT I LIKE.
YOU TRULY LOVE MAGIC, DON'T YOU, MISTRESS FRIEREN?
ONLY SOMEWHAT. JUST LIKE YOU, FERN.

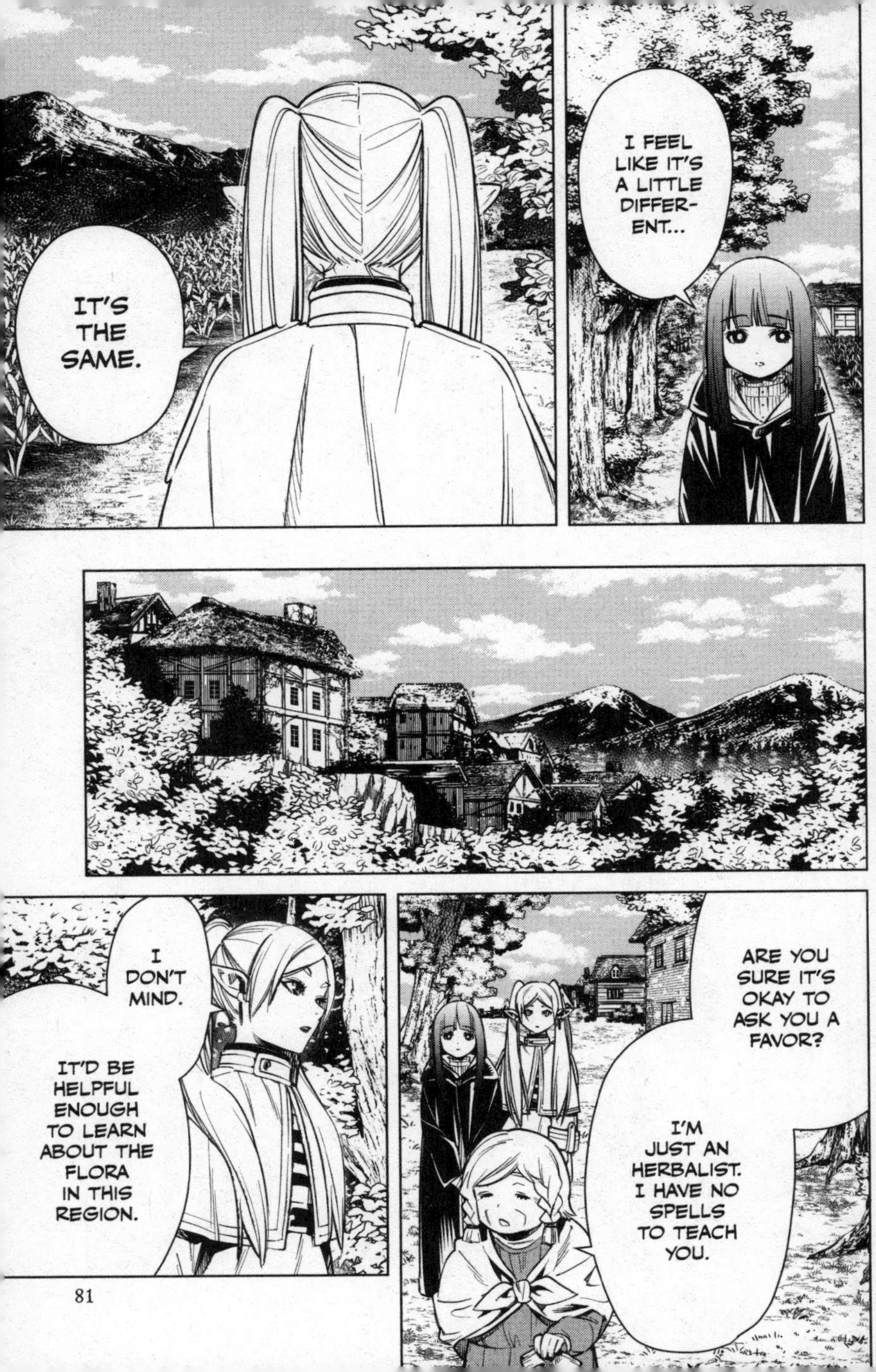
I FEEL LIKE IT'S A LITTLE DIFFERENT...
IT'S THE SAME.
ARE YOU SURE IT'S OKAY TO ASK YOU A FAVOR?
I'M JUST AN HERBALIST. I HAVE NO SPELLS TO TEACH YOU.
I DON'T MIND.
IT'D BE HELPFUL ENOUGH TO LEARN ABOUT THE FLORA IN THIS REGION.

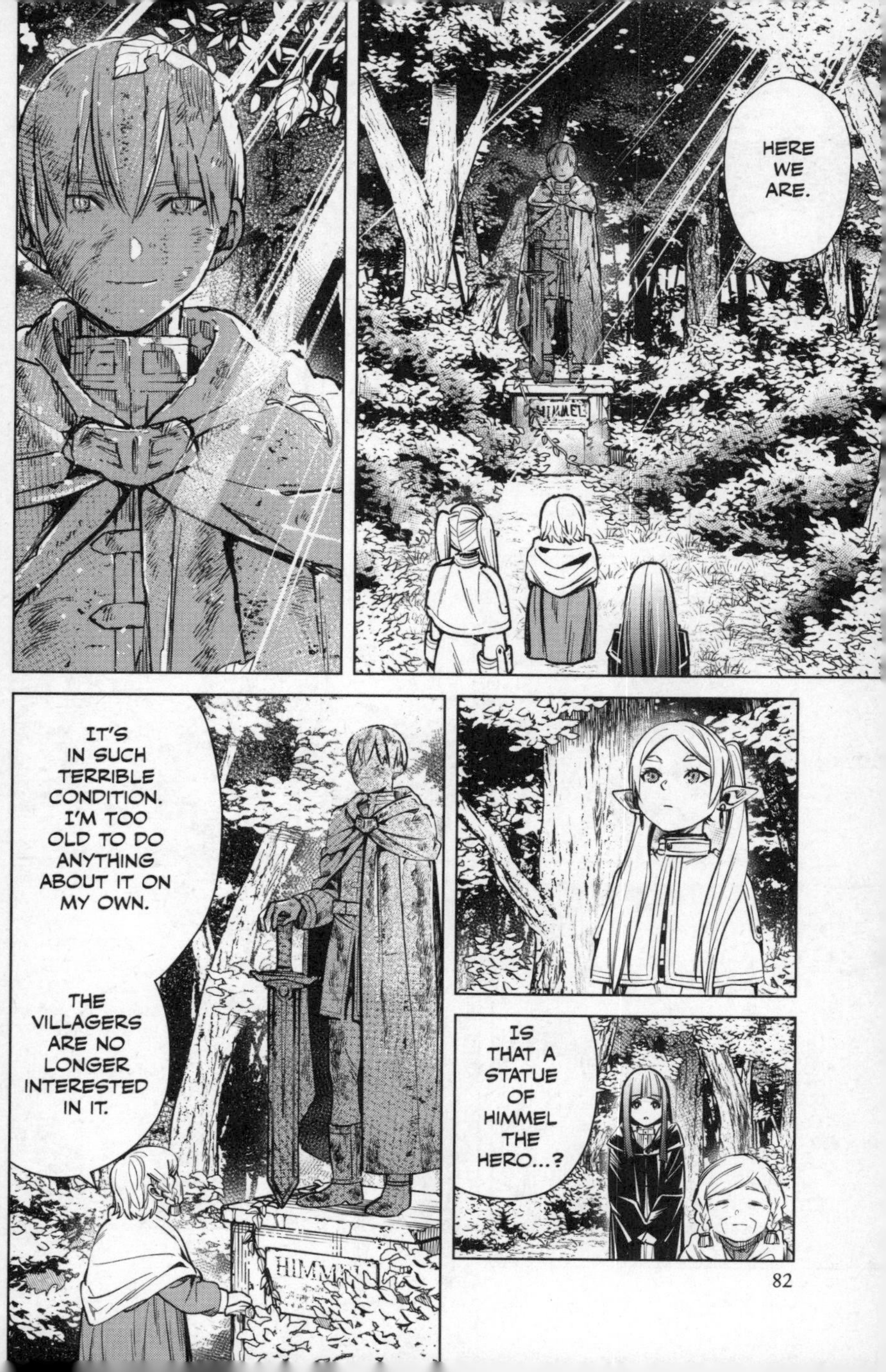
HERE WE ARE.
HIMMEL
IS THAT A STATUE OF HIMMEL THE HERO...?
IT'S IN SUCH TERRIBLE CONDITION. I'M TOO OLD TO DO ANYTHING ABOUT IT ON MY OWN.
THE VILLAGERS ARE NO LONGER INTERESTED IN IT.

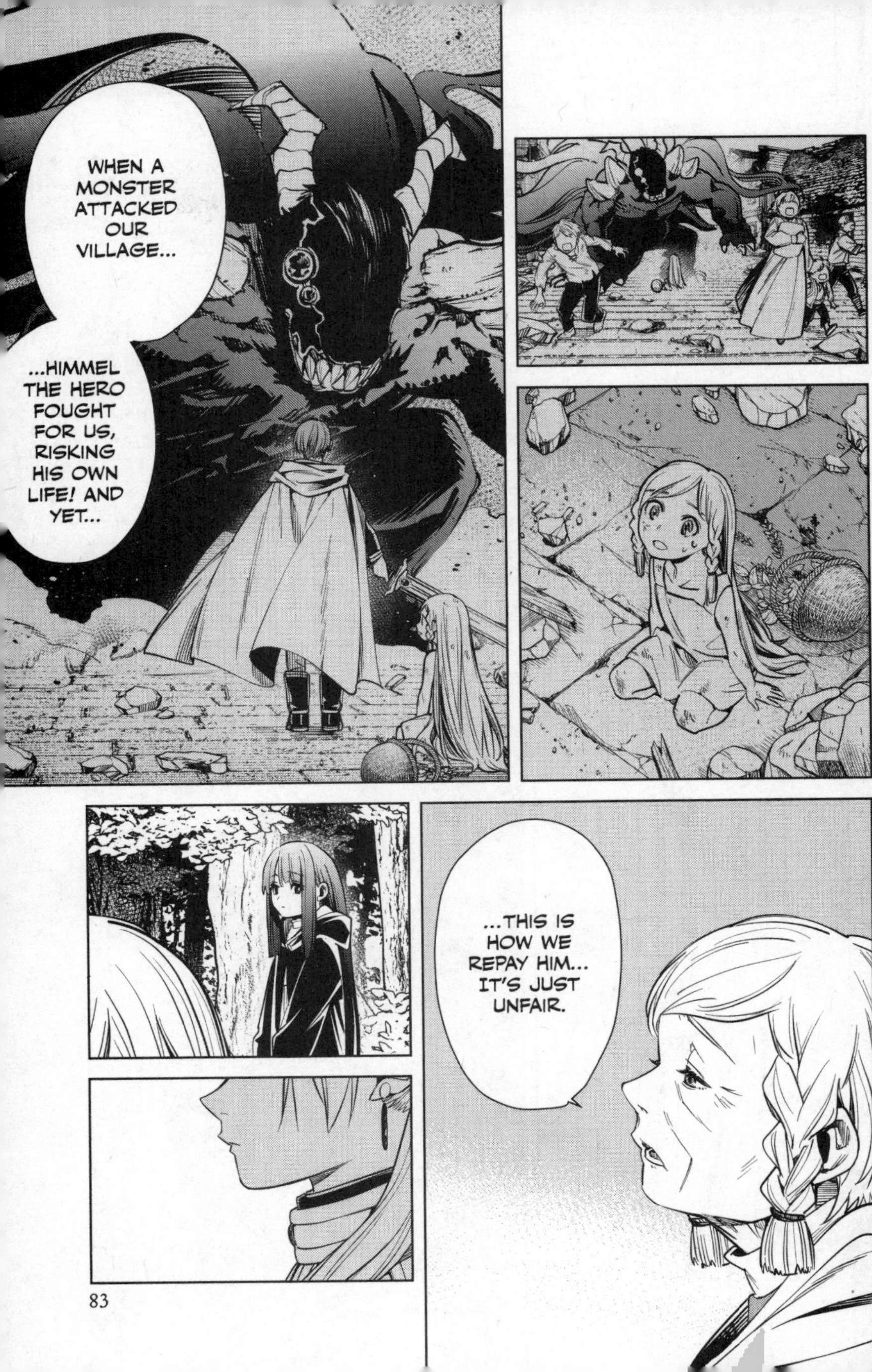
WHEN A MONSTER ATTACKED OUR VILLAGE...
...HIMMEL THE HERO FOUGHT FOR US, RISKING HIS OWN LIFE! AND YET...
...THIS IS HOW WE REPAY HIM... IT'S JUST UNFAIR.

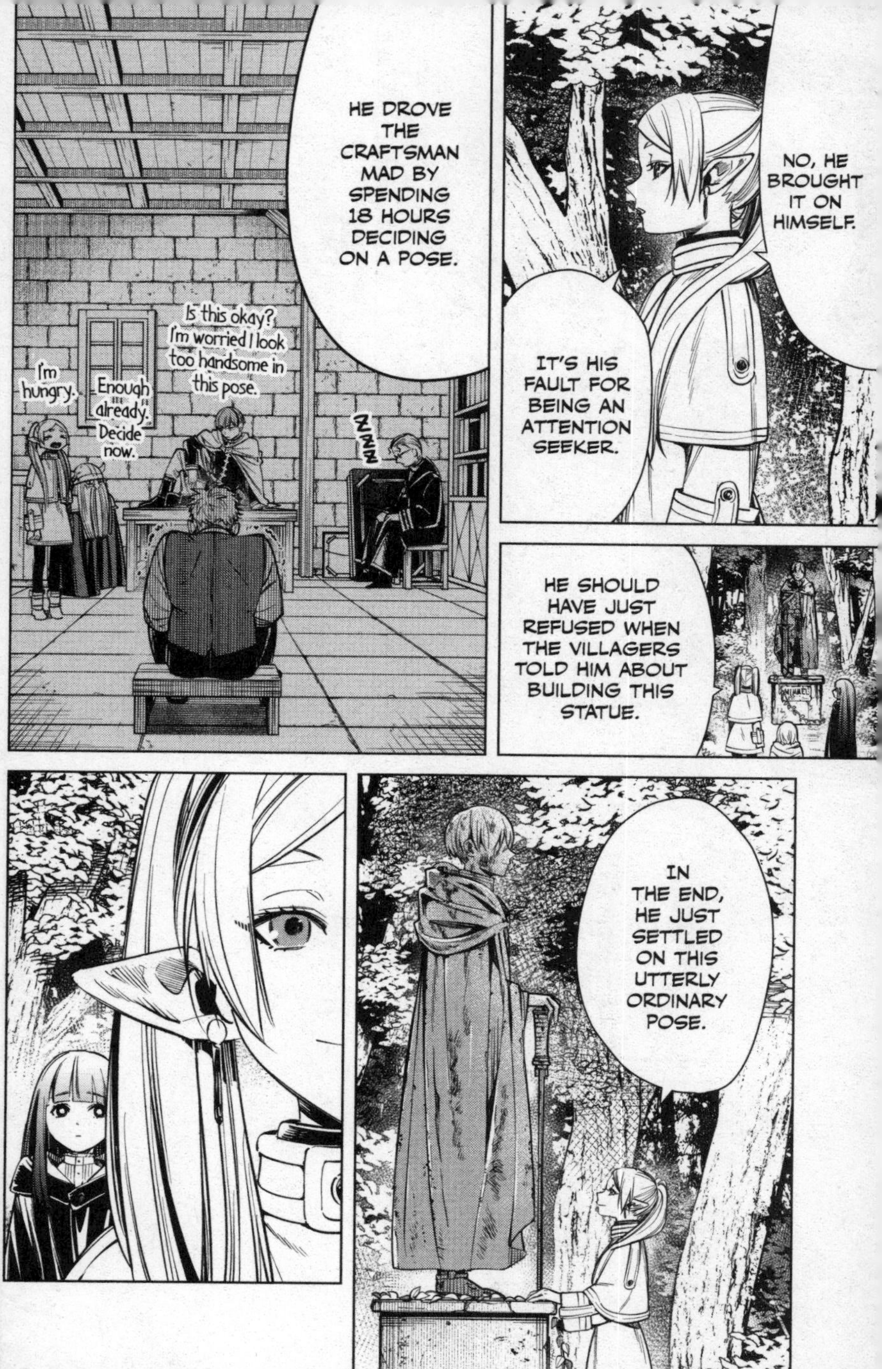
NO, HE BROUGHT IT ON HIMSELF.
IT'S HIS FAULT FOR BEING AN ATTENTION SEEKER.
HE SHOULD HAVE JUST REFUSED WHEN THE VILLAGERS TOLD HIM ABOUT BUILDING THIS STATUE.
HE DROVE THE CRAFTSMAN MAD BY SPENDING 18 HOURS DECIDING ON A POSE.
ZZZ
Is this okay? I'm worried I look too handsome in this pose.
Enough already. Decide now.
I'm hungry.
IN THE END, HE JUST SETTLED ON THIS UTTERLY ORDINARY POSE.

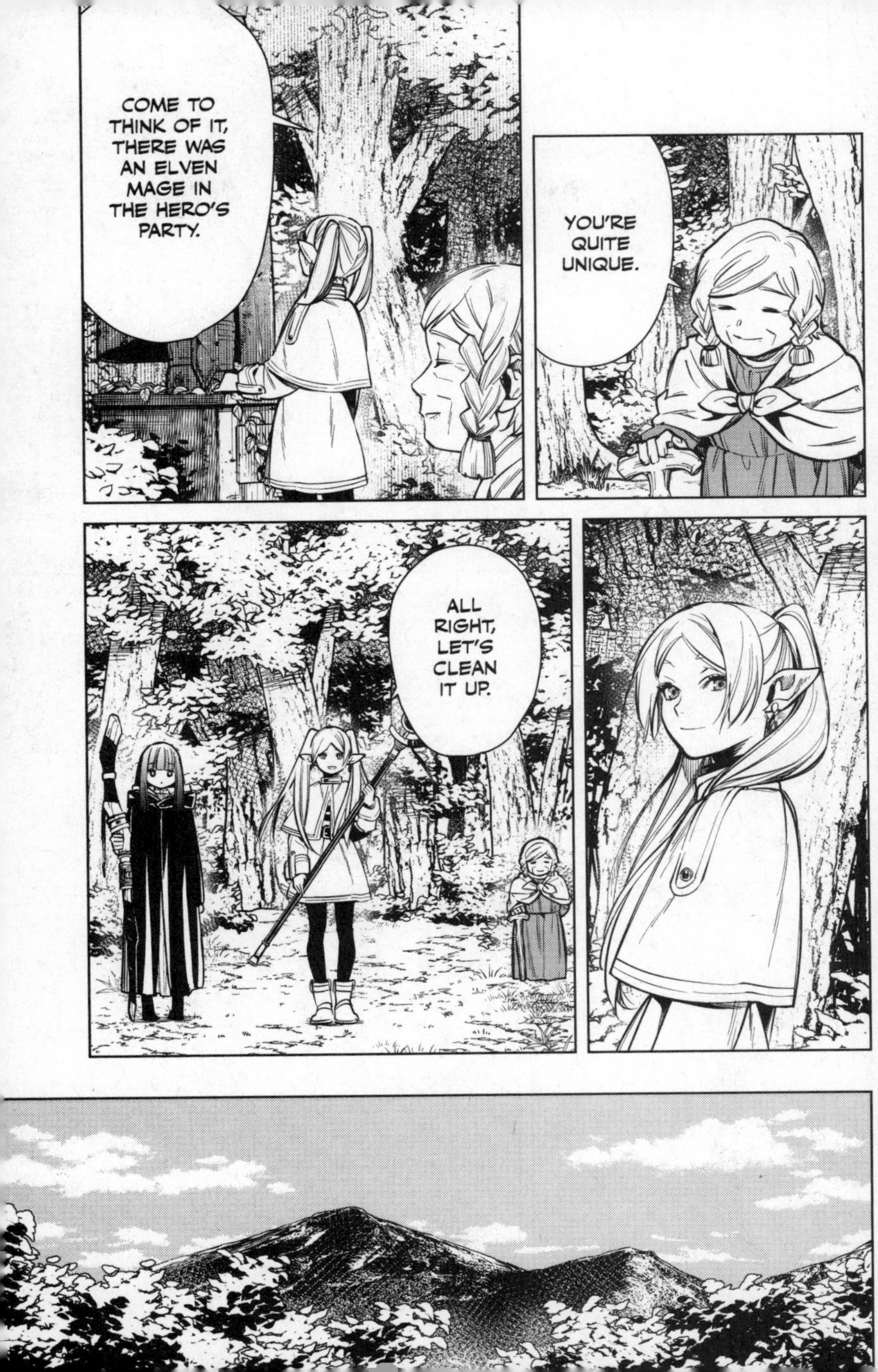
YOU'RE QUITE UNIQUE.
COME TO THINK OF IT, THERE WAS AN ELVEN MAGE IN THE HERO'S PARTY.
ALL RIGHT, LET'S CLEAN IT UP.

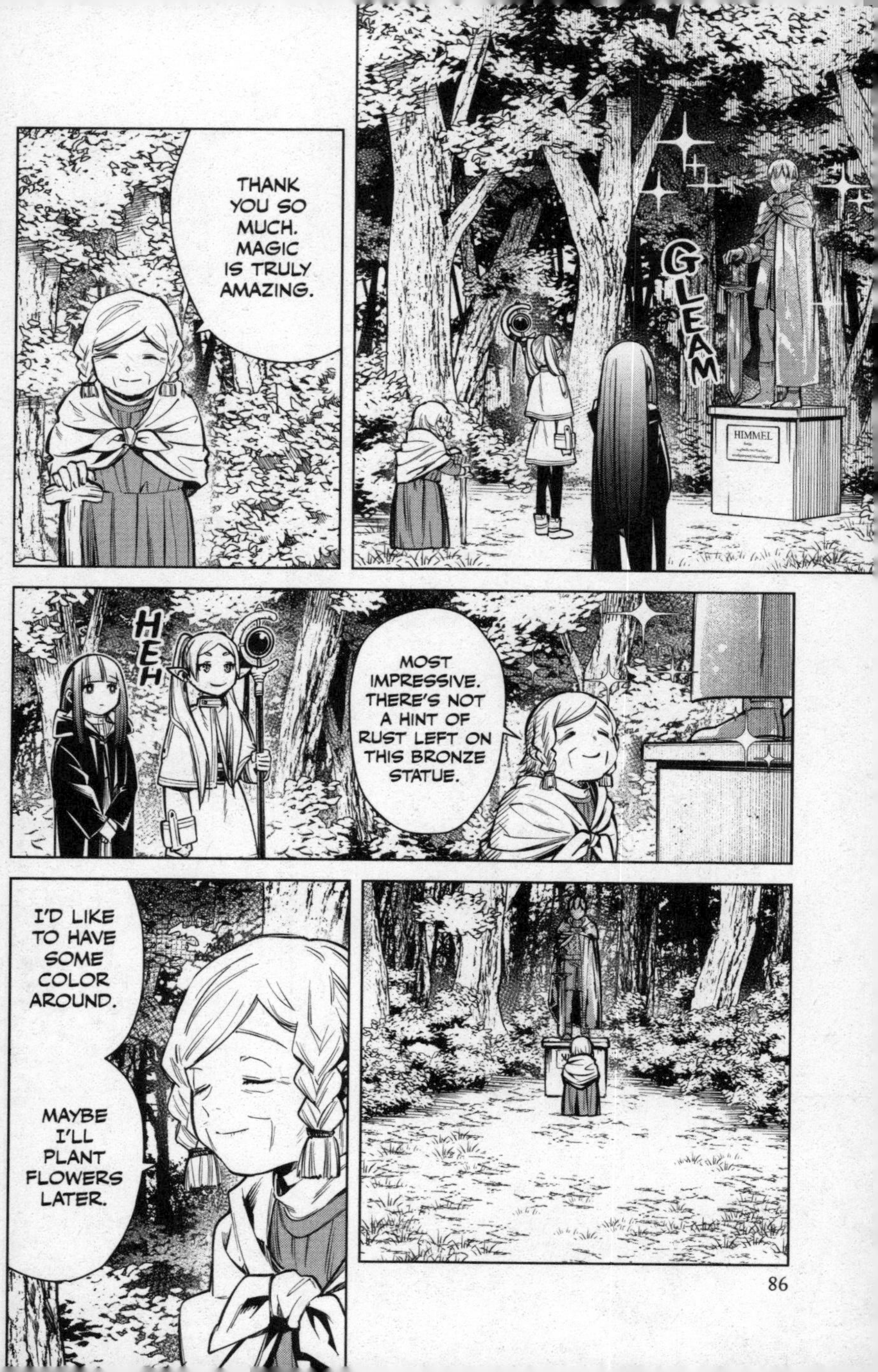
GLEAM
HIMMEL
THANK YOU SO MUCH. MAGIC IS TRULY AMAZING.
MOST IMPRESSIVE. THERE'S NOT A HINT OF RUST LEFT ON THIS BRONZE STATUE.
HEH
I'D LIKE TO HAVE SOME COLOR AROUND.
MAYBE I'LL PLANT FLOWERS LATER.

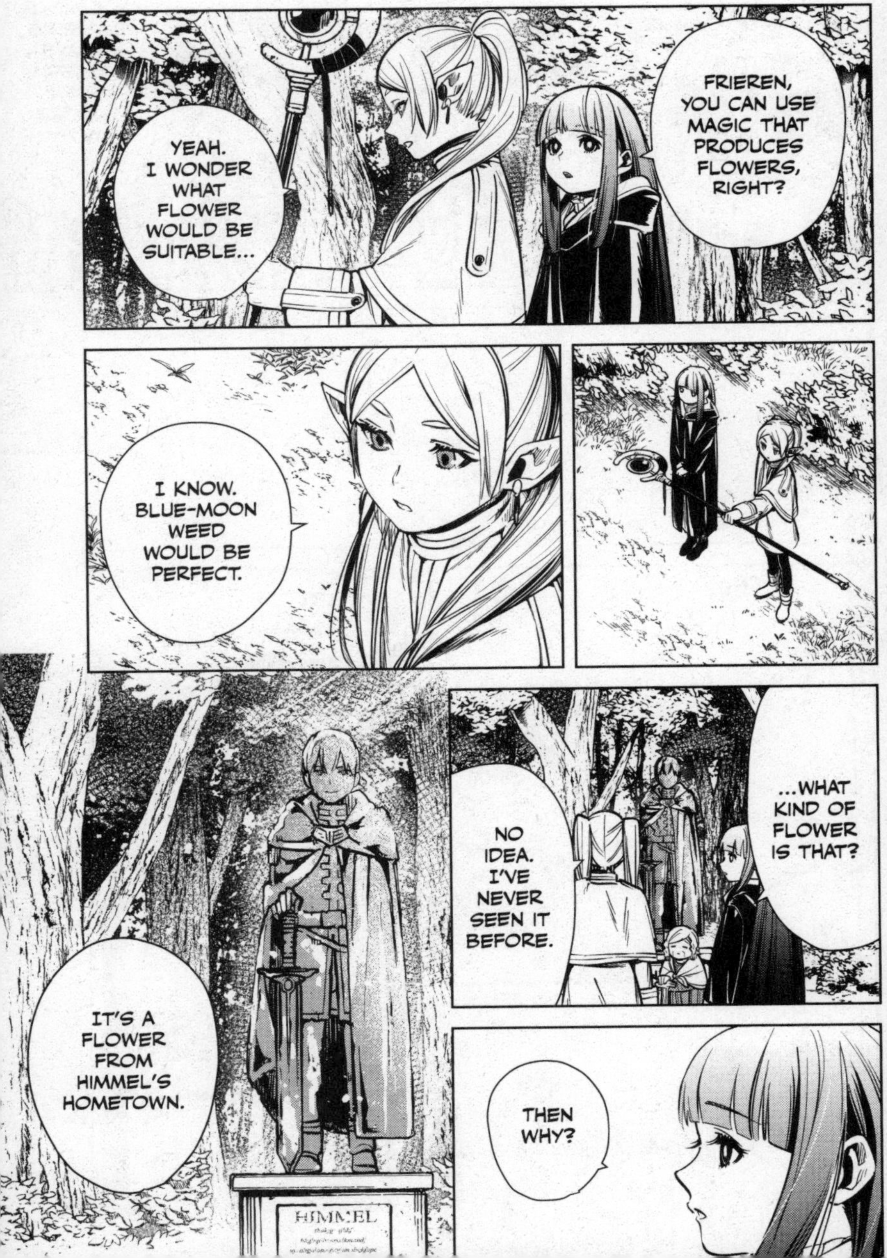
FRIEREN, YOU CAN USE MAGIC THAT PRODUCES FLOWERS, RIGHT?
YEAH. I WONDER WHAT FLOWER WOULD BE SUITABLE...
I KNOW. BLUE-MOON WEED WOULD BE PERFECT.
...WHAT KIND OF FLOWER IS THAT?
NO IDEA. I'VE NEVER SEEN IT BEFORE.
THEN WHY?
IT'S A FLOWER FROM HIMMEL'S HOMETOWN.
HIMMEL

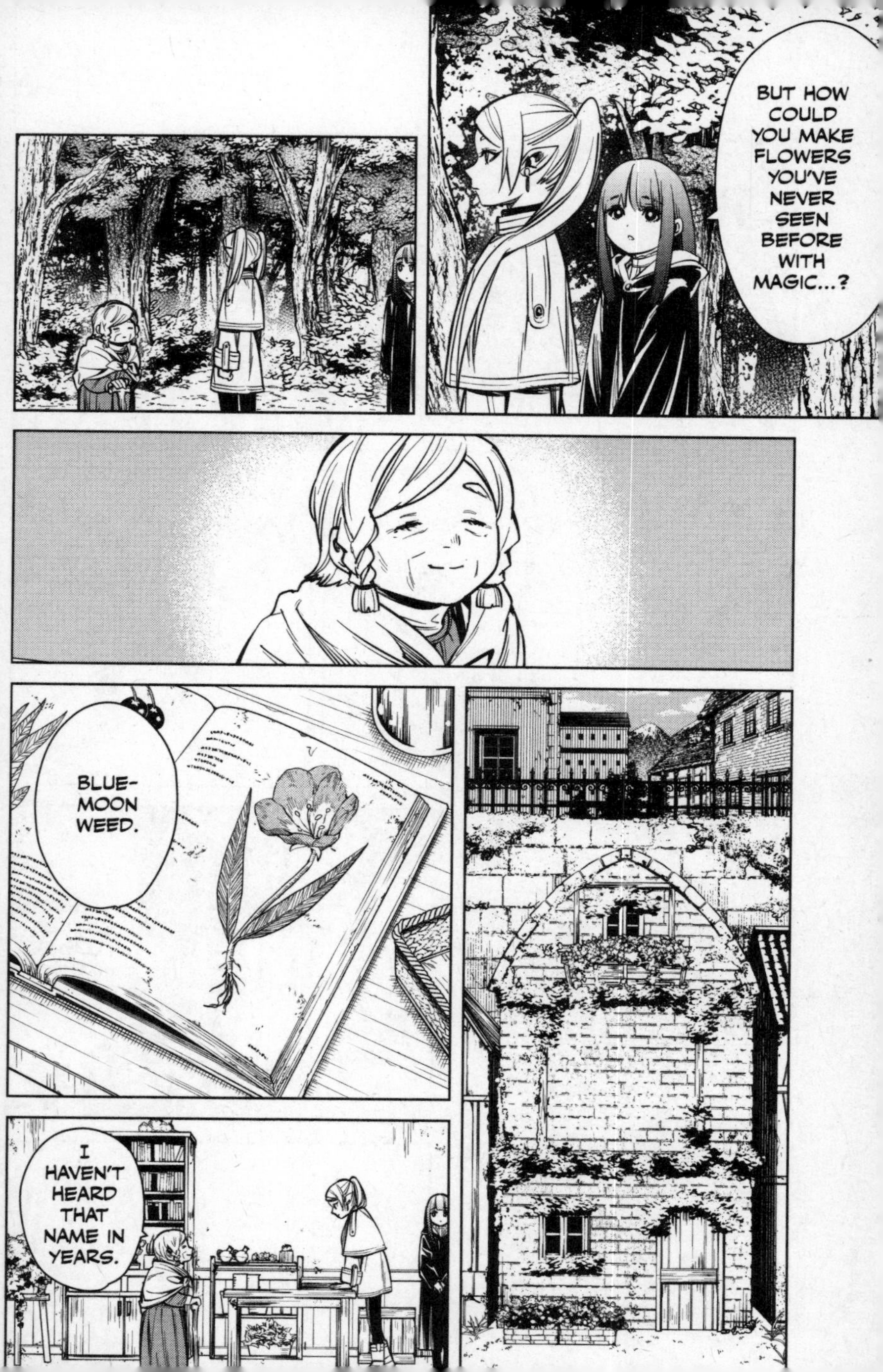
BUT HOW COULD YOU MAKE FLOWERS YOU'VE NEVER SEEN BEFORE WITH MAGIC...?
BLUE-MOON WEED.
I HAVEN'T HEARD THAT NAME IN YEARS.

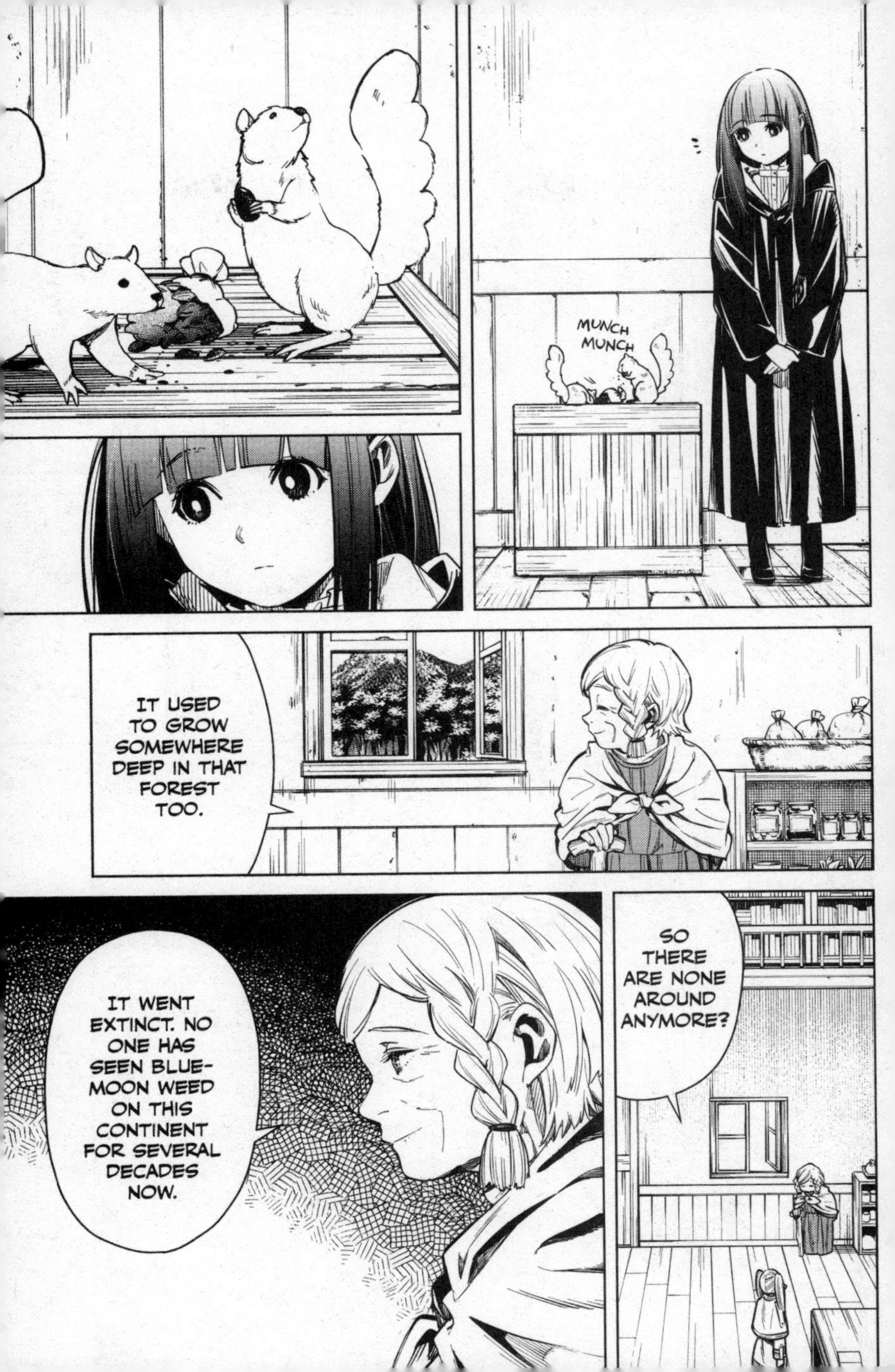
MUNCH MUNCH
IT USED TO GROW SOMEWHERE DEEP IN THAT FOREST TOO.
SO THERE ARE NONE AROUND ANYMORE?
IT WENT EXTINCT. NO ONE HAS SEEN BLUE-MOON WEED ON THIS CONTINENT FOR SEVERAL DECADES NOW.

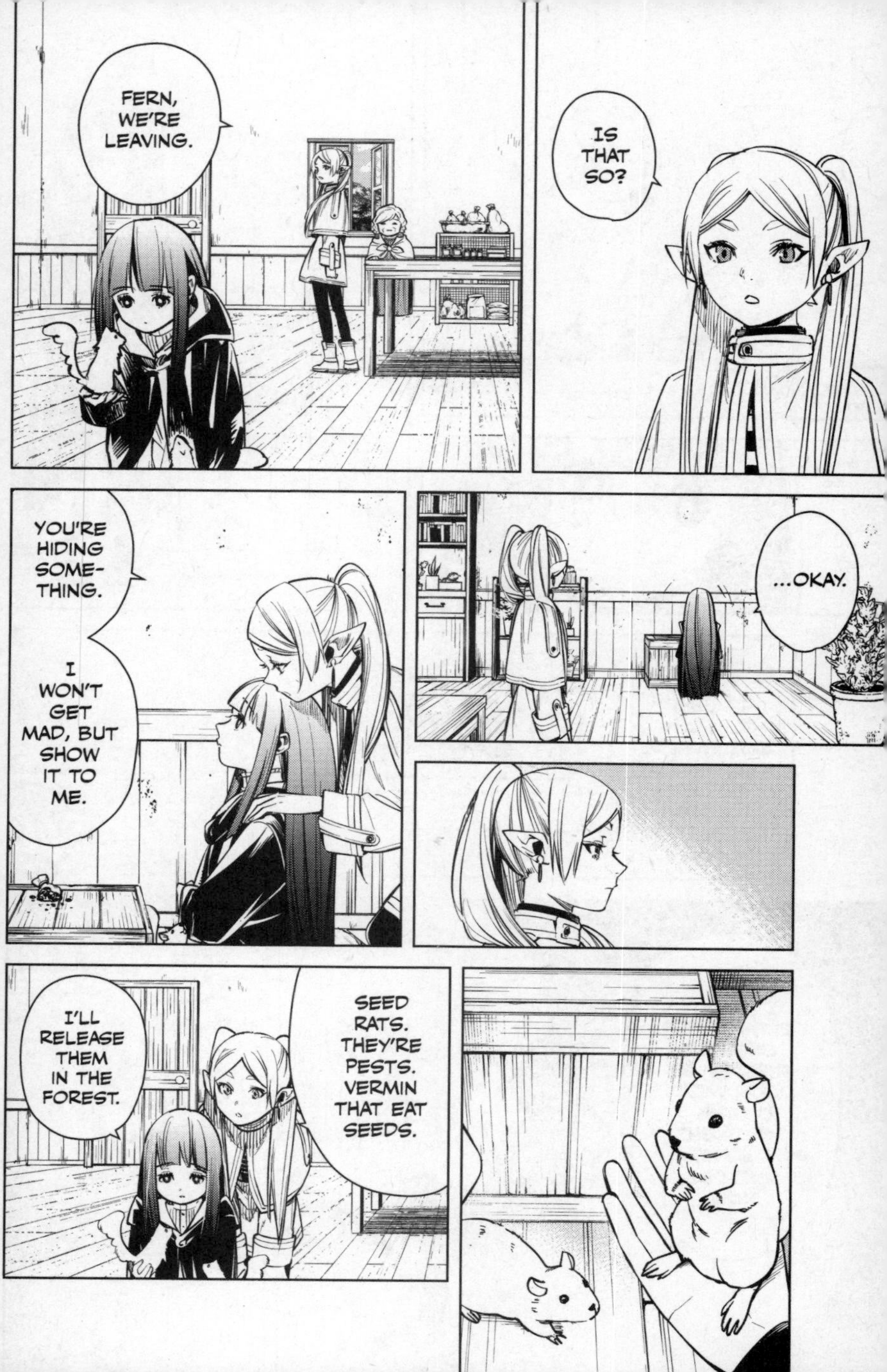

IS THAT SO?
FERN, WE'RE LEAVING.
...OKAY.
YOU'RE HIDING SOME-THING.
I WON'T GET MAD, BUT SHOW IT TO ME.
SEED RATS. THEY'RE PESTS. VERMIN THAT EAT SEEDS.
I'LL RELEASE THEM IN THE FOREST.

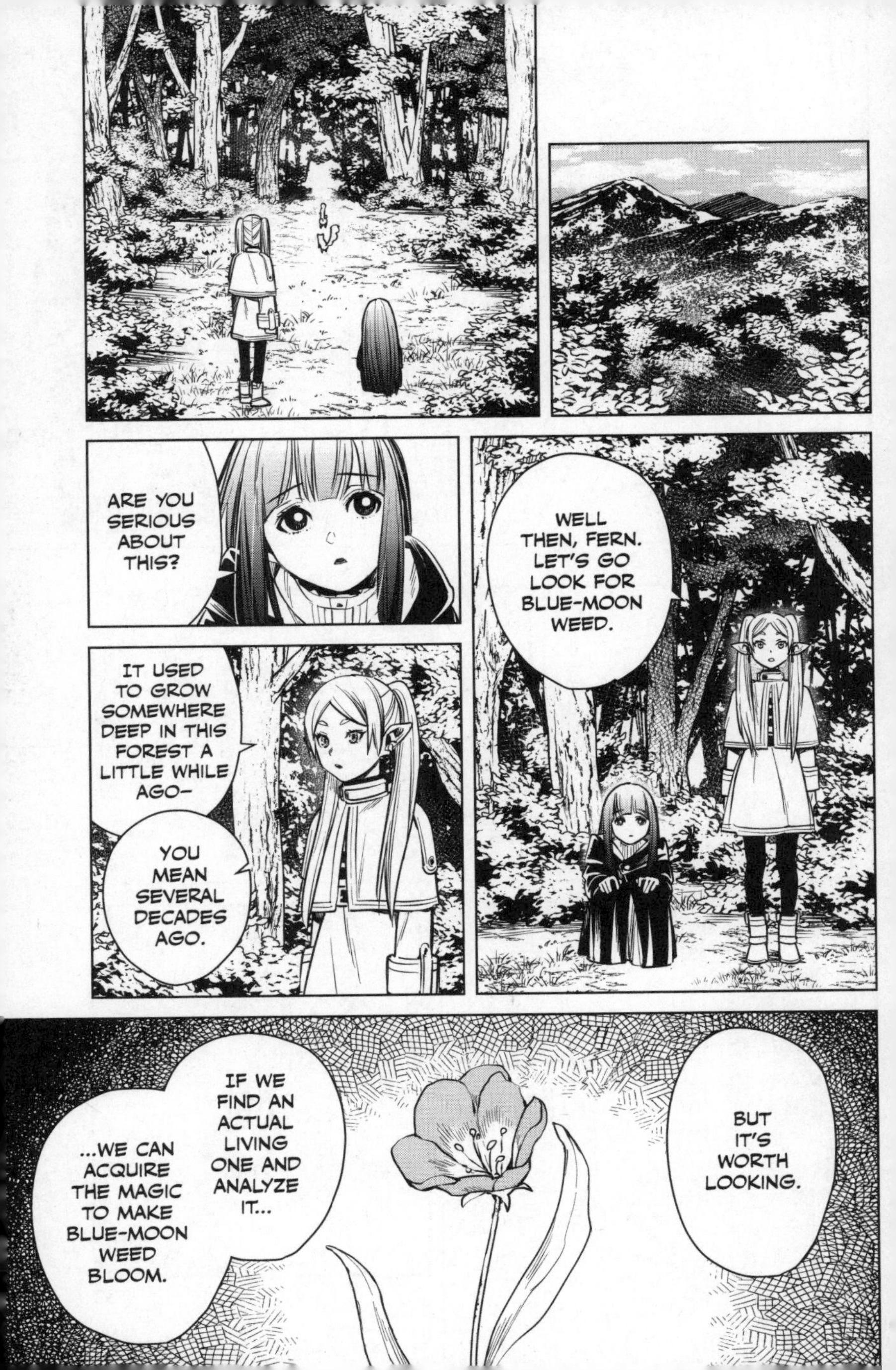
WELL THEN, FERN. LET'S GO LOOK FOR BLUE-MOON WEED.
ARE YOU SERIOUS ABOUT THIS?
IT USED TO GROW SOMEWHERE DEEP IN THIS FOREST A LITTLE WHILE AGO–
YOU MEAN SEVERAL DECADES AGO.
BUT IT'S WORTH LOOKING.
IF WE FIND AN ACTUAL LIVING ONE AND ANALYZE IT...
...WE CAN ACQUIRE THE MAGIC TO MAKE BLUE-MOON WEED BLOOM.

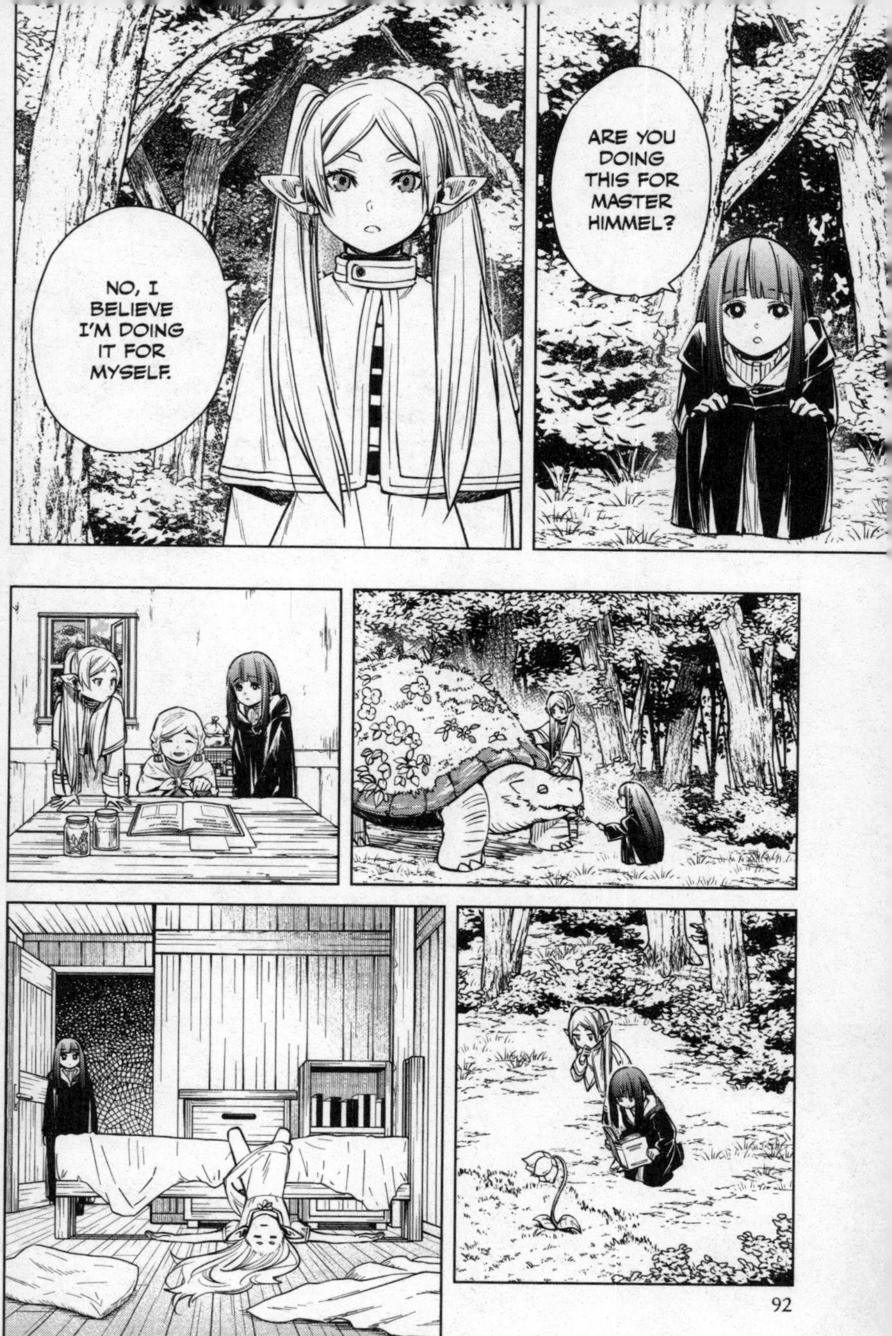
ARE YOU DOING THIS FOR MASTER HIMMEL?
NO, I BELIEVE I'M DOING IT FOR MYSELF.

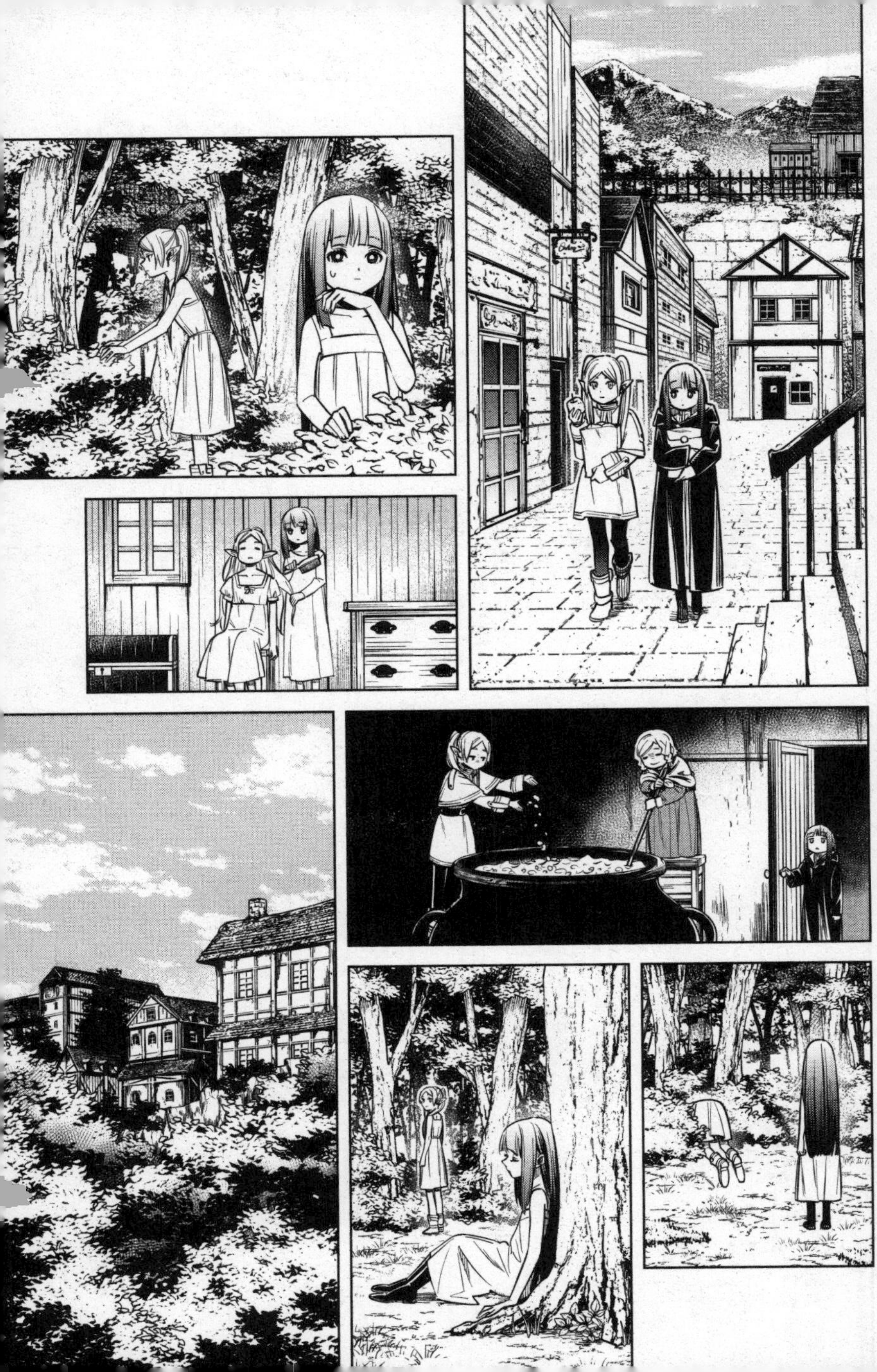

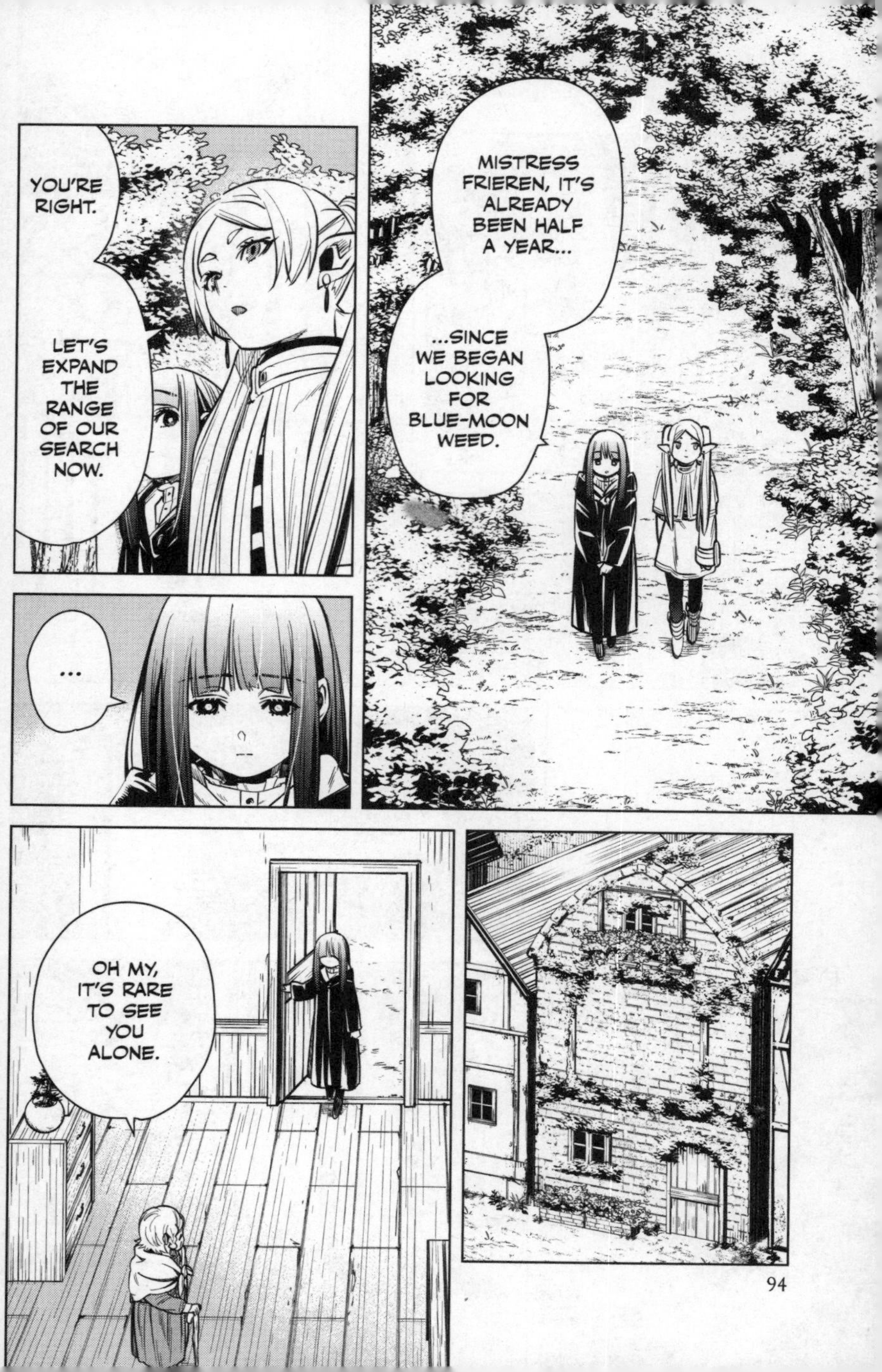
MISTRESS FRIEREN, IT'S ALREADY BEEN HALF A YEAR...
...SINCE WE BEGAN LOOKING FOR BLUE-MOON WEED.
YOU'RE RIGHT.
LET'S EXPAND THE RANGE OF OUR SEARCH NOW.
...
OH MY, IT'S RARE TO SEE YOU ALONE.

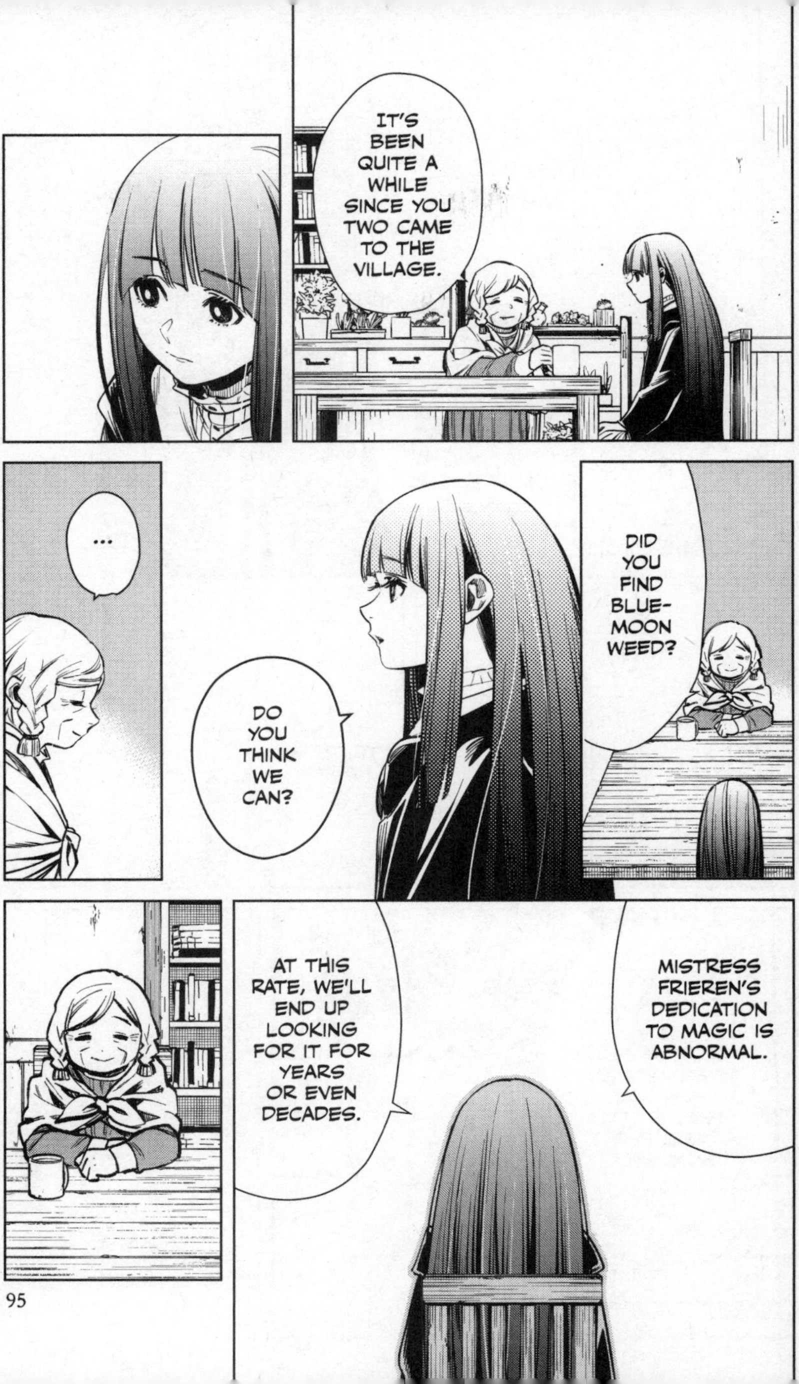
IT'S BEEN QUITE A WHILE SINCE YOU TWO CAME TO THE VILLAGE.
DID YOU FIND BLUE-MOON WEED?
DO YOU THINK WE CAN?
...
MISTRESS FRIEREN'S DEDICATION TO MAGIC IS ABNORMAL.
AT THIS RATE, WE'LL END UP LOOKING FOR IT FOR YEARS OR EVEN DECADES.

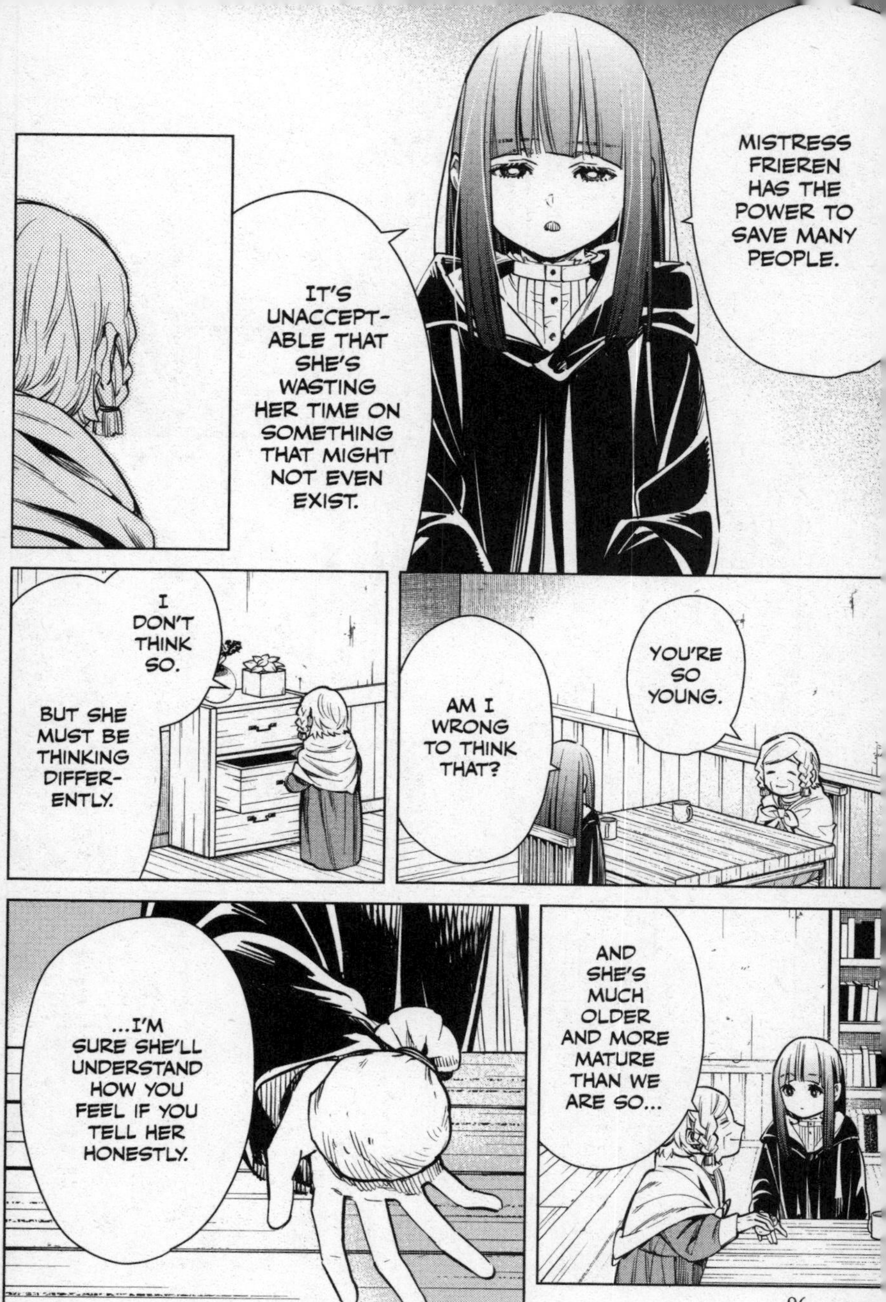
MISTRESS FRIEREN HAS THE POWER TO SAVE MANY PEOPLE.
IT'S UNACCEPTABLE THAT SHE'S WASTING HER TIME ON SOMETHING THAT MIGHT NOT EVEN EXIST.
YOU'RE SO YOUNG.
AM I WRONG TO THINK THAT?
I DON'T THINK SO.
BUT SHE MUST BE THINKING DIFFERENTLY.
AND SHE'S MUCH OLDER AND MORE MATURE THAN WE ARE SO...
...I'M SURE SHE'LL UNDERSTAND HOW YOU FEEL IF YOU TELL HER HONESTLY.

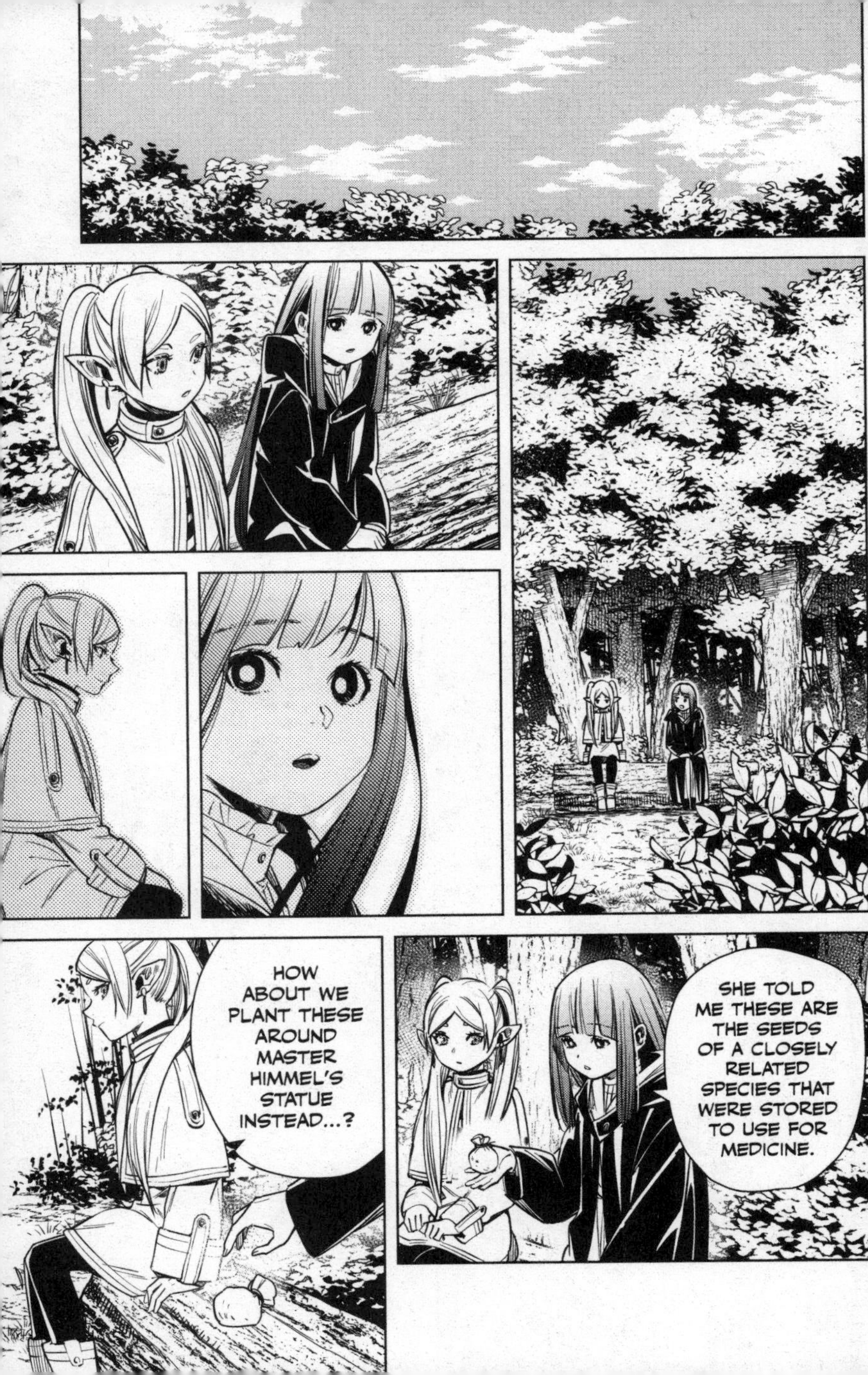
SHE TOLD ME THESE ARE THE SEEDS OF A CLOSELY RELATED SPECIES THAT WERE STORED TO USE FOR MEDICINE.
HOW ABOUT WE PLANT THESE AROUND MASTER HIMMEL'S STATUE INSTEAD...?

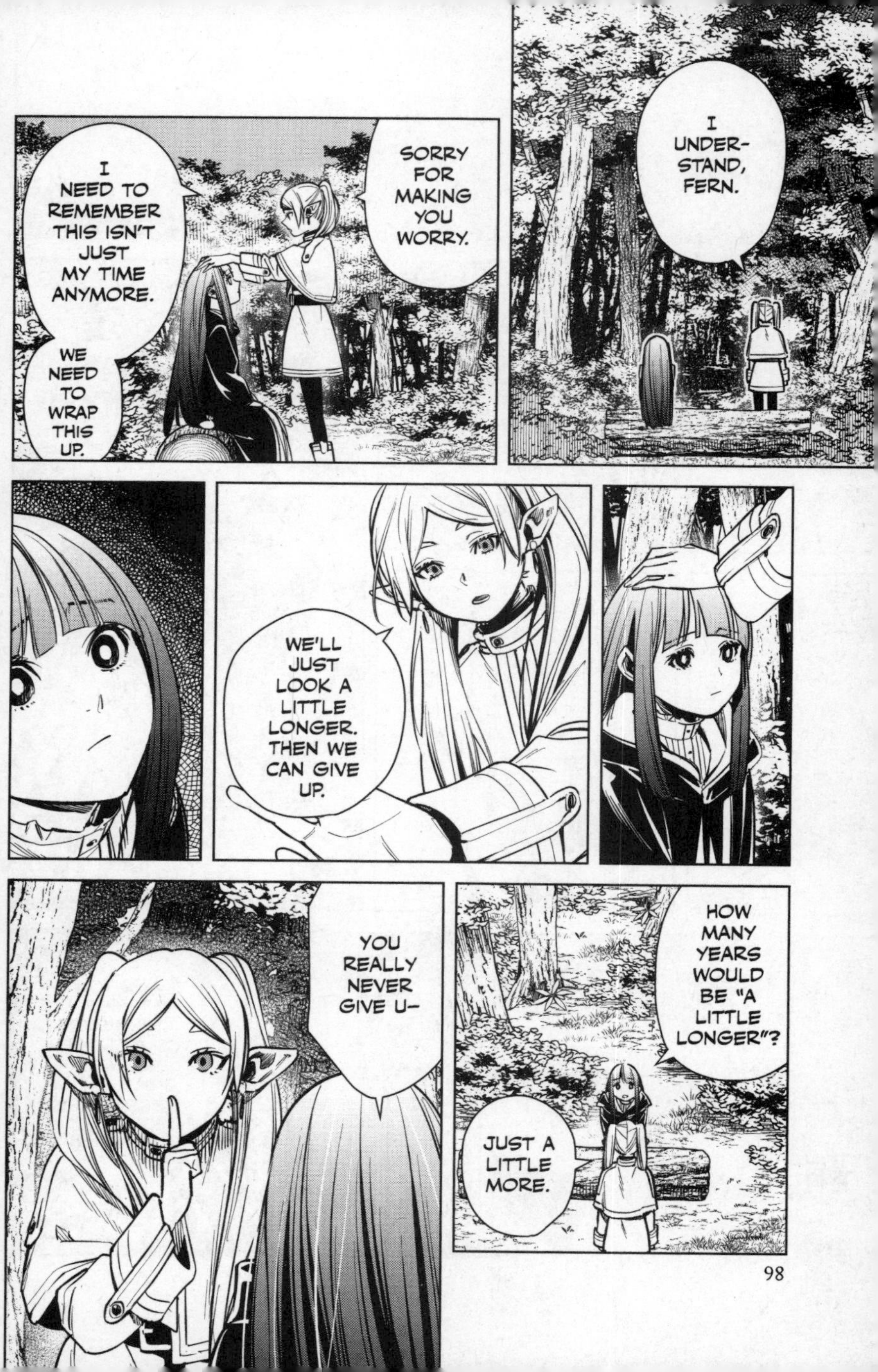
I UNDER-STAND, FERN.
SORRY FOR MAKING YOU WORRY.
I NEED TO REMEMBER THIS ISN'T JUST MY TIME ANYMORE.
WE NEED TO WRAP THIS UP.
WE'LL JUST LOOK A LITTLE LONGER. THEN WE CAN GIVE UP.
HOW MANY YEARS WOULD BE "A LITTLE LONGER"?
JUST A LITTLE MORE.
YOU REALLY NEVER GIVE U-

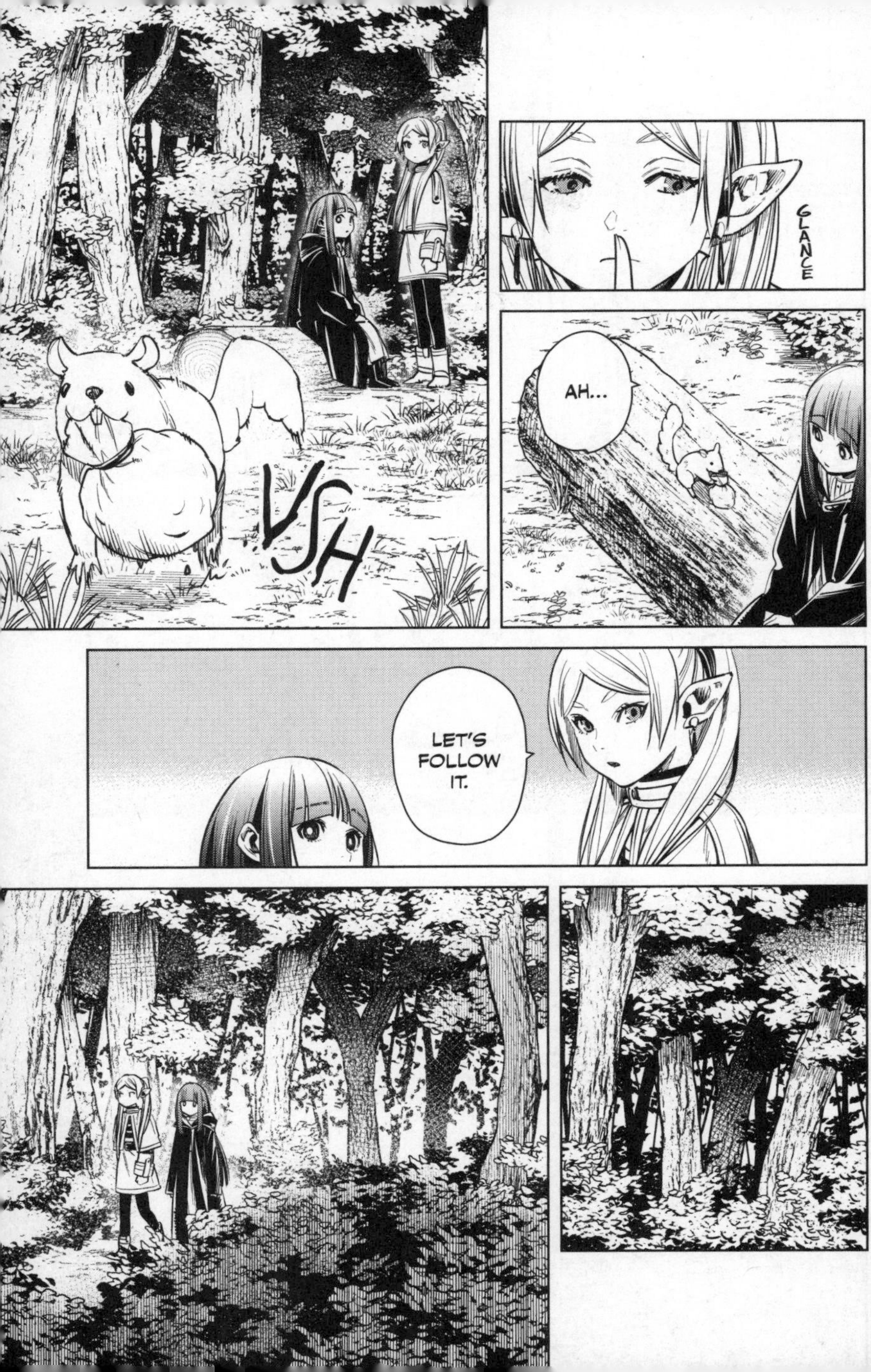
GLANCE
AH...
VSH
LET'S FOLLOW IT.

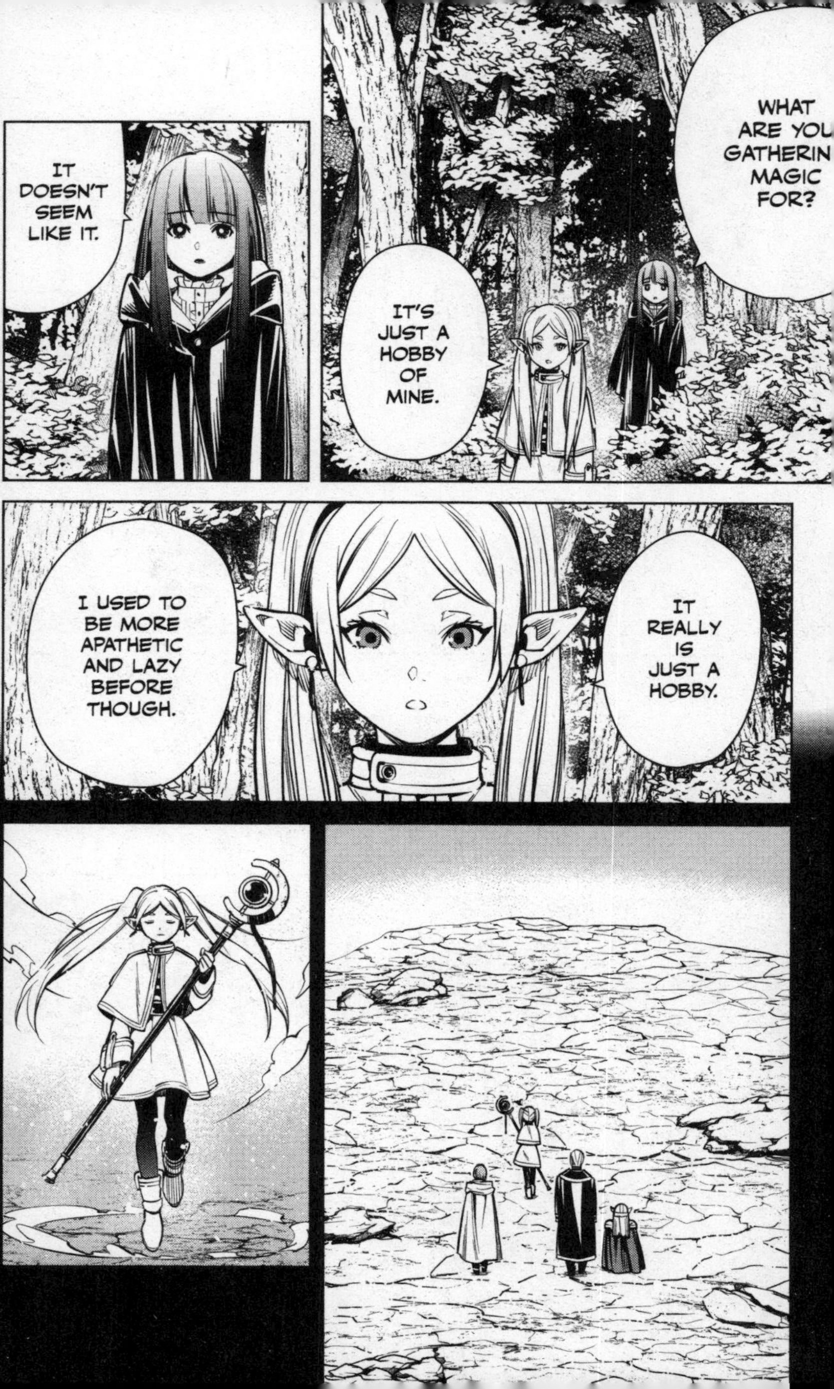
WHAT ARE YOU GATHERIN MAGIC FOR?
IT'S JUST A HOBBY OF MINE.
IT DOESN'T SEEM LIKE IT.
IT REALLY IS JUST A HOBBY.
I USED TO BE MORE APATHETIC AND LAZY BEFORE THOUGH.

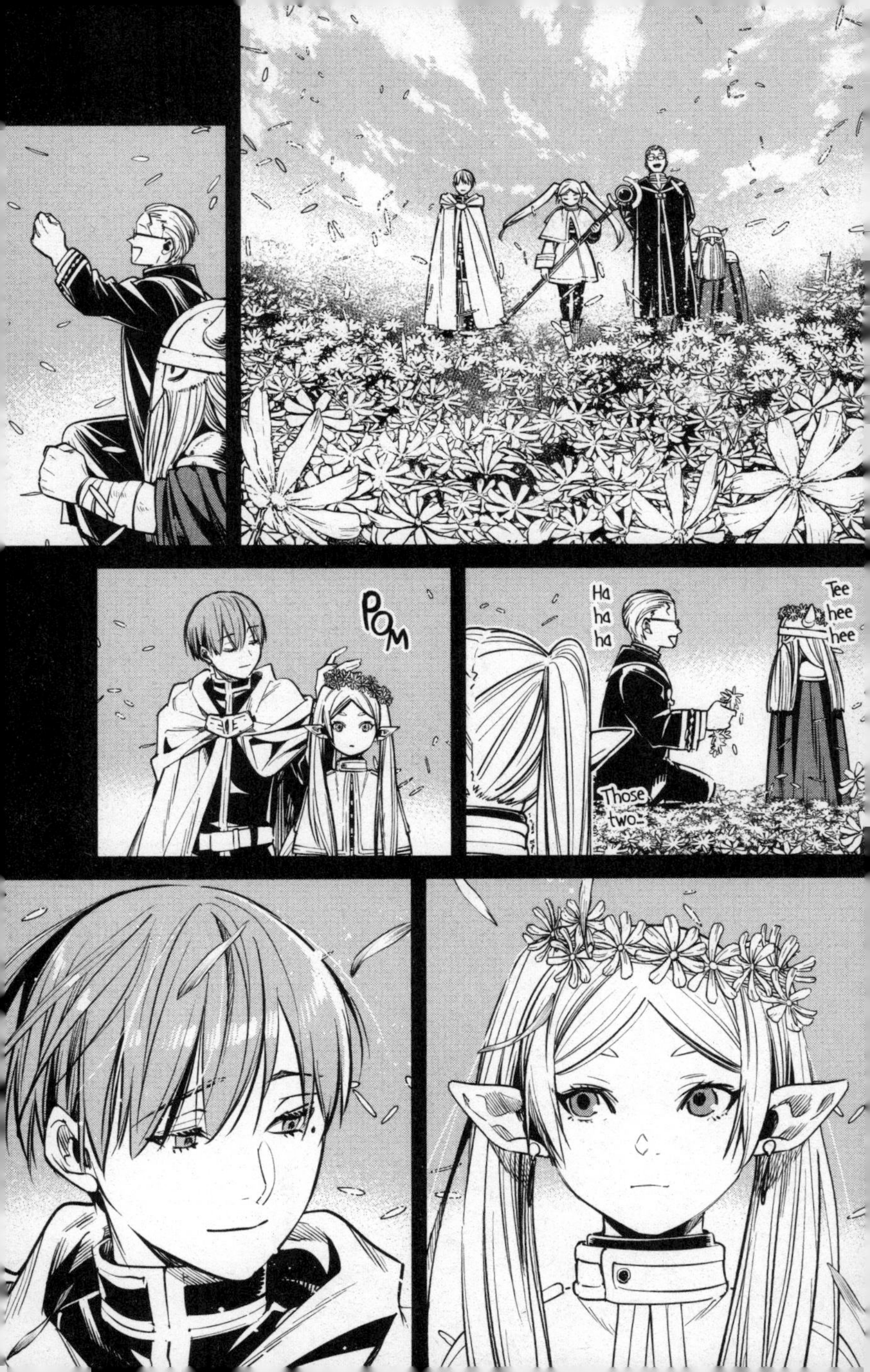
Tee hee hee
Ha ha ha
Those two...
POM

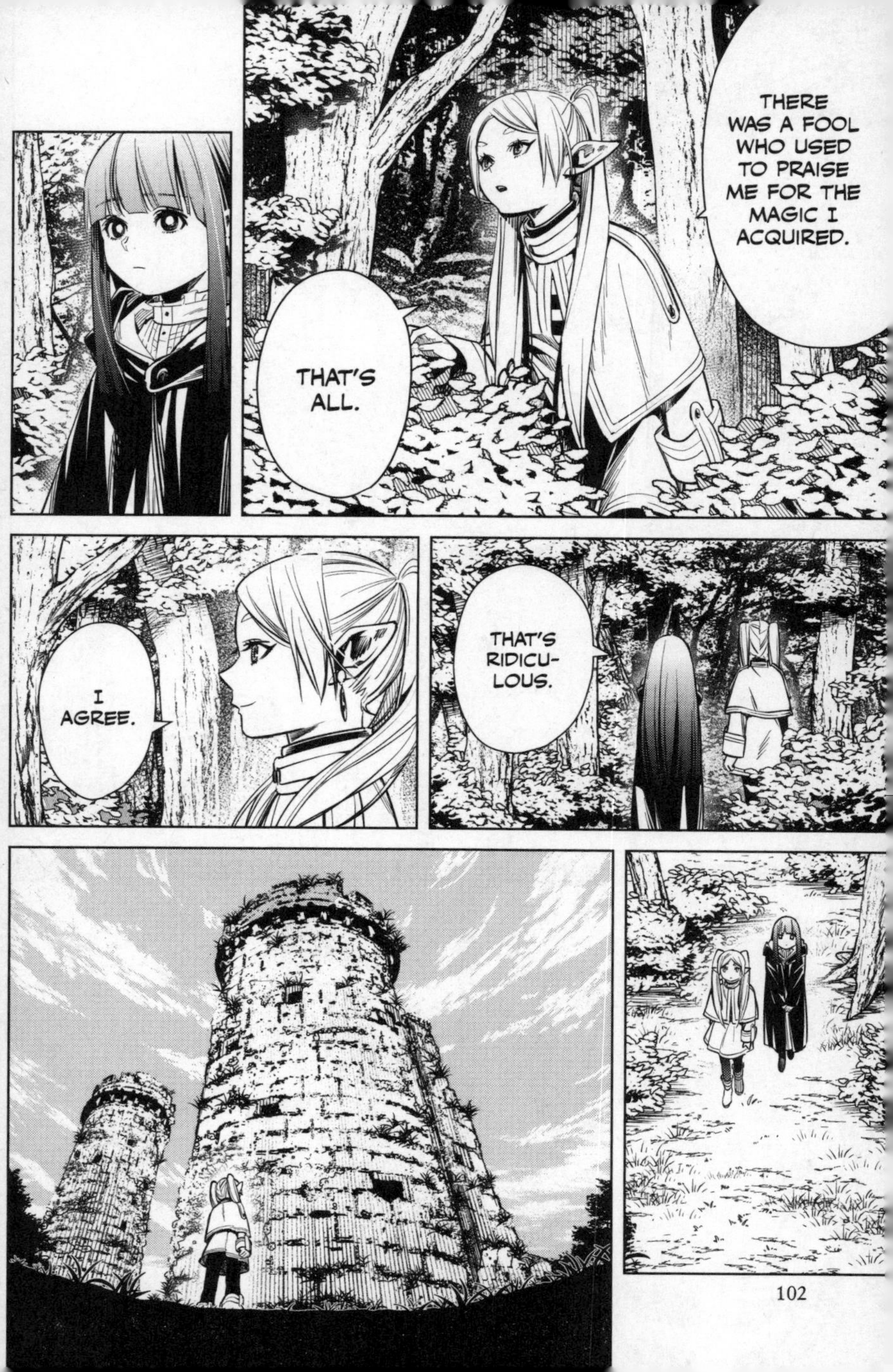
THERE WAS A FOOL WHO USED TO PRAISE ME FOR THE MAGIC I ACQUIRED.
THAT'S ALL.
THAT'S RIDICU-LOUS.
I AGREE.

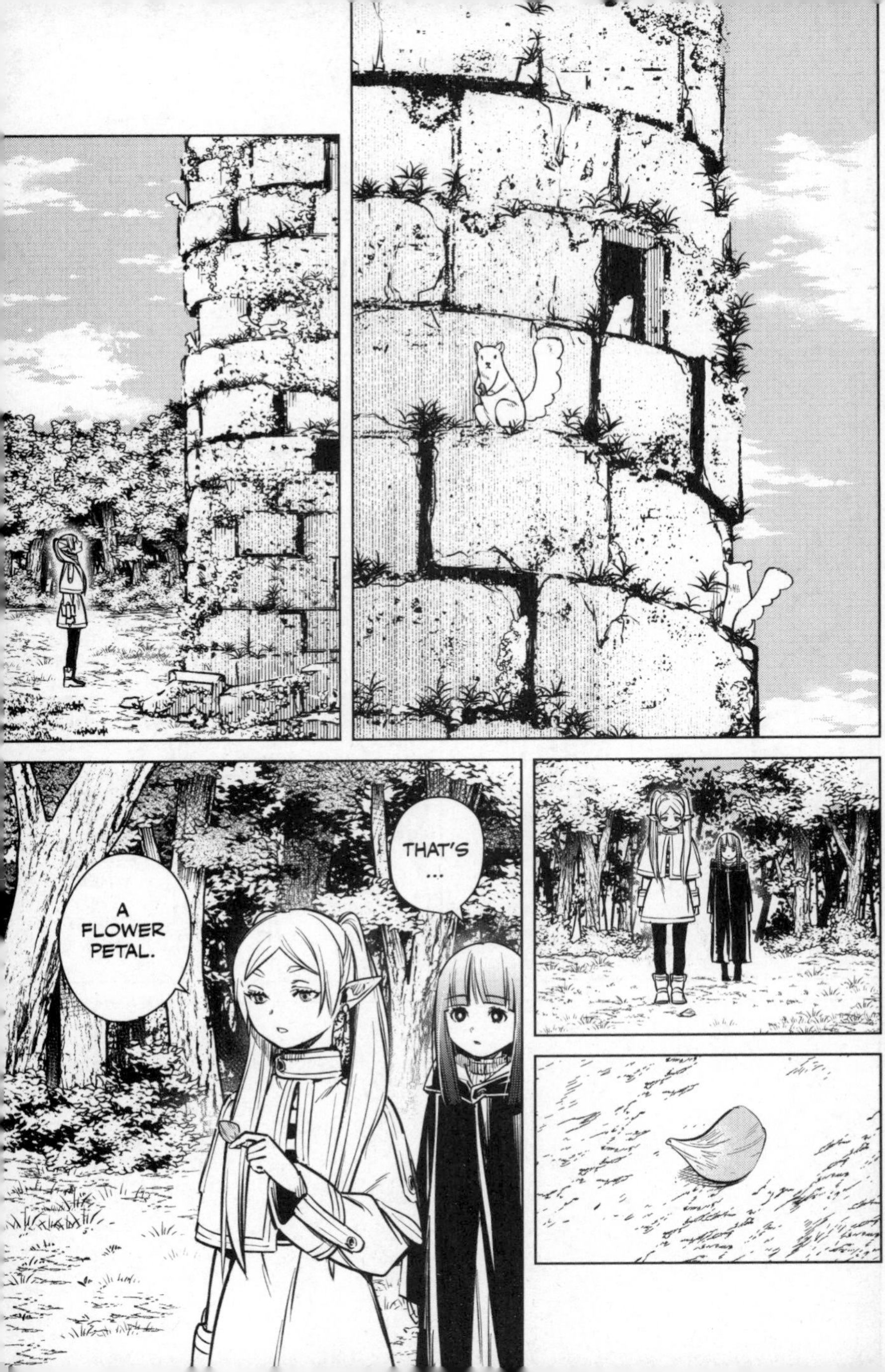
THAT'S ...
A FLOWER PETAL.

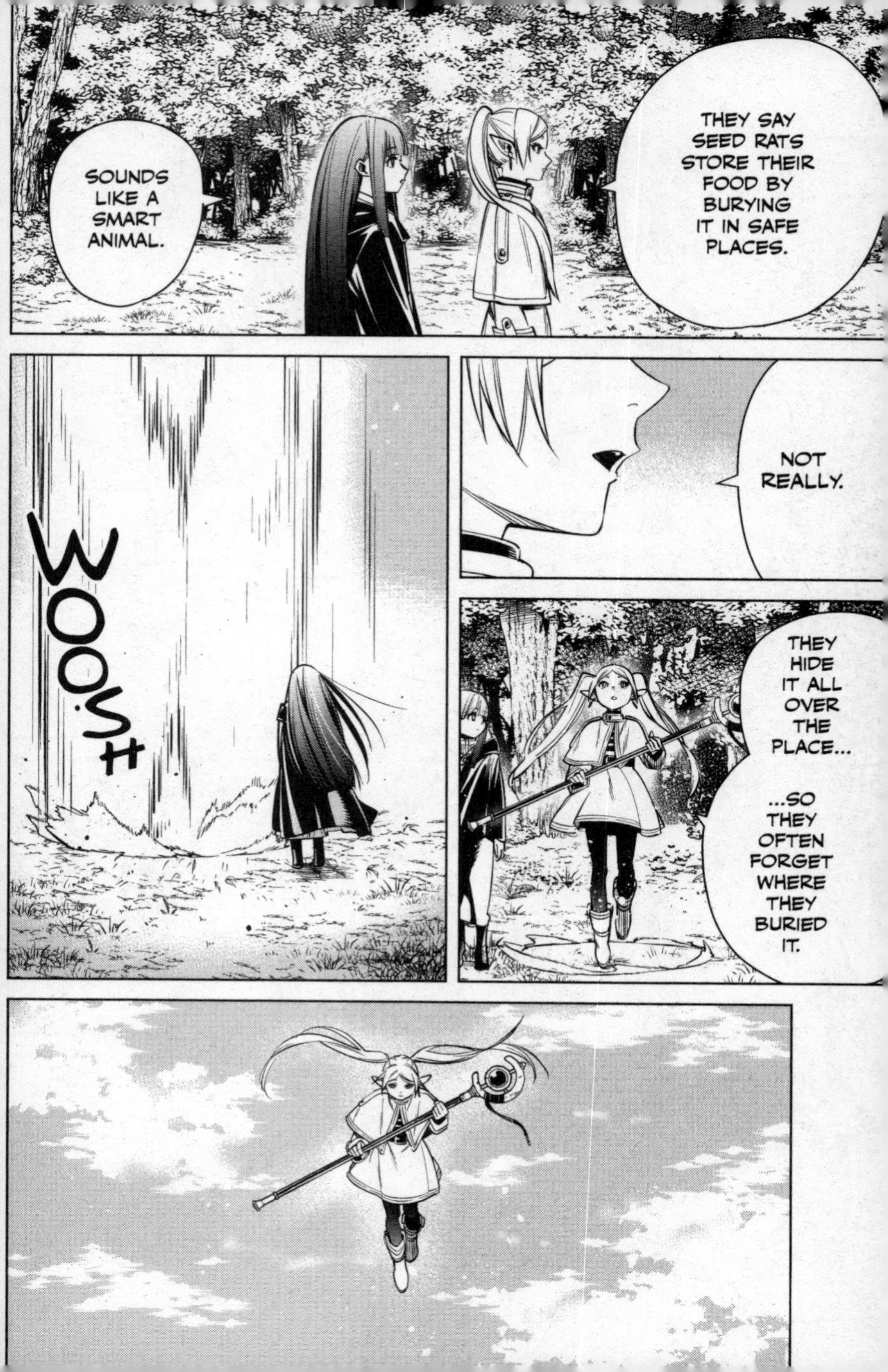
THEY SAY SEED RATS STORE THEIR FOOD BY BURYING IT IN SAFE PLACES.
SOUNDS LIKE A SMART ANIMAL.
NOT REALLY.
THEY HIDE IT ALL OVER THE PLACE...
...SO THEY OFTEN FORGET WHERE THEY BURIED IT.
WOOSH

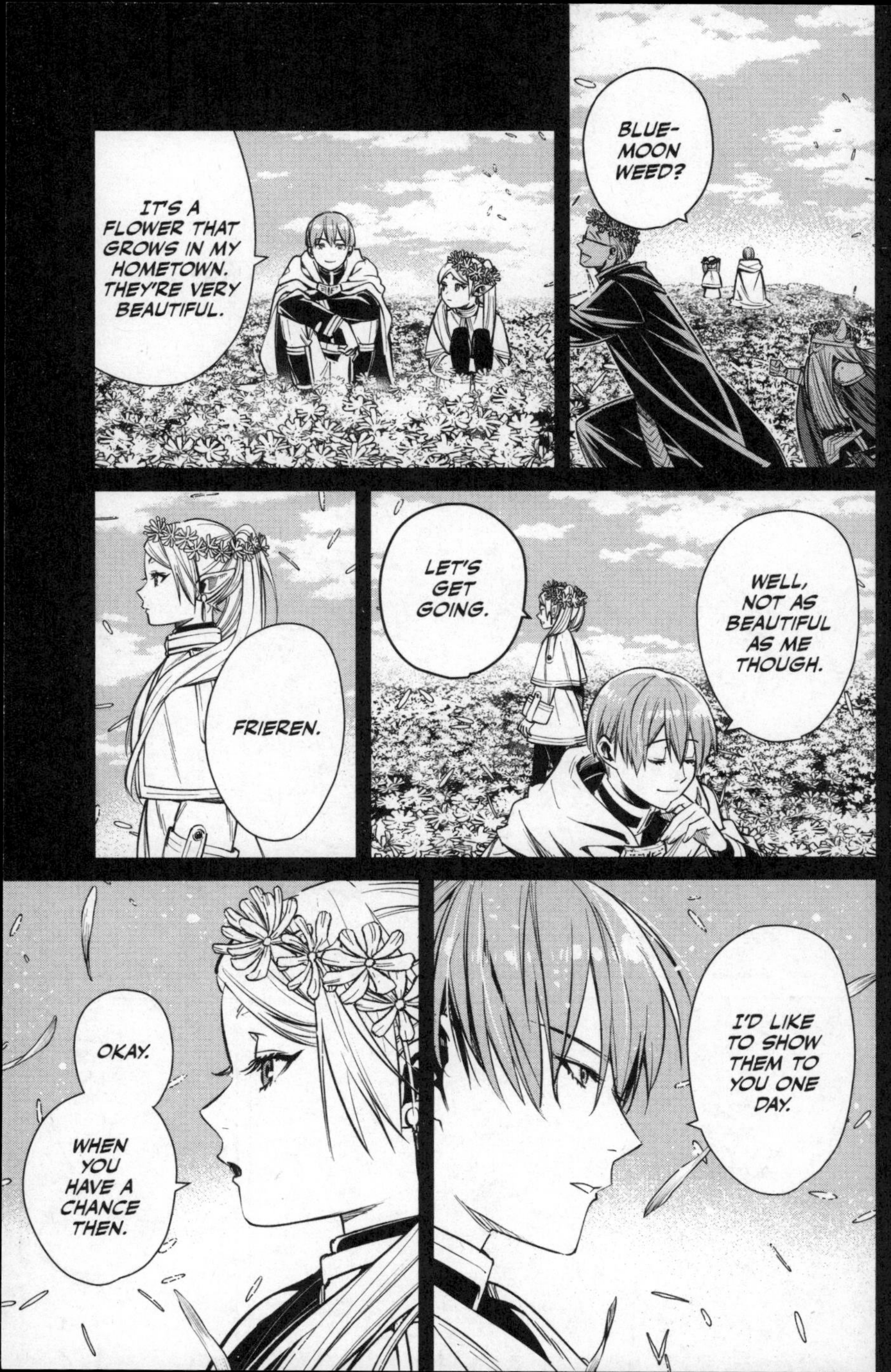
BLUE-MOON WEED?
IT'S A FLOWER THAT GROWS IN MY HOMETOWN. THEY'RE VERY BEAUTIFUL.
WELL, NOT AS BEAUTIFUL AS ME THOUGH.
LET'S GET GOING.
FRIEREN.
I'D LIKE TO SHOW THEM TO YOU ONE DAY.
OKAY.
WHEN YOU HAVE A CHANCE THEN.

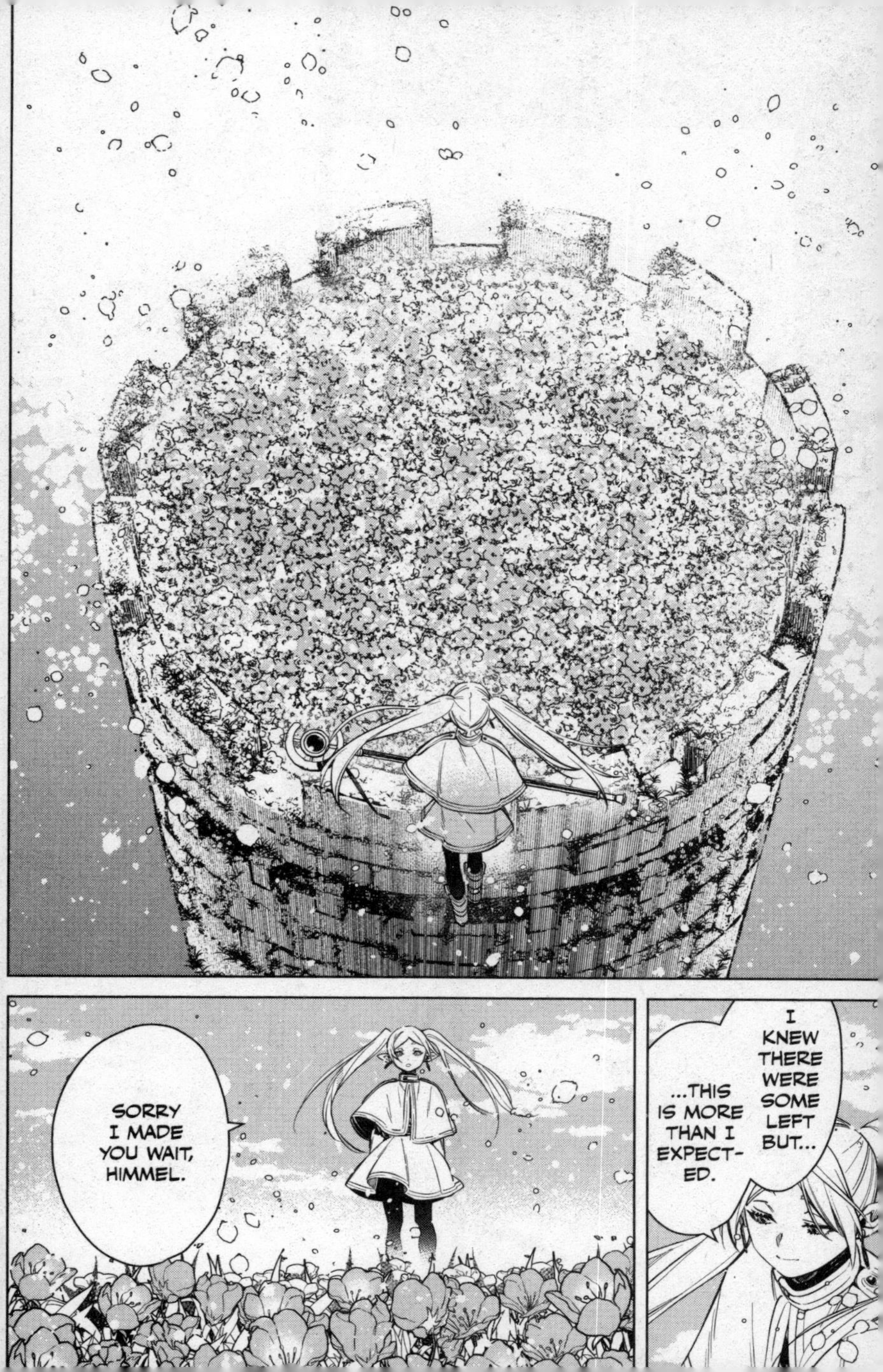
I KNEW THERE WERE SOME LEFT BUT...
...THIS IS MORE THAN I EXPECT-ED.
SORRY I MADE YOU WAIT, HIMMEL.

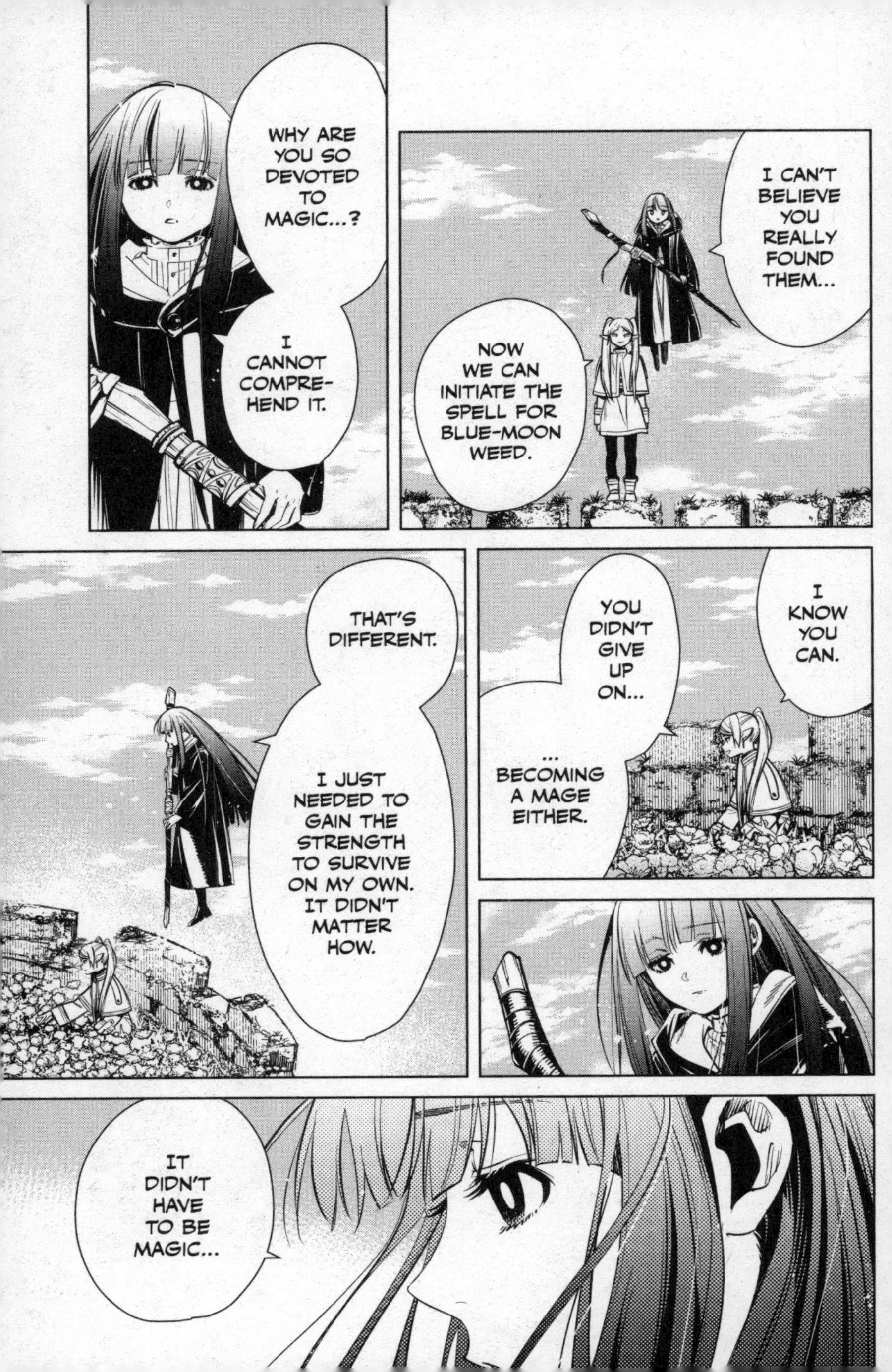
I CAN'T BELIEVE YOU REALLY FOUND THEM...
NOW WE CAN INITIATE THE SPELL FOR BLUE-MOON WEED.
WHY ARE YOU SO DEVOTED TO MAGIC...?
I CANNOT COMPRE-HEND IT.
I KNOW YOU CAN.
YOU DIDN'T GIVE UP ON...
...BECOMING A MAGE EITHER.
THAT'S DIFFERENT.
I JUST NEEDED TO GAIN THE STRENGTH TO SURVIVE ON MY OWN. IT DIDN'T MATTER HOW.
IT DIDN'T HAVE TO BE MAGIC...

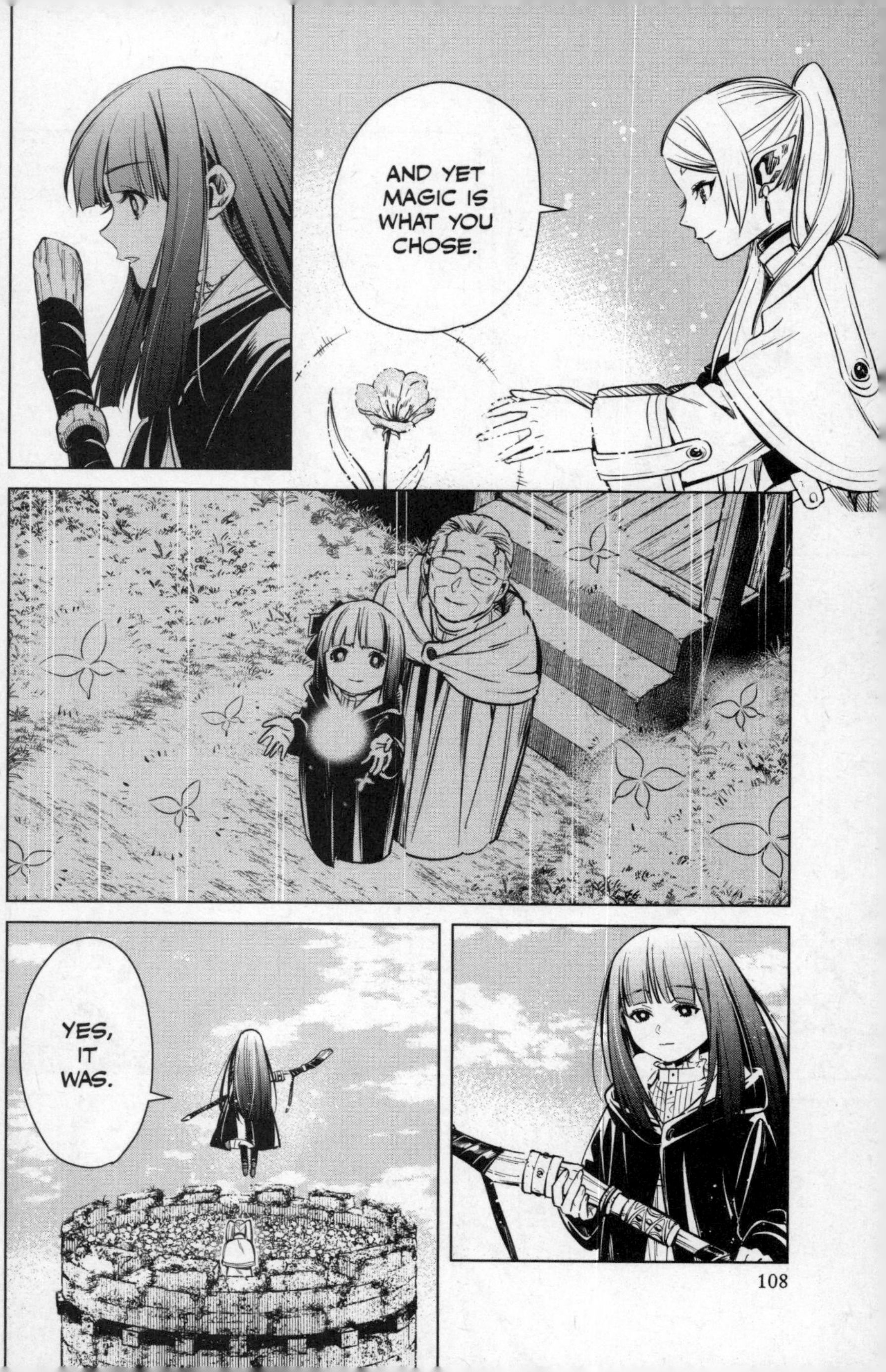
AND YET MAGIC IS WHAT YOU CHOSE.
YES, IT WAS.

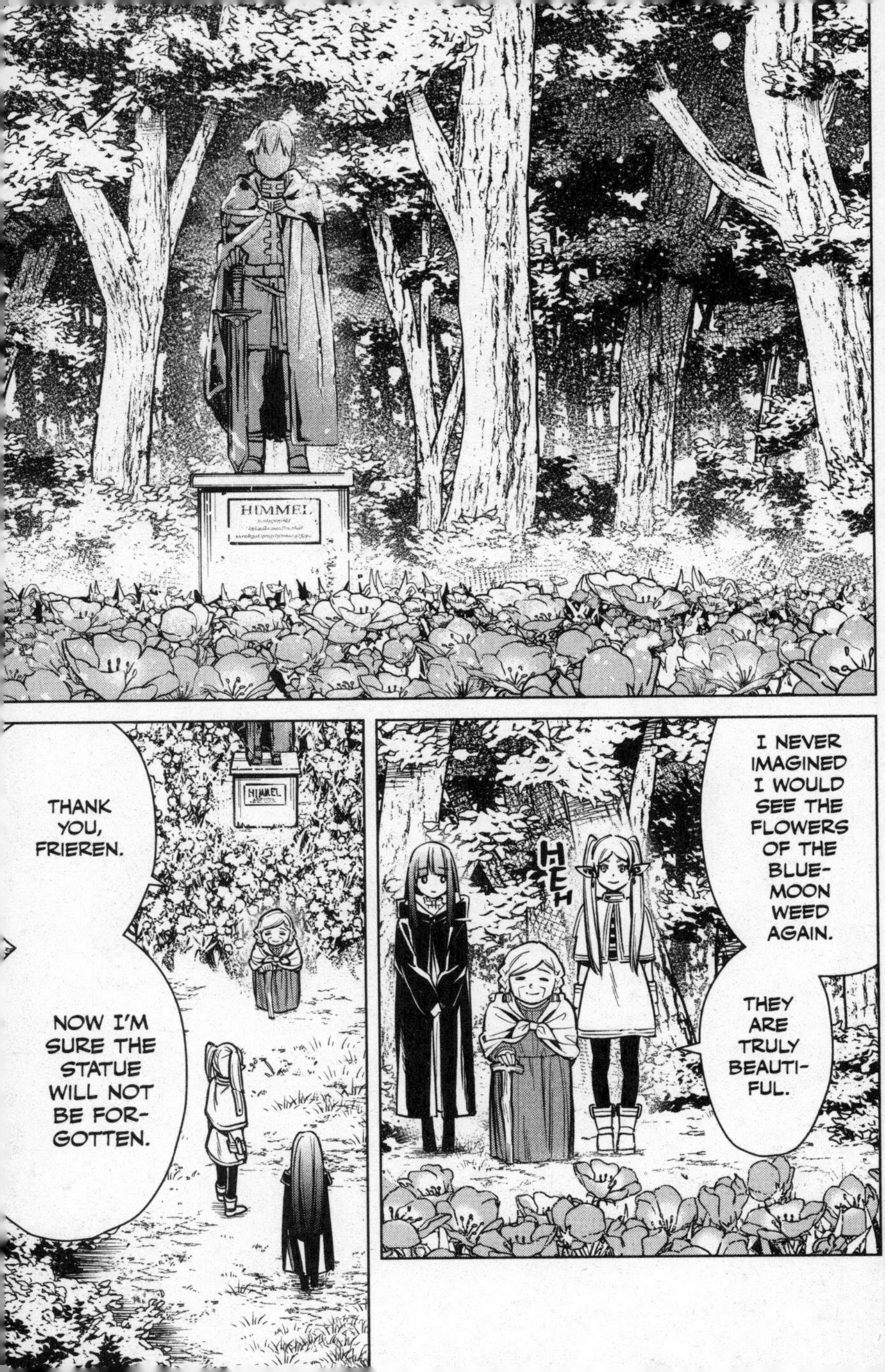
HIMMEL
I NEVER IMAGINED I WOULD SEE THE FLOWERS OF THE BLUE-MOON WEED AGAIN.
HEH
THEY ARE TRULY BEAUTIFUL.
HIMMEL
THANK YOU, FRIEREN.
NOW I'M SURE THE STATUE WILL NOT BE FORGOTTEN.

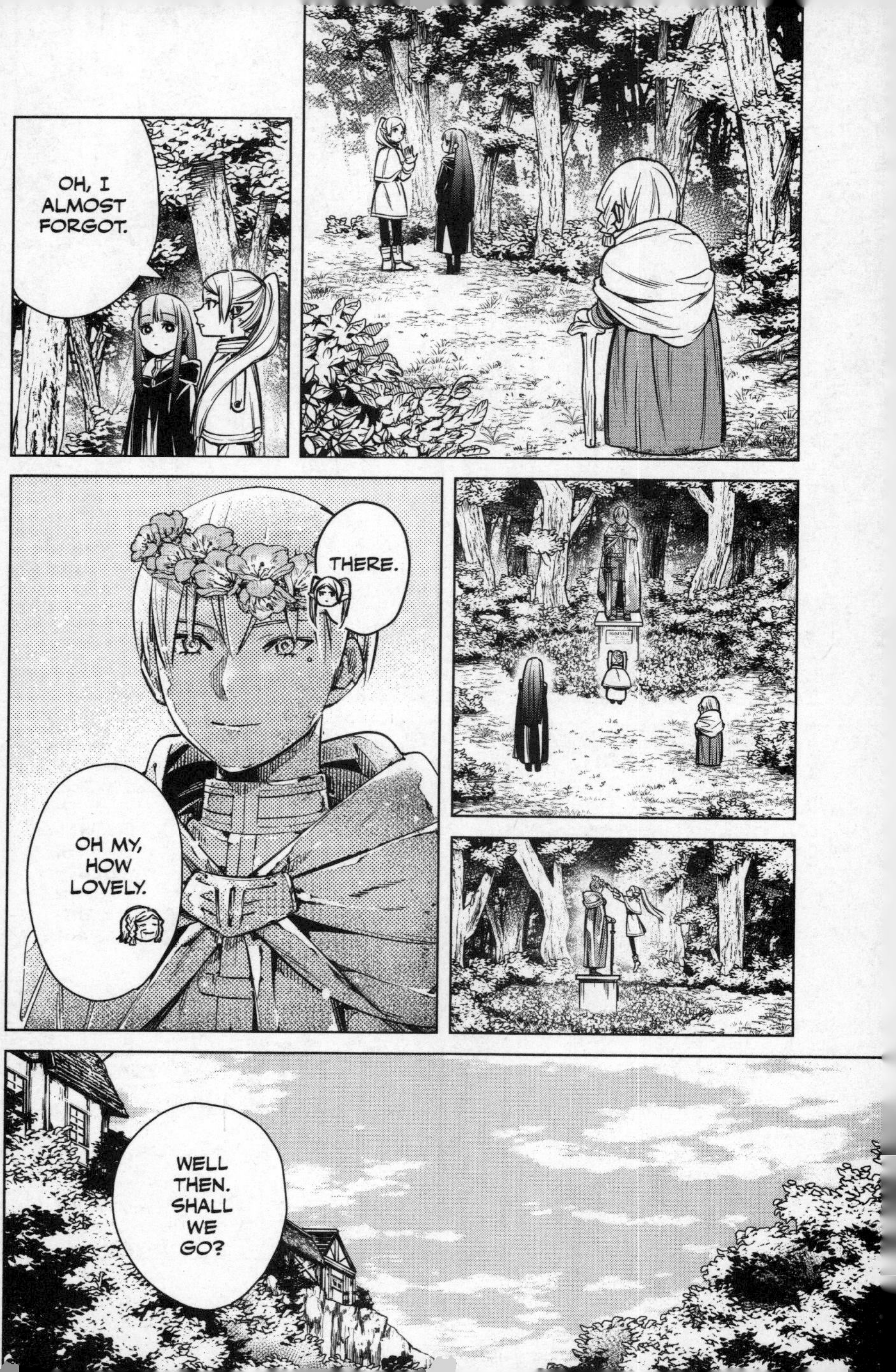
OH, I ALMOST FORGOT.
THERE.
OH MY, HOW LOVELY.
WELL THEN. SHALL WE GO?

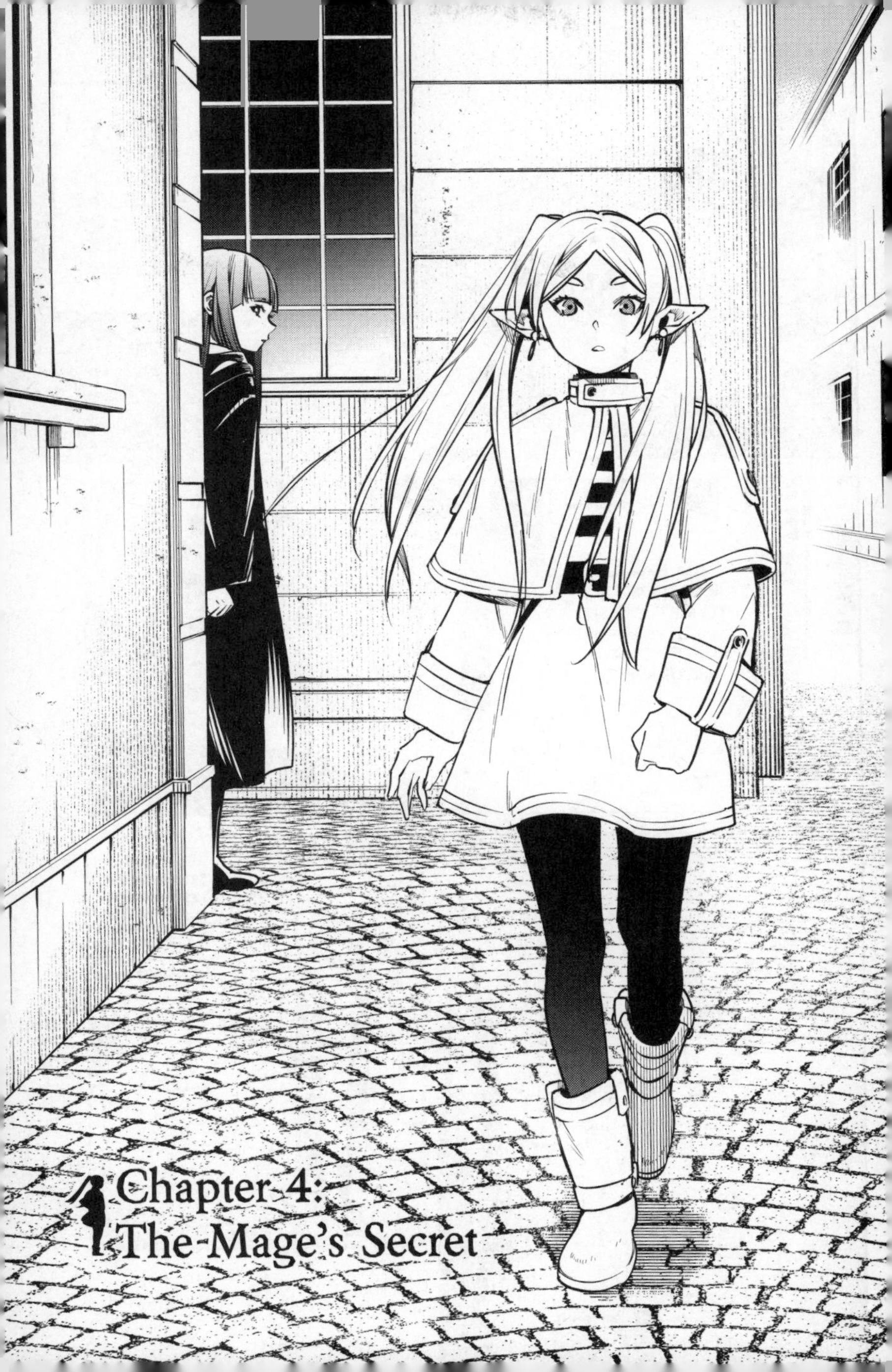
Chapter 4:
The Mage's Secret

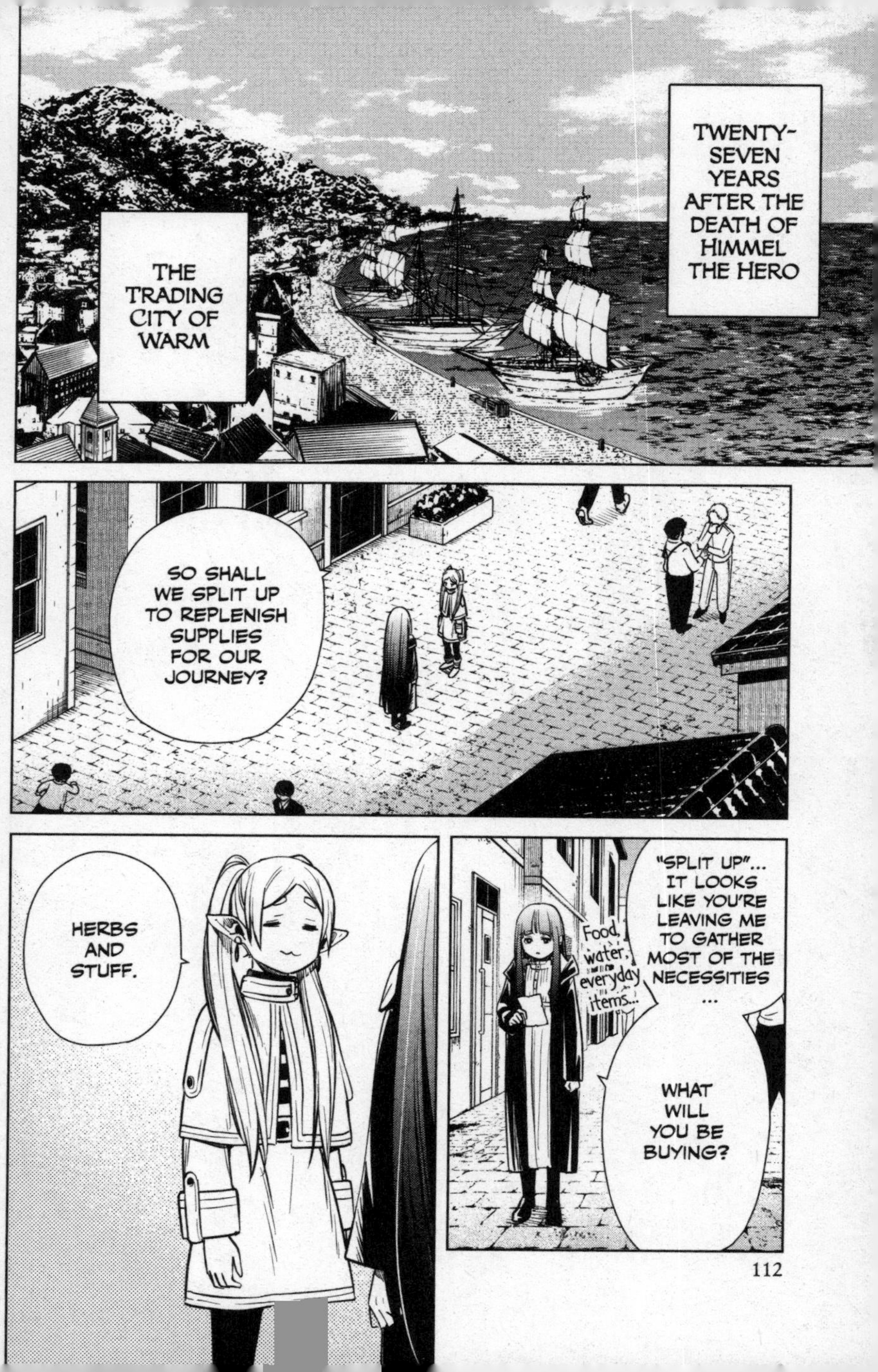
TWENTY-SEVEN YEARS AFTER THE DEATH OF HIMMEL THE HERO
THE TRADING CITY OF WARM
SO SHALL WE SPLIT UP TO REPLENISH SUPPLIES FOR OUR JOURNEY?
"SPLIT UP"... IT LOOKS LIKE YOU'RE LEAVING ME TO GATHER MOST OF THE NECESSITIES ...
Food, water, everyday items...
WHAT WILL YOU BE BUYING?
HERBS AND STUFF.

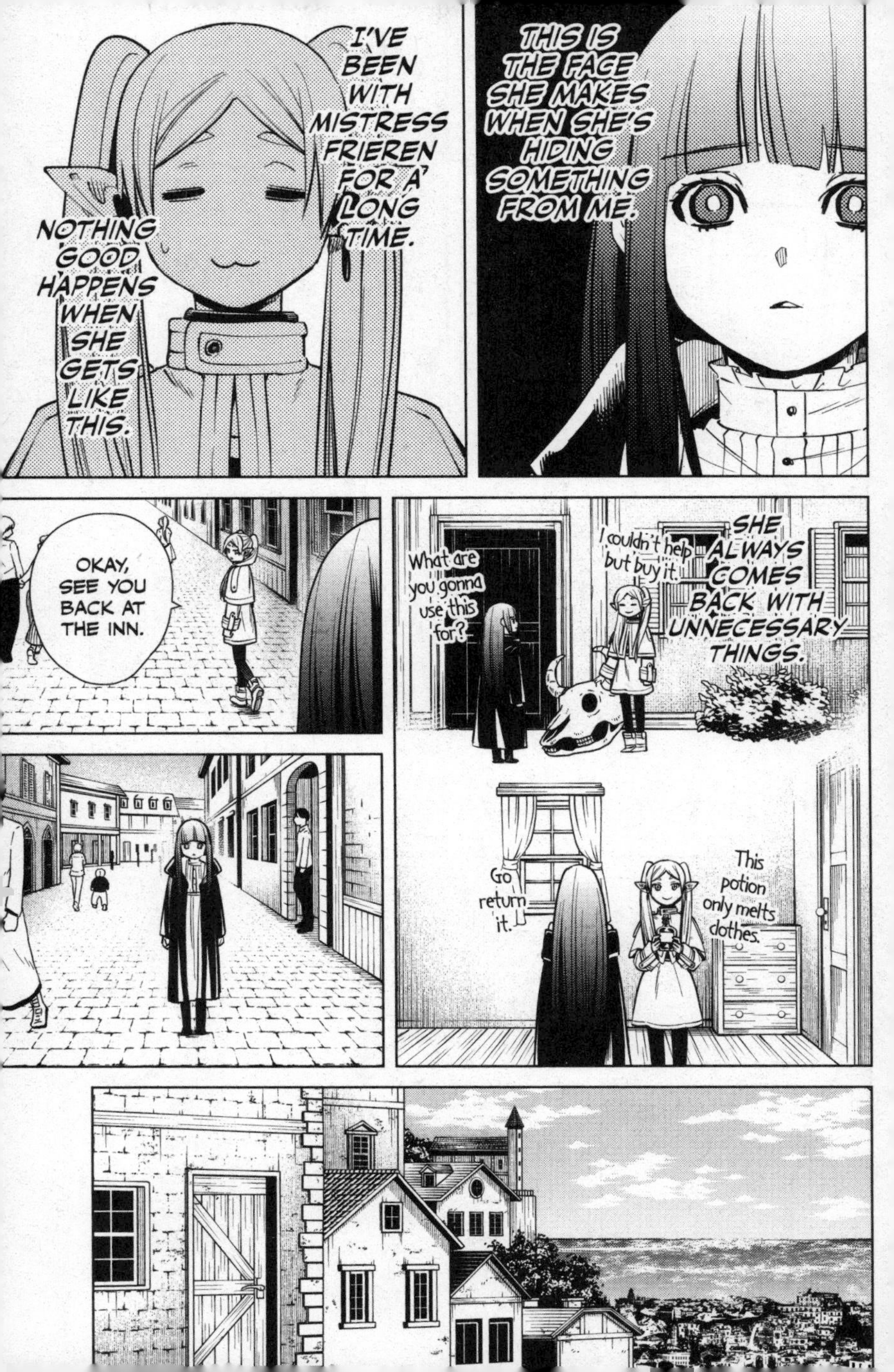
THIS IS THE FACE SHE MAKES WHEN SHE'S HIDING SOMETHING FROM ME.
I'VE BEEN WITH MISTRESS FRIEREN FOR A LONG TIME.
NOTHING GOOD HAPPENS WHEN SHE GETS LIKE THIS.
SHE ALWAYS COMES BACK WITH UNNECESSARY THINGS.
I couldn't help but buy it.
What are you gonna use this for?
This potion only melts clothes.
Go return it.
OKAY, SEE YOU BACK AT THE INN.

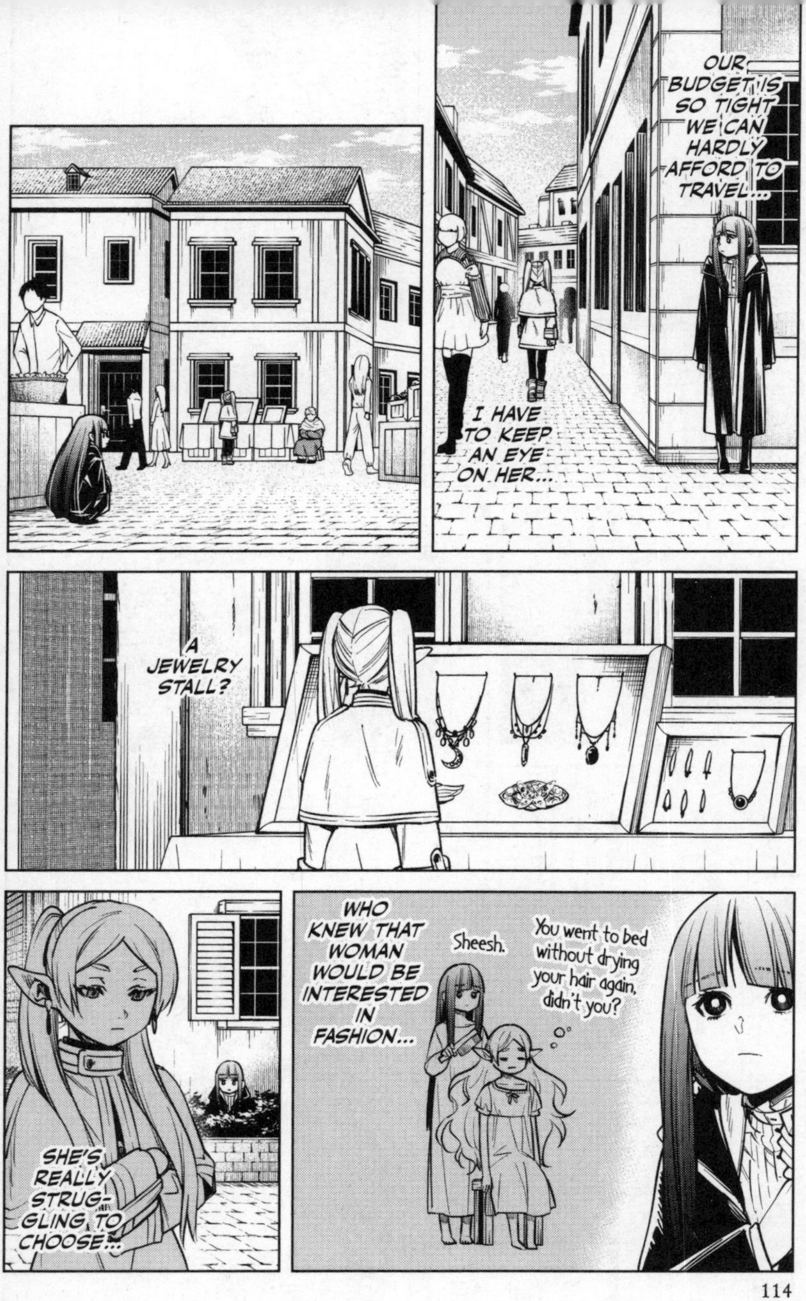
OUR BUDGET IS SO TIGHT WE CAN HARDLY AFFORD TO TRAVEL...
I HAVE TO KEEP AN EYE ON HER...
A JEWELRY STALL?
You went to bed without drying your hair again, didn't you?
Sheesh.
WHO KNEW THAT WOMAN WOULD BE INTERESTED IN FASHION...
SHE'S REALLY STRUG-GLING TO CHOOSE...

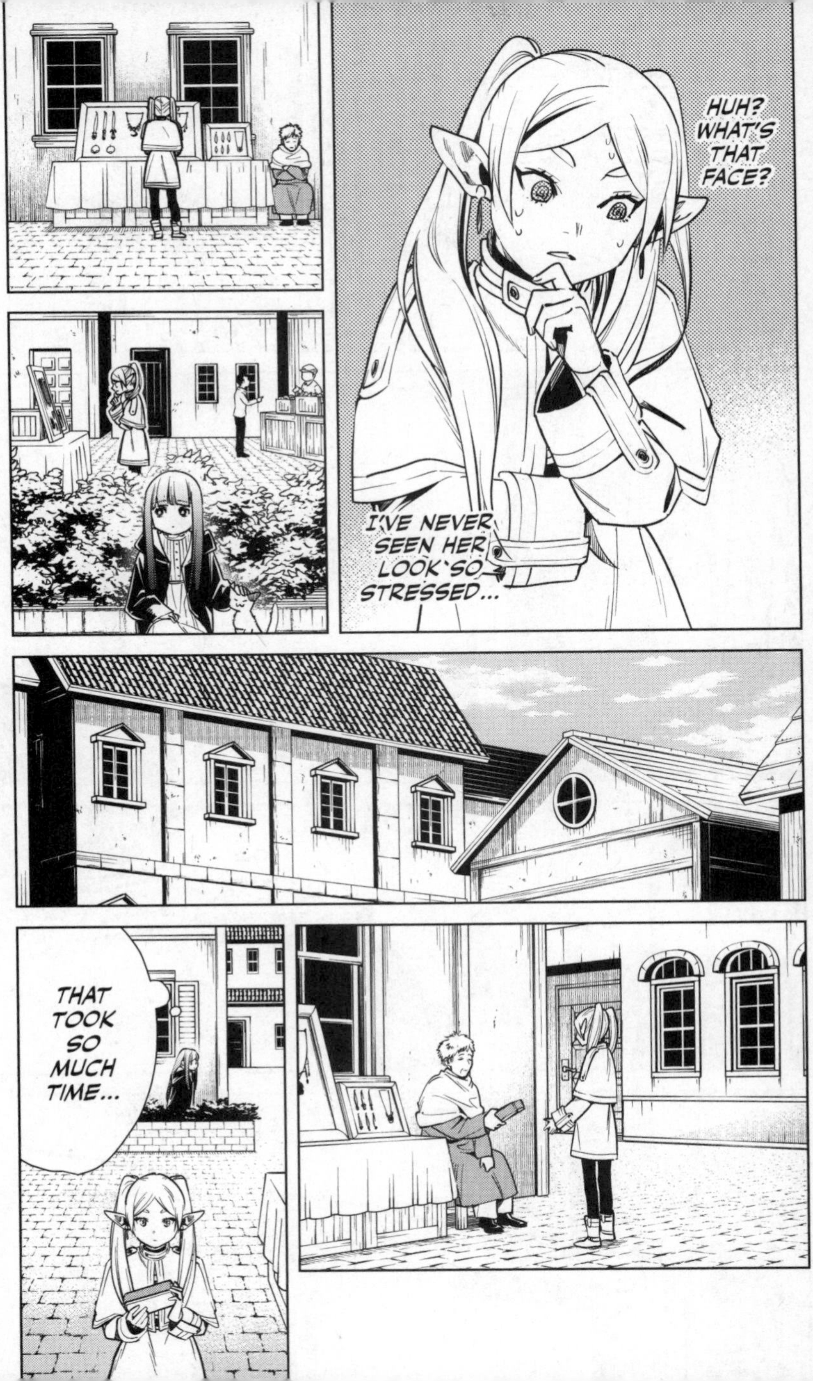
HUH? WHAT'S THAT FACE?
I'VE NEVER SEEN HER LOOK SO STRESSED...
THAT TOOK SO MUCH TIME...

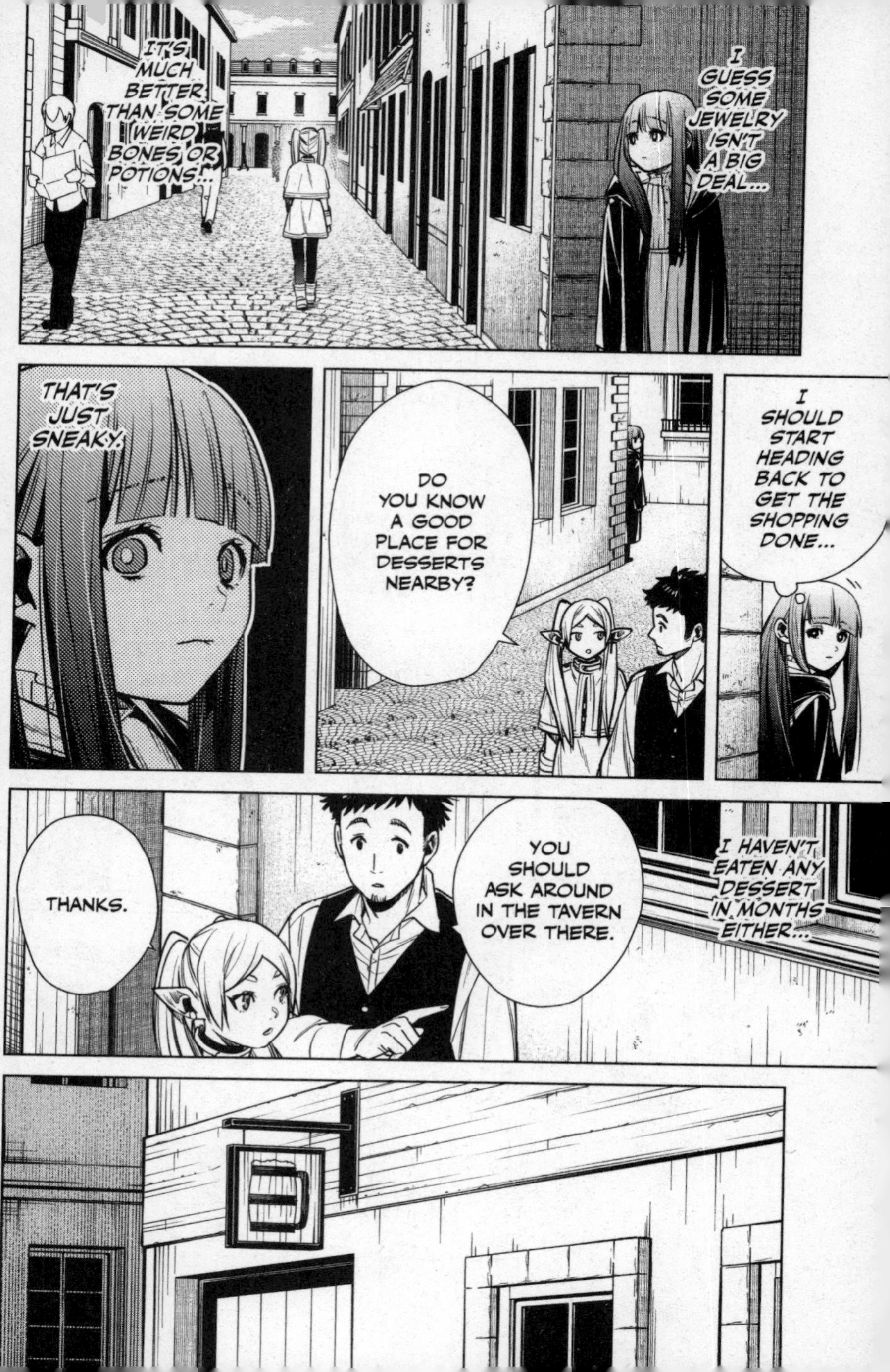
I GUESS SOME JEWELRY ISN'T A BIG DEAL...
IT'S MUCH BETTER THAN SOME WEIRD BONES OR POTIONS...
I SHOULD START HEADING BACK TO GET THE SHOPPING DONE...
DO YOU KNOW A GOOD PLACE FOR DESSERTS NEARBY?
THAT'S JUST SNEAKY.
I HAVEN'T EATEN ANY DESSERT IN MONTHS EITHER...
YOU SHOULD ASK AROUND IN THE TAVERN OVER THERE.
THANKS.

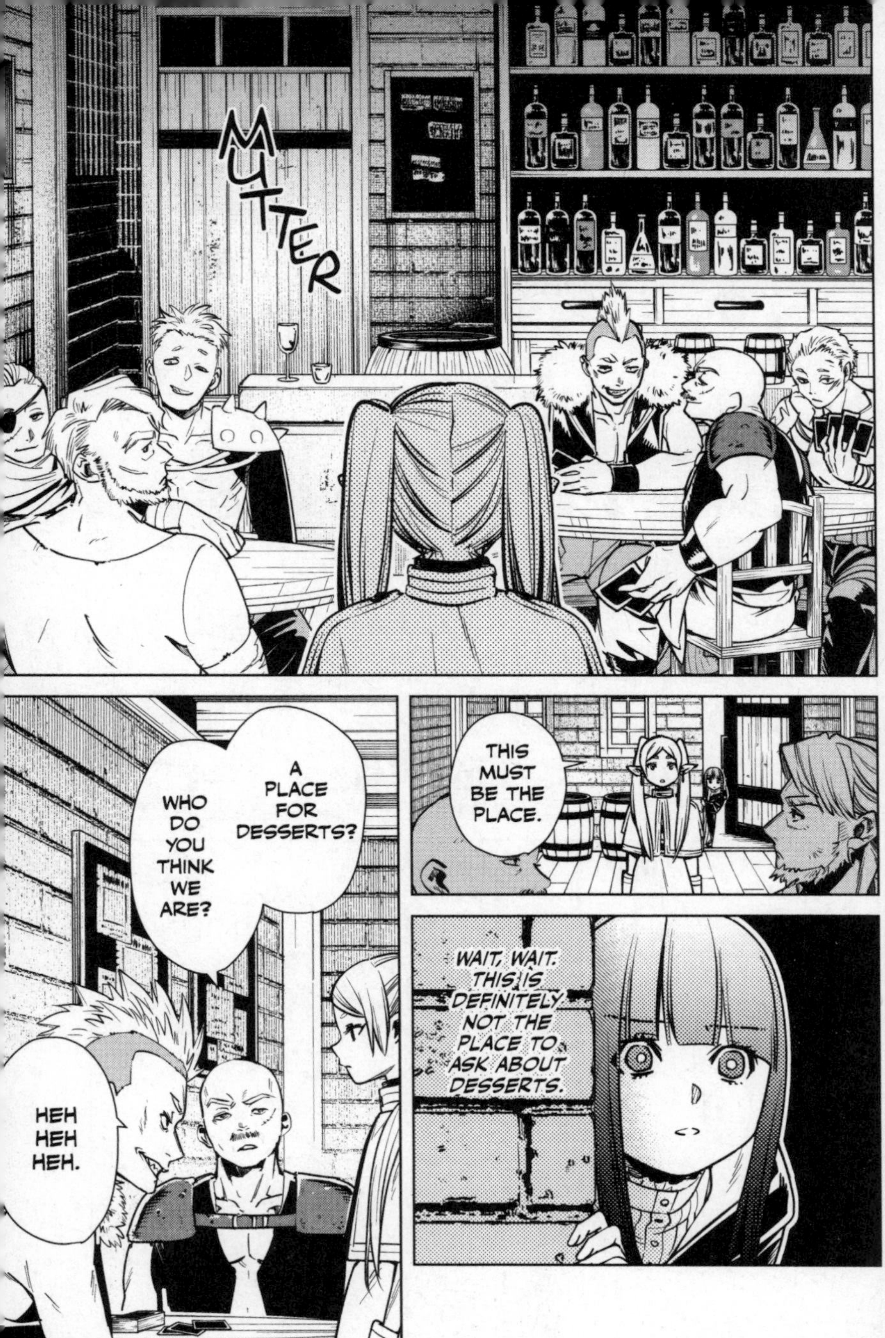
MUTTER
THIS MUST BE THE PLACE.
WAIT, WAIT. THIS IS DEFINITELY NOT THE PLACE TO ASK ABOUT DESSERTS.
A PLACE FOR DESSERTS?
WHO DO YOU THINK WE ARE?
HEH HEH HEH.

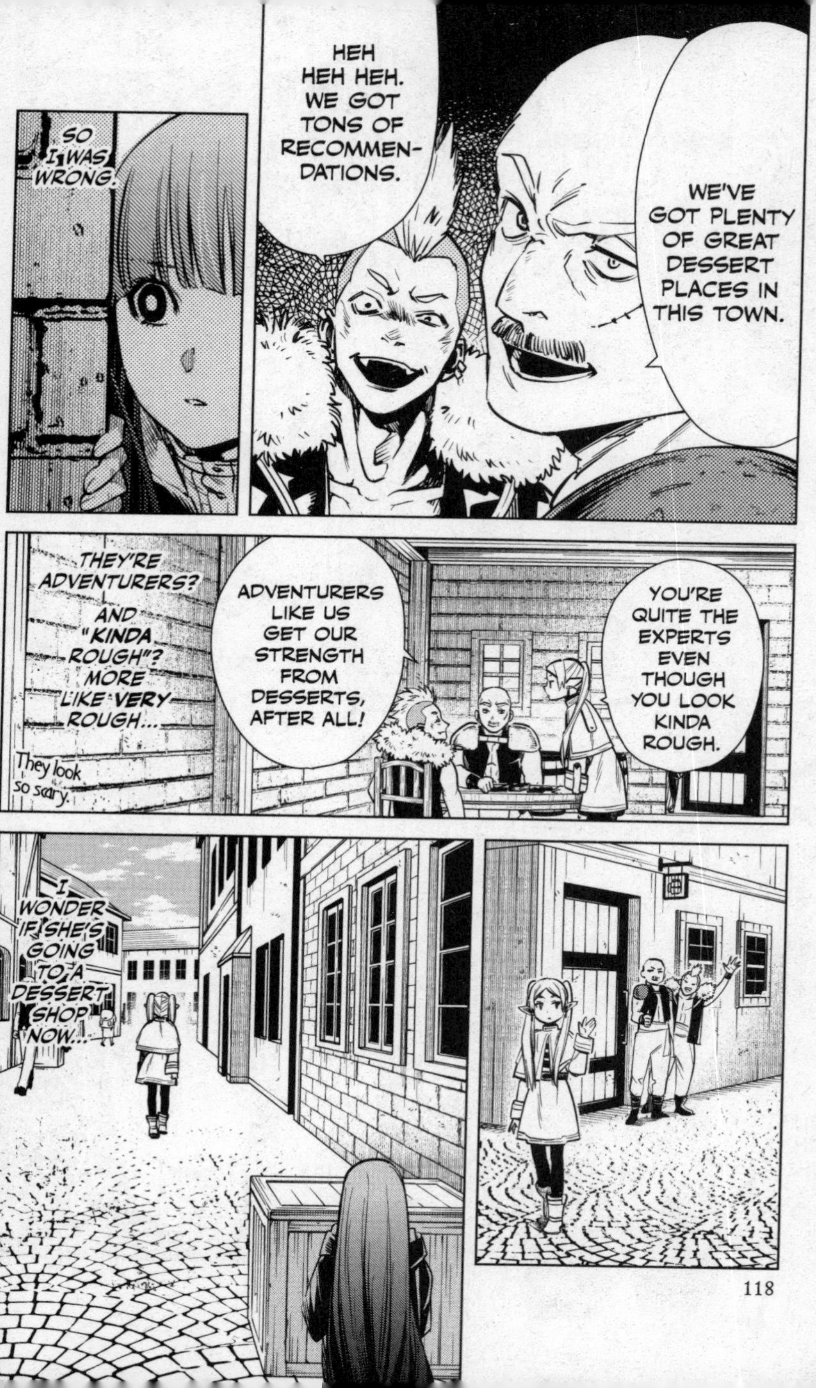
WE'VE GOT PLENTY OF GREAT DESSERT PLACES IN THIS TOWN.
HEH HEH HEH. WE GOT TONS OF RECOMMENDATIONS.
SO I WAS WRONG.
YOU'RE QUITE THE EXPERTS EVEN THOUGH YOU LOOK KINDA ROUGH.
ADVENTURERS LIKE US GET OUR STRENGTH FROM DESSERTS, AFTER ALL!
THEY'RE ADVENTURERS? AND "KINDA ROUGH"? MORE LIKE VERY ROUGH...
They look so scary.
I WONDER IF SHE'S GOING TO A DESSERT SHOP NOW...

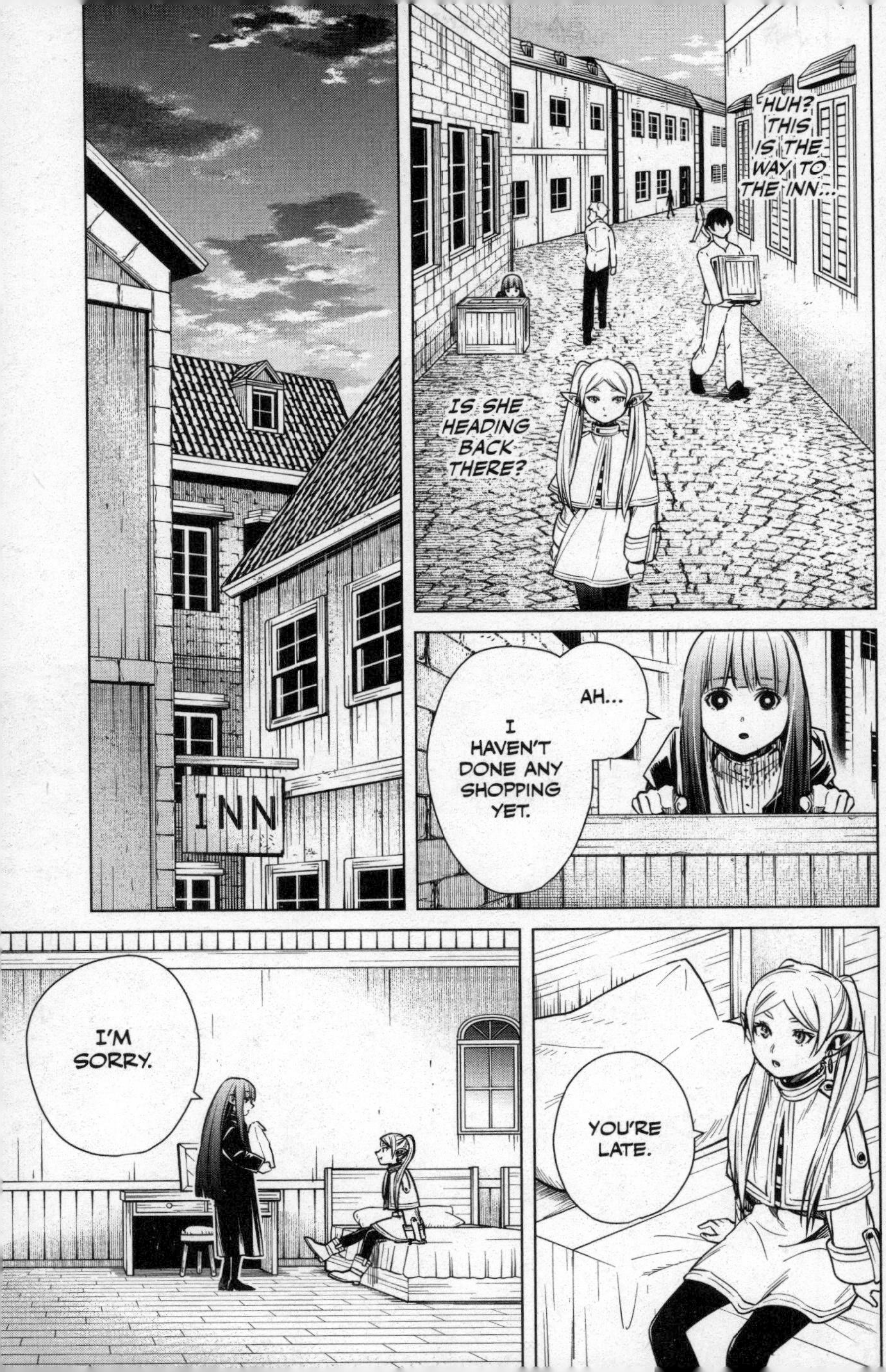
HUH? THIS IS THE WAY TO THE INN...
IS SHE HEADING BACK THERE?
AH...
I HAVEN'T DONE ANY SHOPPING YET.
INN
YOU'RE LATE.
I'M SORRY.

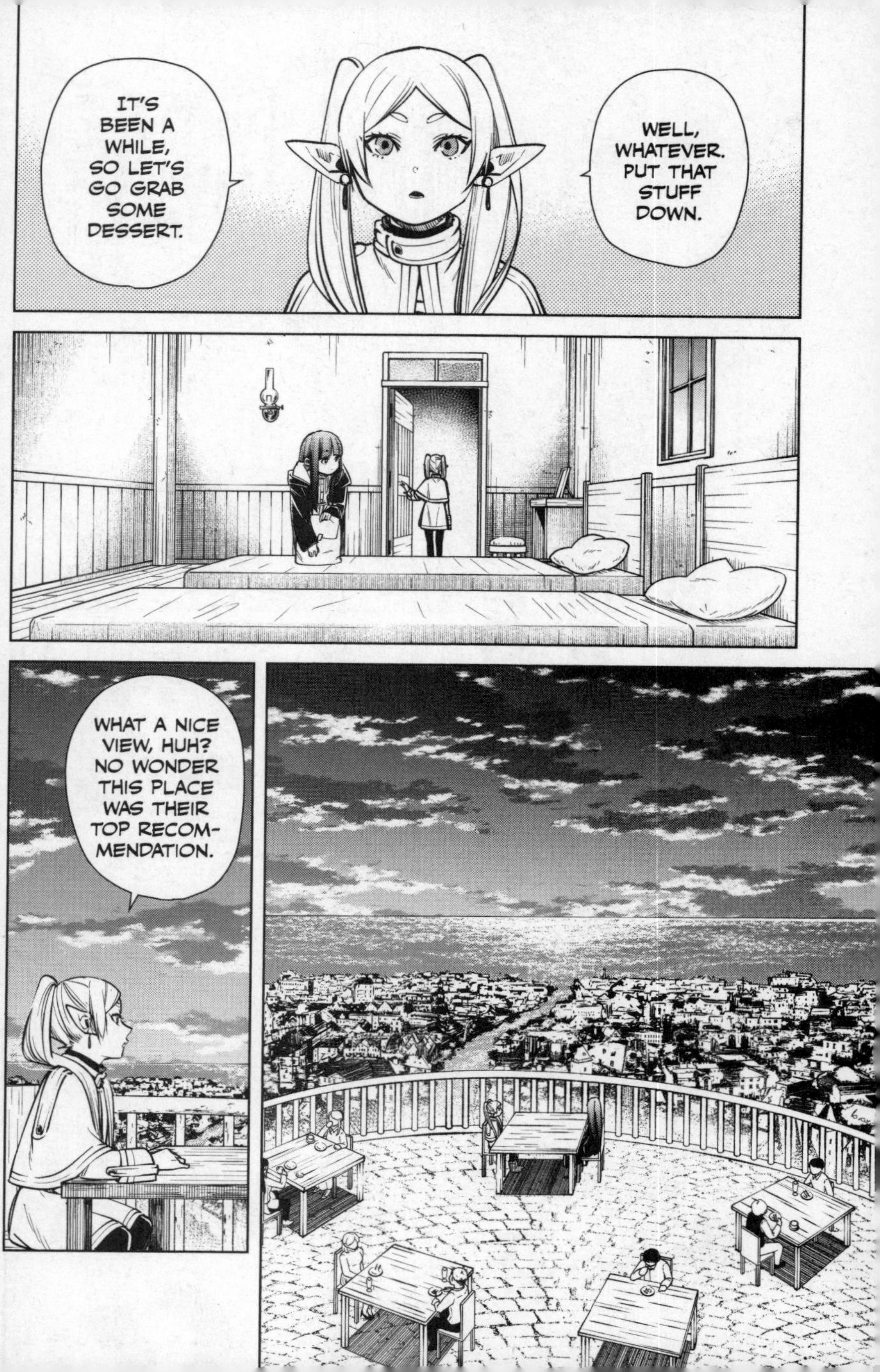
WELL, WHATEVER. PUT THAT STUFF DOWN.
IT'S BEEN A WHILE, SO LET'S GO GRAB SOME DESSERT.
WHAT A NICE VIEW, HUH? NO WONDER THIS PLACE WAS THEIR TOP RECOM-MENDATION.

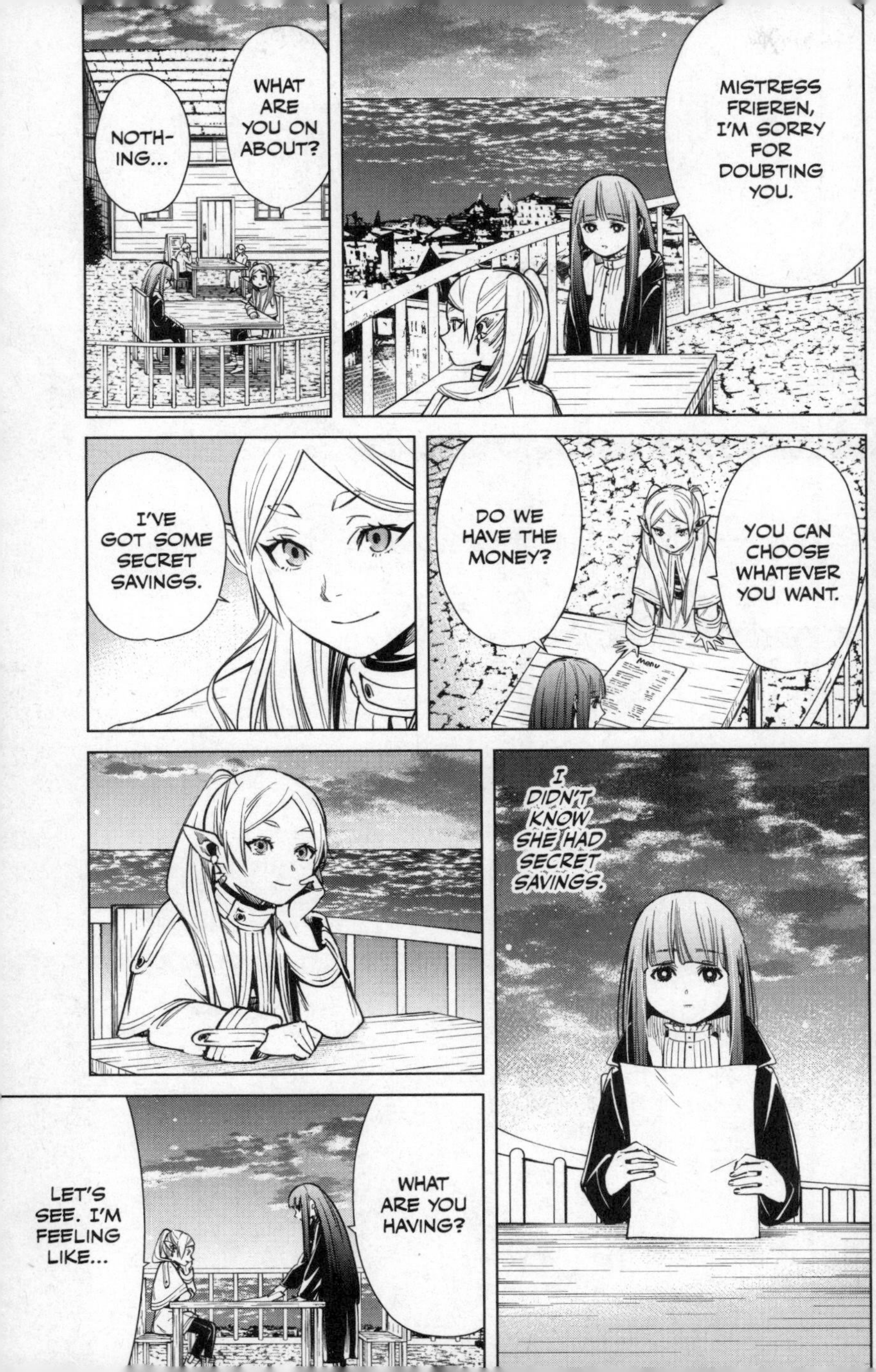
MISTRESS FRIEREN, I'M SORRY FOR DOUBTING YOU.
WHAT ARE YOU ON ABOUT?
NOTH-ING...
YOU CAN CHOOSE WHATEVER YOU WANT.
DO WE HAVE THE MONEY?
I'VE GOT SOME SECRET SAVINGS.
I DIDN'T KNOW SHE HAD SECRET SAVINGS.
WHAT ARE YOU HAVING?
LET'S SEE. I'M FEELING LIKE...

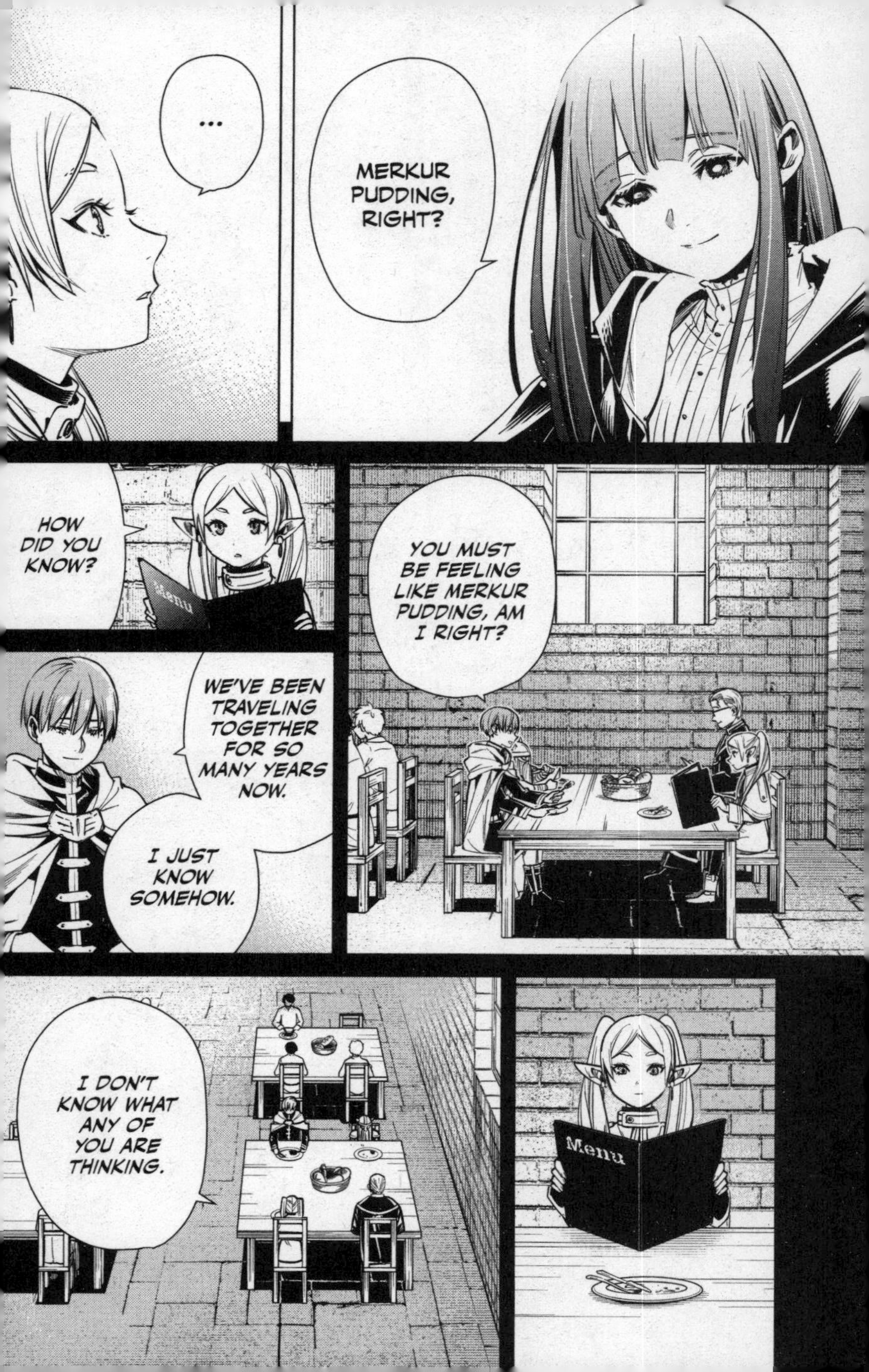
MERKUR PUDDING, RIGHT?
...
YOU MUST BE FEELING LIKE MERKUR PUDDING, AM I RIGHT?
HOW DID YOU KNOW?
WE'VE BEEN TRAVELING TOGETHER FOR SO MANY YEARS NOW.
I JUST KNOW SOMEHOW.
Menu
I DON'T KNOW WHAT ANY OF YOU ARE THINKING.

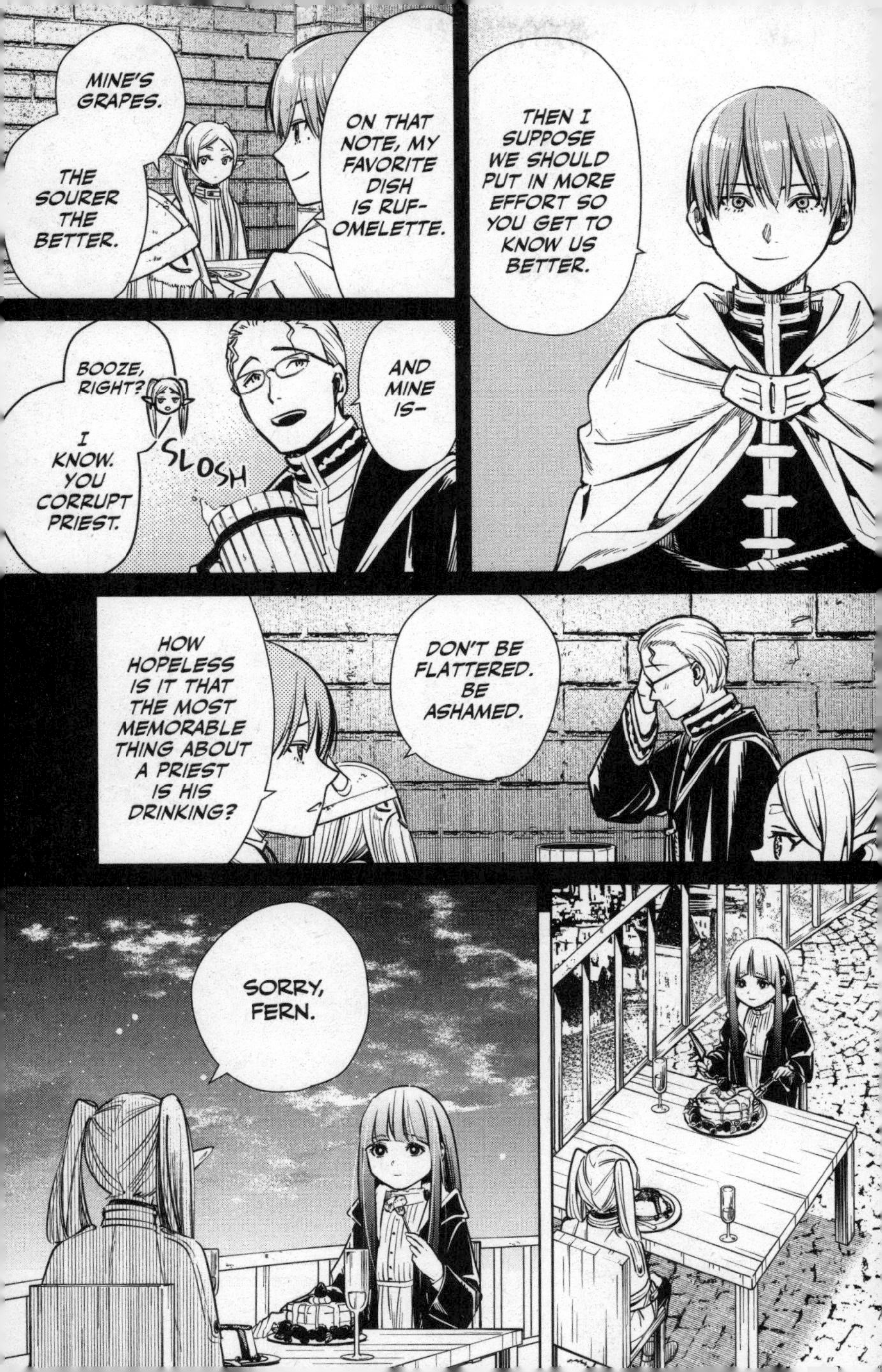
THEN I SUPPOSE WE SHOULD PUT IN MORE EFFORT SO YOU GET TO KNOW US BETTER.
ON THAT NOTE, MY FAVORITE DISH IS RUF-OMELETTE.
MINE'S GRAPES.
THE SOURER THE BETTER.
AND MINE IS-
BOOZE, RIGHT?
I KNOW. YOU CORRUPT PRIEST.
SLOSH
HOW HOPELESS IS IT THAT THE MOST MEMORABLE THING ABOUT A PRIEST IS HIS DRINKING?
DON'T BE FLATTERED. BE ASHAMED.
SORRY, FERN.

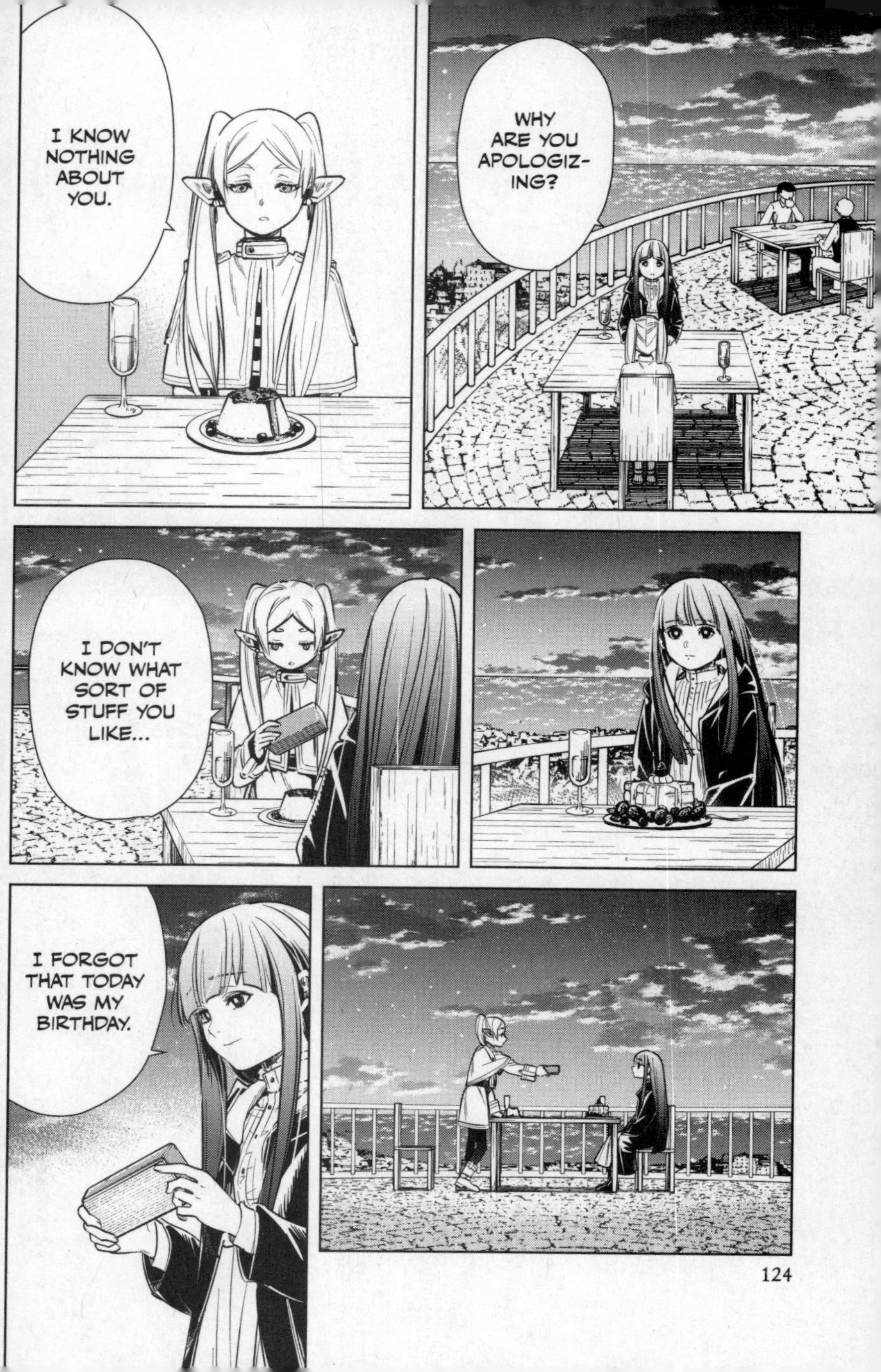
WHY ARE YOU APOLOGIZ-ING?
I KNOW NOTHING ABOUT YOU.
I DON'T KNOW WHAT SORT OF STUFF YOU LIKE...
I FORGOT THAT TODAY WAS MY BIRTHDAY.

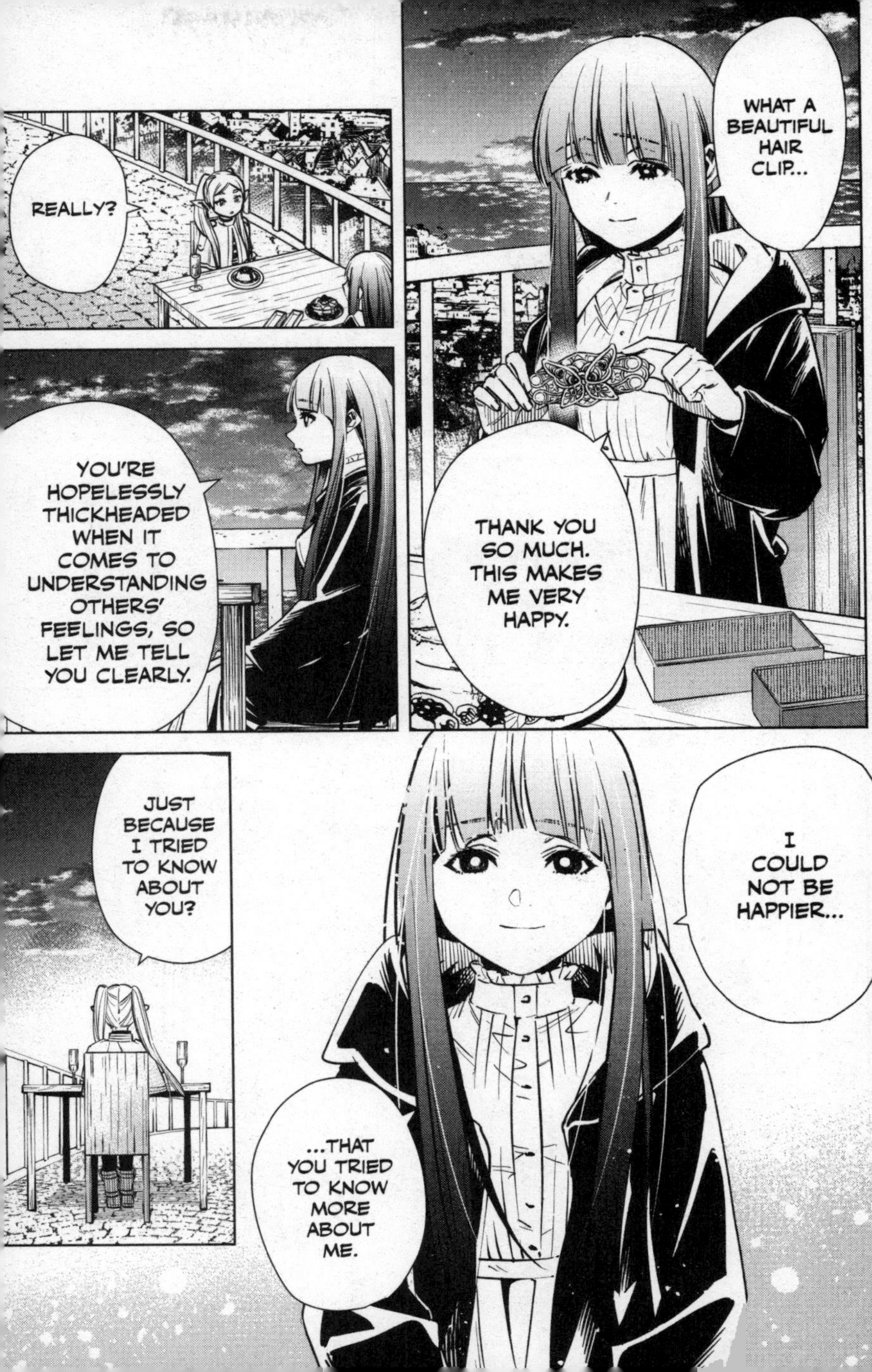
WHAT A BEAUTIFUL HAIR CLIP...
THANK YOU SO MUCH. THIS MAKES ME VERY HAPPY.
REALLY?
YOU'RE HOPELESSLY THICKHEADED WHEN IT COMES TO UNDERSTANDING OTHERS' FEELINGS, SO LET ME TELL YOU CLEARLY.
I COULD NOT BE HAPPIER...
...THAT YOU TRIED TO KNOW MORE ABOUT ME.
JUST BECAUSE I TRIED TO KNOW ABOUT YOU?

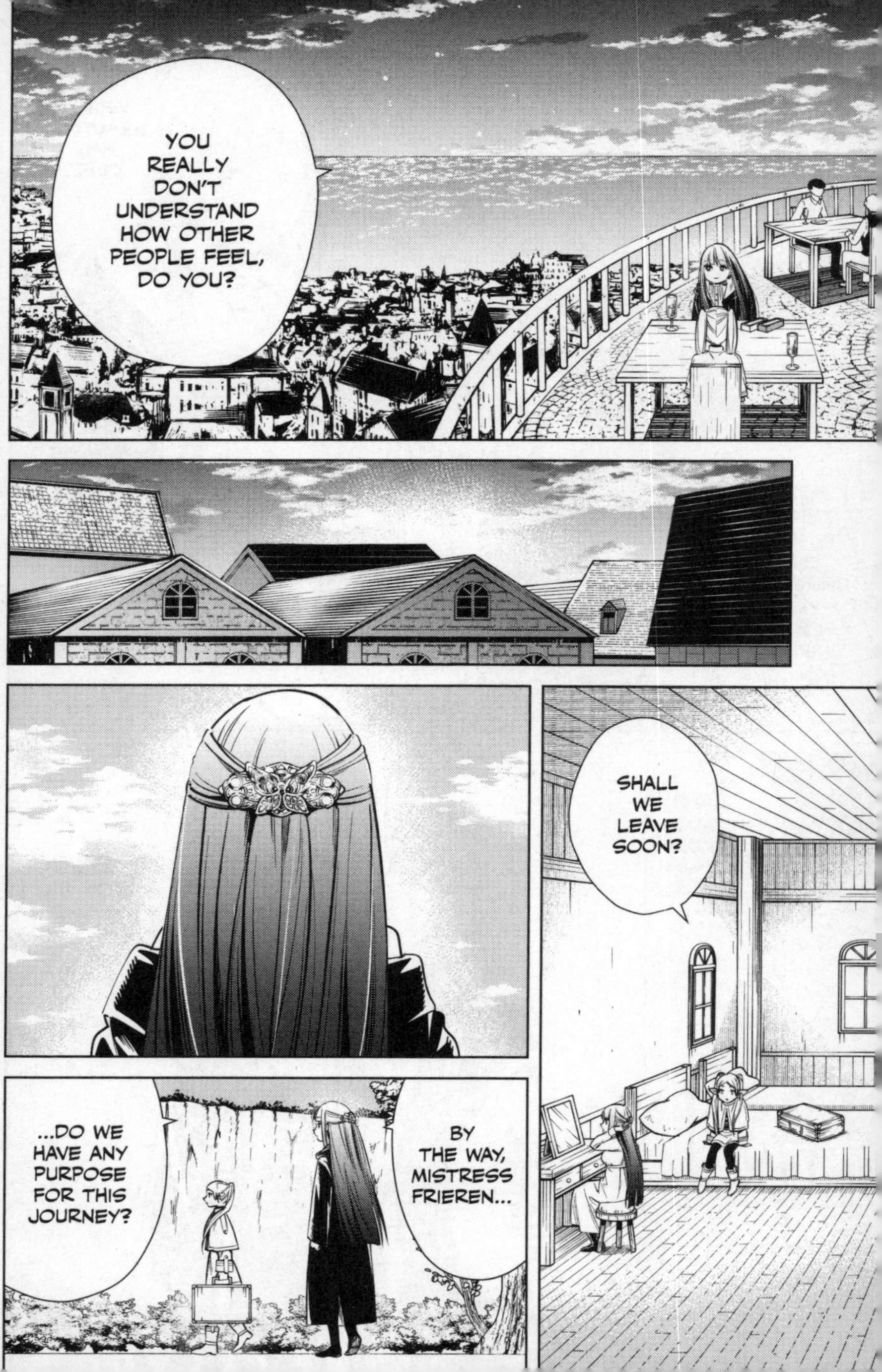
YOU REALLY DON'T UNDERSTAND HOW OTHER PEOPLE FEEL, DO YOU?
SHALL WE LEAVE SOON?
BY THE WAY, MISTRESS FRIEREN...
...DO WE HAVE ANY PURPOSE FOR THIS JOURNEY?

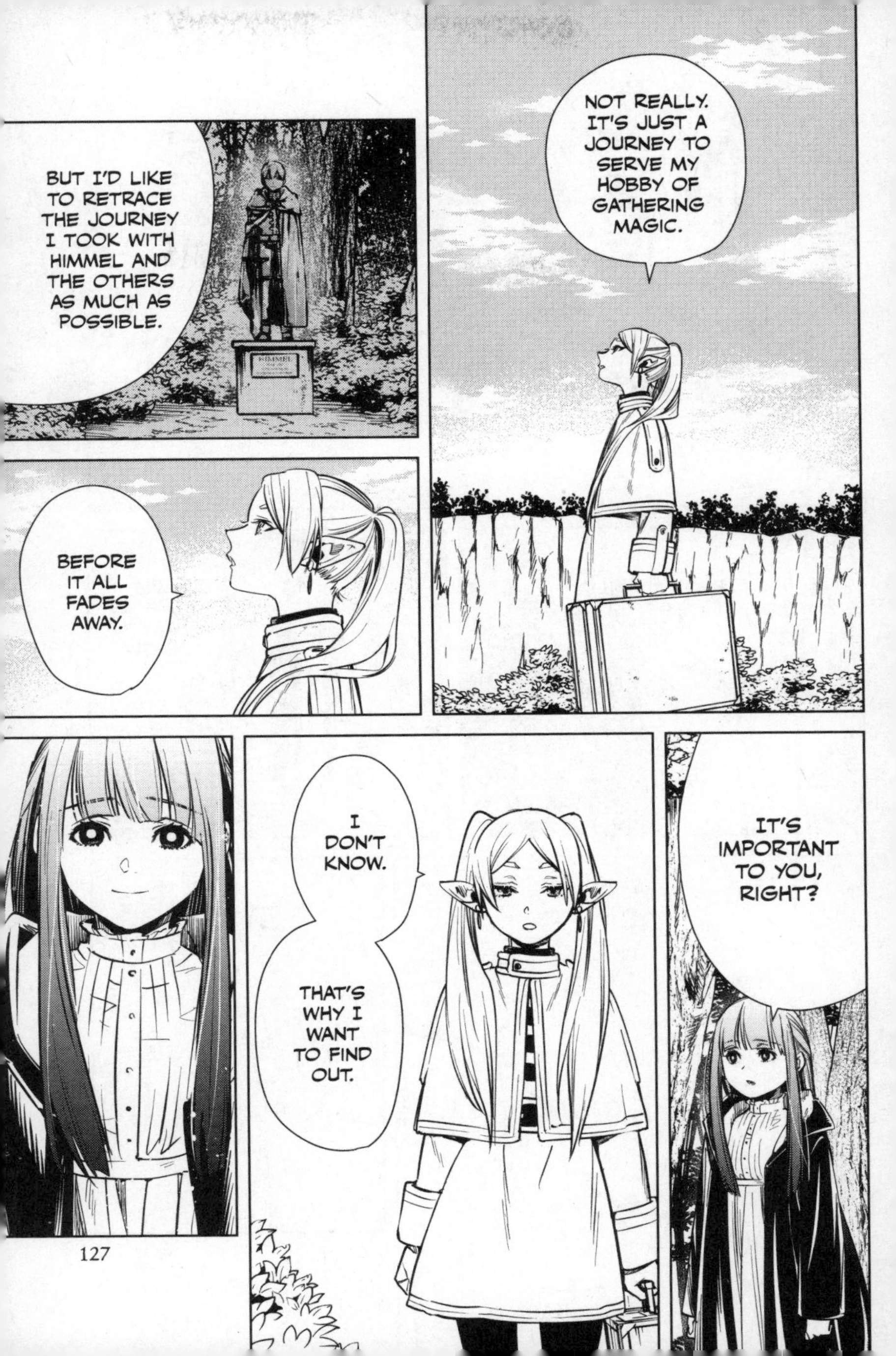
NOT REALLY. IT'S JUST A JOURNEY TO SERVE MY HOBBY OF GATHERING MAGIC.
BUT I'D LIKE TO RETRACE THE JOURNEY I TOOK WITH HIMMEL AND THE OTHERS AS MUCH AS POSSIBLE.
BEFORE IT ALL FADES AWAY.
IT'S IMPORTANT TO YOU, RIGHT?
I DON'T KNOW.
THAT'S WHY I WANT TO FIND OUT.

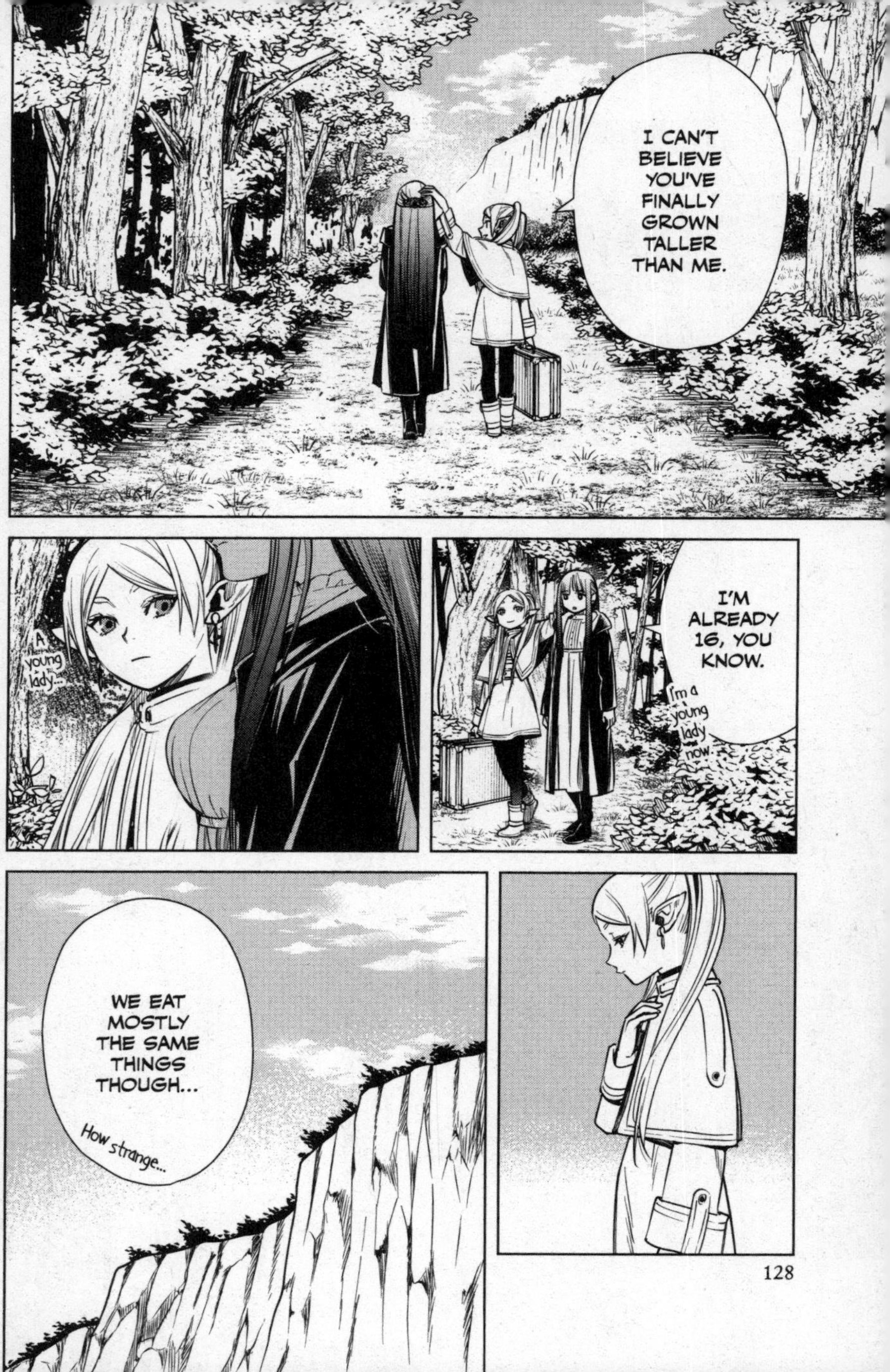
I CAN'T BELIEVE YOU'VE FINALLY GROWN TALLER THAN ME.
I'M ALREADY 16, YOU KNOW.
I'm a young lady now.
A young lady...
WE EAT MOSTLY THE SAME THINGS THOUGH...
How strange...

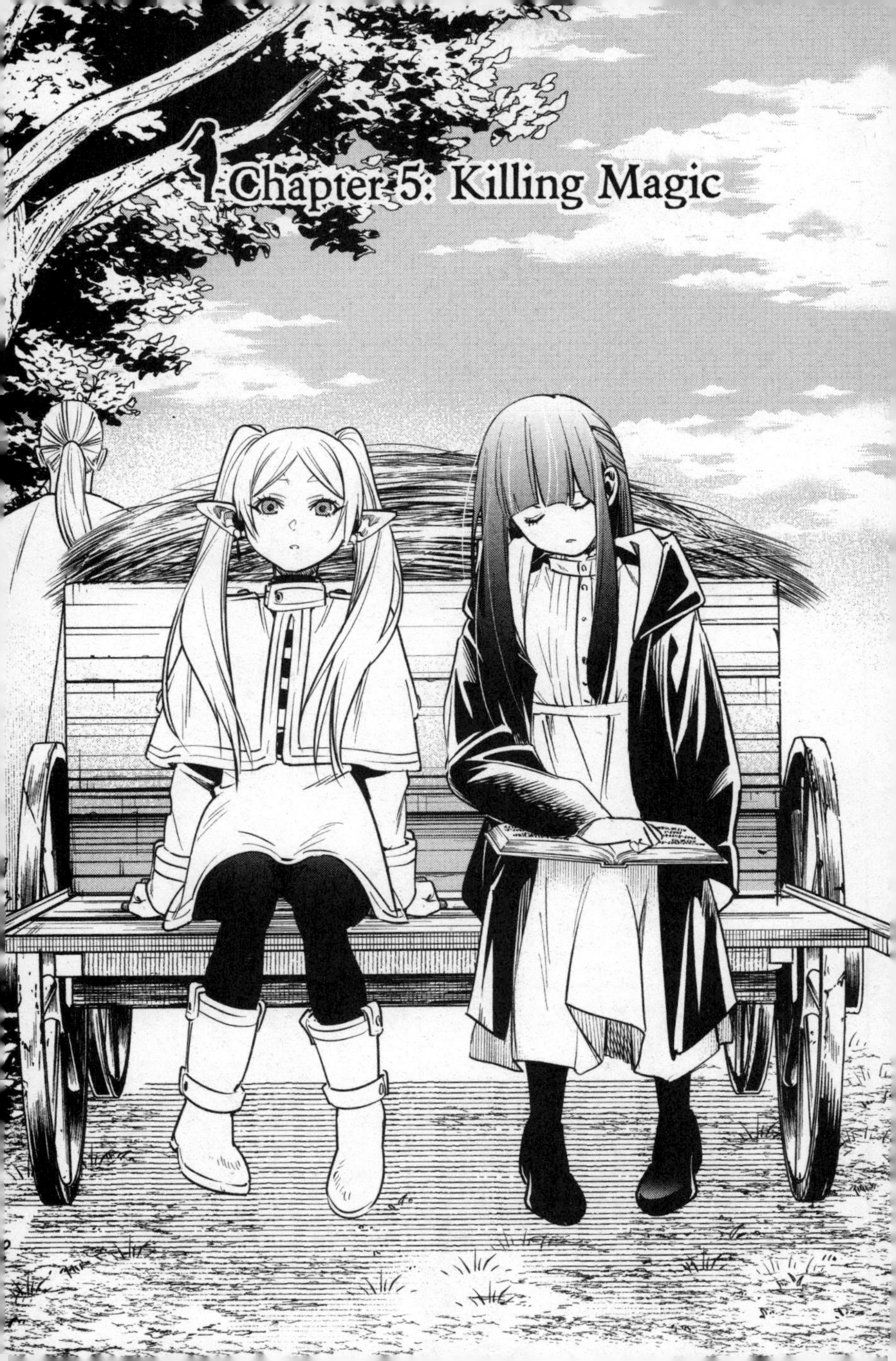
Chapter 5: Killing Magic

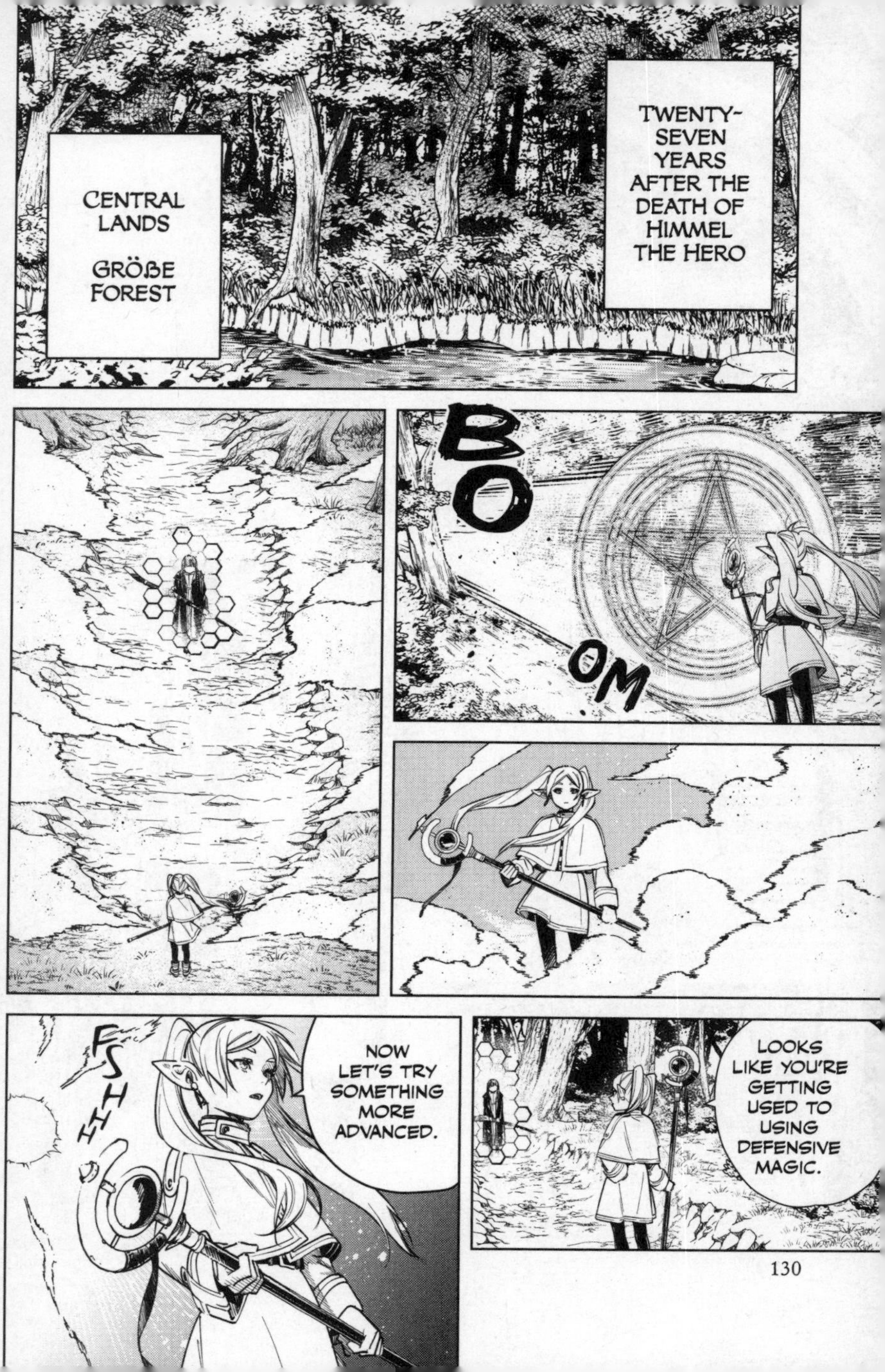
TWENTY-SEVEN YEARS AFTER THE DEATH OF HIMMEL THE HERO
CENTRAL LANDS
GRÖßE FOREST
BOOM
LOOKS LIKE YOU'RE GETTING USED TO USING DEFENSIVE MAGIC.
NOW LET'S TRY SOMETHING MORE ADVANCED.
FSHHH

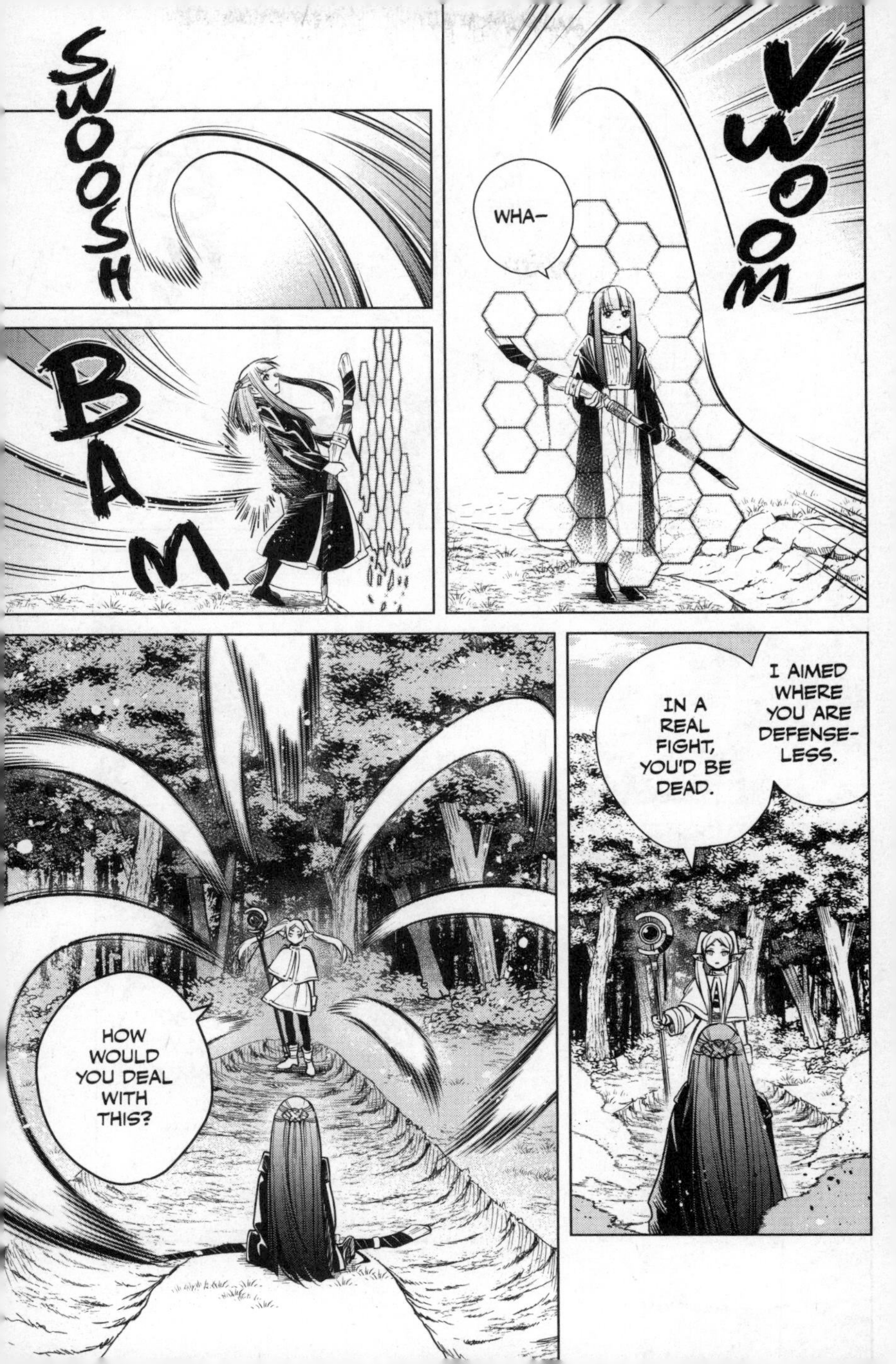
VWOOM
WHA-
SWOOSH
BAM
I AIMED WHERE YOU ARE DEFENSELESS.
IN A REAL FIGHT, YOU'D BE DEAD.
HOW WOULD YOU DEAL WITH THIS?

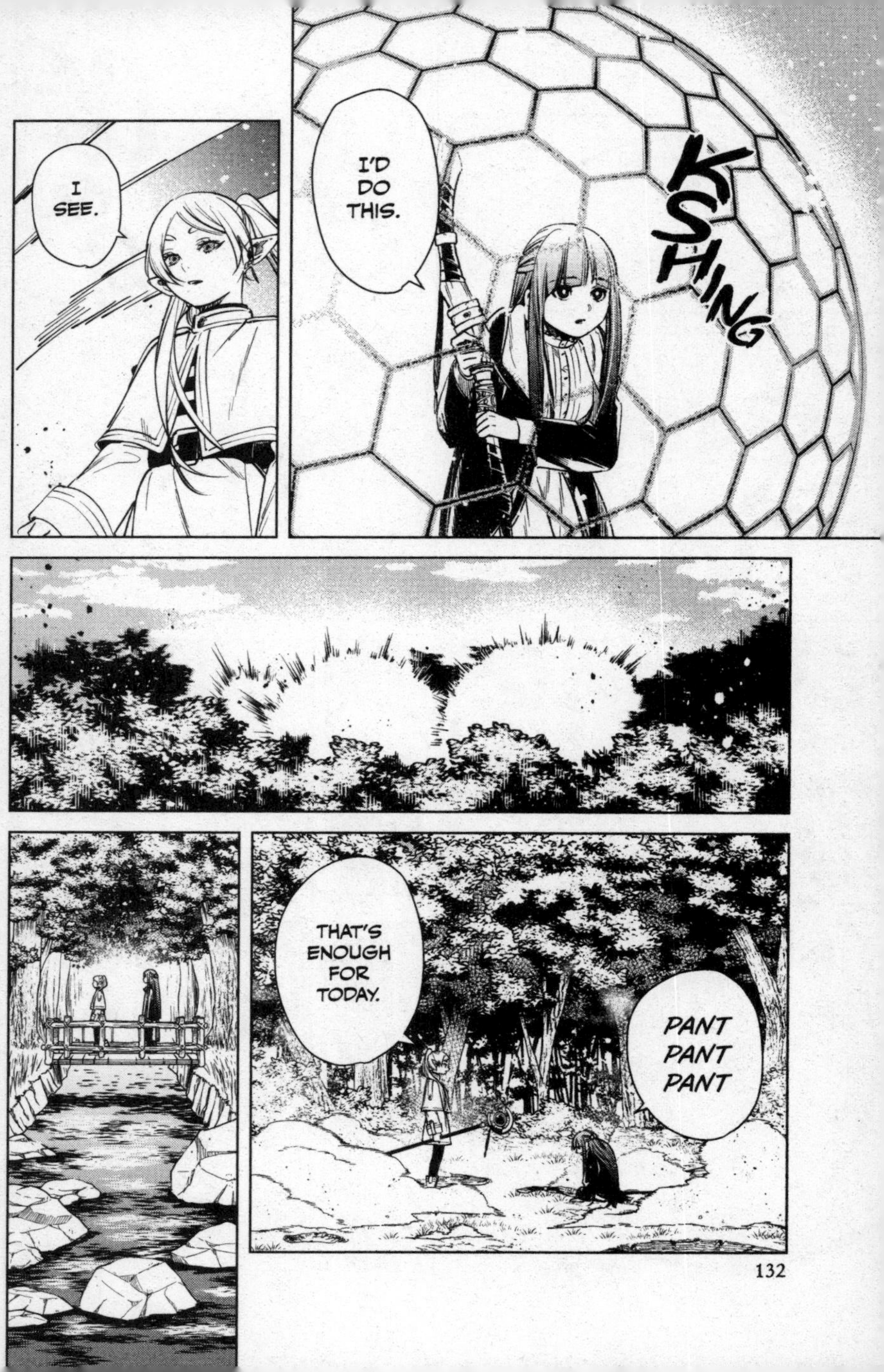
I'D DO THIS.
KSHING
I SEE.
THAT'S ENOUGH FOR TODAY.
PANT PANT PANT

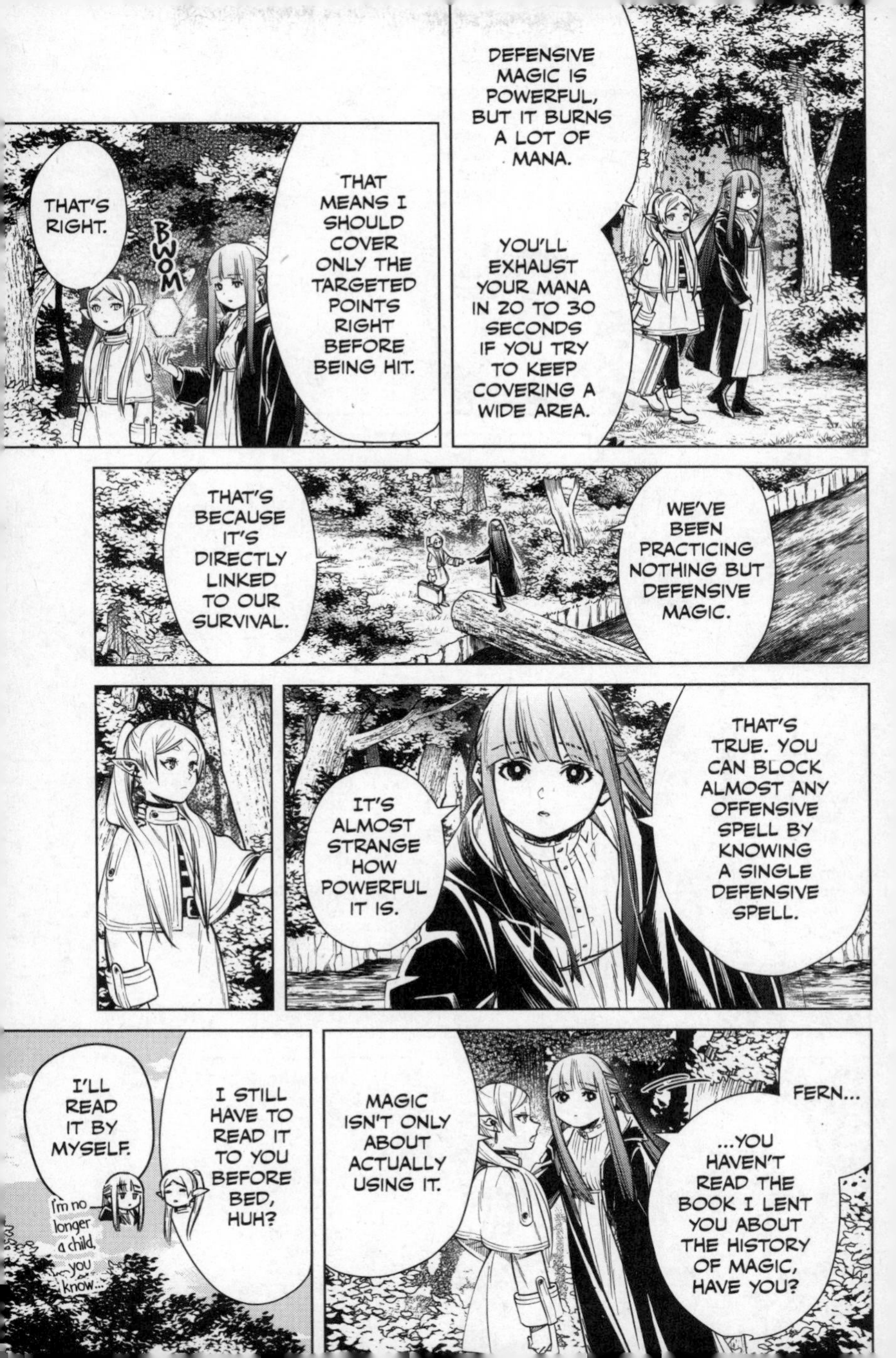
DEFENSIVE MAGIC IS POWERFUL, BUT IT BURNS A LOT OF MANA.
YOU'LL EXHAUST YOUR MANA IN 20 TO 30 SECONDS IF YOU TRY TO KEEP COVERING A WIDE AREA.
THAT MEANS I SHOULD COVER ONLY THE TARGETED POINTS RIGHT BEFORE BEING HIT.
BWOM
THAT'S RIGHT.
WE'VE BEEN PRACTICING NOTHING BUT DEFENSIVE MAGIC.
THAT'S BECAUSE IT'S DIRECTLY LINKED TO OUR SURVIVAL.
THAT'S TRUE. YOU CAN BLOCK ALMOST ANY OFFENSIVE SPELL BY KNOWING A SINGLE DEFENSIVE SPELL.
IT'S ALMOST STRANGE HOW POWERFUL IT IS.
FERN...
...YOU HAVEN'T READ THE BOOK I LENT YOU ABOUT THE HISTORY OF MAGIC, HAVE YOU?
MAGIC ISN'T ONLY ABOUT ACTUALLY USING IT.
I STILL HAVE TO READ IT TO YOU BEFORE BED, HUH?
I'LL READ IT BY MYSELF.
I'm no longer a child, you know...

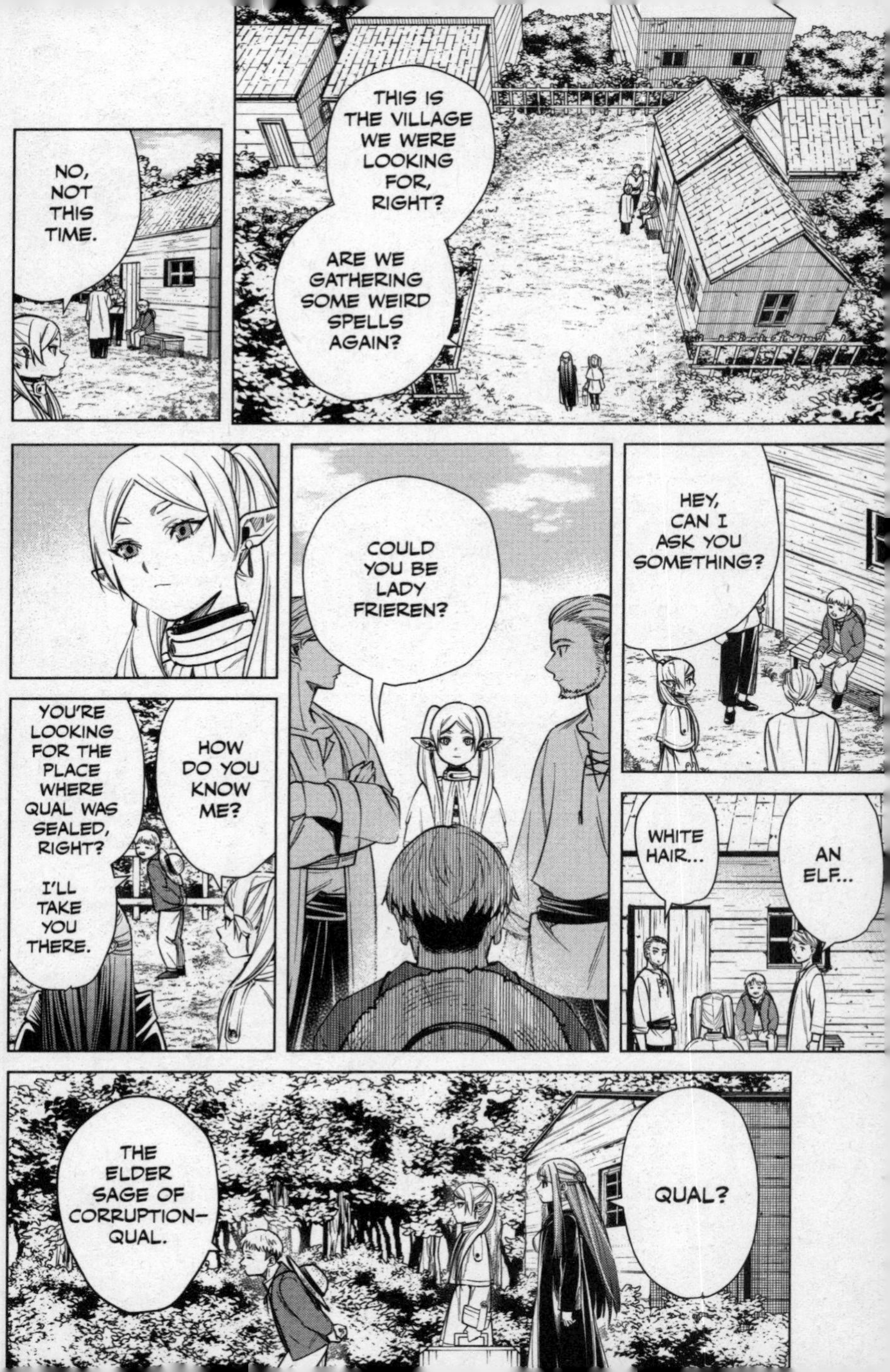

THIS IS THE VILLAGE WE WERE LOOKING FOR, RIGHT?
ARE WE GATHERING SOME WEIRD SPELLS AGAIN?
NO, NOT THIS TIME.
HEY, CAN I ASK YOU SOMETHING?
AN ELF...
WHITE HAIR...
COULD YOU BE LADY FRIEREN?
HOW DO YOU KNOW ME?
YOU'RE LOOKING FOR THE PLACE WHERE QUAL WAS SEALED, RIGHT?
I'LL TAKE YOU THERE.
QUAL?
THE ELDER SAGE OF CORRUPTION—QUAL.

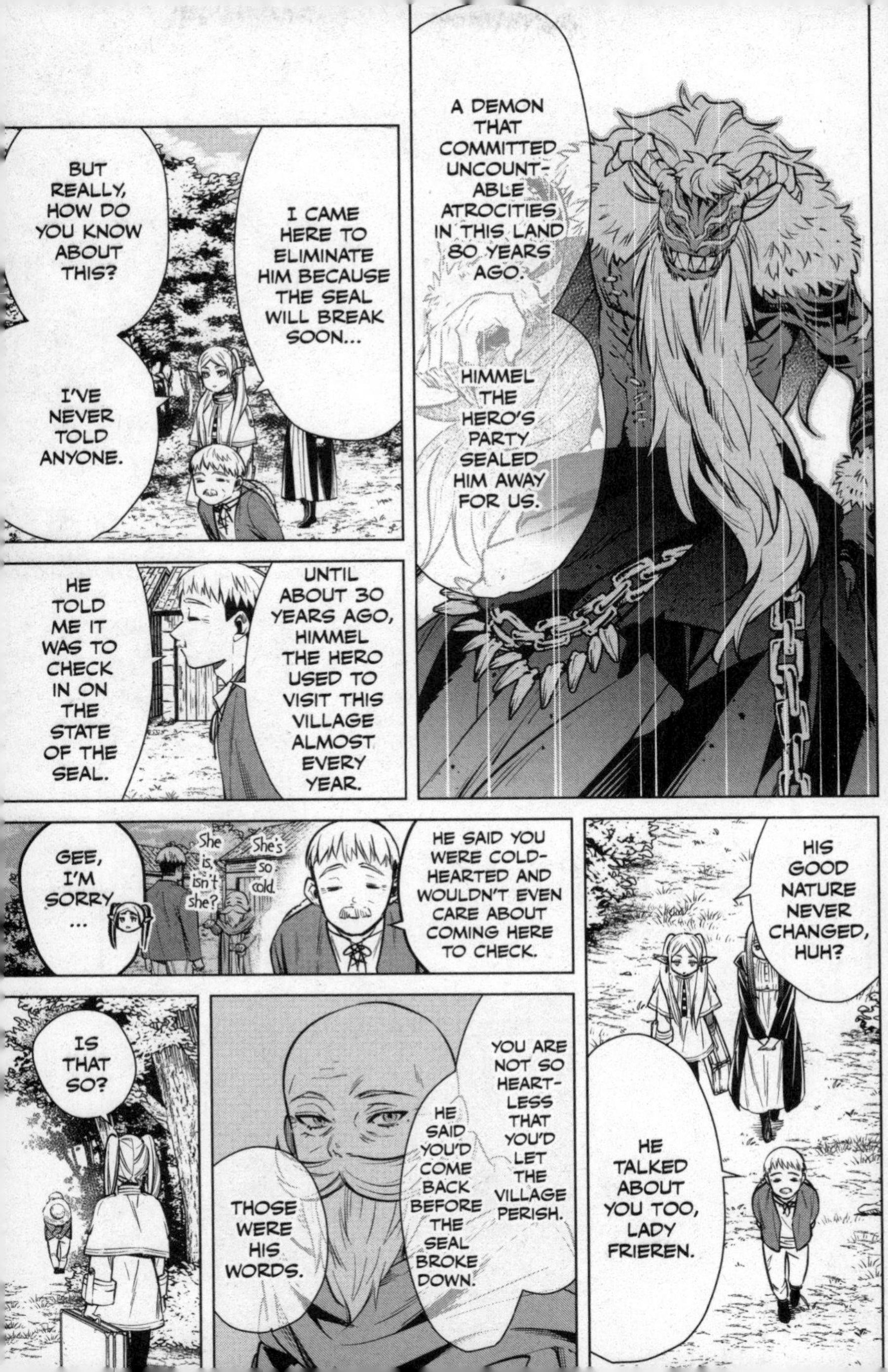
A DEMON THAT COMMITTED UNCOUNT-ABLE ATROCITIES IN THIS LAND 80 YEARS AGO.
HIMMEL THE HERO'S PARTY SEALED HIM AWAY FOR US.
I CAME HERE TO ELIMINATE HIM BECAUSE THE SEAL WILL BREAK SOON...
BUT REALLY, HOW DO YOU KNOW ABOUT THIS?
I'VE NEVER TOLD ANYONE.
UNTIL ABOUT 30 YEARS AGO, HIMMEL THE HERO USED TO VISIT THIS VILLAGE ALMOST EVERY YEAR.
HE TOLD ME IT WAS TO CHECK IN ON THE STATE OF THE SEAL.
HIS GOOD NATURE NEVER CHANGED, HUH?
HE TALKED ABOUT YOU TOO, LADY FRIEREN.
HE SAID YOU WERE COLD-HEARTED AND WOULDN'T EVEN CARE ABOUT COMING HERE TO CHECK.
She's so cold.
She is, isn't she?
GEE, I'M SORRY...
YOU ARE NOT SO HEART-LESS THAT YOU'D LET THE VILLAGE PERISH.
HE SAID YOU'D COME BACK BEFORE THE SEAL BROKE DOWN.
THOSE WERE HIS WORDS.
IS THAT SO?

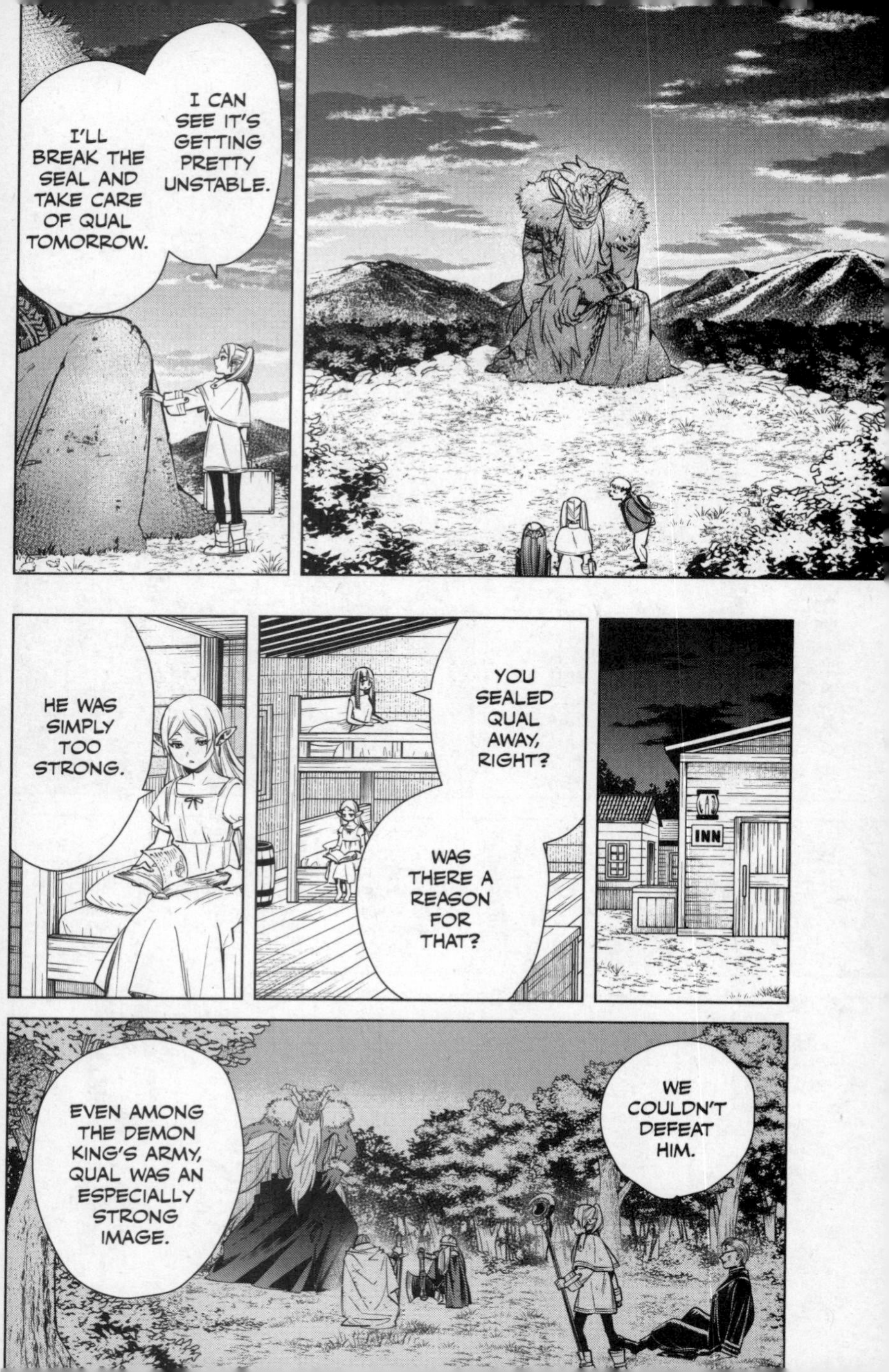
I CAN SEE IT'S GETTING PRETTY UNSTABLE.
I'LL BREAK THE SEAL AND TAKE CARE OF QUAL TOMORROW.
YOU SEALED QUAL AWAY, RIGHT?
WAS THERE A REASON FOR THAT?
HE WAS SIMPLY TOO STRONG.
INN
WE COULDN'T DEFEAT HIM.
EVEN AMONG THE DEMON KING'S ARMY, QUAL WAS AN ESPECIALLY STRONG IMAGE.

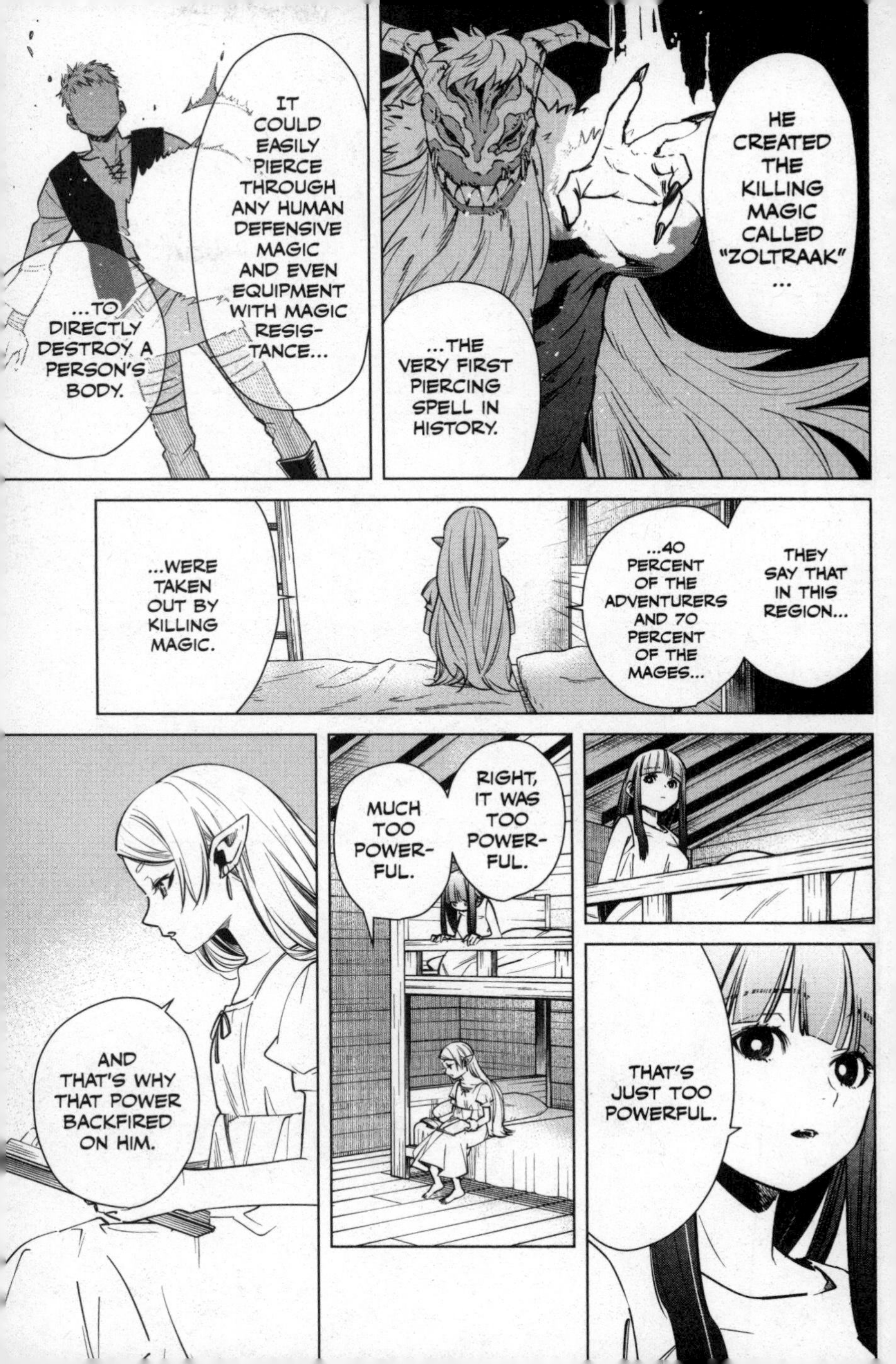
HE CREATED THE KILLING MAGIC CALLED "ZOLTRAAK"...
...THE VERY FIRST PIERCING SPELL IN HISTORY.
IT COULD EASILY PIERCE THROUGH ANY HUMAN DEFENSIVE MAGIC AND EVEN EQUIPMENT WITH MAGIC RESISTANCE...
...TO DIRECTLY DESTROY A PERSON'S BODY.
THEY SAY THAT IN THIS REGION...
...40 PERCENT OF THE ADVENTURERS AND 70 PERCENT OF THE MAGES...
...WERE TAKEN OUT BY KILLING MAGIC.
THAT'S JUST TOO POWERFUL.
RIGHT, IT WAS TOO POWERFUL.
MUCH TOO POWERFUL.
AND THAT'S WHY THAT POWER BACKFIRED ON HIM.

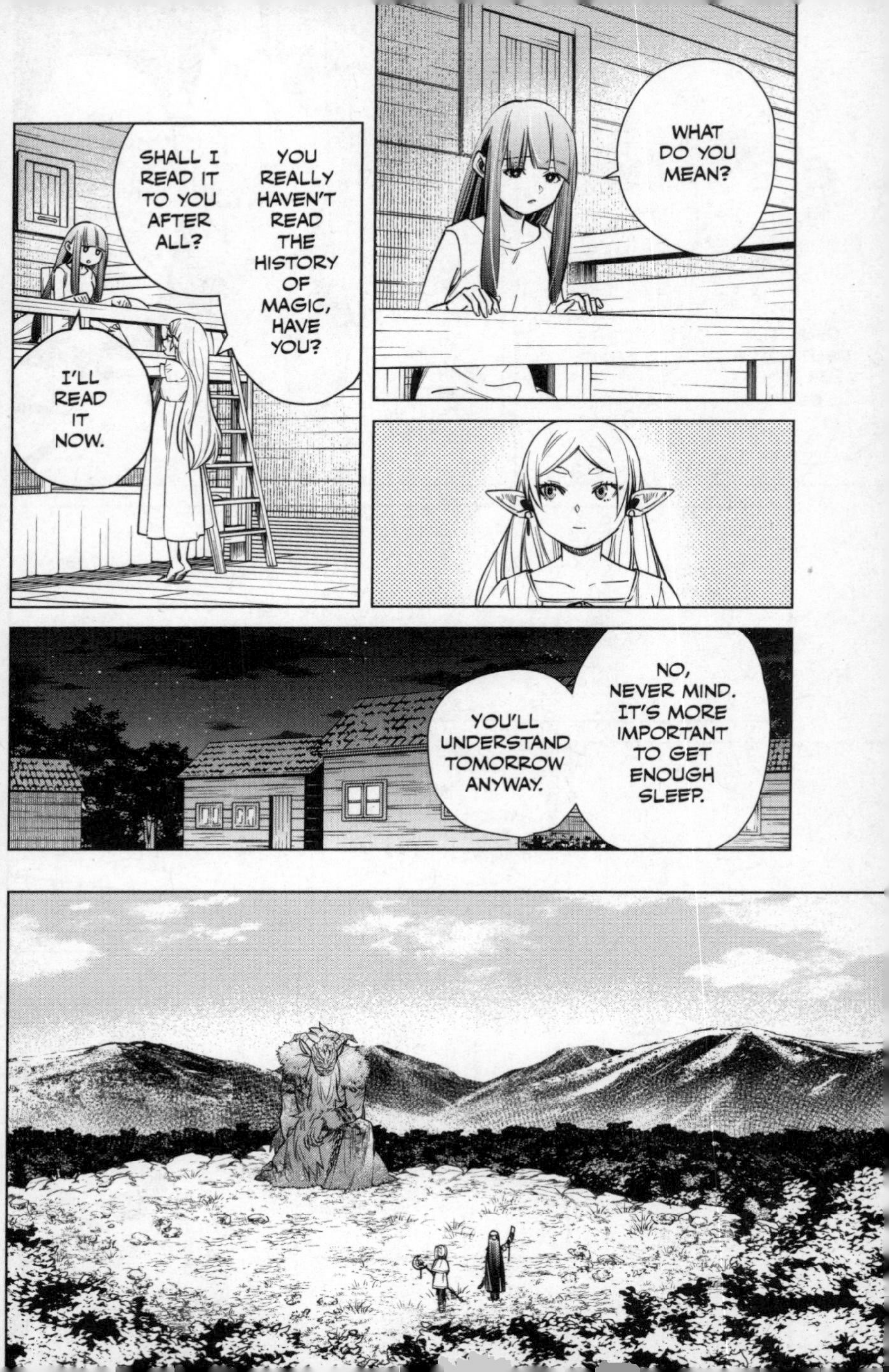
WHAT DO YOU MEAN?
YOU REALLY HAVEN'T READ THE HISTORY OF MAGIC, HAVE YOU?
SHALL I READ IT TO YOU AFTER ALL?
I'LL READ IT NOW.
NO, NEVER MIND. IT'S MORE IMPORTANT TO GET ENOUGH SLEEP.
YOU'LL UNDERSTAND TOMORROW ANYWAY.

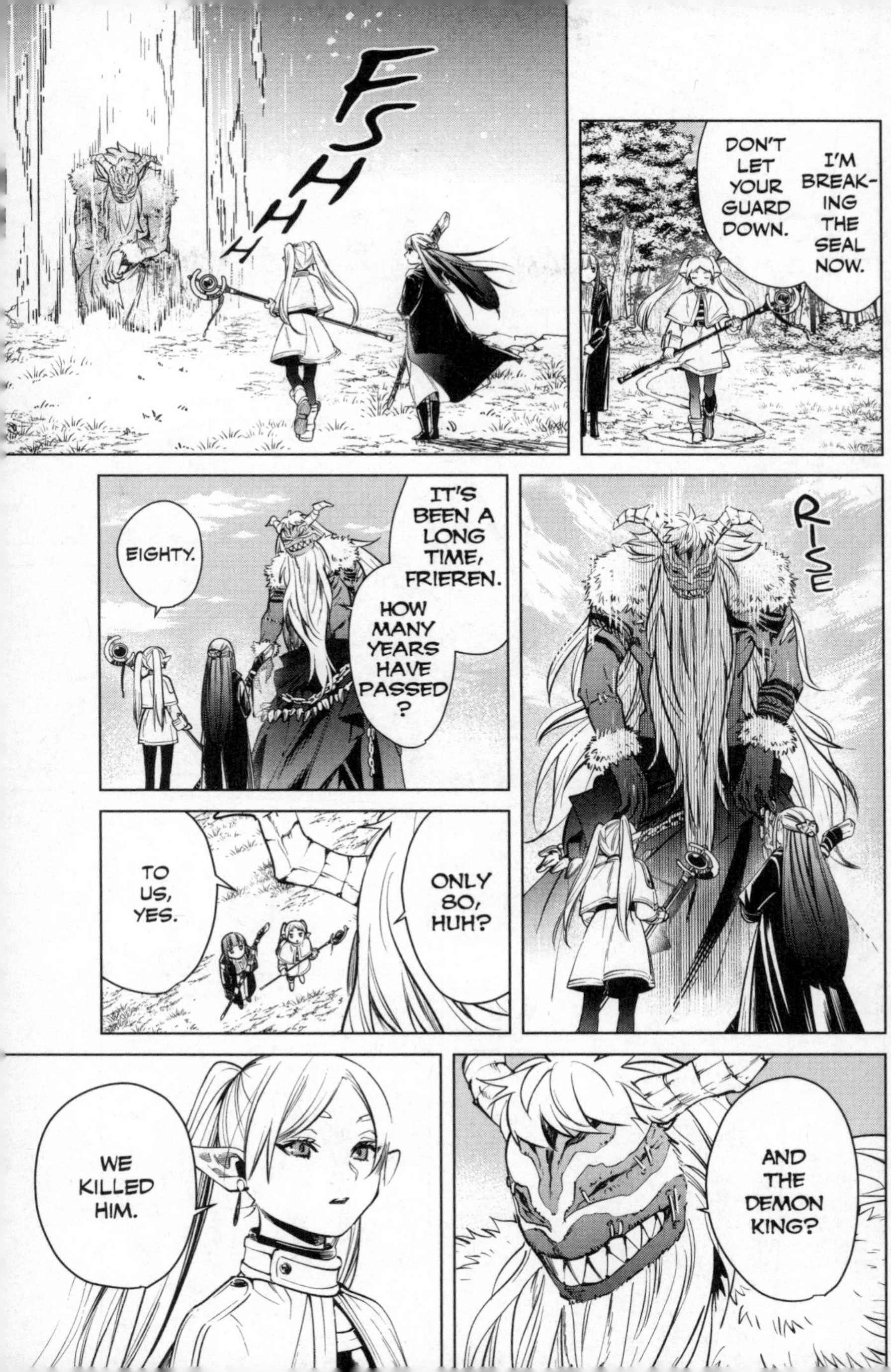
I'M BREAKING THE SEAL NOW.
DON'T LET YOUR GUARD DOWN.
FSHHH
RISE
IT'S BEEN A LONG TIME, FRIEREN.
HOW MANY YEARS HAVE PASSED?
EIGHTY.
ONLY 80, HUH?
TO US, YES.
AND THE DEMON KING?
WE KILLED HIM.

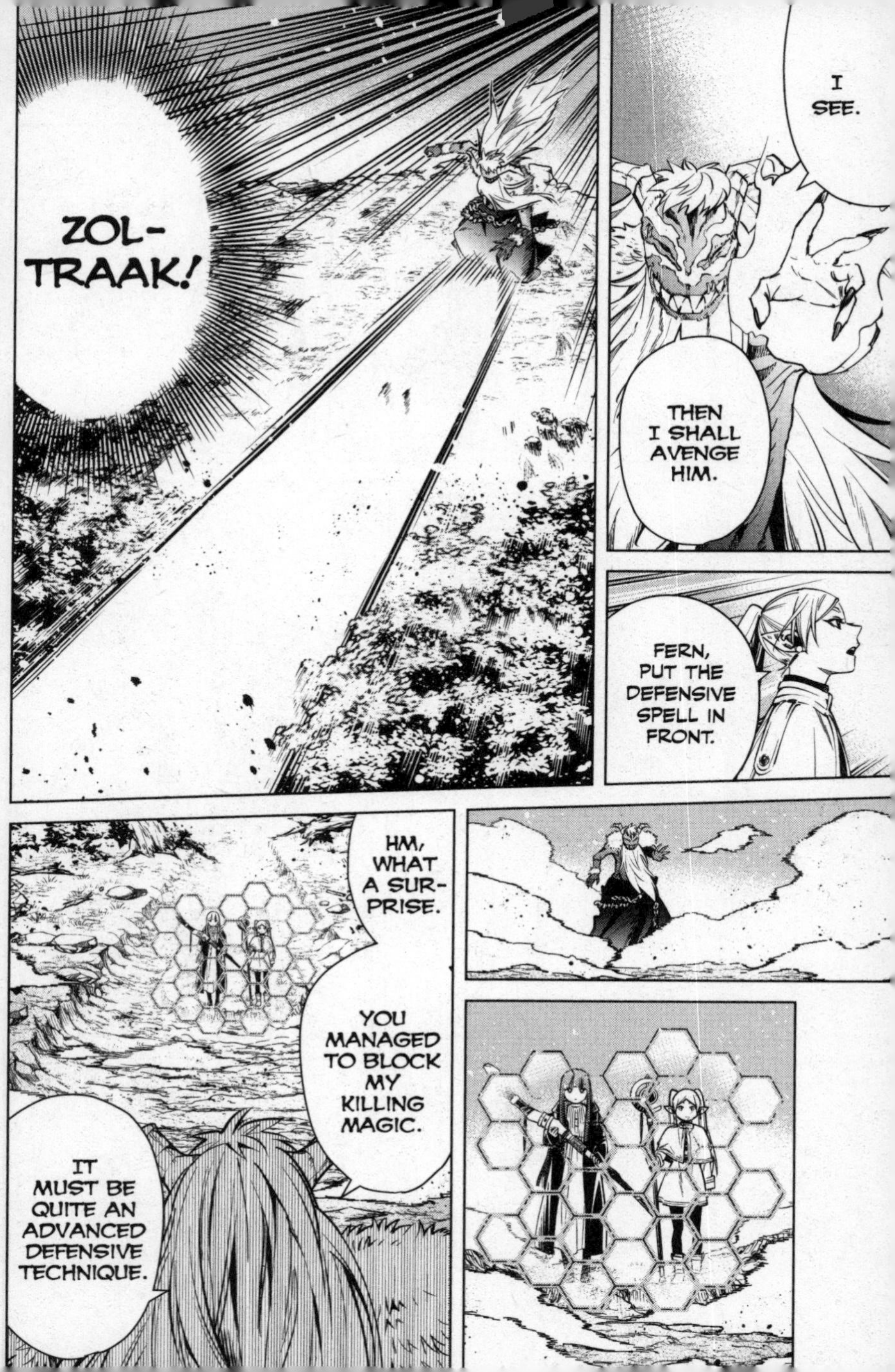
I SEE.
THEN I SHALL AVENGE HIM.
FERN, PUT THE DEFENSIVE SPELL IN FRONT.
ZOL-TRAAK!
HM, WHAT A SUR-PRISE.
YOU MANAGED TO BLOCK MY KILLING MAGIC.
IT MUST BE QUITE AN ADVANCED DEFENSIVE TECHNIQUE.

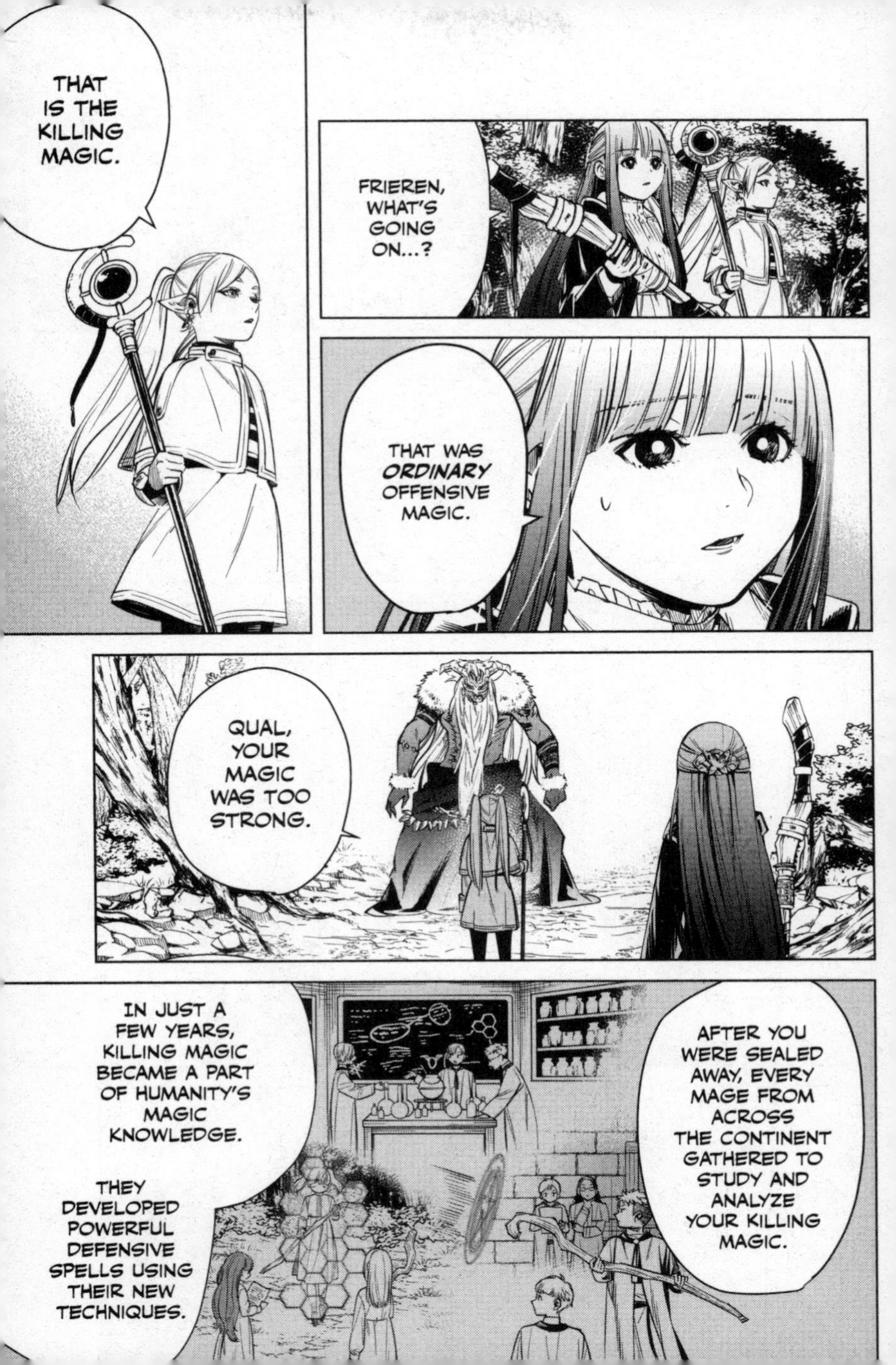
FRIEREN, WHAT'S GOING ON...?
THAT WAS *ORDINARY* OFFENSIVE MAGIC.
THAT IS THE KILLING MAGIC.
QUAL, YOUR MAGIC WAS TOO STRONG.
AFTER YOU WERE SEALED AWAY, EVERY MAGE FROM ACROSS THE CONTINENT GATHERED TO STUDY AND ANALYZE YOUR KILLING MAGIC.
IN JUST A FEW YEARS, KILLING MAGIC BECAME A PART OF HUMANITY'S MAGIC KNOWLEDGE.
THEY DEVELOPED POWERFUL DEFENSIVE SPELLS USING THEIR NEW TECHNIQUES.

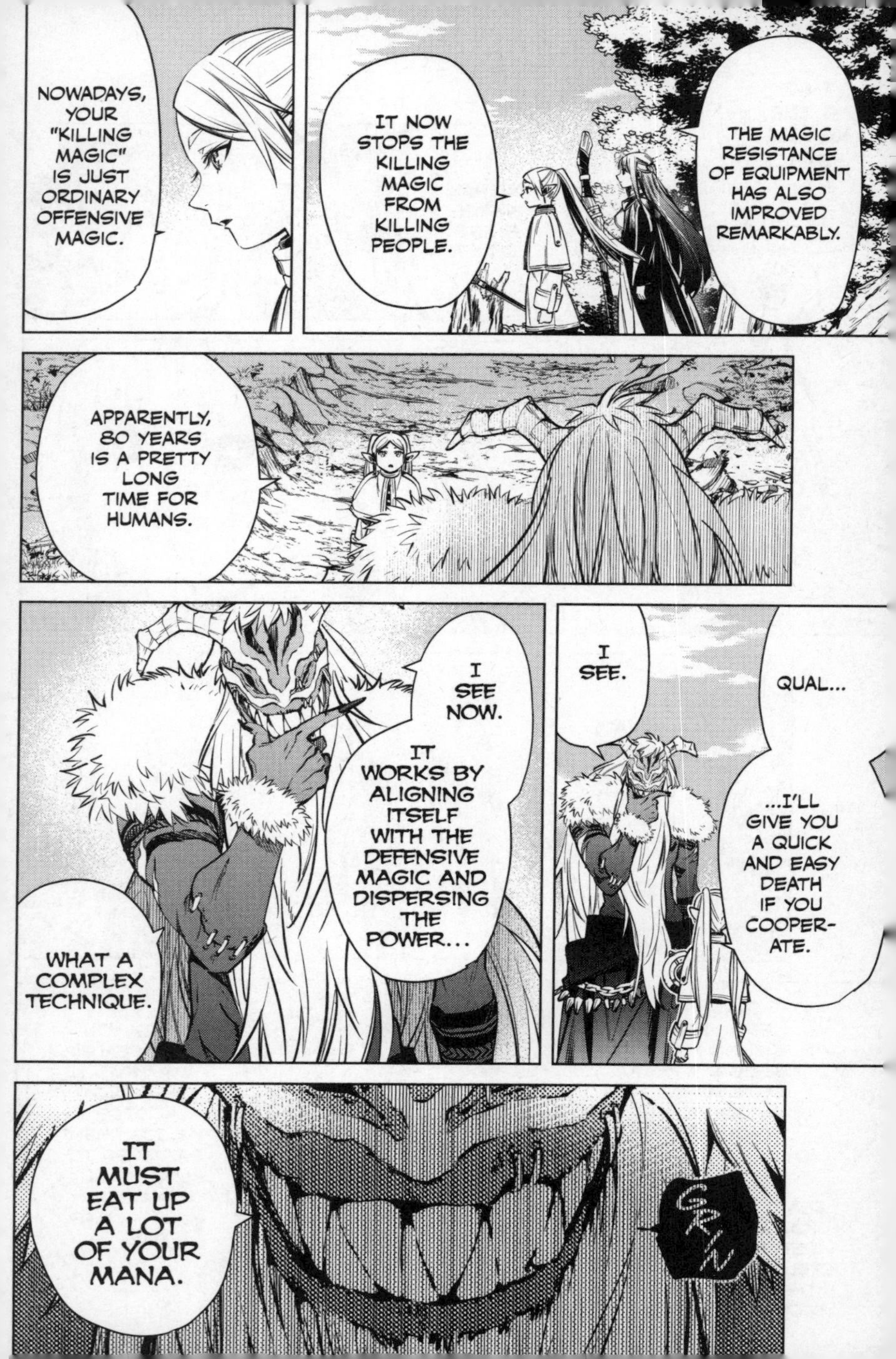
THE MAGIC RESISTANCE OF EQUIPMENT HAS ALSO IMPROVED REMARKABLY.
IT NOW STOPS THE KILLING MAGIC FROM KILLING PEOPLE.
NOWADAYS, YOUR "KILLING MAGIC" IS JUST ORDINARY OFFENSIVE MAGIC.
APPARENTLY, 80 YEARS IS A PRETTY LONG TIME FOR HUMANS.
QUAL...
...I'LL GIVE YOU A QUICK AND EASY DEATH IF YOU COOPERATE.
I SEE.
I SEE NOW.
IT WORKS BY ALIGNING ITSELF WITH THE DEFENSIVE MAGIC AND DISPERSING THE POWER...
WHAT A COMPLEX TECHNIQUE.
GRN
IT MUST EAT UP A LOT OF YOUR MANA.

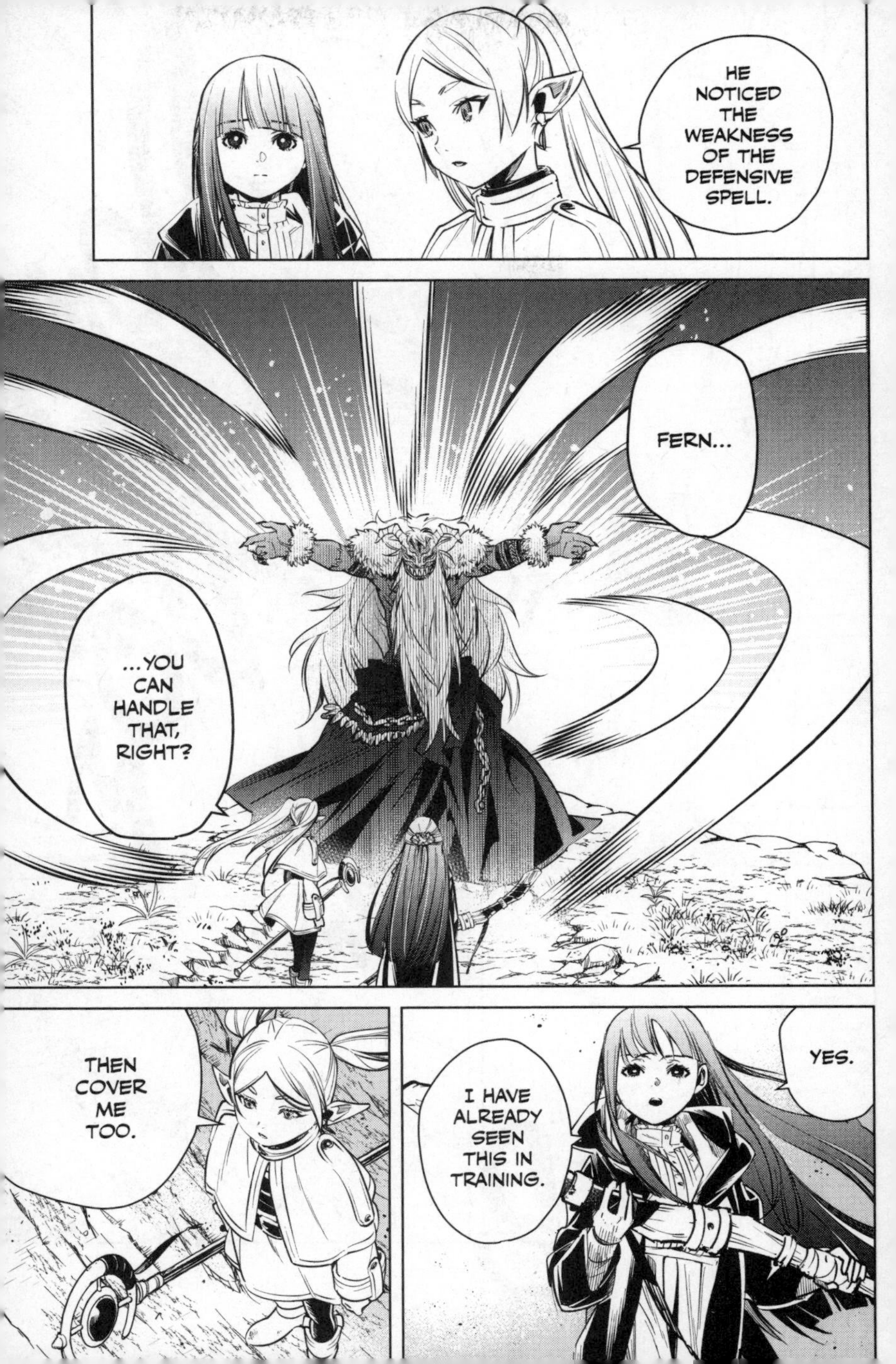
HE NOTICED THE WEAKNESS OF THE DEFENSIVE SPELL.
FERN...
...YOU CAN HANDLE THAT, RIGHT?
YES.
I HAVE ALREADY SEEN THIS IN TRAINING.
THEN COVER ME TOO.

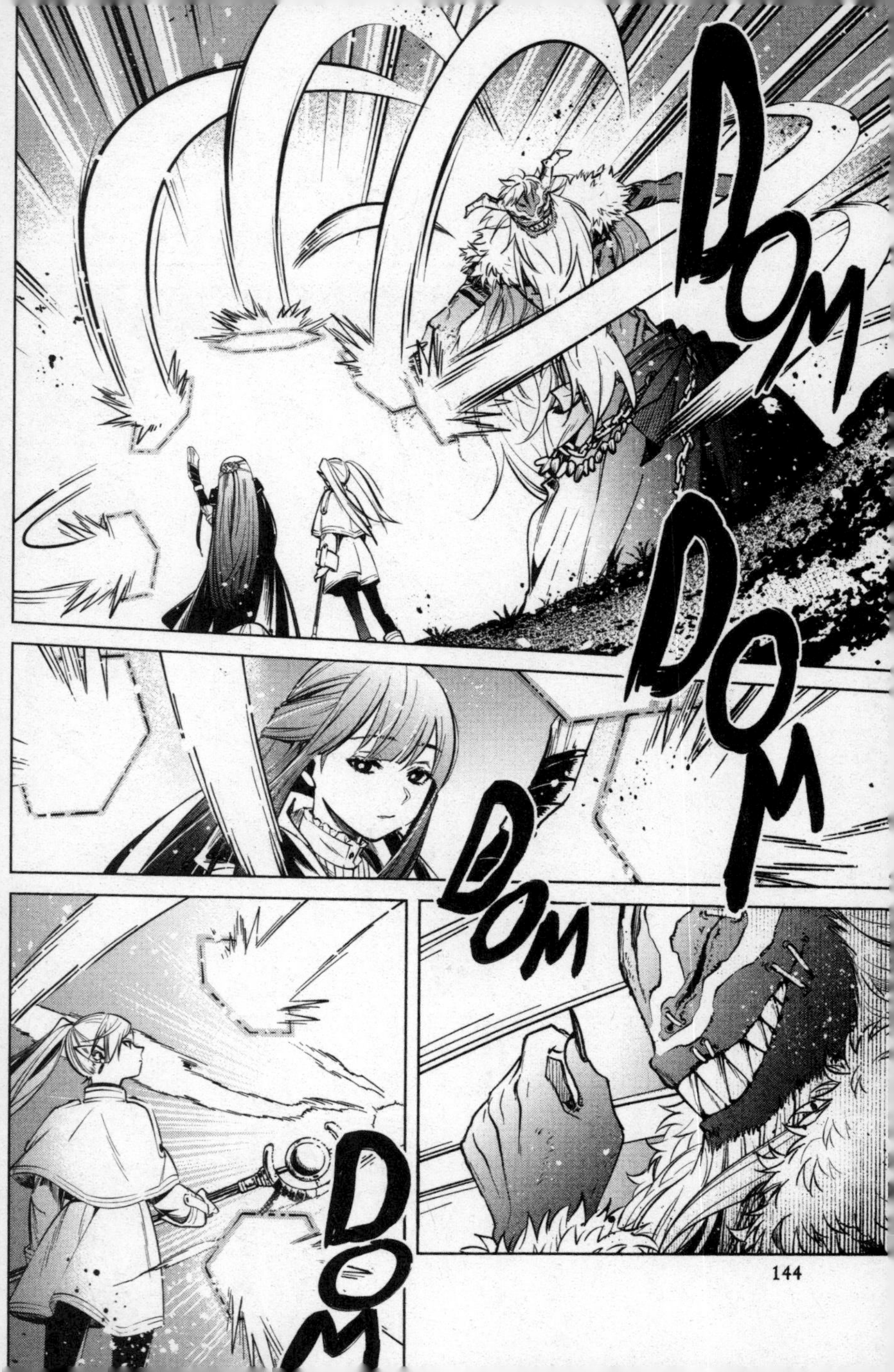
DOM
DOM
DOM
DOM
DOM

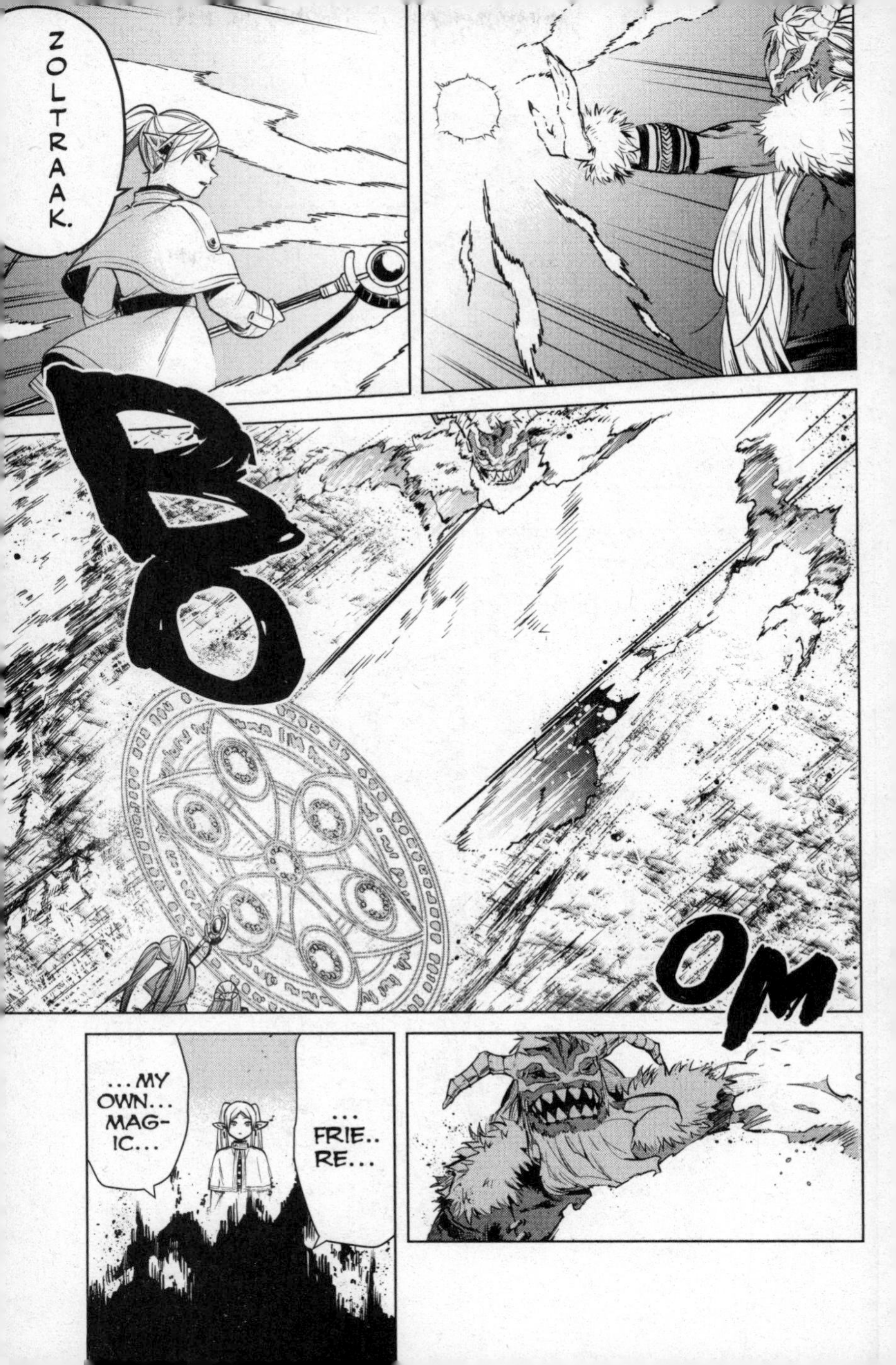
ZOLTRAAK.
BOOM
...FRIE.. RE...
...MY OWN... MAGIC...

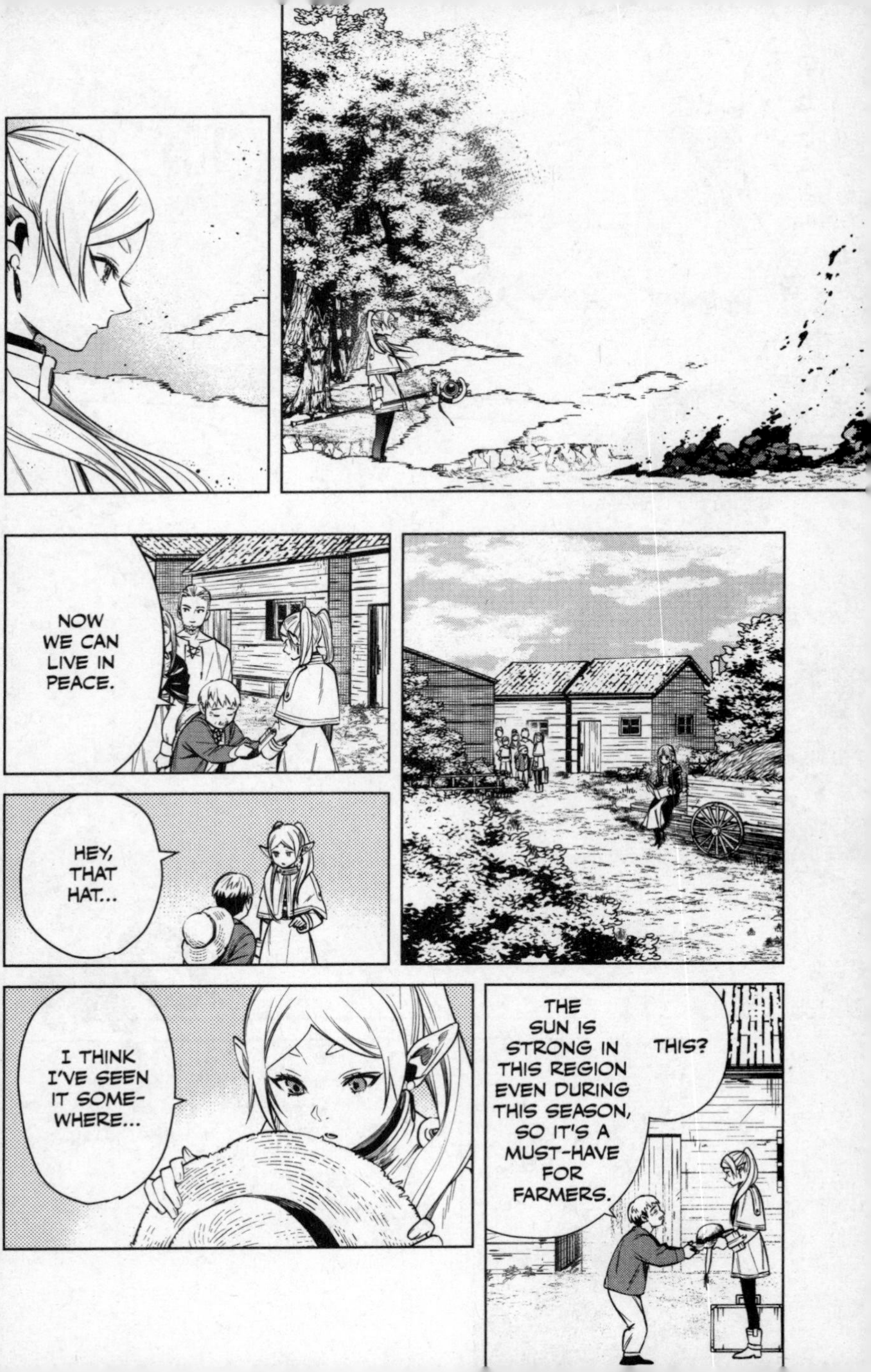
NOW WE CAN LIVE IN PEACE.
HEY, THAT HAT...
THIS?
THE SUN IS STRONG IN THIS REGION EVEN DURING THIS SEASON, SO IT'S A MUST-HAVE FOR FARMERS.
I THINK I'VE SEEN IT SOME-WHERE...

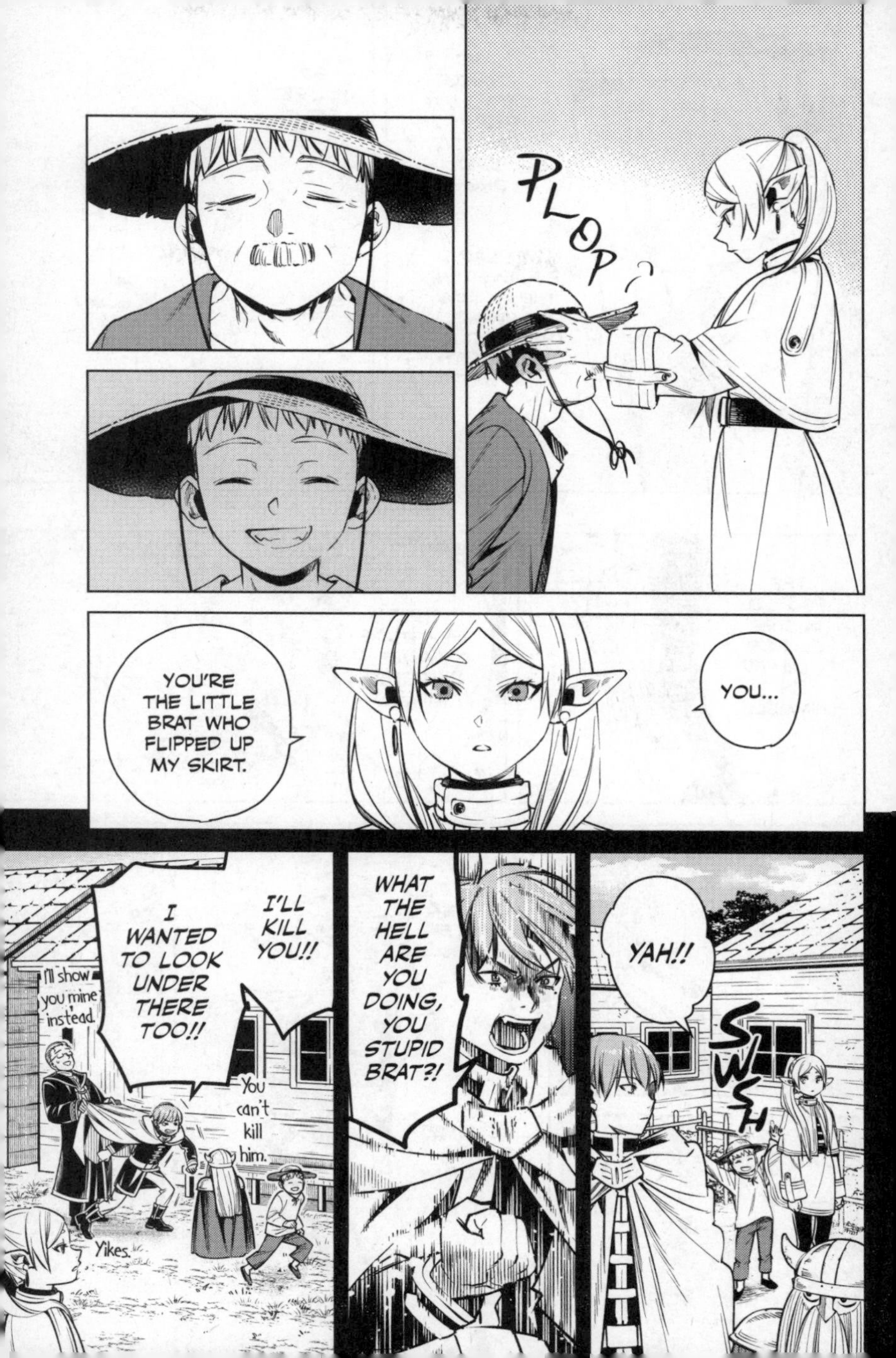
PLOP
YOU...
YOU'RE THE LITTLE BRAT WHO FLIPPED UP MY SKIRT.
YAH!!
SWSH
WHAT THE HELL ARE YOU DOING, YOU STUPID BRAT?!
I'LL KILL YOU!!
I WANTED TO LOOK UNDER THERE TOO!!
I'll show you mine instead.
You can't kill him.
Yikes.

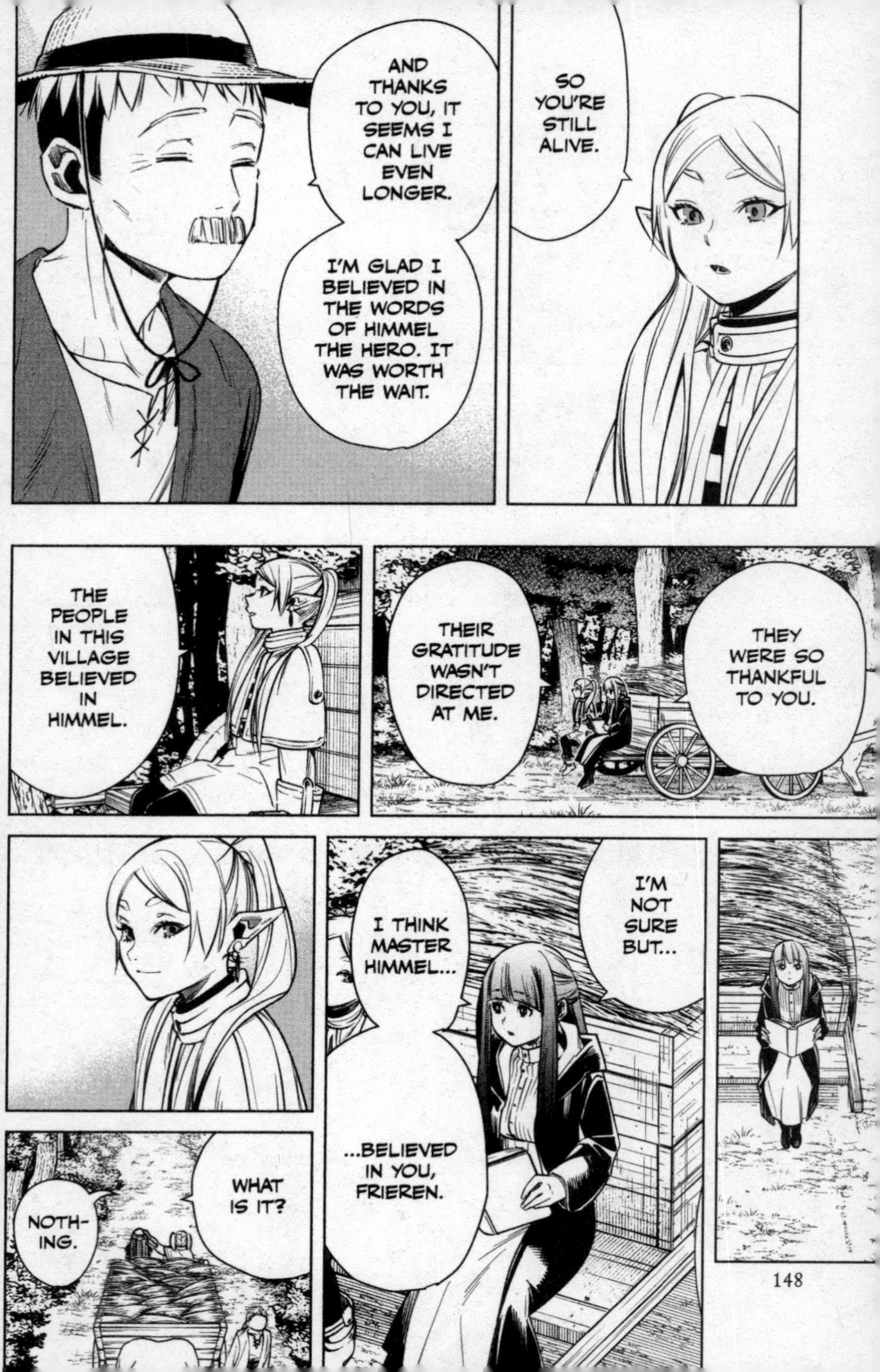
SO YOU'RE STILL ALIVE.
AND THANKS TO YOU, IT SEEMS I CAN LIVE EVEN LONGER.
I'M GLAD I BELIEVED IN THE WORDS OF HIMMEL THE HERO. IT WAS WORTH THE WAIT.
THEY WERE SO THANKFUL TO YOU.
THEIR GRATITUDE WASN'T DIRECTED AT ME.
THE PEOPLE IN THIS VILLAGE BELIEVED IN HIMMEL.
I'M NOT SURE BUT...
I THINK MASTER HIMMEL...
...BELIEVED IN YOU, FRIEREN.
WHAT IS IT?
NOTH-ING.

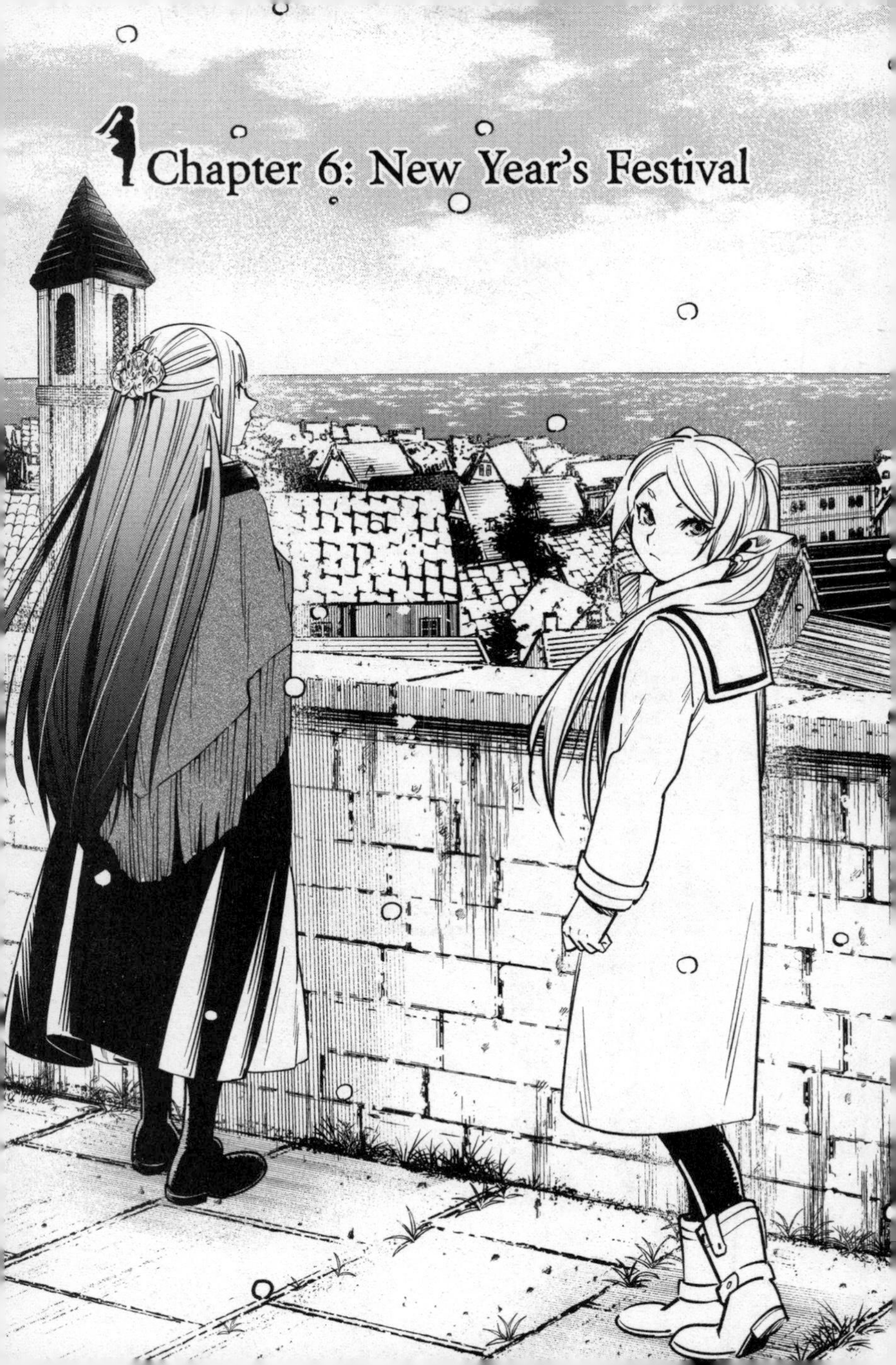
Chapter 6: New Year's Festival

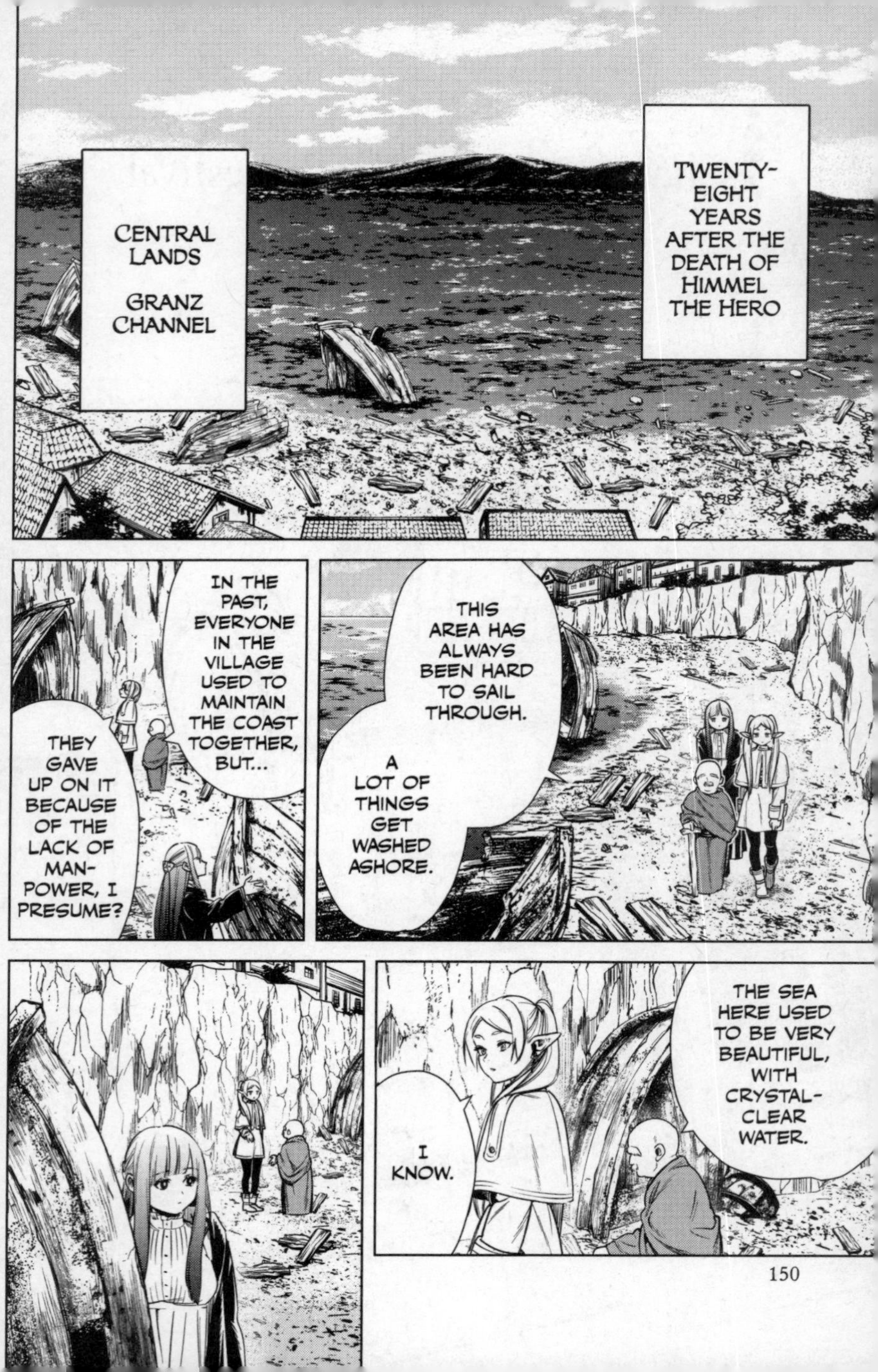
TWENTY-EIGHT YEARS AFTER THE DEATH OF HIMMEL THE HERO
CENTRAL LANDS
GRANZ CHANNEL
THIS AREA HAS ALWAYS BEEN HARD TO SAIL THROUGH.
A LOT OF THINGS GET WASHED ASHORE.
IN THE PAST, EVERYONE IN THE VILLAGE USED TO MAINTAIN THE COAST TOGETHER, BUT...
THEY GAVE UP ON IT BECAUSE OF THE LACK OF MAN-POWER, I PRESUME?
THE SEA HERE USED TO BE VERY BEAUTIFUL, WITH CRYSTAL-CLEAR WATER.
I KNOW.

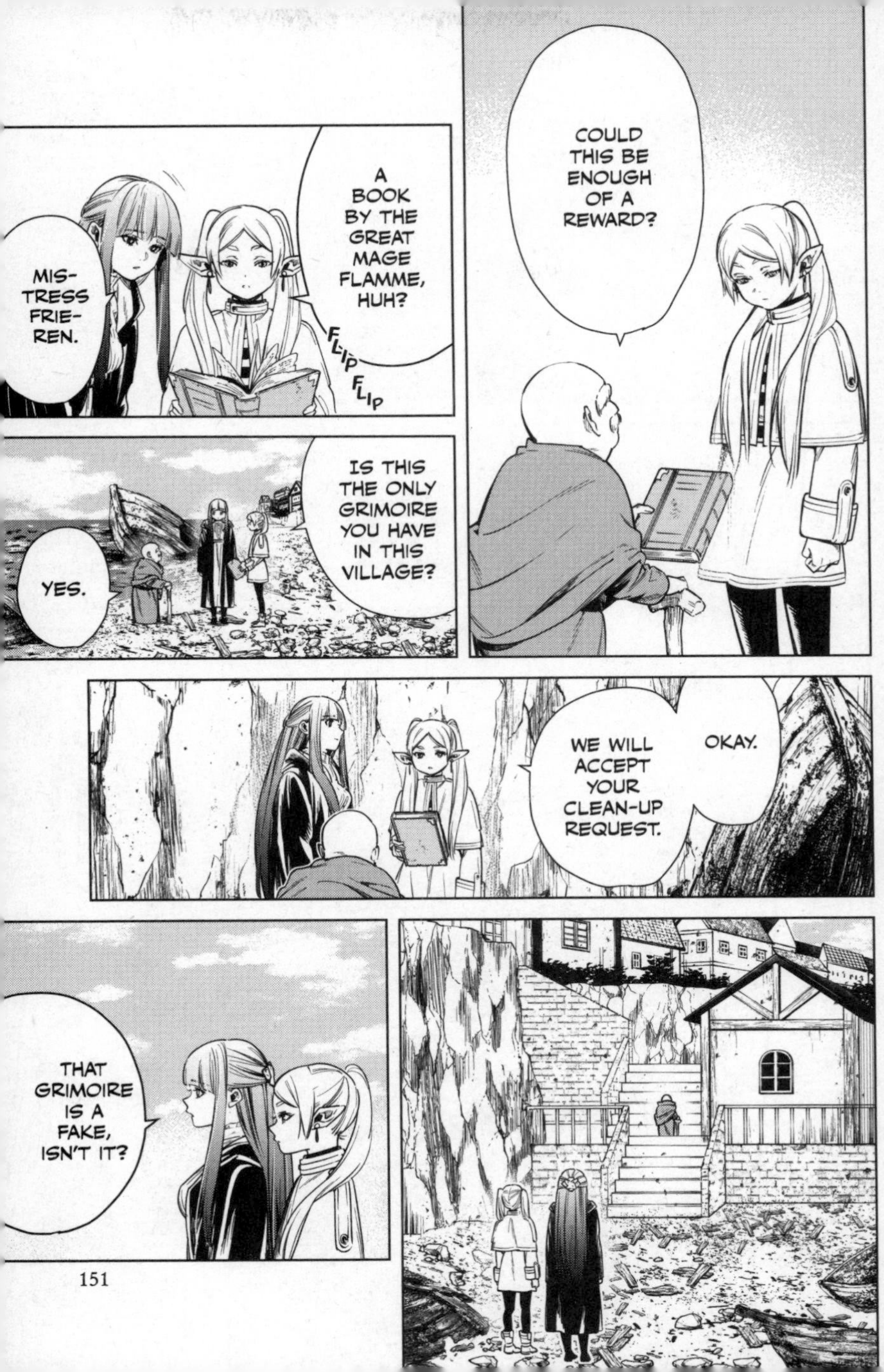
COULD THIS BE ENOUGH OF A REWARD?
A BOOK BY THE GREAT MAGE FLAMME, HUH?
FLIP FLIP
MIS-TRESS FRIE-REN.
IS THIS THE ONLY GRIMOIRE YOU HAVE IN THIS VILLAGE?
YES.
OKAY.
WE WILL ACCEPT YOUR CLEAN-UP REQUEST.
THAT GRIMOIRE IS A FAKE, ISN'T IT?

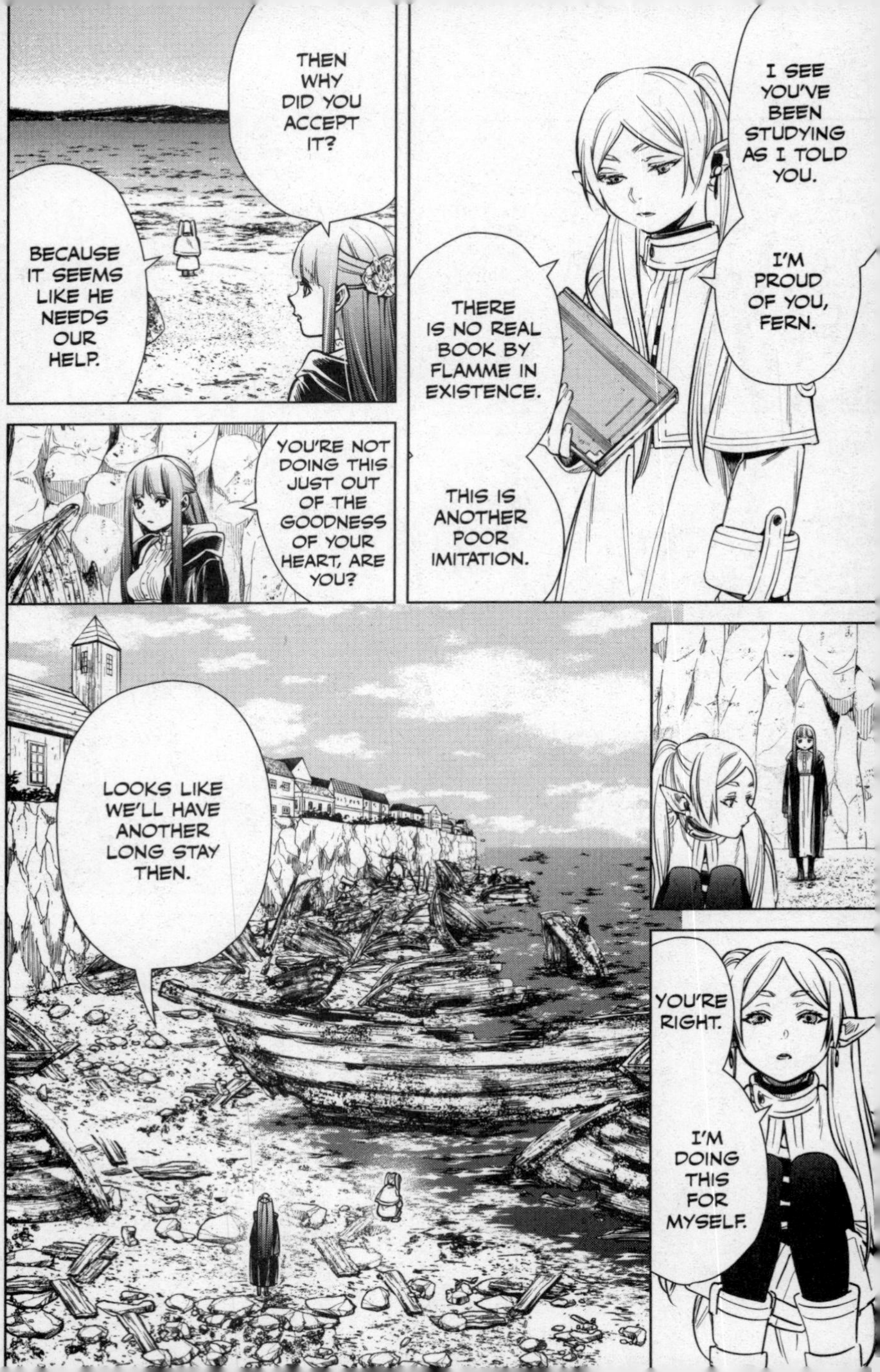
I SEE YOU'VE BEEN STUDYING AS I TOLD YOU.
I'M PROUD OF YOU, FERN.
THERE IS NO REAL BOOK BY FLAMME IN EXISTENCE.
THIS IS ANOTHER POOR IMITATION.
THEN WHY DID YOU ACCEPT IT?
BECAUSE IT SEEMS LIKE HE NEEDS OUR HELP.
YOU'RE NOT DOING THIS JUST OUT OF THE GOODNESS OF YOUR HEART, ARE YOU?
YOU'RE RIGHT.
I'M DOING THIS FOR MYSELF.
LOOKS LIKE WE'LL HAVE ANOTHER LONG STAY THEN.

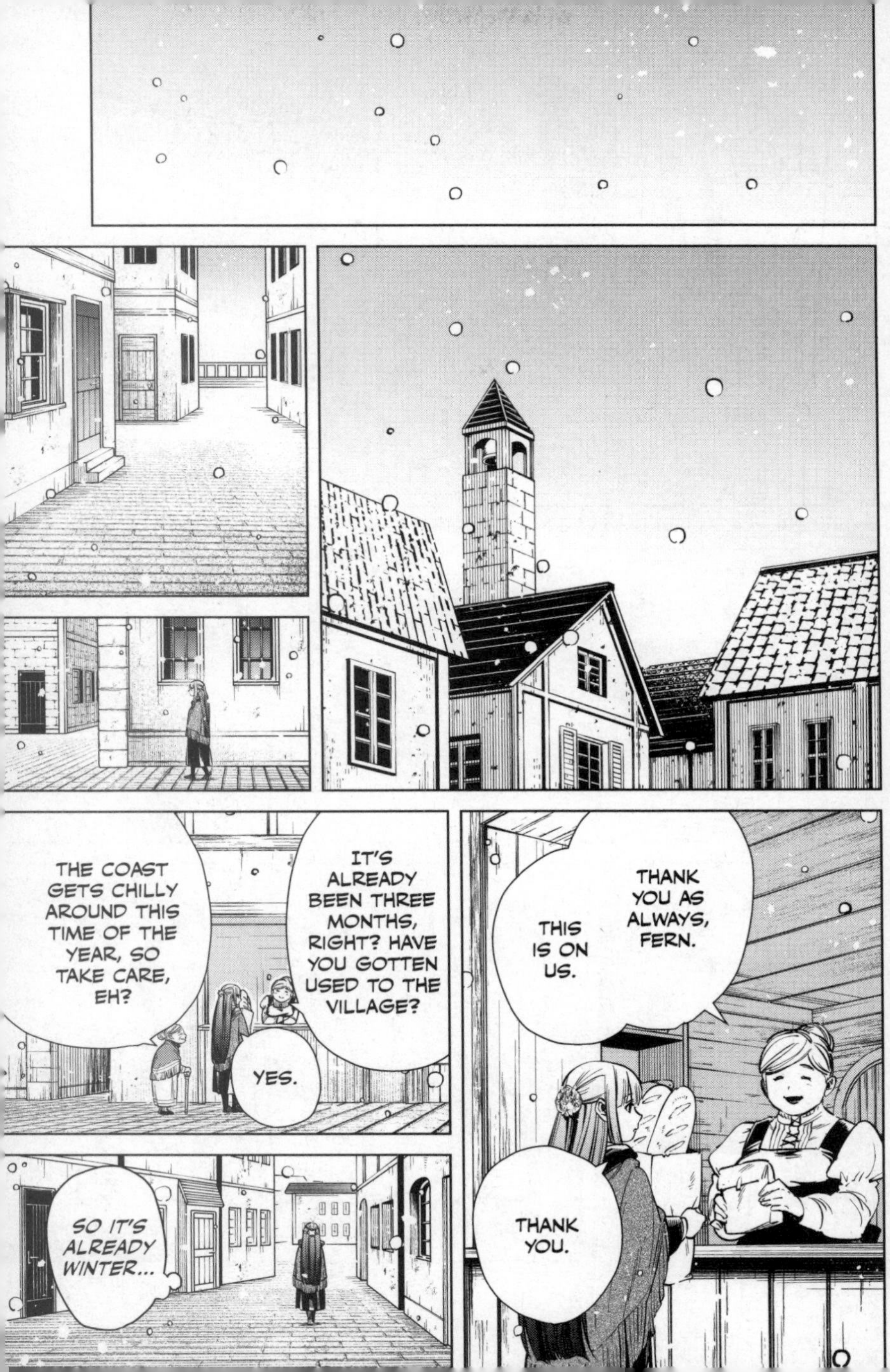
THANK YOU AS ALWAYS, FERN.
THIS IS ON US.
THANK YOU.
IT'S ALREADY BEEN THREE MONTHS, RIGHT? HAVE YOU GOTTEN USED TO THE VILLAGE?
THE COAST GETS CHILLY AROUND THIS TIME OF THE YEAR, SO TAKE CARE, EH?
YES.
SO IT'S ALREADY WINTER...

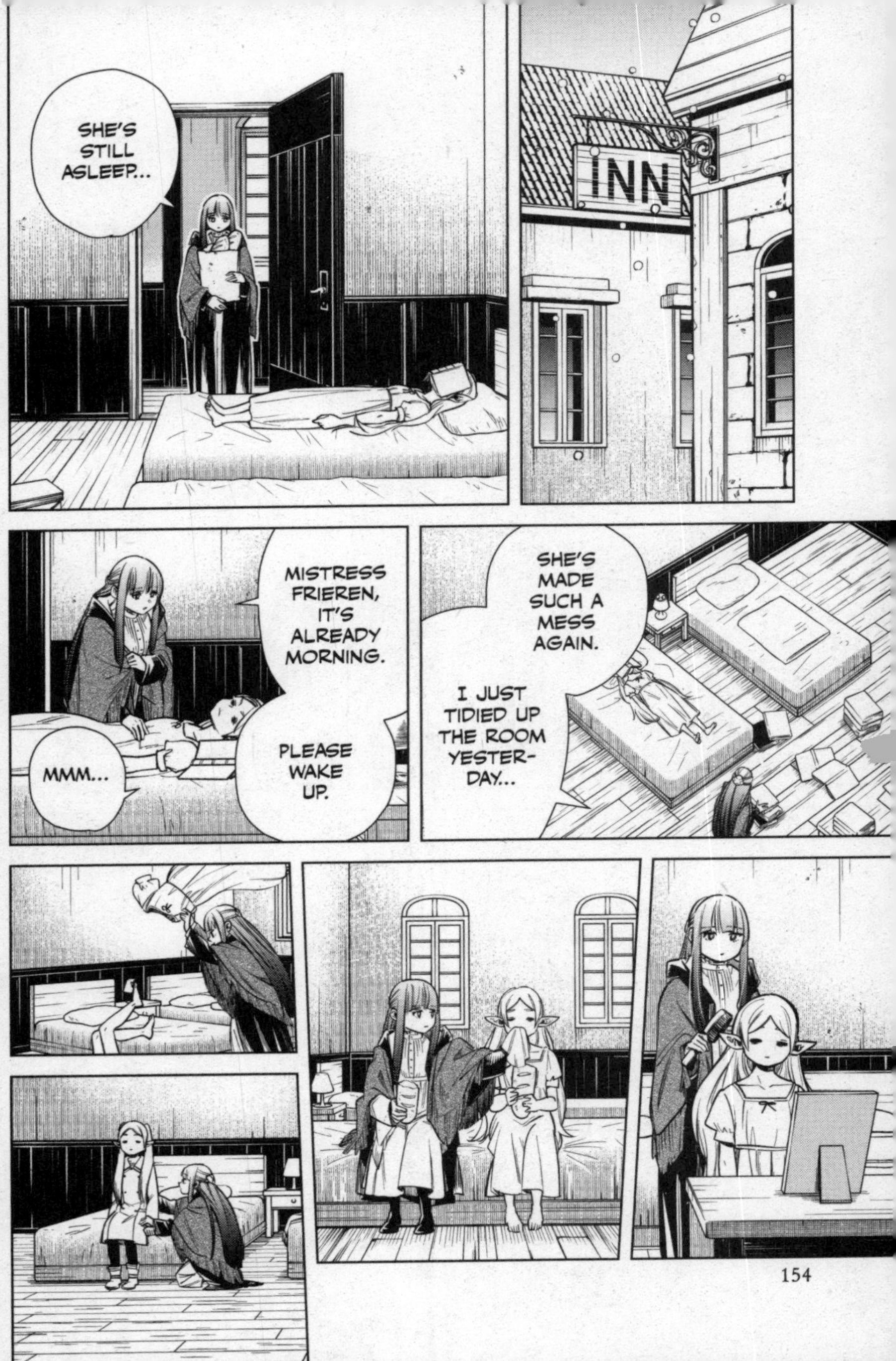
INN
SHE'S STILL ASLEEP...
SHE'S MADE SUCH A MESS AGAIN.
I JUST TIDIED UP THE ROOM YESTER-DAY...
MISTRESS FRIEREN, IT'S ALREADY MORNING.
PLEASE WAKE UP.
MMM...

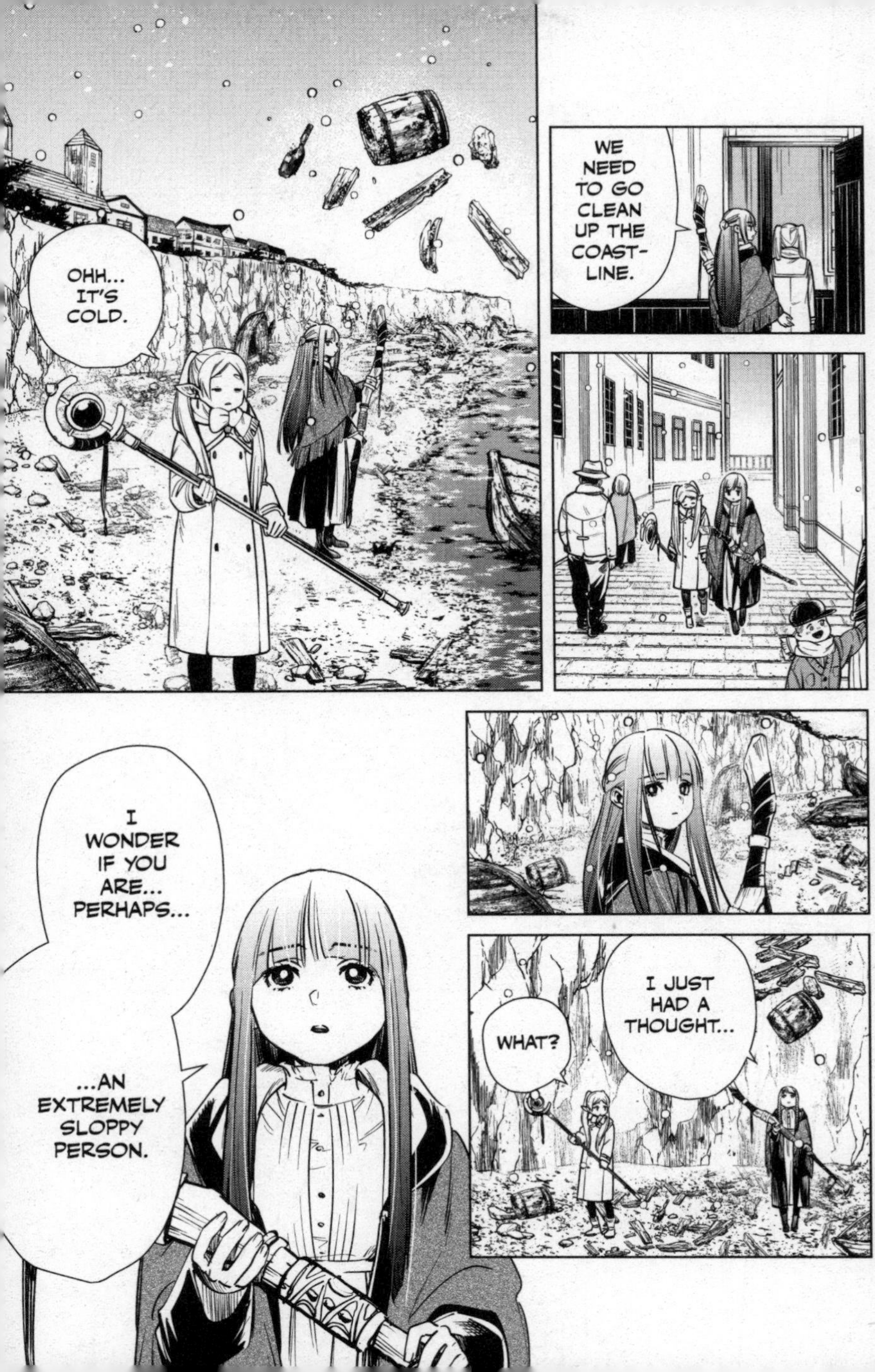
WE NEED TO GO CLEAN UP THE COAST-LINE.
OHH... IT'S COLD.
I JUST HAD A THOUGHT...
WHAT?
I WONDER IF YOU ARE... PERHAPS...
...AN EXTREMELY SLOPPY PERSON.

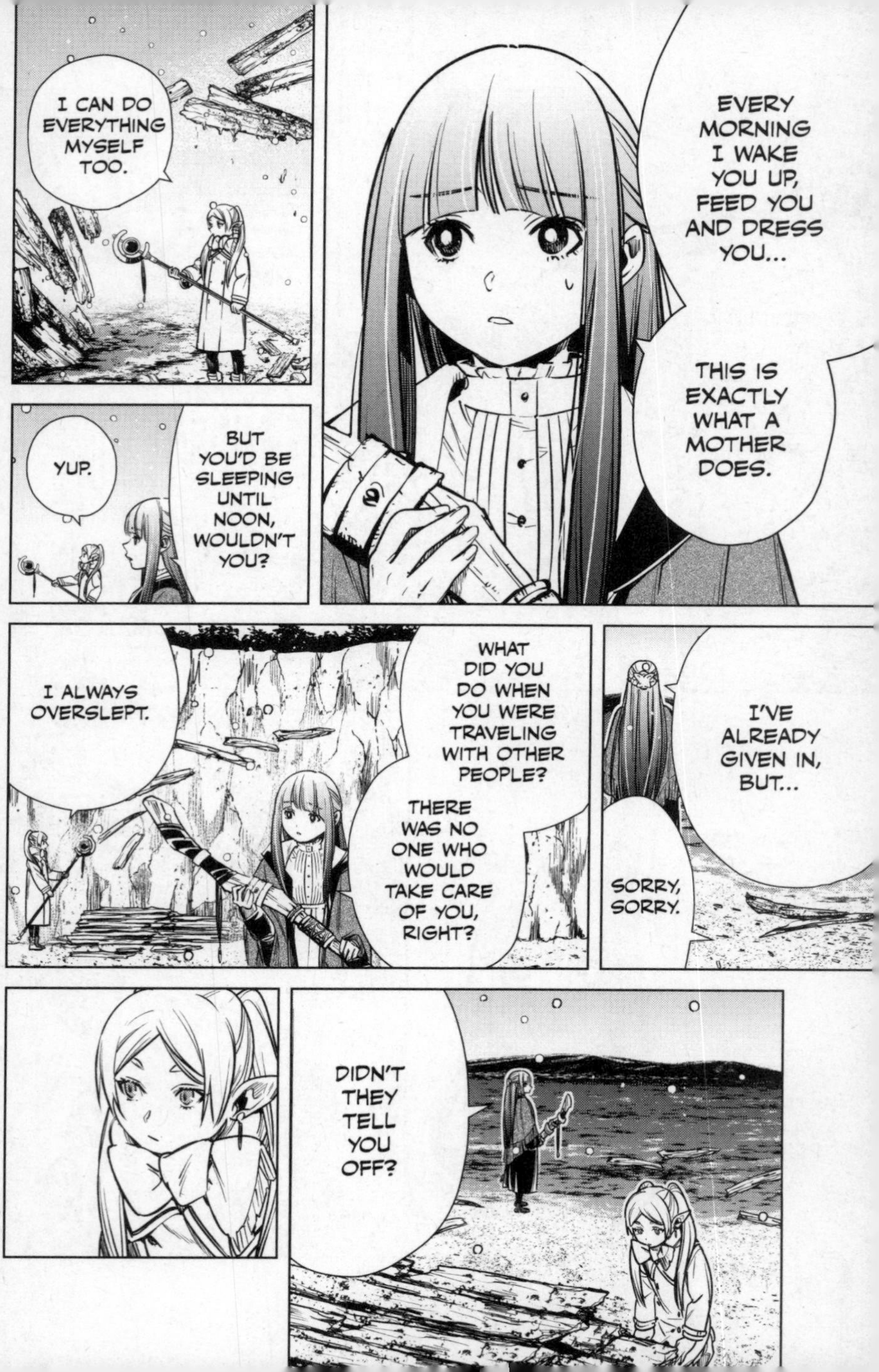
EVERY MORNING I WAKE YOU UP, FEED YOU AND DRESS YOU...
THIS IS EXACTLY WHAT A MOTHER DOES.
I CAN DO EVERYTHING MYSELF TOO.
BUT YOU'D BE SLEEPING UNTIL NOON, WOULDN'T YOU?
YUP.
I'VE ALREADY GIVEN IN, BUT...
SORRY, SORRY.
WHAT DID YOU DO WHEN YOU WERE TRAVELING WITH OTHER PEOPLE?
THERE WAS NO ONE WHO WOULD TAKE CARE OF YOU, RIGHT?
I ALWAYS OVERSLEPT.
DIDN'T THEY TELL YOU OFF?

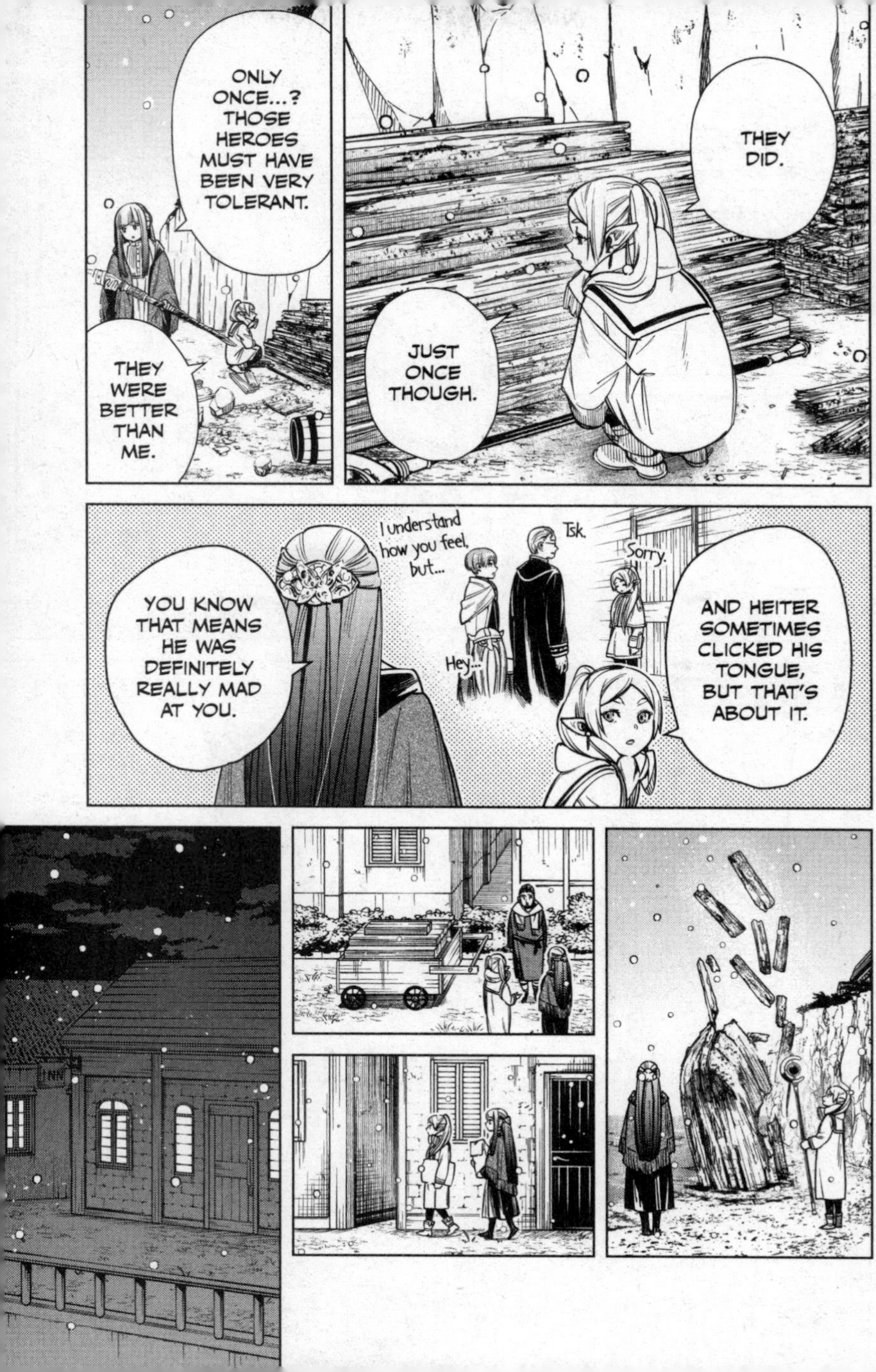
THEY DID.
JUST ONCE THOUGH.
ONLY ONCE...? THOSE HEROES MUST HAVE BEEN VERY TOLERANT.
THEY WERE BETTER THAN ME.
AND HEITER SOMETIMES CLICKED HIS TONGUE, BUT THAT'S ABOUT IT.
Sorry.
Tsk.
I understand how you feel, but...
Hey...
YOU KNOW THAT MEANS HE WAS DEFINITELY REALLY MAD AT YOU.
INN

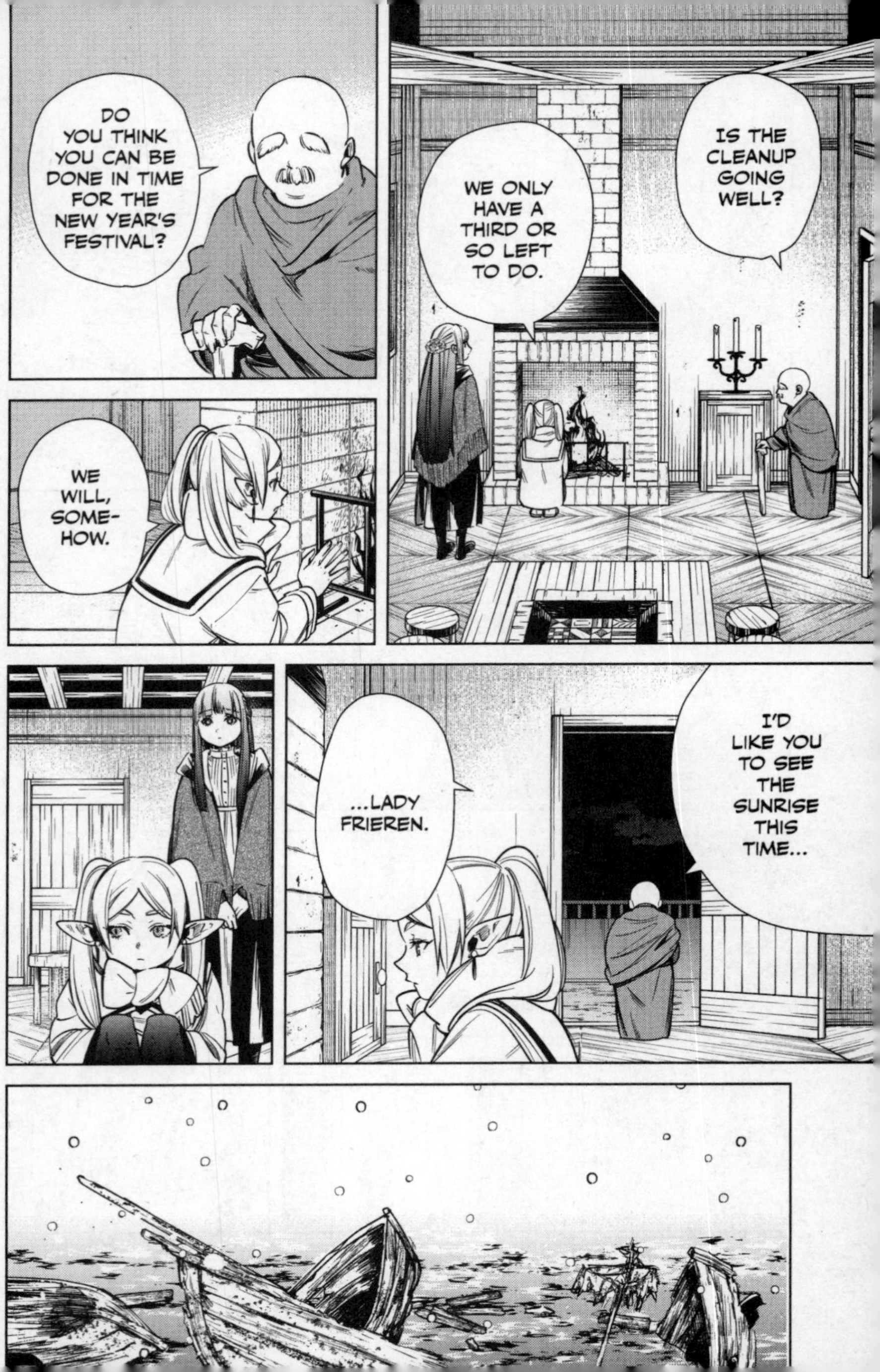
IS THE CLEANUP GOING WELL?
WE ONLY HAVE A THIRD OR SO LEFT TO DO.
DO YOU THINK YOU CAN BE DONE IN TIME FOR THE NEW YEAR'S FESTIVAL?
WE WILL, SOME-HOW.
I'D LIKE YOU TO SEE THE SUNRISE THIS TIME...
...LADY FRIEREN.

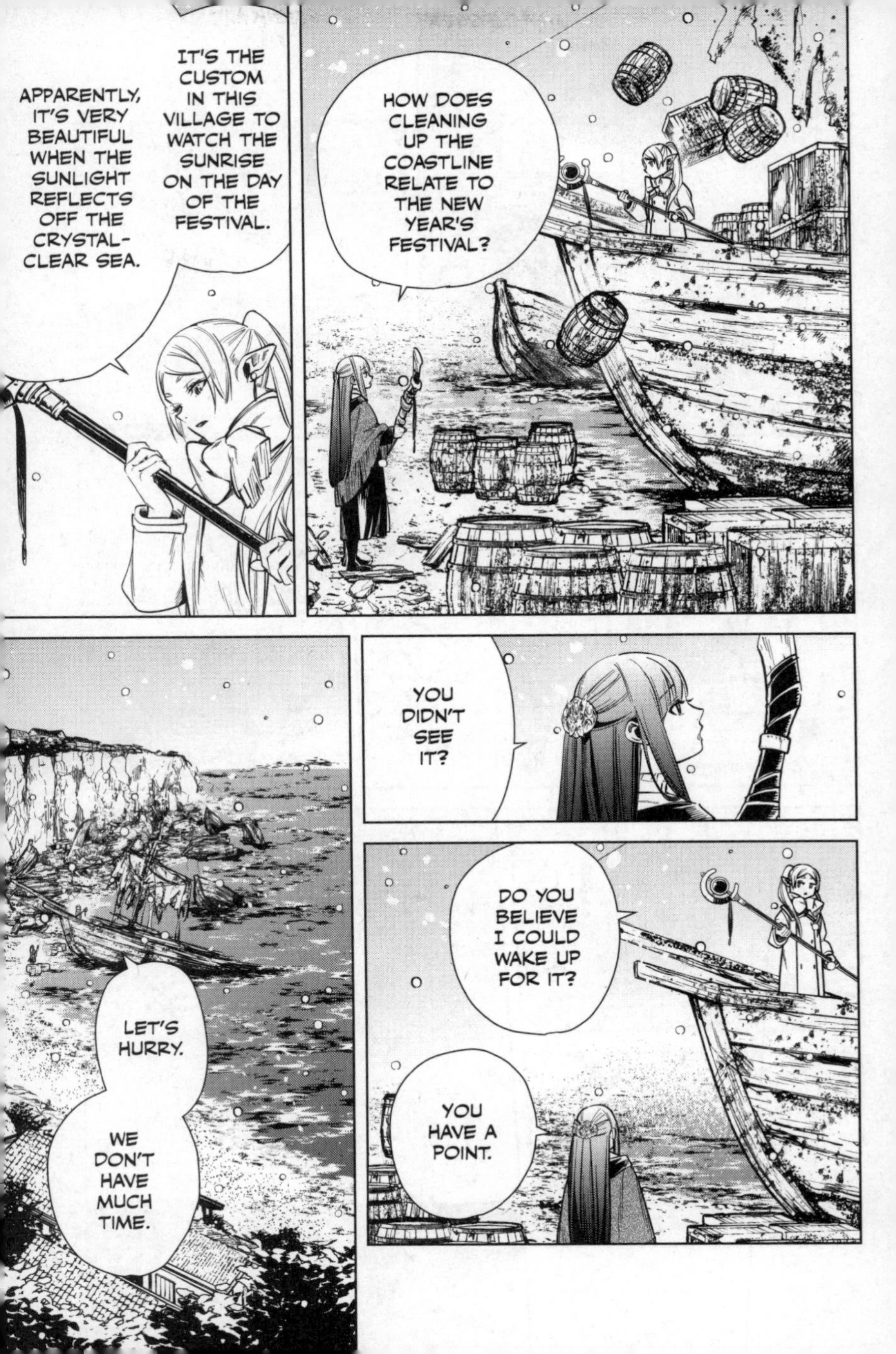
HOW DOES CLEANING UP THE COASTLINE RELATE TO THE NEW YEAR'S FESTIVAL?
IT'S THE CUSTOM IN THIS VILLAGE TO WATCH THE SUNRISE ON THE DAY OF THE FESTIVAL.
APPARENTLY, IT'S VERY BEAUTIFUL WHEN THE SUNLIGHT REFLECTS OFF THE CRYSTAL-CLEAR SEA.
YOU DIDN'T SEE IT?
DO YOU BELIEVE I COULD WAKE UP FOR IT?
YOU HAVE A POINT.
LET'S HURRY.
WE DON'T HAVE MUCH TIME.

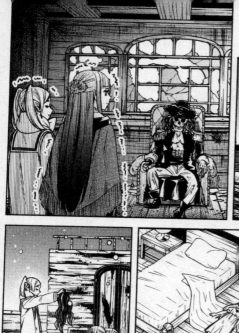

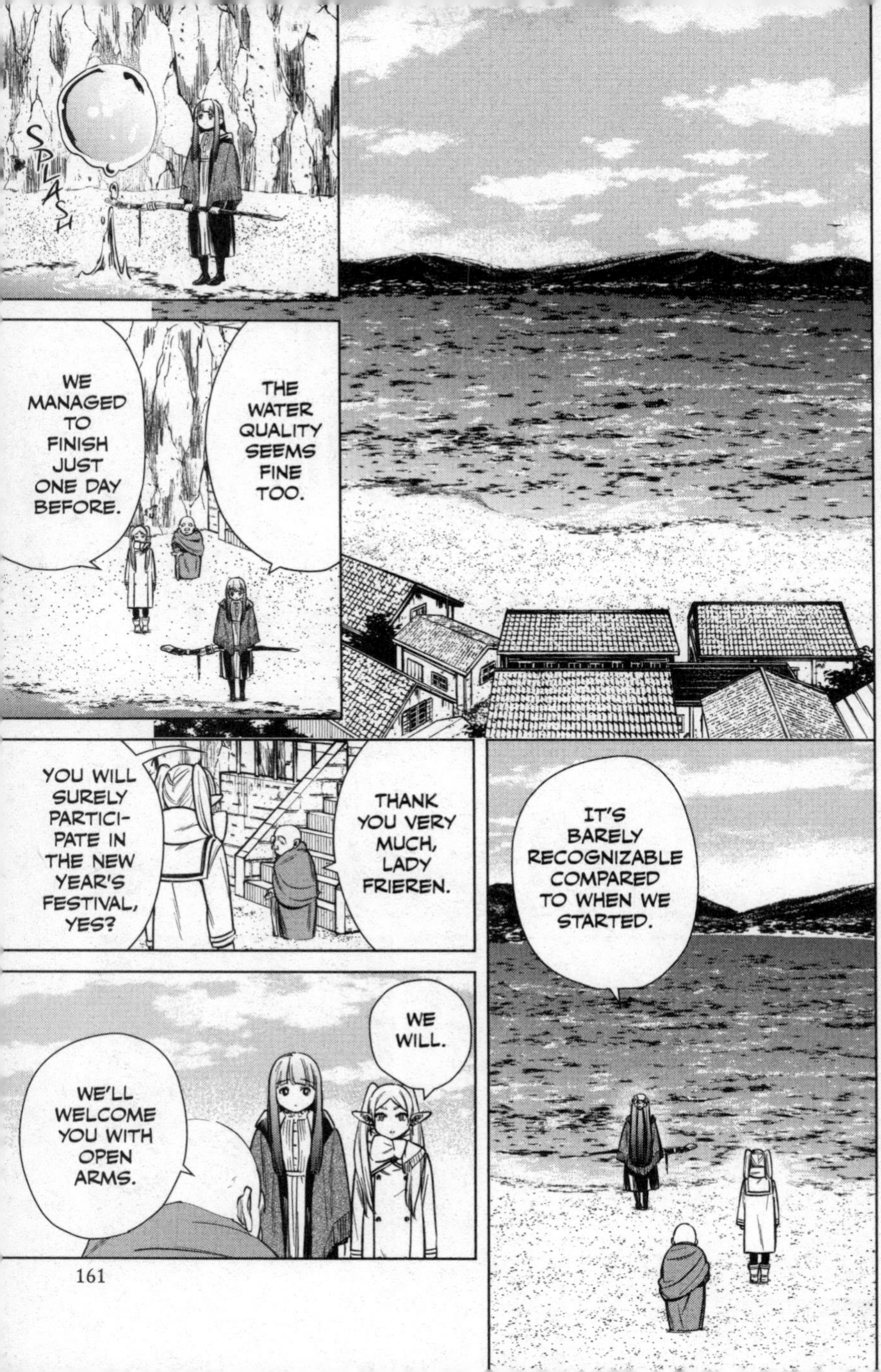
SPLASH
THE WATER QUALITY SEEMS FINE TOO.
WE MANAGED TO FINISH JUST ONE DAY BEFORE.
IT'S BARELY RECOGNIZABLE COMPARED TO WHEN WE STARTED.
THANK YOU VERY MUCH, LADY FRIEREN.
YOU WILL SURELY PARTICI-PATE IN THE NEW YEAR'S FESTIVAL, YES?
WE WILL.
WE'LL WELCOME YOU WITH OPEN ARMS.

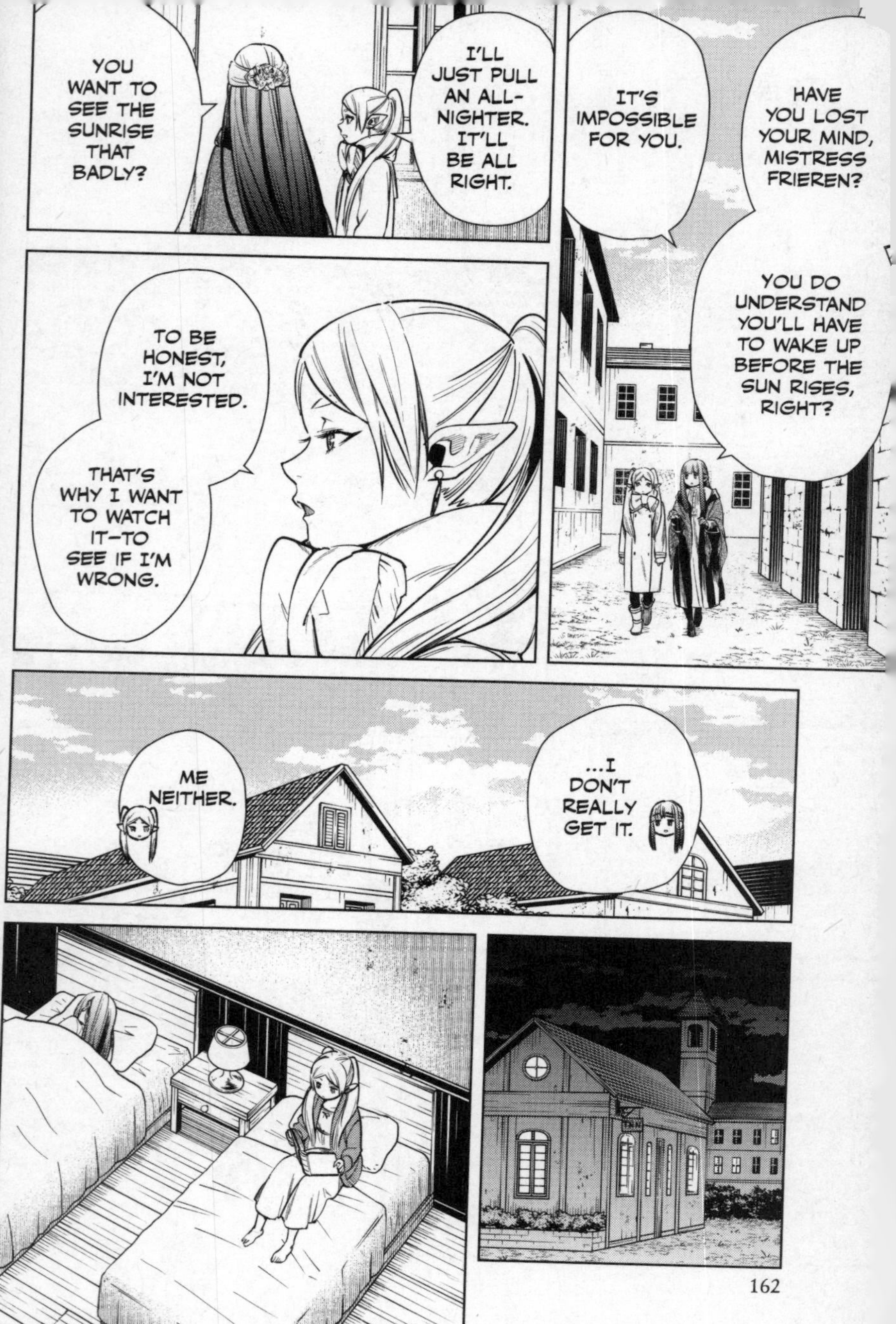
HAVE YOU LOST YOUR MIND, MISTRESS FRIEREN?
IT'S IMPOSSIBLE FOR YOU.
YOU DO UNDERSTAND YOU'LL HAVE TO WAKE UP BEFORE THE SUN RISES, RIGHT?
I'LL JUST PULL AN ALL-NIGHTER. IT'LL BE ALL RIGHT.
YOU WANT TO SEE THE SUNRISE THAT BADLY?
TO BE HONEST, I'M NOT INTERESTED.
THAT'S WHY I WANT TO WATCH IT—TO SEE IF I'M WRONG.
...I DON'T REALLY GET IT.
ME NEITHER.

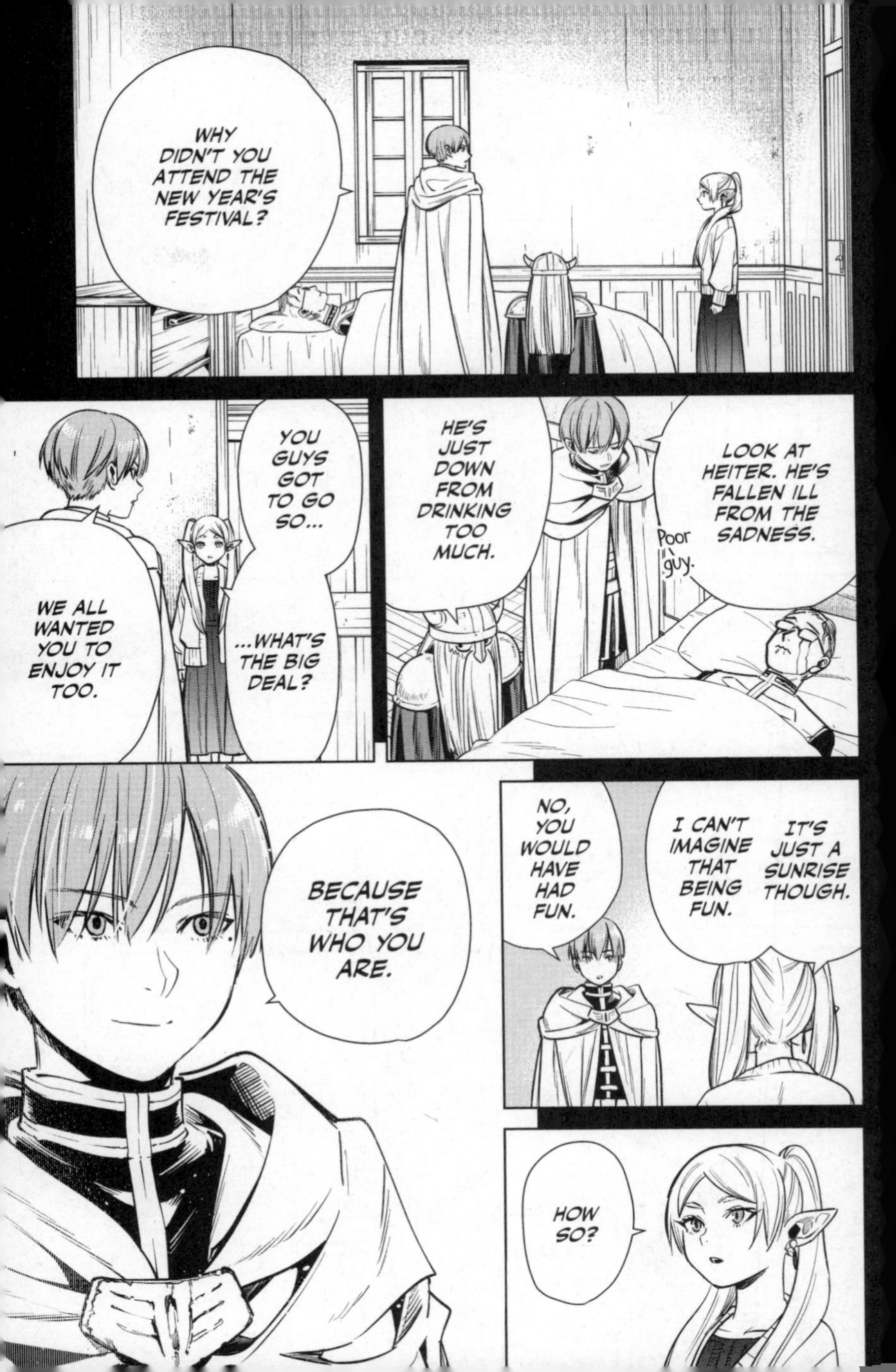
WHY DIDN'T YOU ATTEND THE NEW YEAR'S FESTIVAL?
LOOK AT HEITER. HE'S FALLEN ILL FROM THE SADNESS.
Poor guy.
HE'S JUST DOWN FROM DRINKING TOO MUCH.
YOU GUYS GOT TO GO SO... ...WHAT'S THE BIG DEAL?
WE ALL WANTED YOU TO ENJOY IT TOO.
IT'S JUST A SUNRISE THOUGH.
I CAN'T IMAGINE THAT BEING FUN.
NO, YOU WOULD HAVE HAD FUN.
HOW SO?
BECAUSE THAT'S WHO YOU ARE.

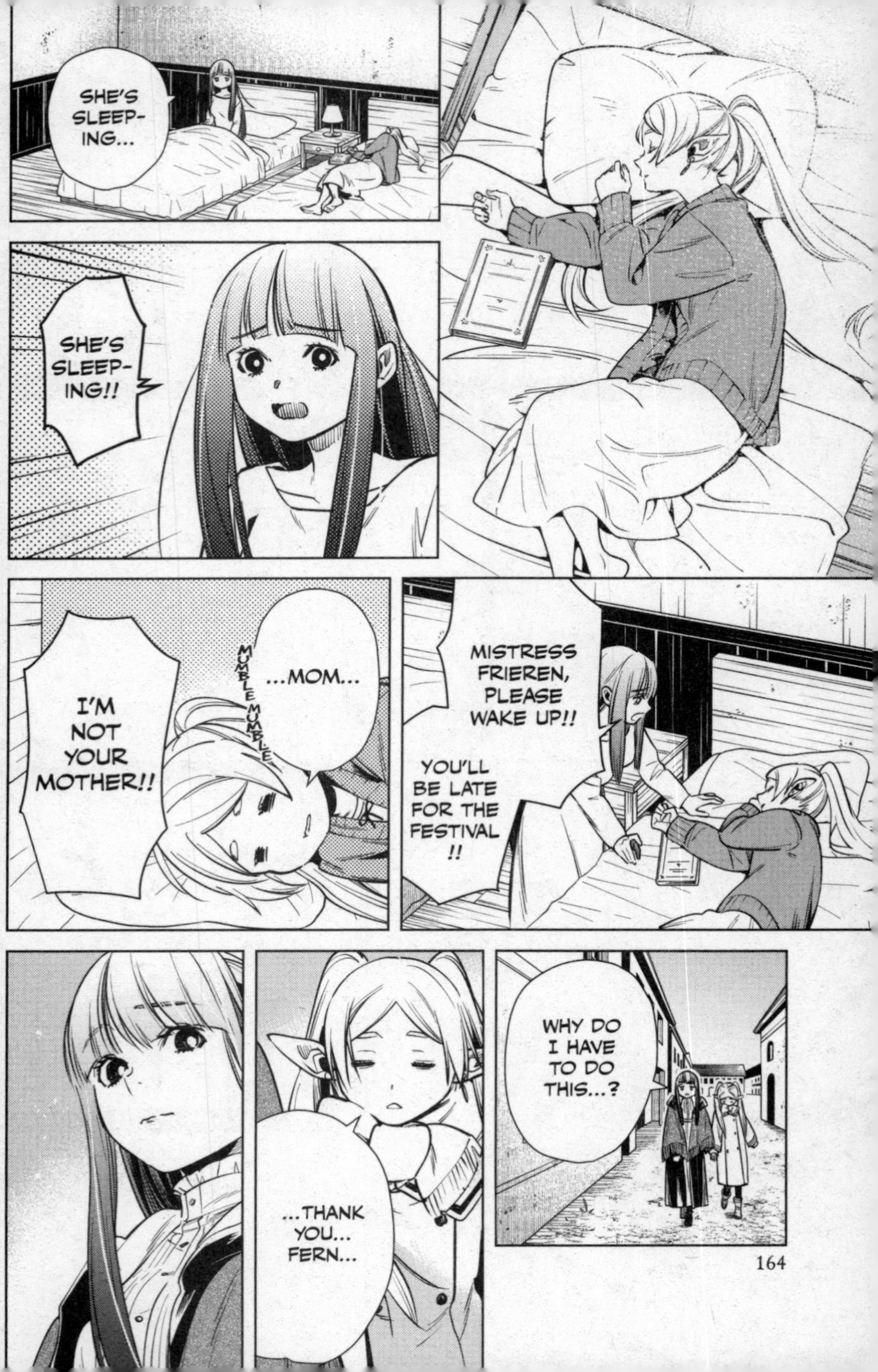
SHE'S SLEEPING...
SHE'S SLEEPING!!
MISTRESS FRIEREN, PLEASE WAKE UP!!
YOU'LL BE LATE FOR THE FESTIVAL!!
...MOM...
MUMBLE MUMBLE
I'M NOT YOUR MOTHER!!
WHY DO I HAVE TO DO THIS...?
...THANK YOU... FERN...

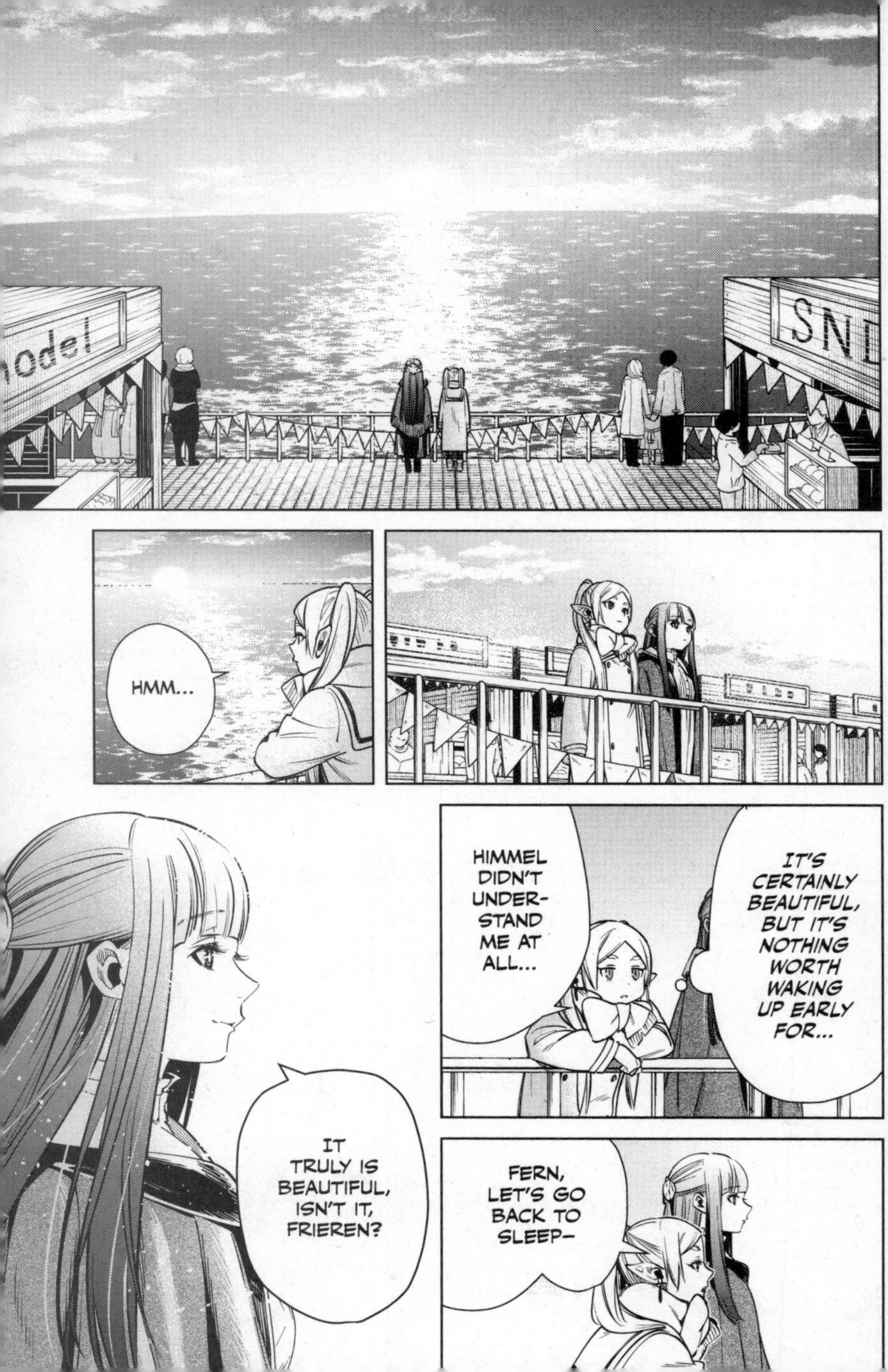
HMM...
IT'S CERTAINLY BEAUTIFUL, BUT IT'S NOTHING WORTH WAKING UP EARLY FOR...
HIMMEL DIDN'T UNDER-STAND ME AT ALL...
FERN, LET'S GO BACK TO SLEEP–
IT TRULY IS BEAUTIFUL, ISN'T IT, FRIEREN?

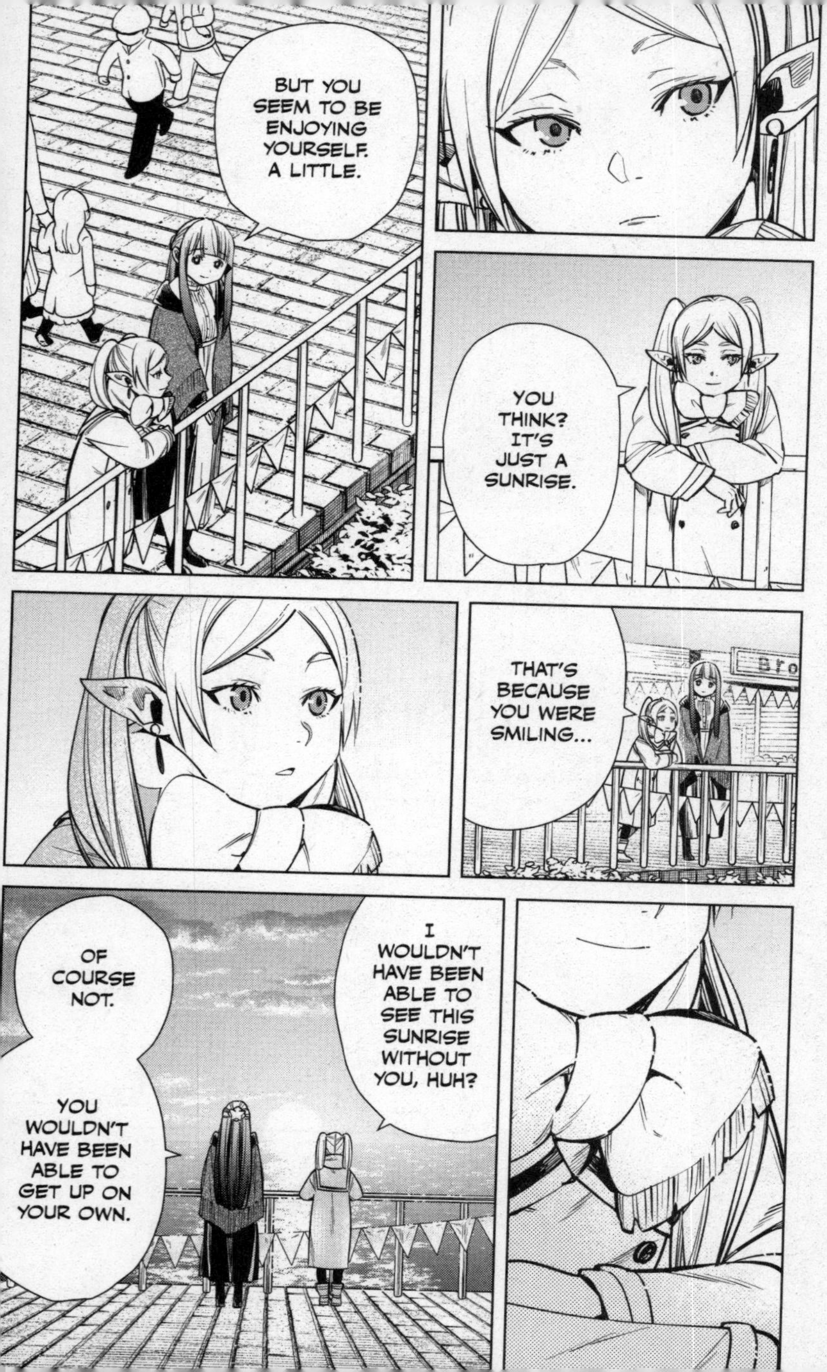
YOU THINK? IT'S JUST A SUNRISE.
BUT YOU SEEM TO BE ENJOYING YOURSELF. A LITTLE.
THAT'S BECAUSE YOU WERE SMILING...
I WOULDN'T HAVE BEEN ABLE TO SEE THIS SUNRISE WITHOUT YOU, HUH?
OF COURSE NOT.
YOU WOULDN'T HAVE BEEN ABLE TO GET UP ON YOUR OWN.

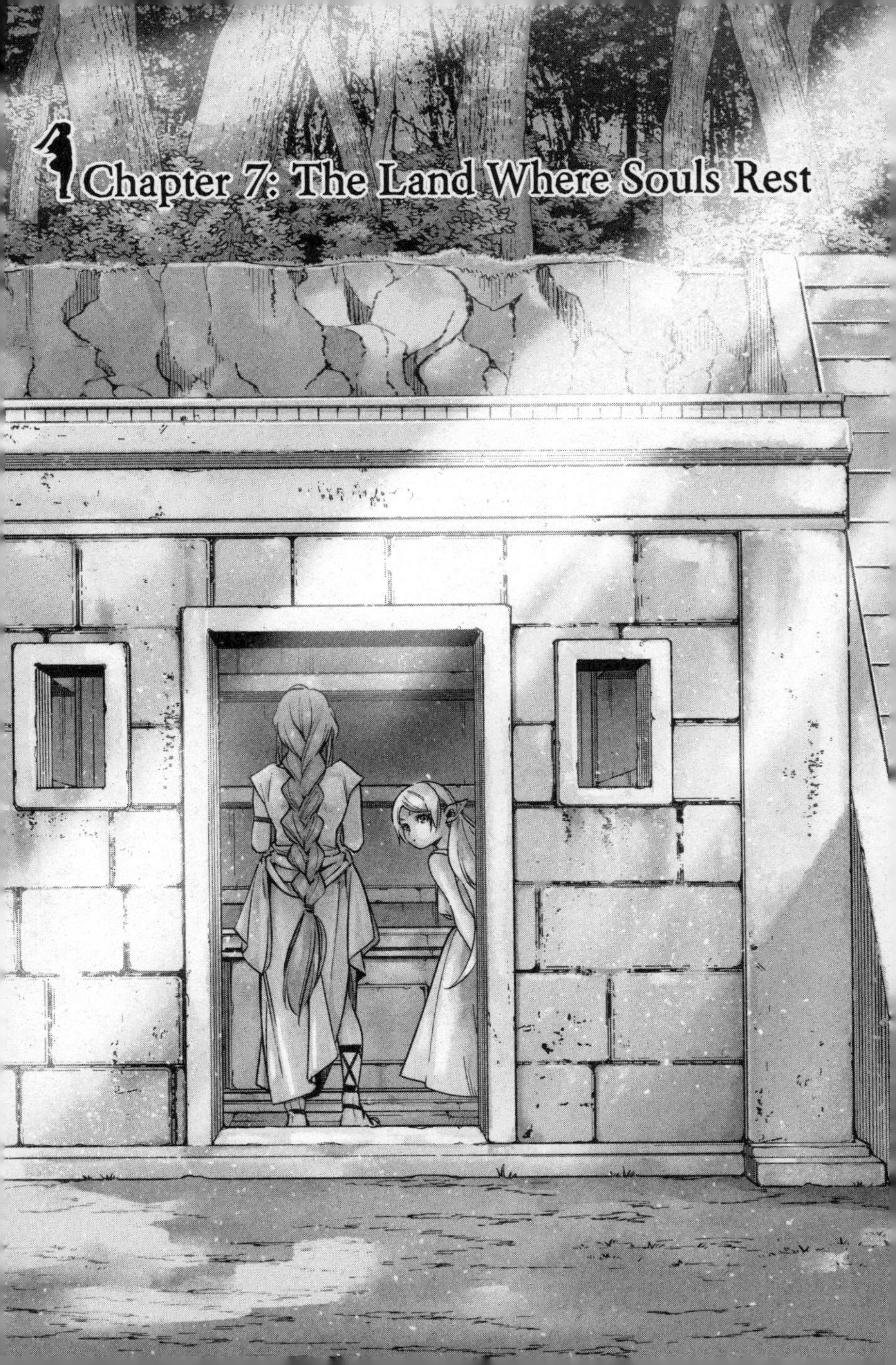
Chapter 7: The Land Where Souls Rest

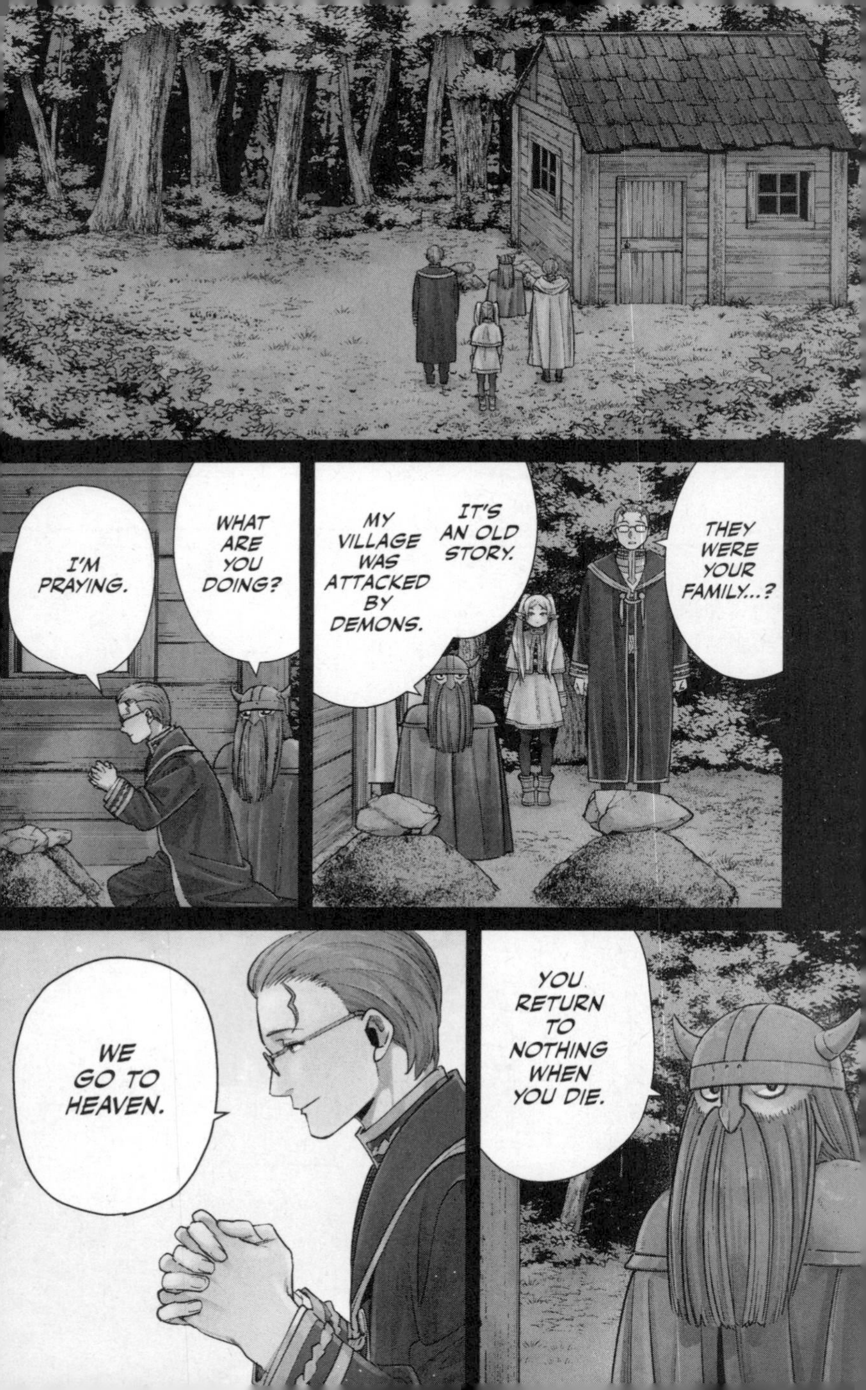
THEY WERE YOUR FAMILY...?
IT'S AN OLD STORY.
MY VILLAGE WAS ATTACKED BY DEMONS.
WHAT ARE YOU DOING?
I'M PRAYING.
YOU RETURN TO NOTHING WHEN YOU DIE.
WE GO TO HEAVEN.

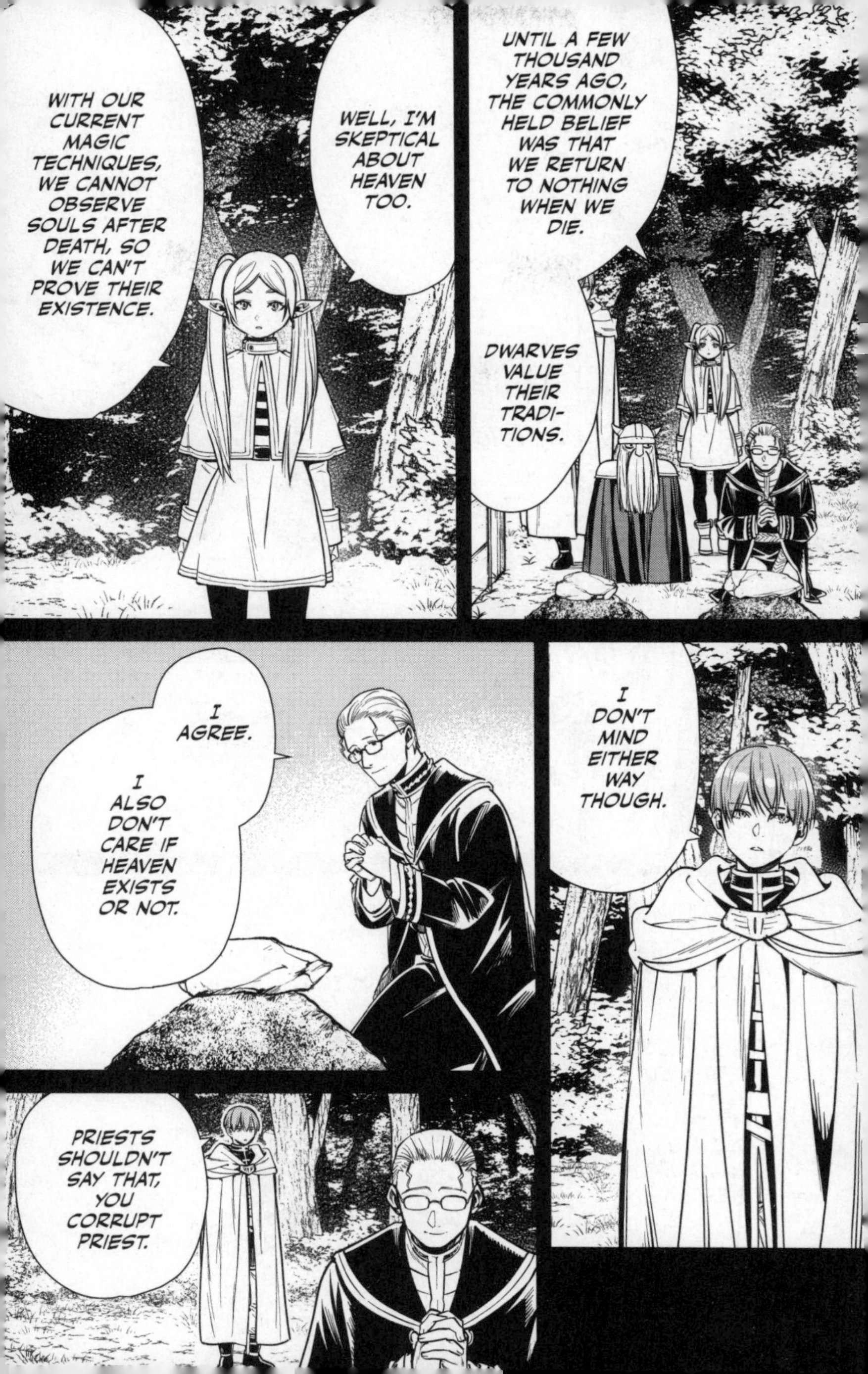
UNTIL A FEW THOUSAND YEARS AGO, THE COMMONLY HELD BELIEF WAS THAT WE RETURN TO NOTHING WHEN WE DIE.
DWARVES VALUE THEIR TRADITIONS.
WELL, I'M SKEPTICAL ABOUT HEAVEN TOO.
WITH OUR CURRENT MAGIC TECHNIQUES, WE CANNOT OBSERVE SOULS AFTER DEATH, SO WE CAN'T PROVE THEIR EXISTENCE.
I DON'T MIND EITHER WAY THOUGH.
I AGREE.
I ALSO DON'T CARE IF HEAVEN EXISTS OR NOT.
PRIESTS SHOULDN'T SAY THAT, YOU CORRUPT PRIEST.

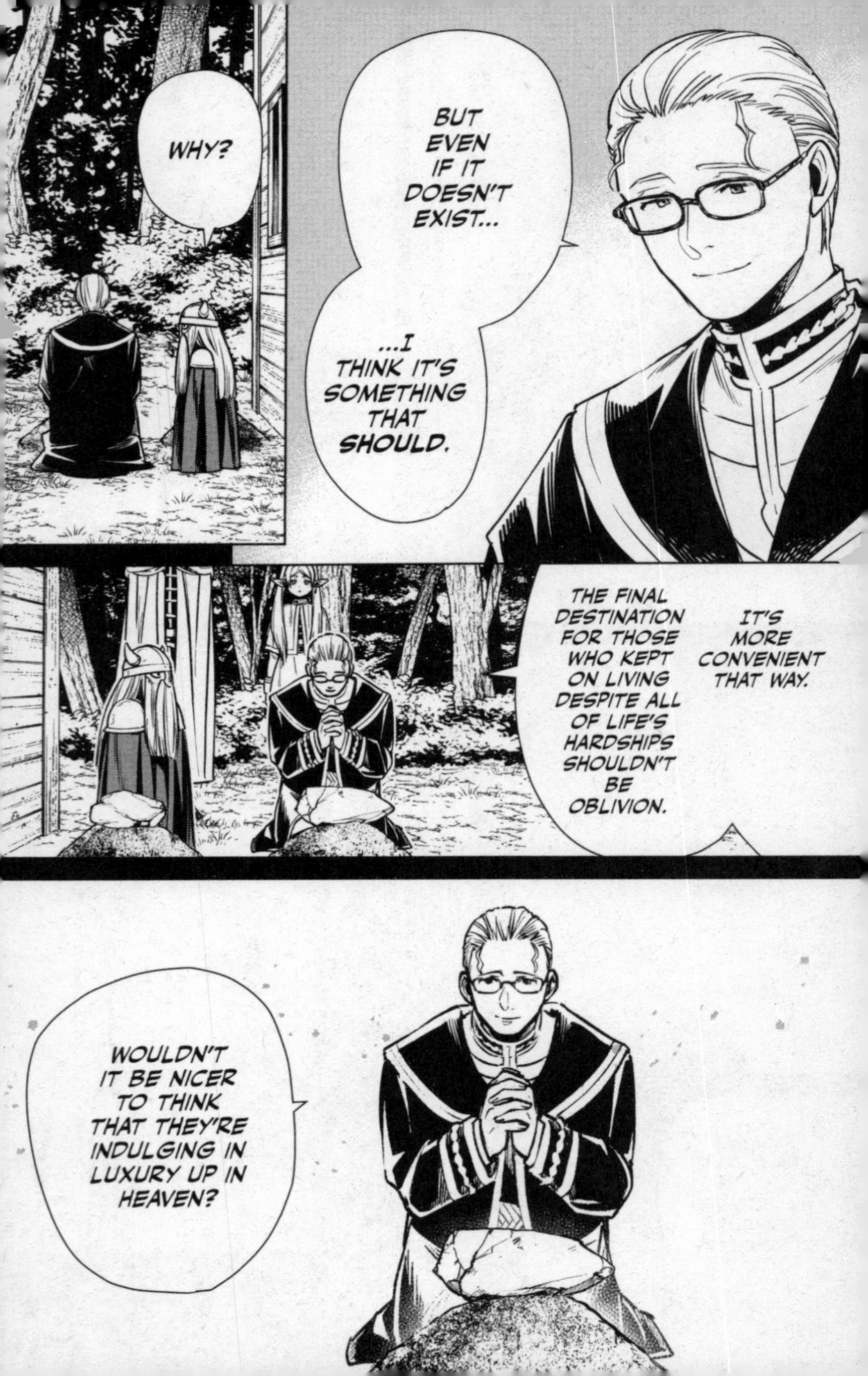
BUT EVEN IF IT DOESN'T EXIST...
...I THINK IT'S SOMETHING THAT SHOULD.
WHY?
IT'S MORE CONVENIENT THAT WAY.
THE FINAL DESTINATION FOR THOSE WHO KEPT ON LIVING DESPITE ALL OF LIFE'S HARDSHIPS SHOULDN'T BE OBLIVION.
WOULDN'T IT BE NICER TO THINK THAT THEY'RE INDULGING IN LUXURY UP IN HEAVEN?

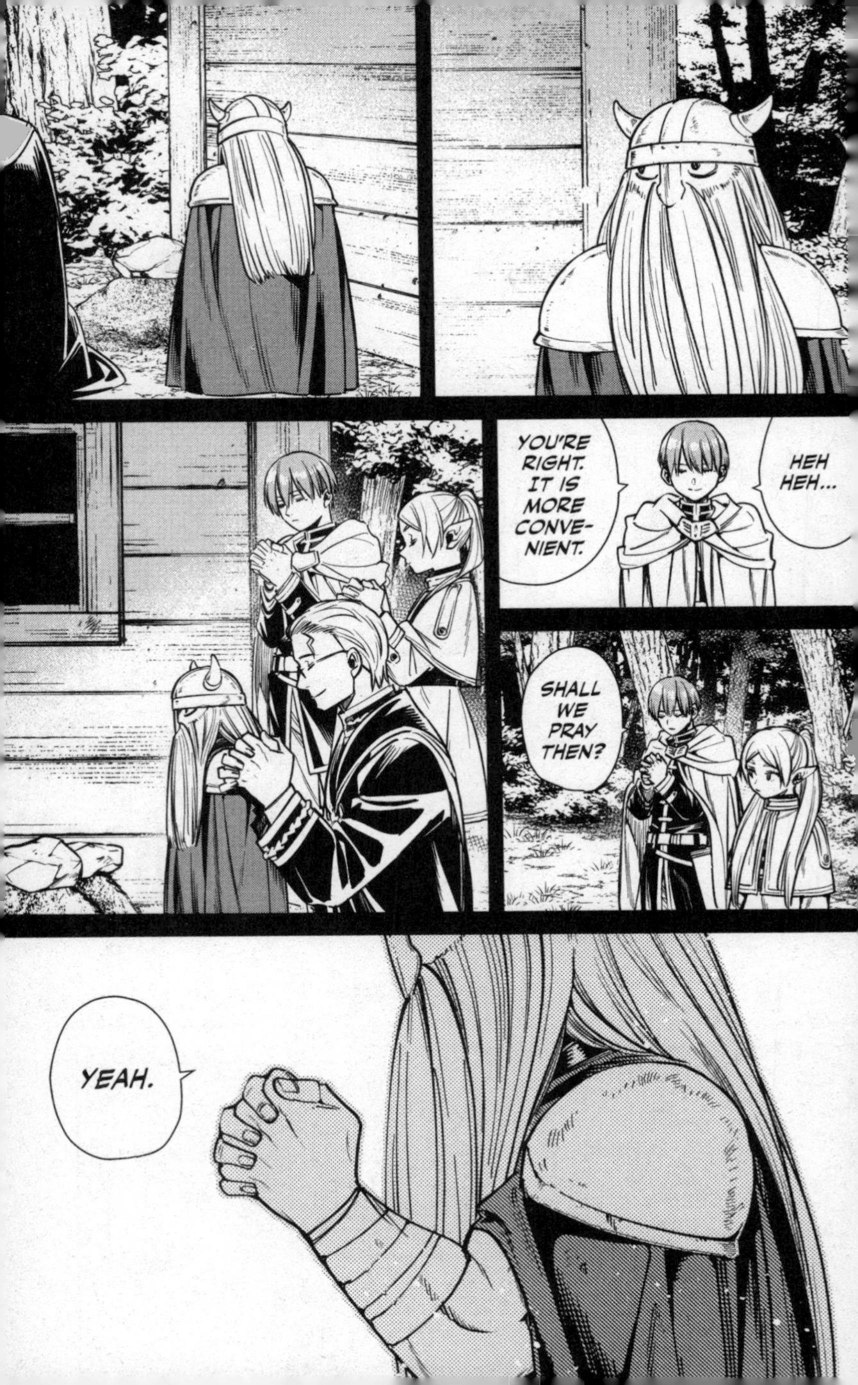
HEH HEH...
YOU'RE RIGHT. IT IS MORE CONVE- NIENT.
SHALL WE PRAY THEN?
YEAH.

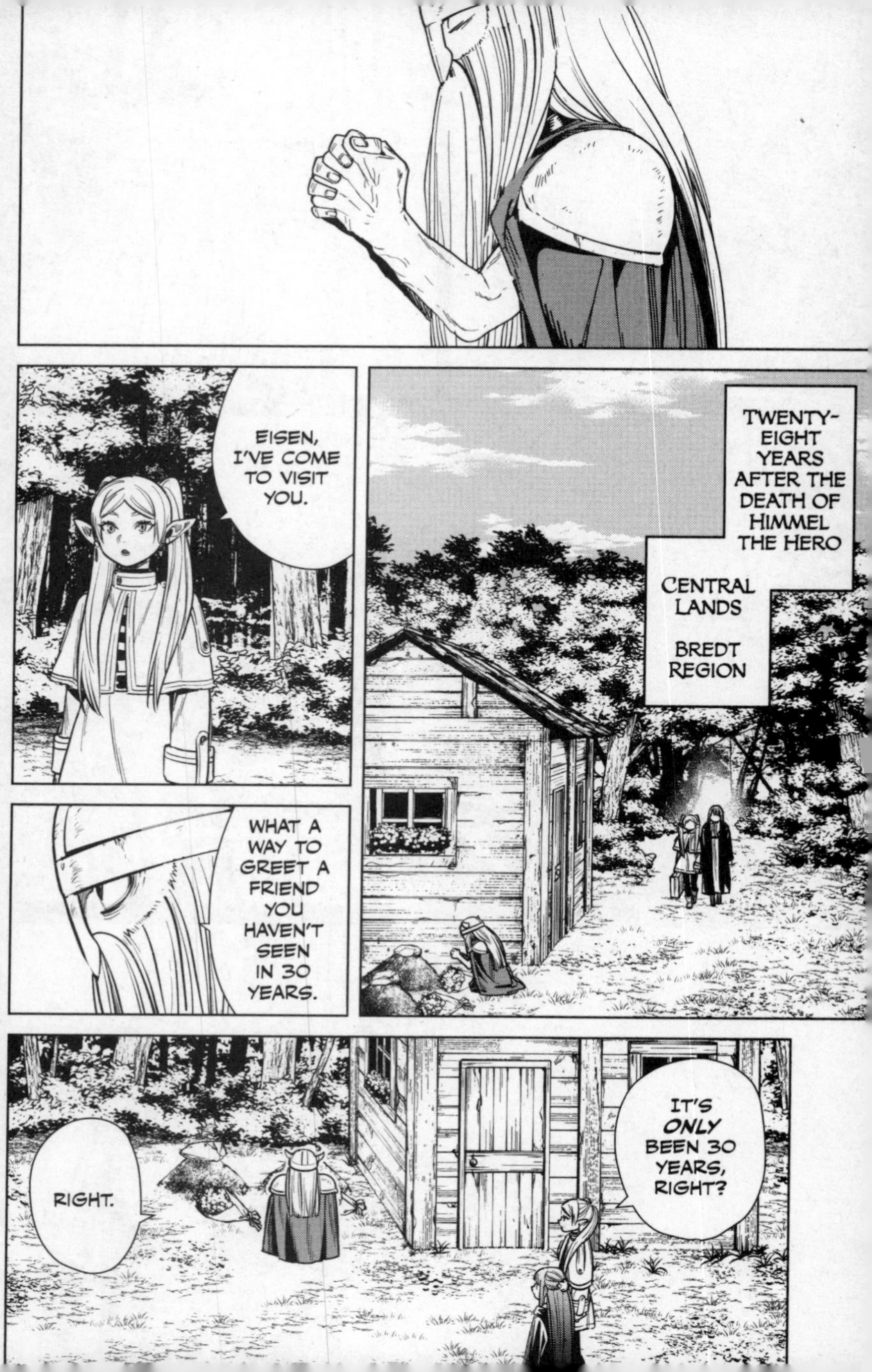
TWENTY-EIGHT YEARS AFTER THE DEATH OF HIMMEL THE HERO
CENTRAL LANDS
BREDT REGION
EISEN, I'VE COME TO VISIT YOU.
WHAT A WAY TO GREET A FRIEND YOU HAVEN'T SEEN IN 30 YEARS.
IT'S *ONLY* BEEN 30 YEARS, RIGHT?
RIGHT.

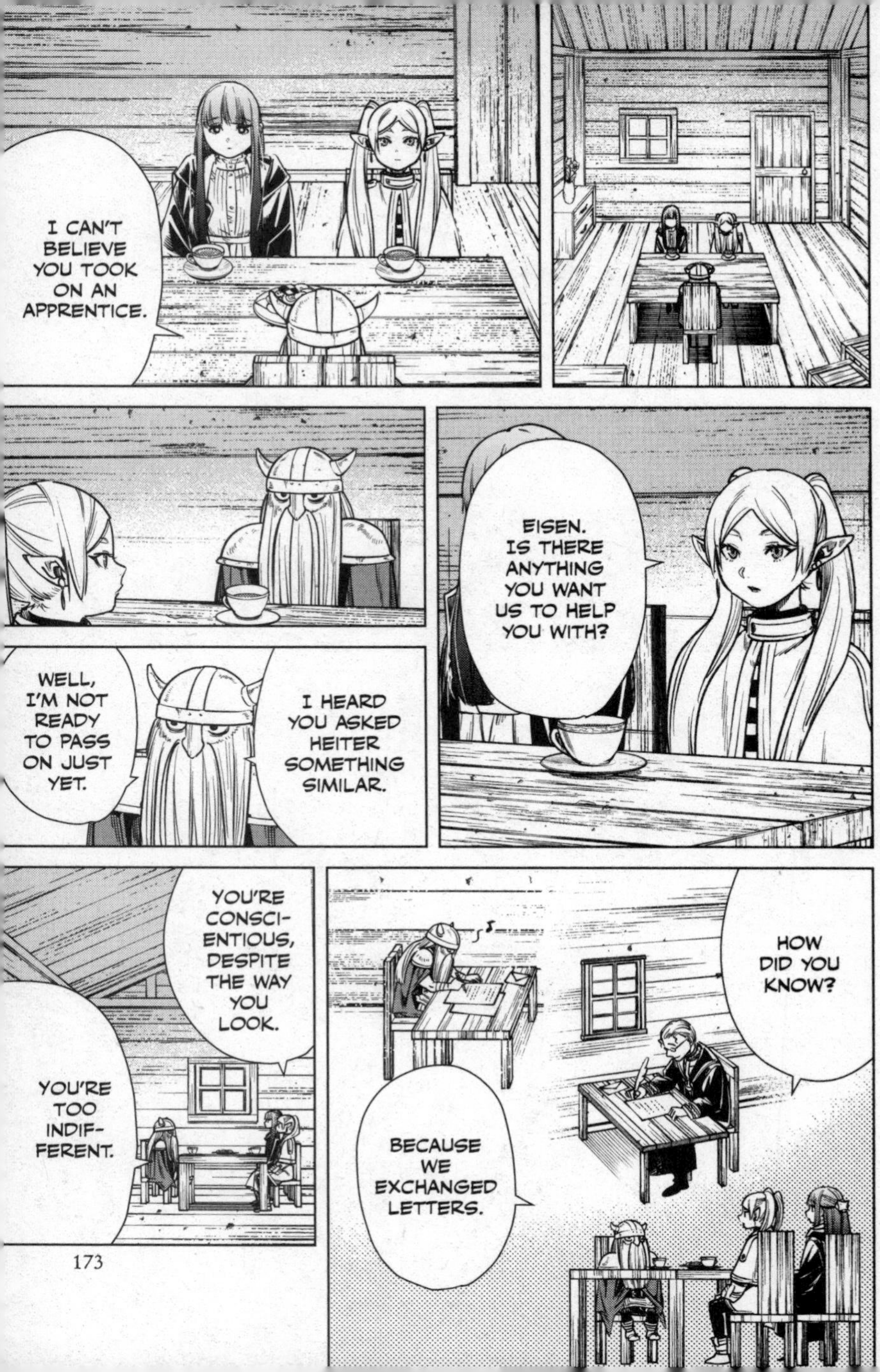
I CAN'T BELIEVE YOU TOOK ON AN APPRENTICE.
EISEN. IS THERE ANYTHING YOU WANT US TO HELP YOU WITH?
I HEARD YOU ASKED HEITER SOMETHING SIMILAR.
WELL, I'M NOT READY TO PASS ON JUST YET.
HOW DID YOU KNOW?
BECAUSE WE EXCHANGED LETTERS.
YOU'RE CONSCI-ENTIOUS, DESPITE THE WAY YOU LOOK.
YOU'RE TOO INDIF-FERENT.

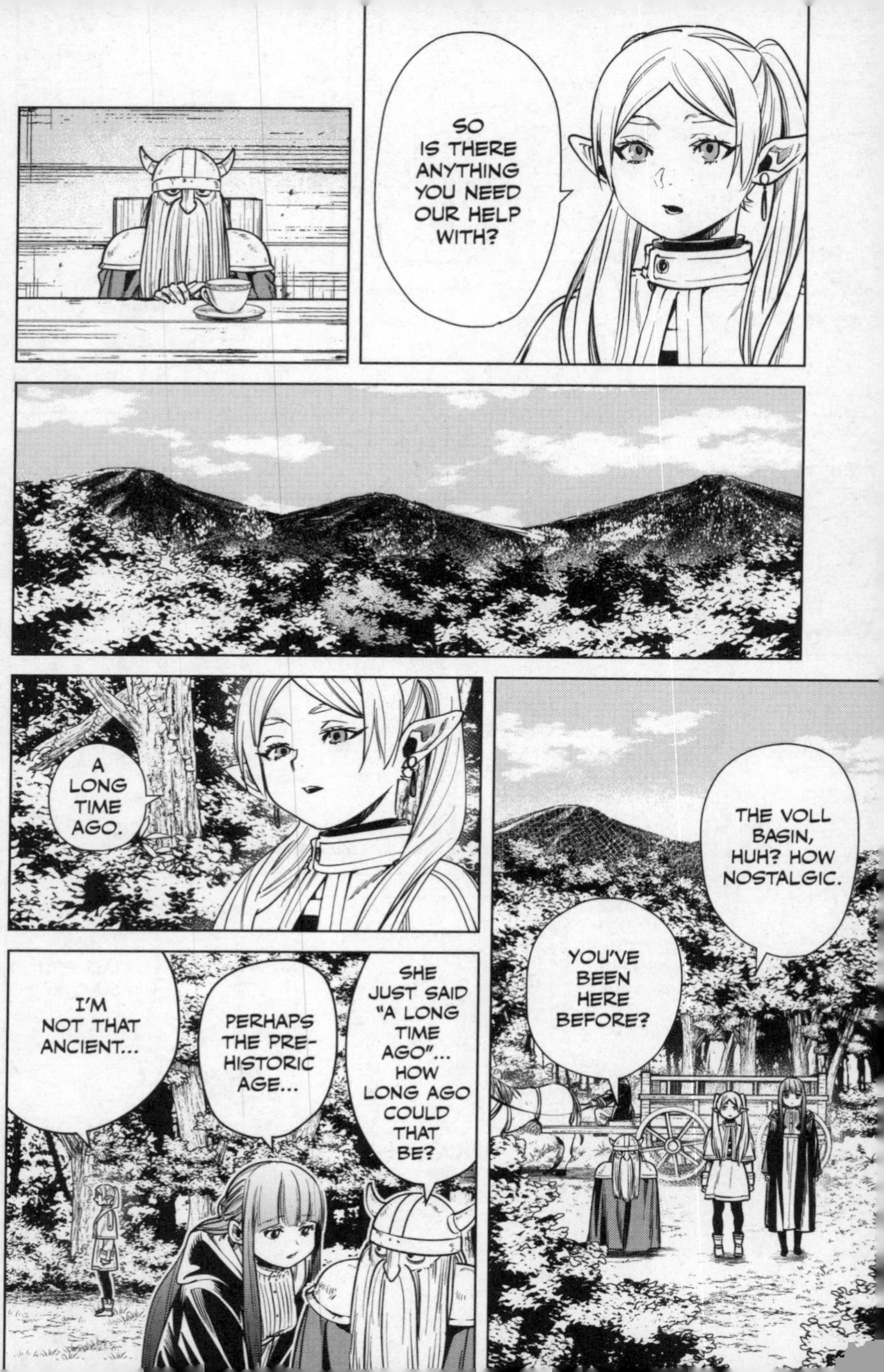
SO IS THERE ANYTHING YOU NEED OUR HELP WITH?
THE VOLL BASIN, HUH? HOW NOSTALGIC.
YOU'VE BEEN HERE BEFORE?
A LONG TIME AGO.
SHE JUST SAID "A LONG TIME AGO"... HOW LONG AGO COULD THAT BE?
PERHAPS THE PRE-HISTORIC AGE...
I'M NOT THAT ANCIENT...

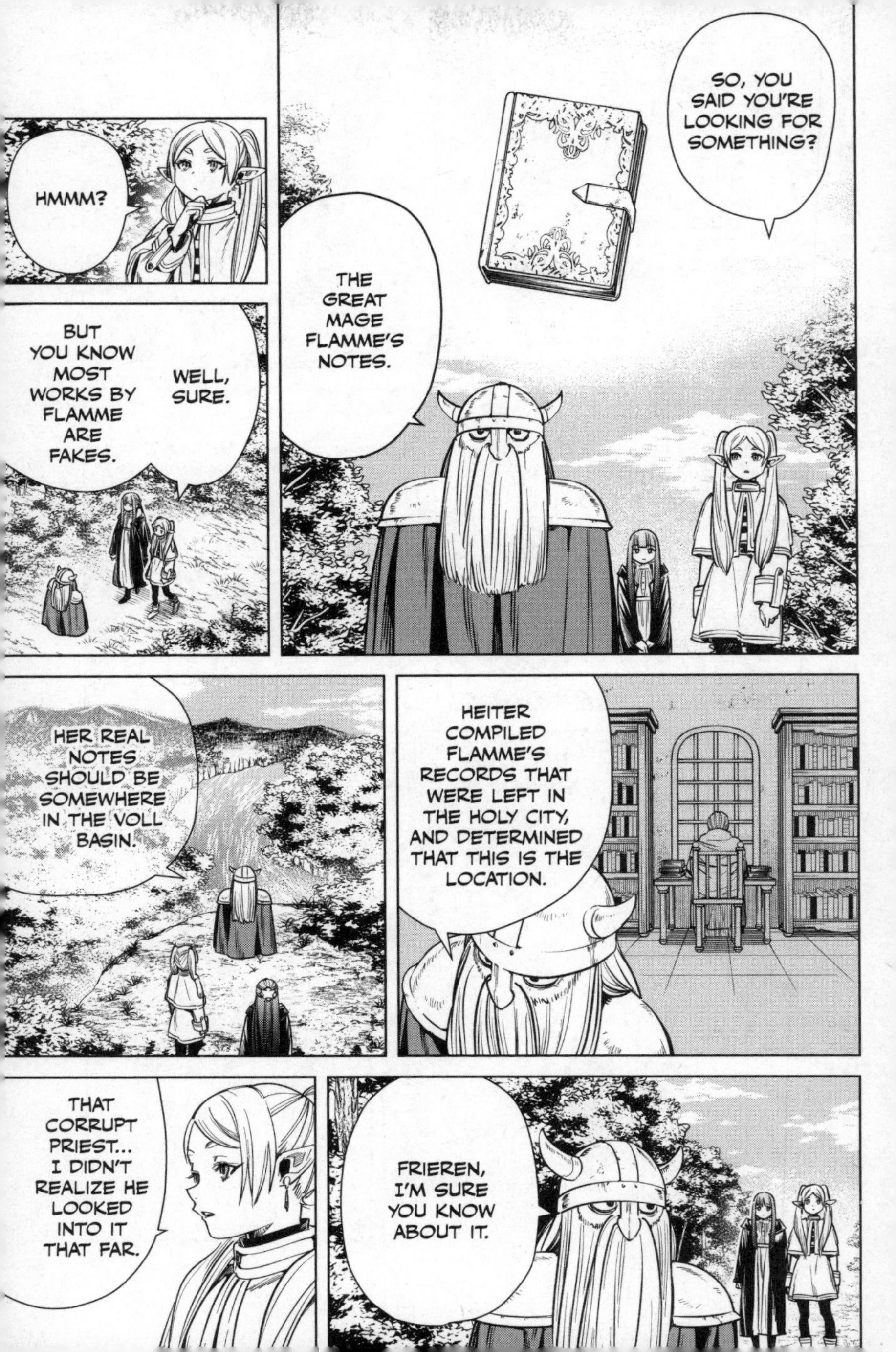
SO, YOU SAID YOU'RE LOOKING FOR SOMETHING?
THE GREAT MAGE FLAMME'S NOTES.
HMMM?
WELL, SURE.
BUT YOU KNOW MOST WORKS BY FLAMME ARE FAKES.
HEITER COMPILED FLAMME'S RECORDS THAT WERE LEFT IN THE HOLY CITY, AND DETERMINED THAT THIS IS THE LOCATION.
HER REAL NOTES SHOULD BE SOMEWHERE IN THE VOLL BASIN.
FRIEREN, I'M SURE YOU KNOW ABOUT IT.
THAT CORRUPT PRIEST... I DIDN'T REALIZE HE LOOKED INTO IT THAT FAR.

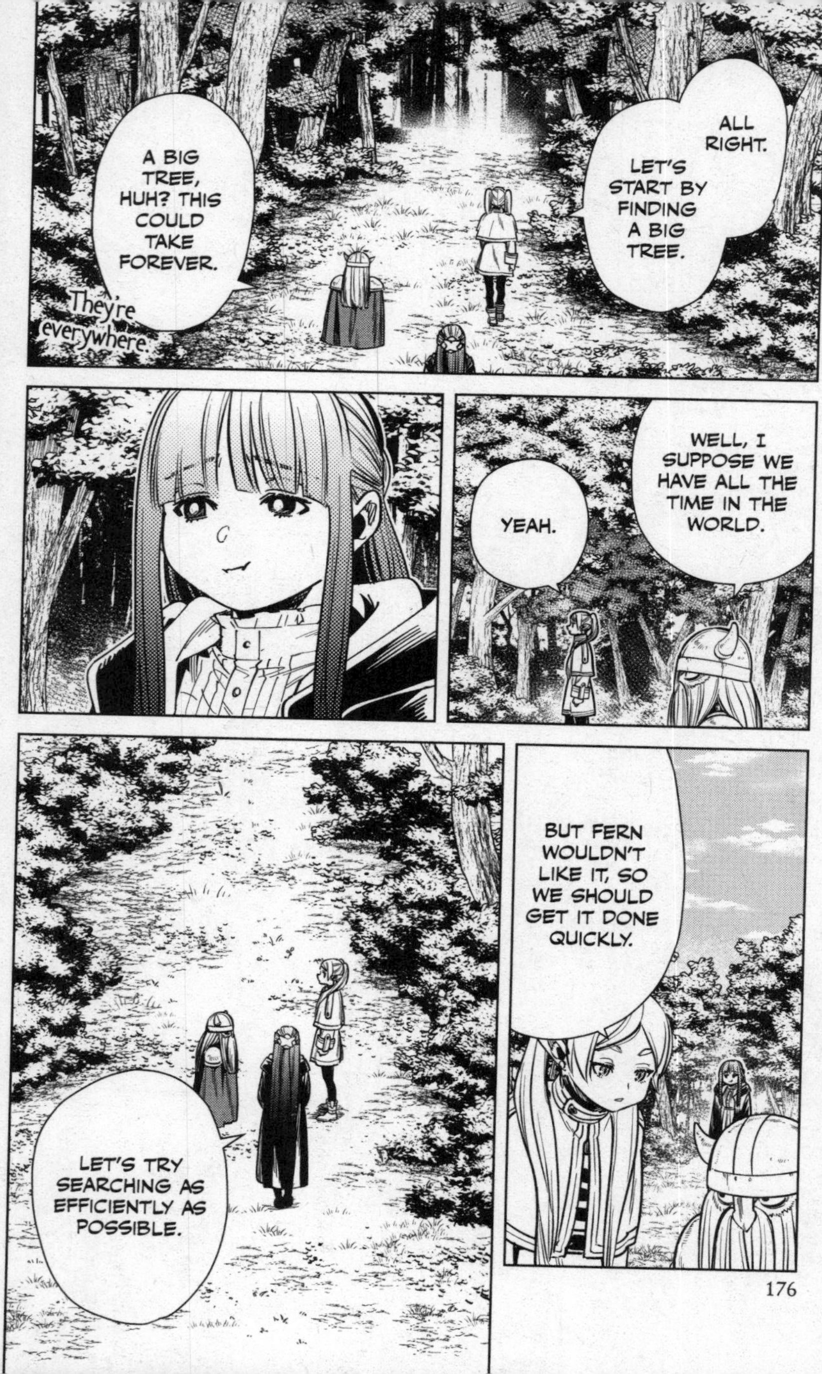
ALL RIGHT.
LET'S START BY FINDING A BIG TREE.
A BIG TREE, HUH? THIS COULD TAKE FOREVER.
They're everywhere.
WELL, I SUPPOSE WE HAVE ALL THE TIME IN THE WORLD.
YEAH.
BUT FERN WOULDN'T LIKE IT, SO WE SHOULD GET IT DONE QUICKLY.
LET'S TRY SEARCHING AS EFFICIENTLY AS POSSIBLE.

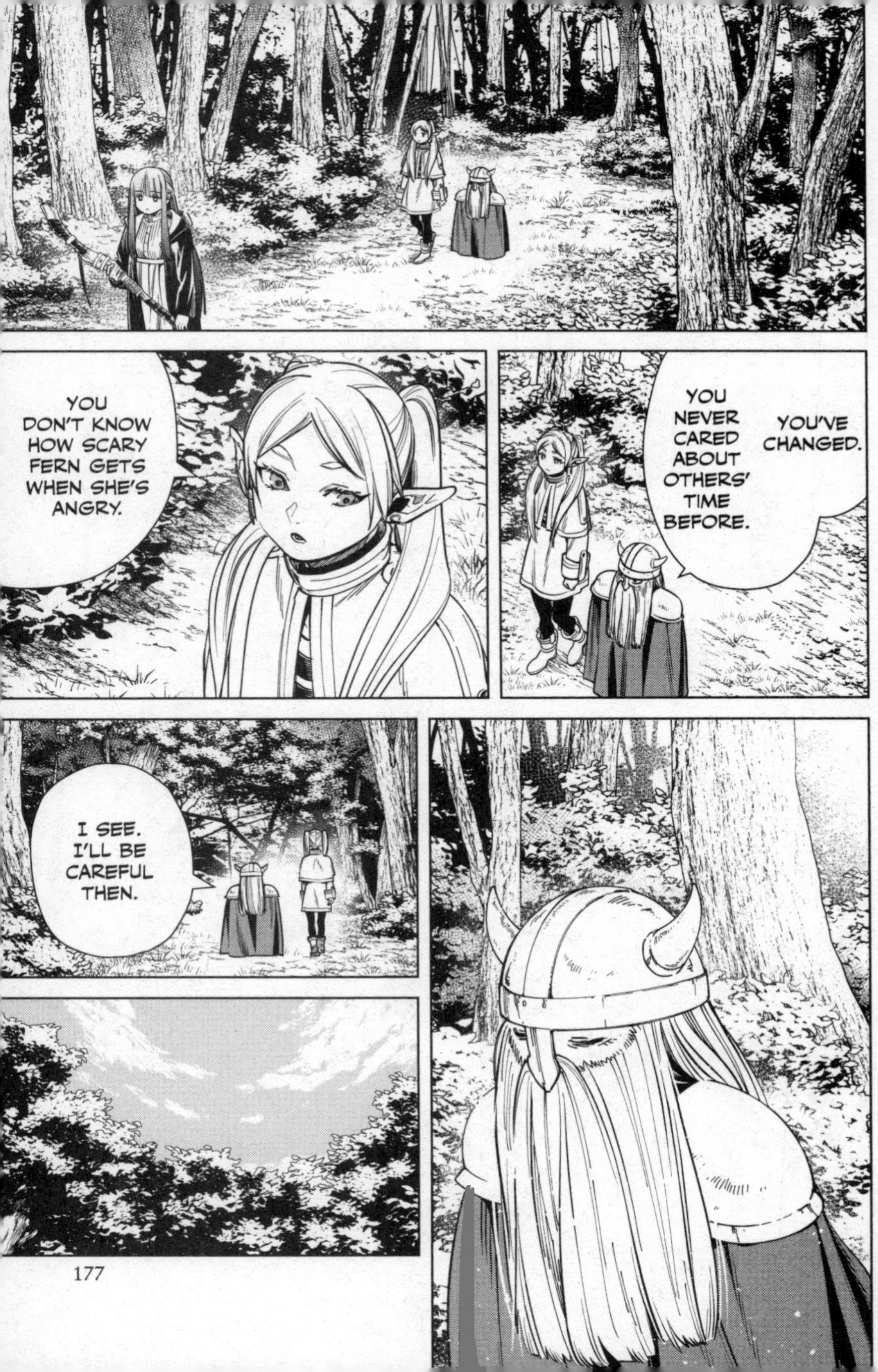
YOU'VE CHANGED.
YOU NEVER CARED ABOUT OTHERS' TIME BEFORE.
YOU DON'T KNOW HOW SCARY FERN GETS WHEN SHE'S ANGRY.
I SEE. I'LL BE CAREFUL THEN.

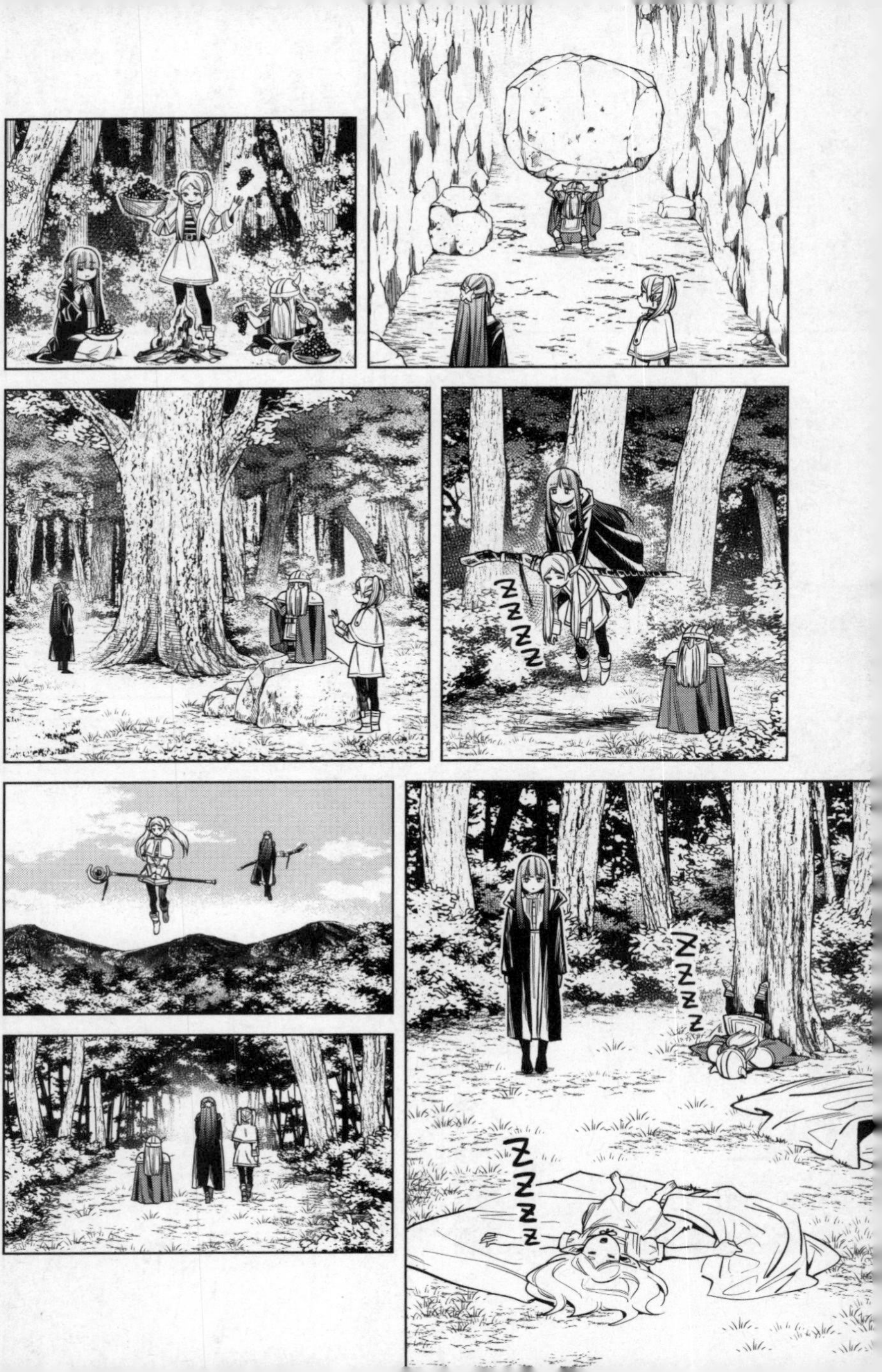
ZZZZ
ZZZZ
ZZZZ

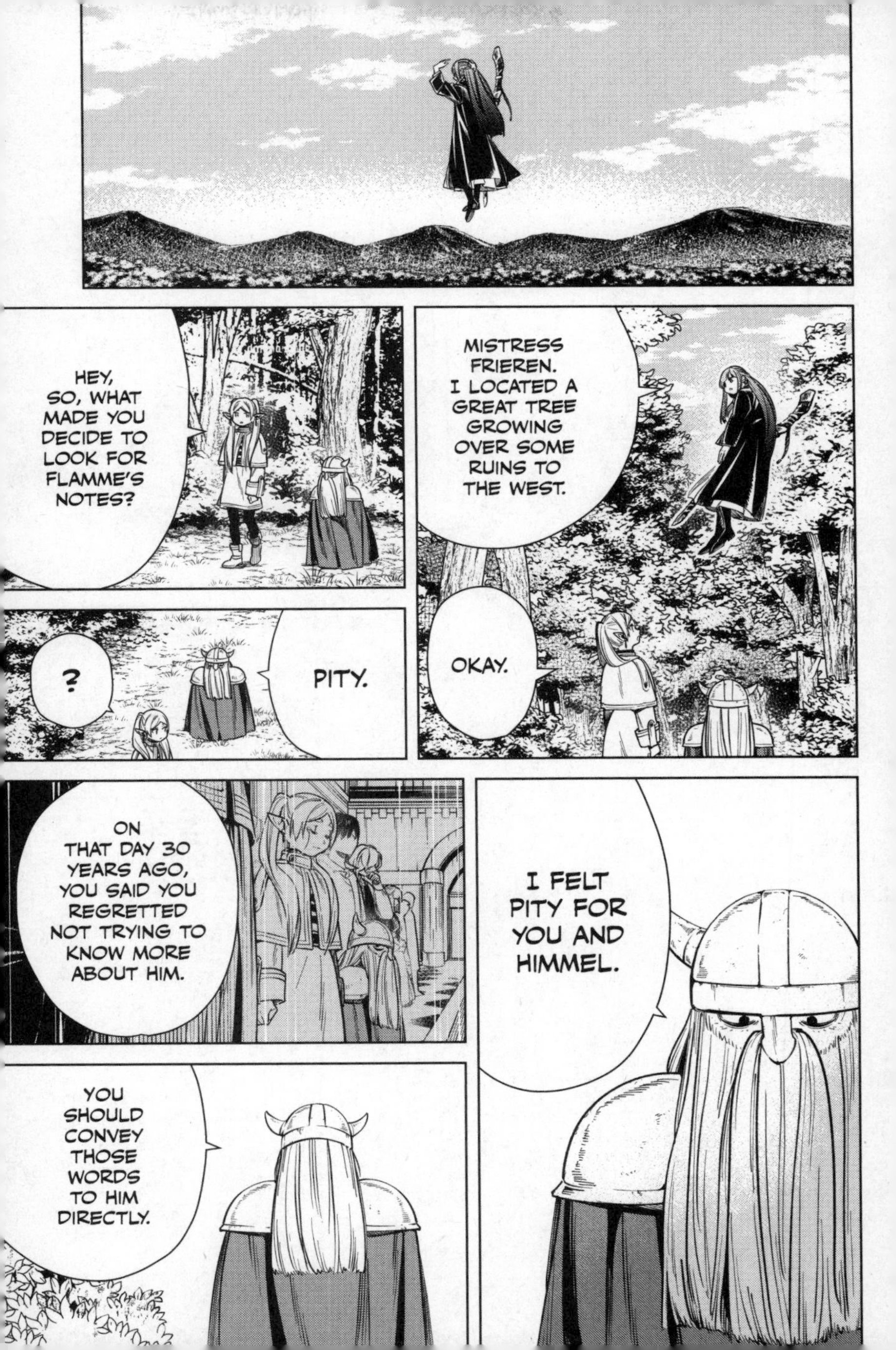
MISTRESS FRIEREN. I LOCATED A GREAT TREE GROWING OVER SOME RUINS TO THE WEST.
OKAY.
HEY, SO, WHAT MADE YOU DECIDE TO LOOK FOR FLAMME'S NOTES?
PITY.
?
I FELT PITY FOR YOU AND HIMMEL.
ON THAT DAY 30 YEARS AGO, YOU SAID YOU REGRETTED NOT TRYING TO KNOW MORE ABOUT HIM.
YOU SHOULD CONVEY THOSE WORDS TO HIM DIRECTLY.

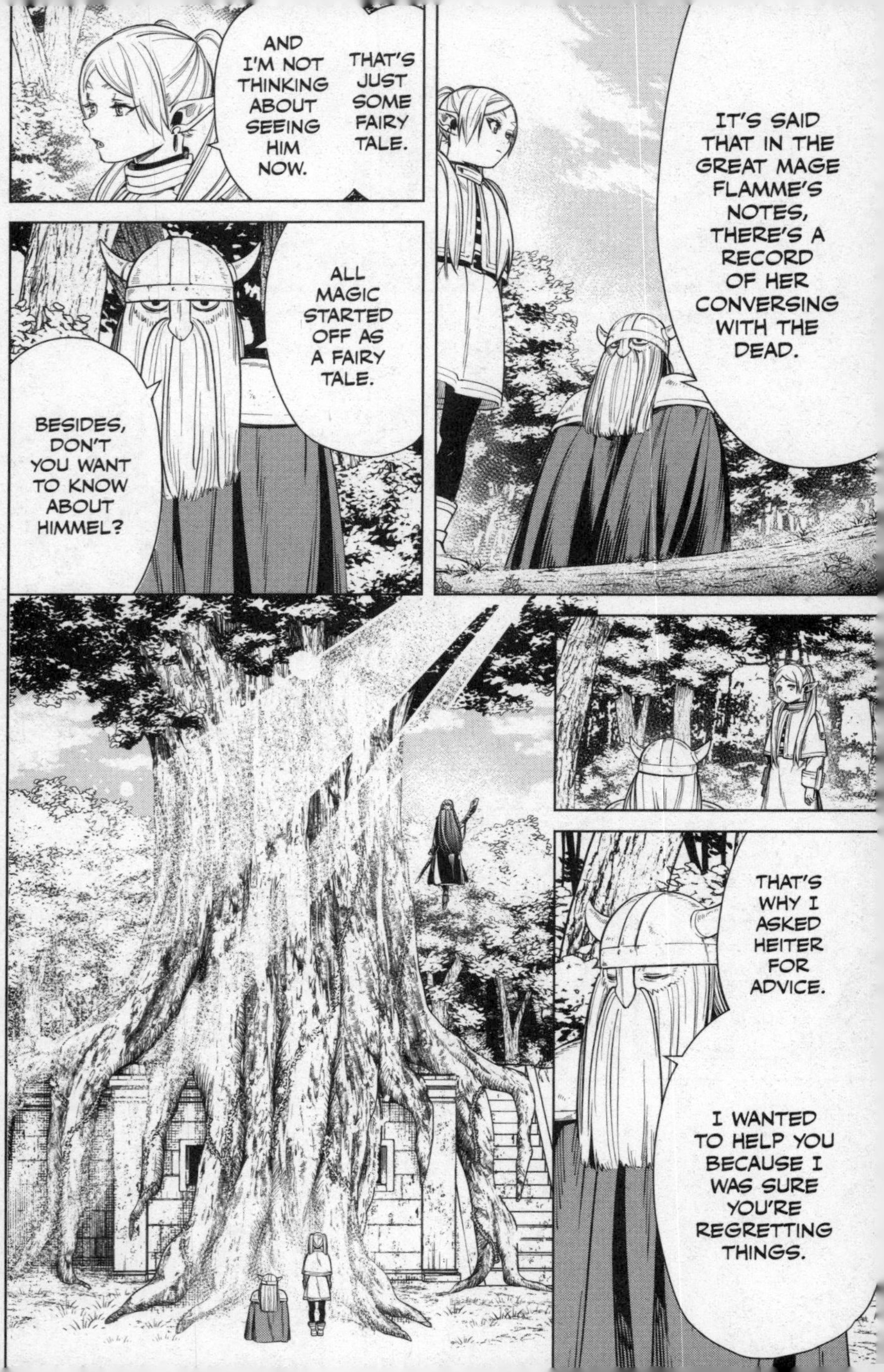
IT'S SAID THAT IN THE GREAT MAGE FLAMME'S NOTES, THERE'S A RECORD OF HER CONVERSING WITH THE DEAD.
THAT'S JUST SOME FAIRY TALE.
AND I'M NOT THINKING ABOUT SEEING HIM NOW.
ALL MAGIC STARTED OFF AS A FAIRY TALE.
BESIDES, DON'T YOU WANT TO KNOW ABOUT HIMMEL?
THAT'S WHY I ASKED HEITER FOR ADVICE.
I WANTED TO HELP YOU BECAUSE I WAS SURE YOU'RE REGRETTING THINGS.

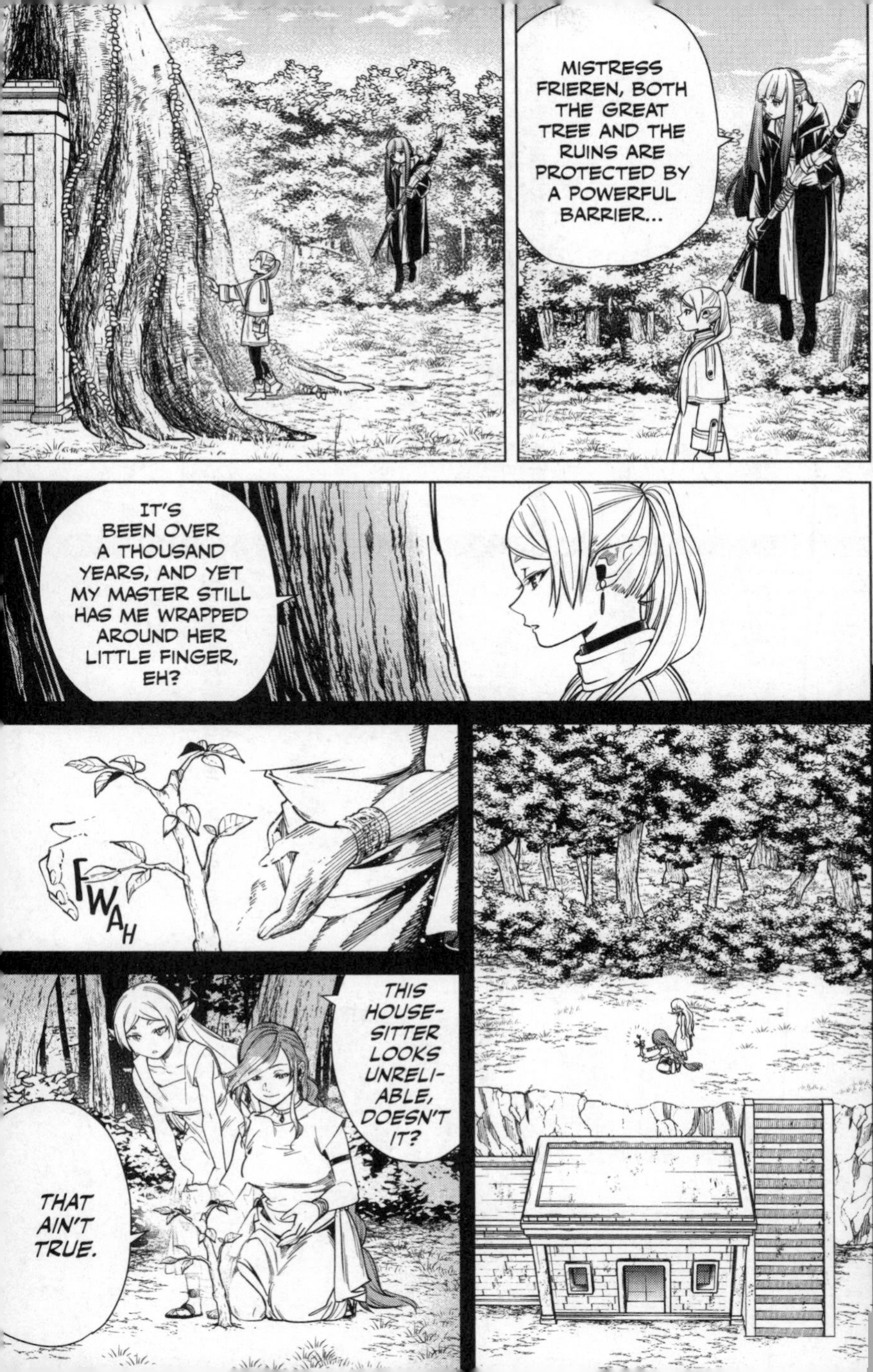
MISTRESS FRIEREN, BOTH THE GREAT TREE AND THE RUINS ARE PROTECTED BY A POWERFUL BARRIER...
IT'S BEEN OVER A THOUSAND YEARS, AND YET MY MASTER STILL HAS ME WRAPPED AROUND HER LITTLE FINGER, EH?
FWAH
THIS HOUSE-SITTER LOOKS UNRELI-ABLE, DOESN'T IT?
THAT AIN'T TRUE.

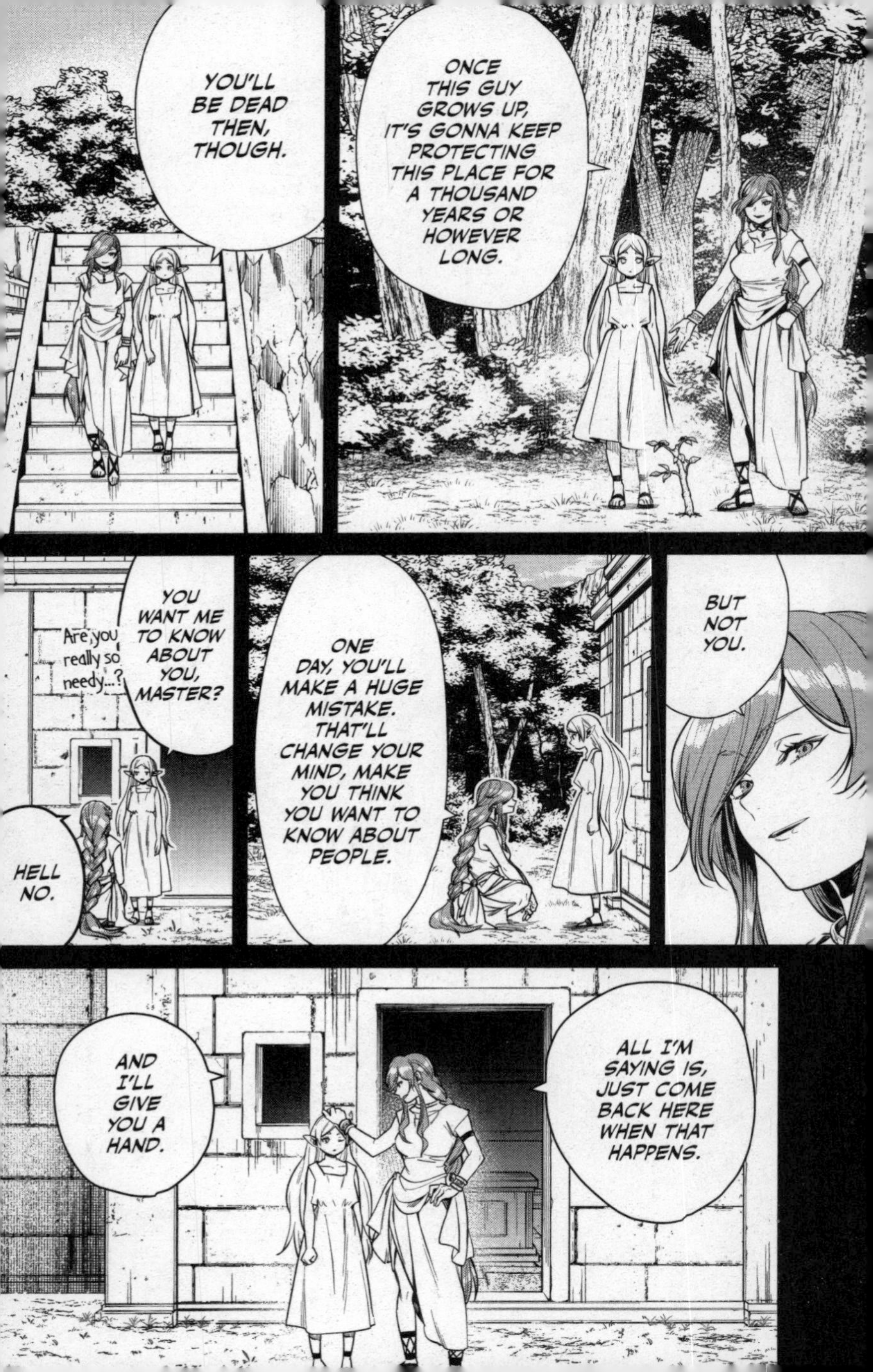
ONCE THIS GUY GROWS UP, IT'S GONNA KEEP PROTECTING THIS PLACE FOR A THOUSAND YEARS OR HOWEVER LONG.
YOU'LL BE DEAD THEN, THOUGH.
BUT NOT YOU.
ONE DAY, YOU'LL MAKE A HUGE MISTAKE. THAT'LL CHANGE YOUR MIND, MAKE YOU THINK YOU WANT TO KNOW ABOUT PEOPLE.
YOU WANT ME TO KNOW ABOUT YOU, MASTER?
Are you really so needy...?
HELL NO.
ALL I'M SAYING IS, JUST COME BACK HERE WHEN THAT HAPPENS.
AND I'LL GIVE YOU A HAND.

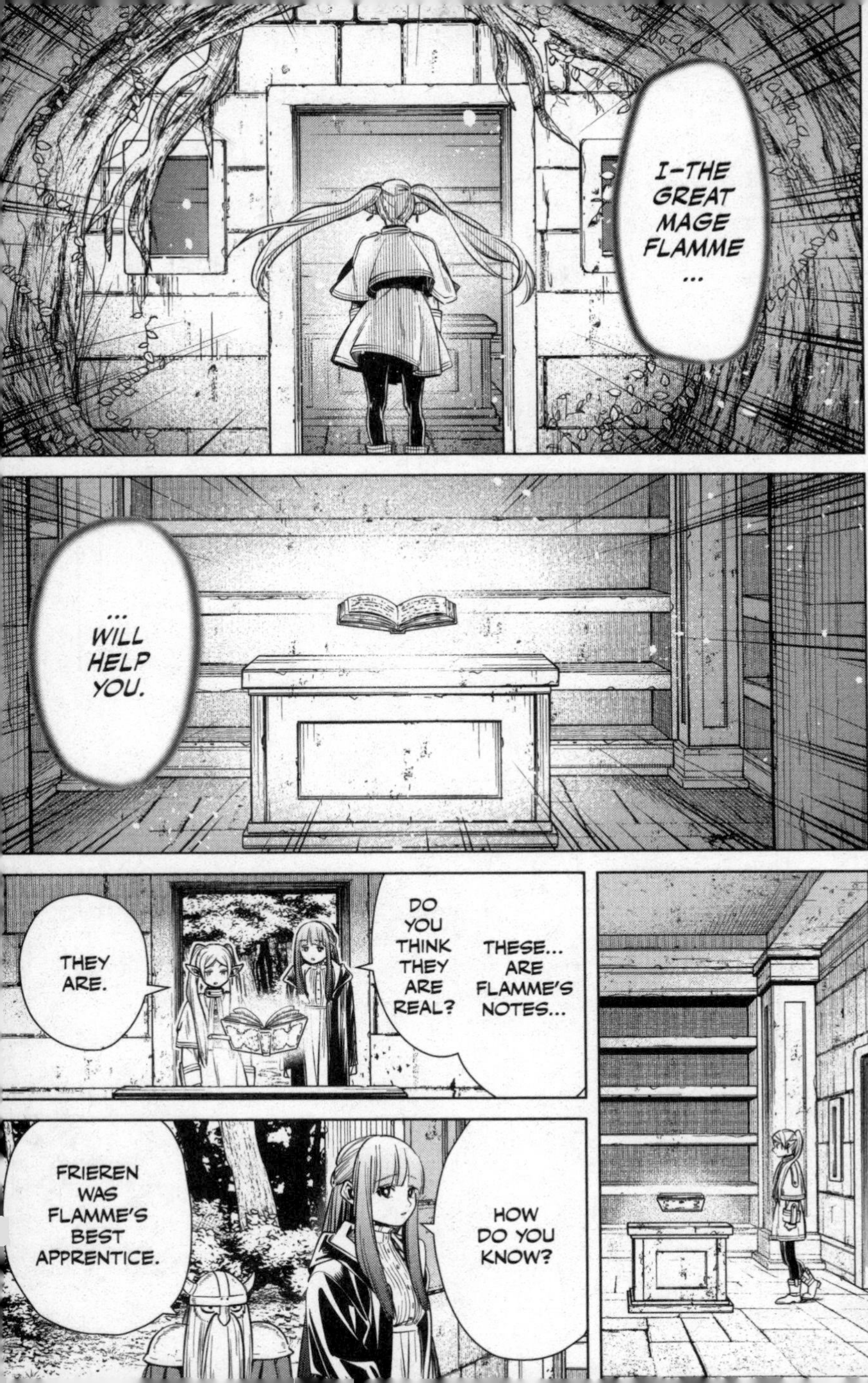
I—THE GREAT MAGE FLAMME ...
... WILL HELP YOU.
THESE... ARE FLAMME'S NOTES...
DO YOU THINK THEY ARE REAL?
THEY ARE.
HOW DO YOU KNOW?
FRIEREN WAS FLAMME'S BEST APPRENTICE.

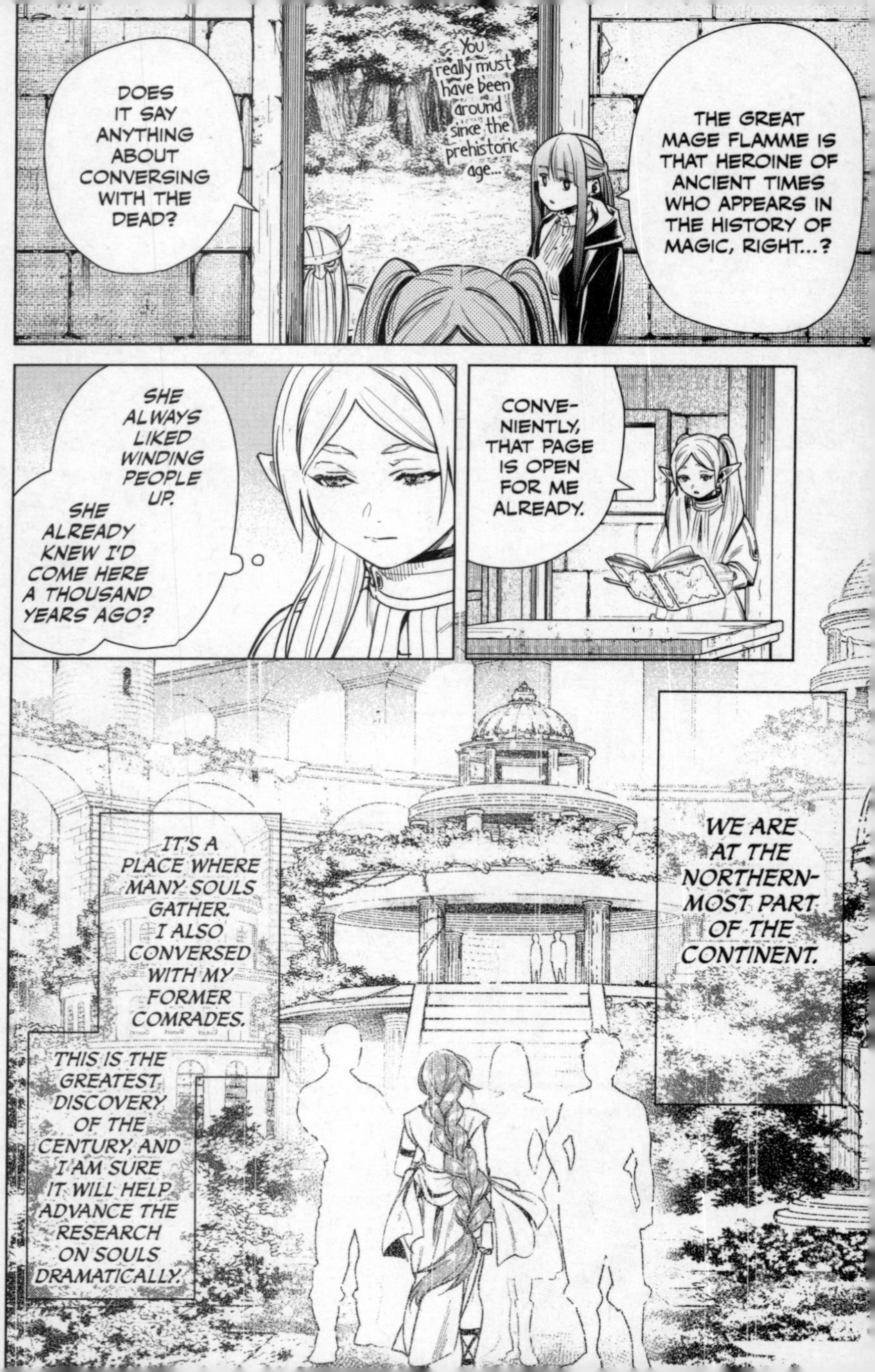
THE GREAT MAGE FLAMME IS THAT HEROINE OF ANCIENT TIMES WHO APPEARS IN THE HISTORY OF MAGIC, RIGHT...?
You really must have been around since the prehistoric age...
DOES IT SAY ANYTHING ABOUT CONVERSING WITH THE DEAD?
CONVE-NIENTLY, THAT PAGE IS OPEN FOR ME ALREADY.
SHE ALWAYS LIKED WINDING PEOPLE UP.
SHE ALREADY KNEW I'D COME HERE A THOUSAND YEARS AGO?
WE ARE AT THE NORTHERN-MOST PART OF THE CONTINENT.
IT'S A PLACE WHERE MANY SOULS GATHER. I ALSO CONVERSED WITH MY FORMER COMRADES.
THIS IS THE GREATEST DISCOVERY OF THE CENTURY, AND I AM SURE IT WILL HELP ADVANCE THE RESEARCH ON SOULS DRAMATICALLY.

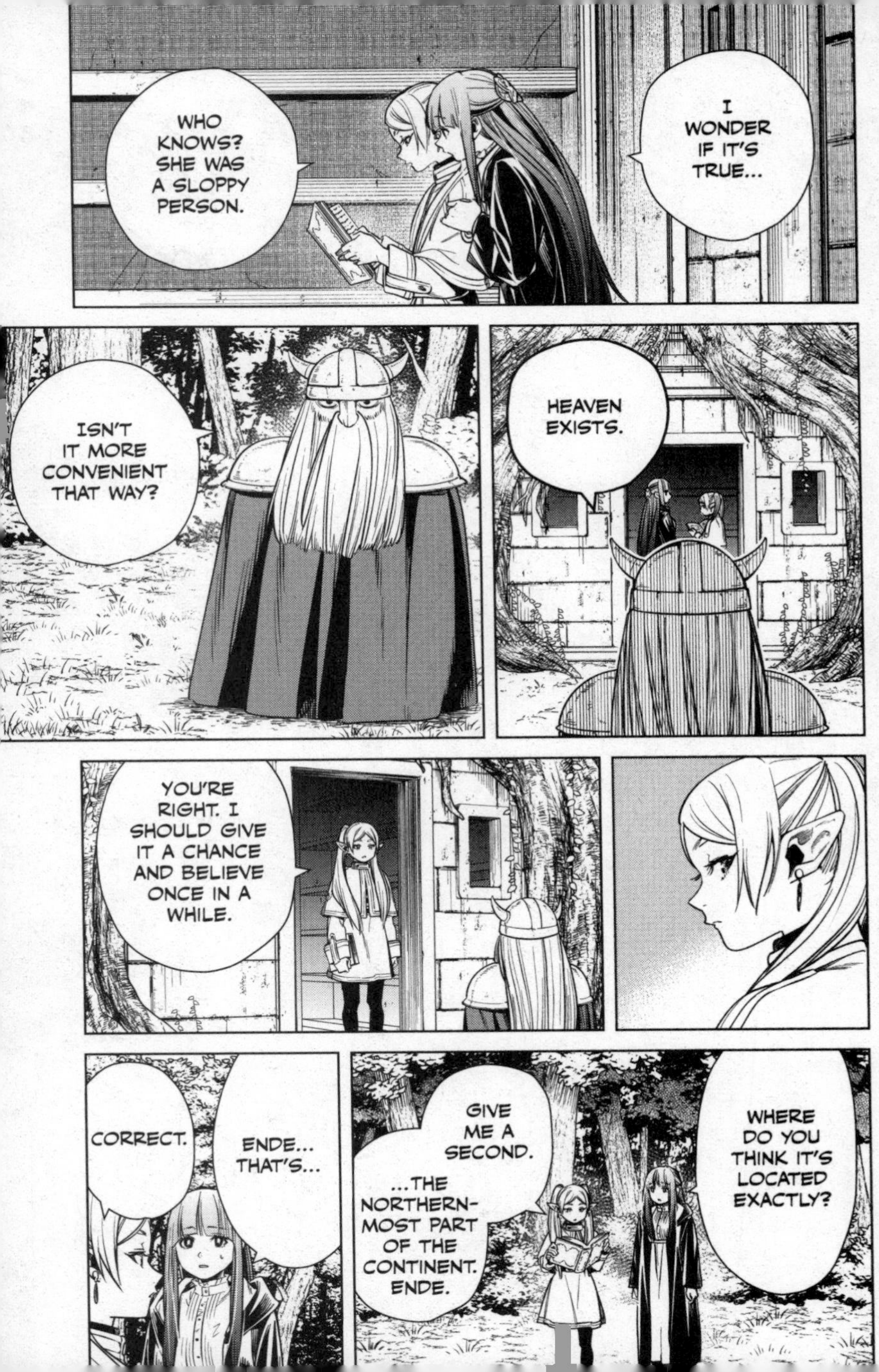
I WONDER IF IT'S TRUE...
WHO KNOWS? SHE WAS A SLOPPY PERSON.
HEAVEN EXISTS.
ISN'T IT MORE CONVENIENT THAT WAY?
YOU'RE RIGHT. I SHOULD GIVE IT A CHANCE AND BELIEVE ONCE IN A WHILE.
WHERE DO YOU THINK IT'S LOCATED EXACTLY?
GIVE ME A SECOND.
...THE NORTHERN-MOST PART OF THE CONTINENT. ENDE.
ENDE... THAT'S...
CORRECT.

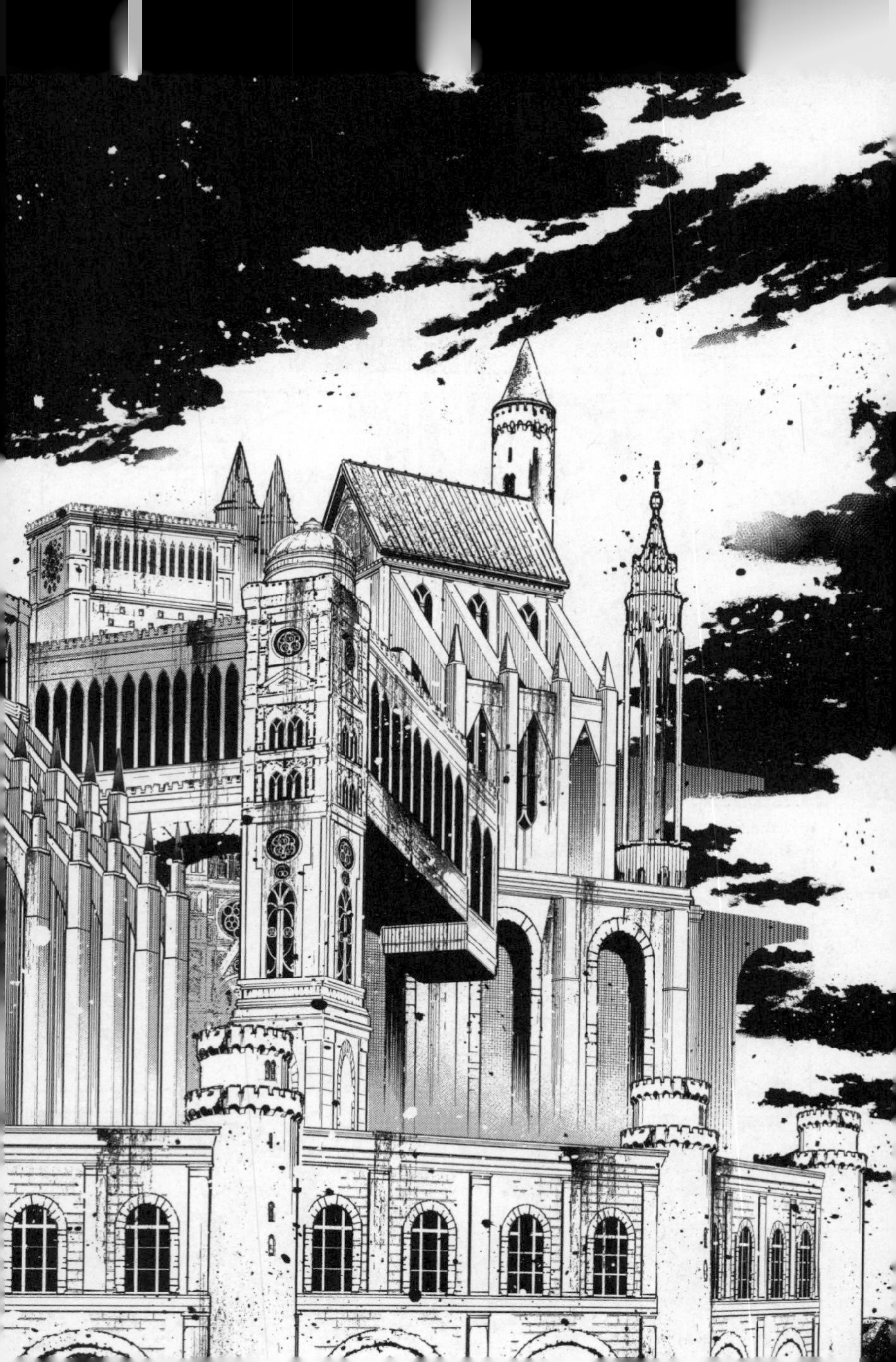

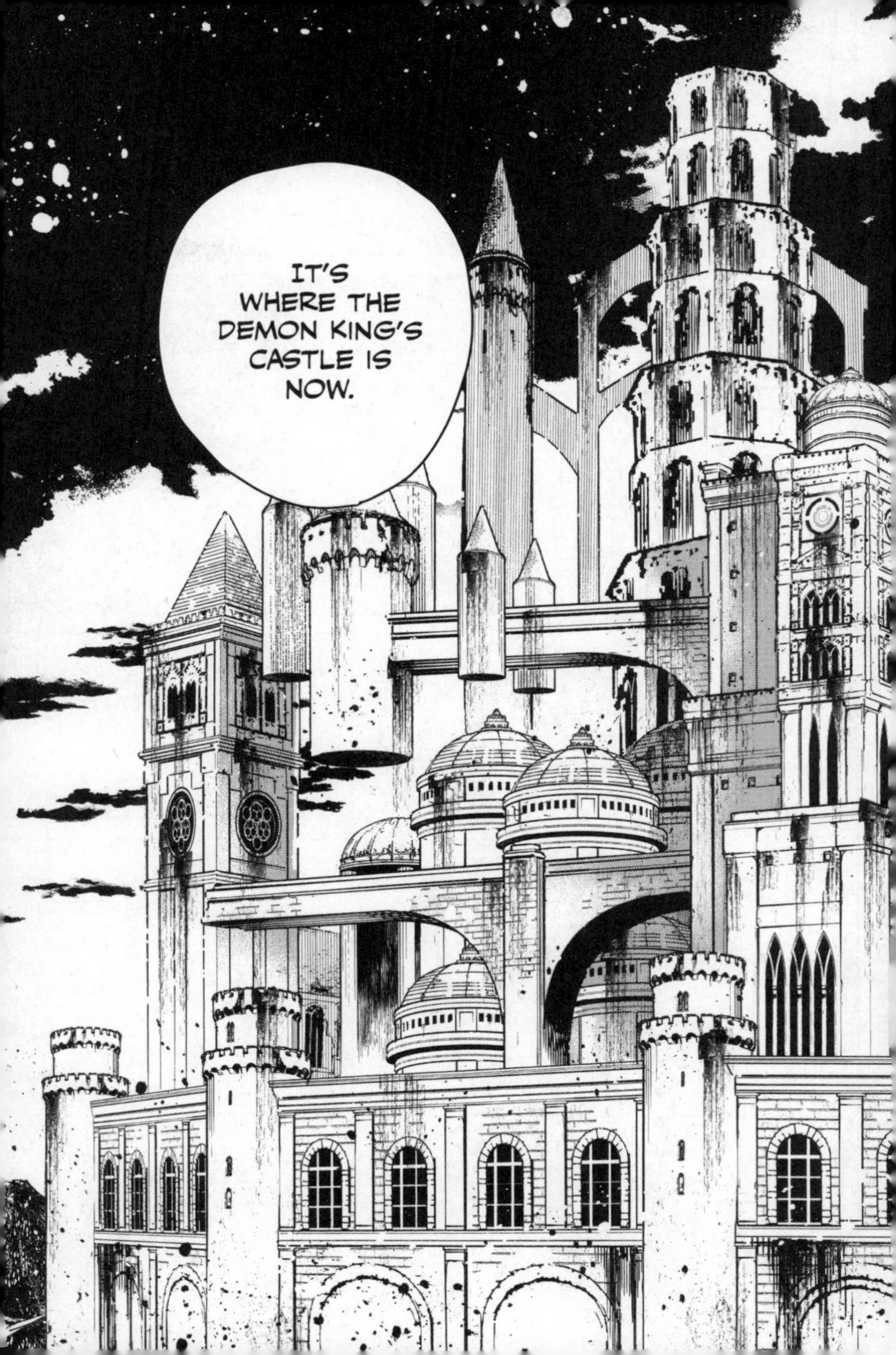
IT'S WHERE THE DEMON KING'S CASTLE IS NOW.

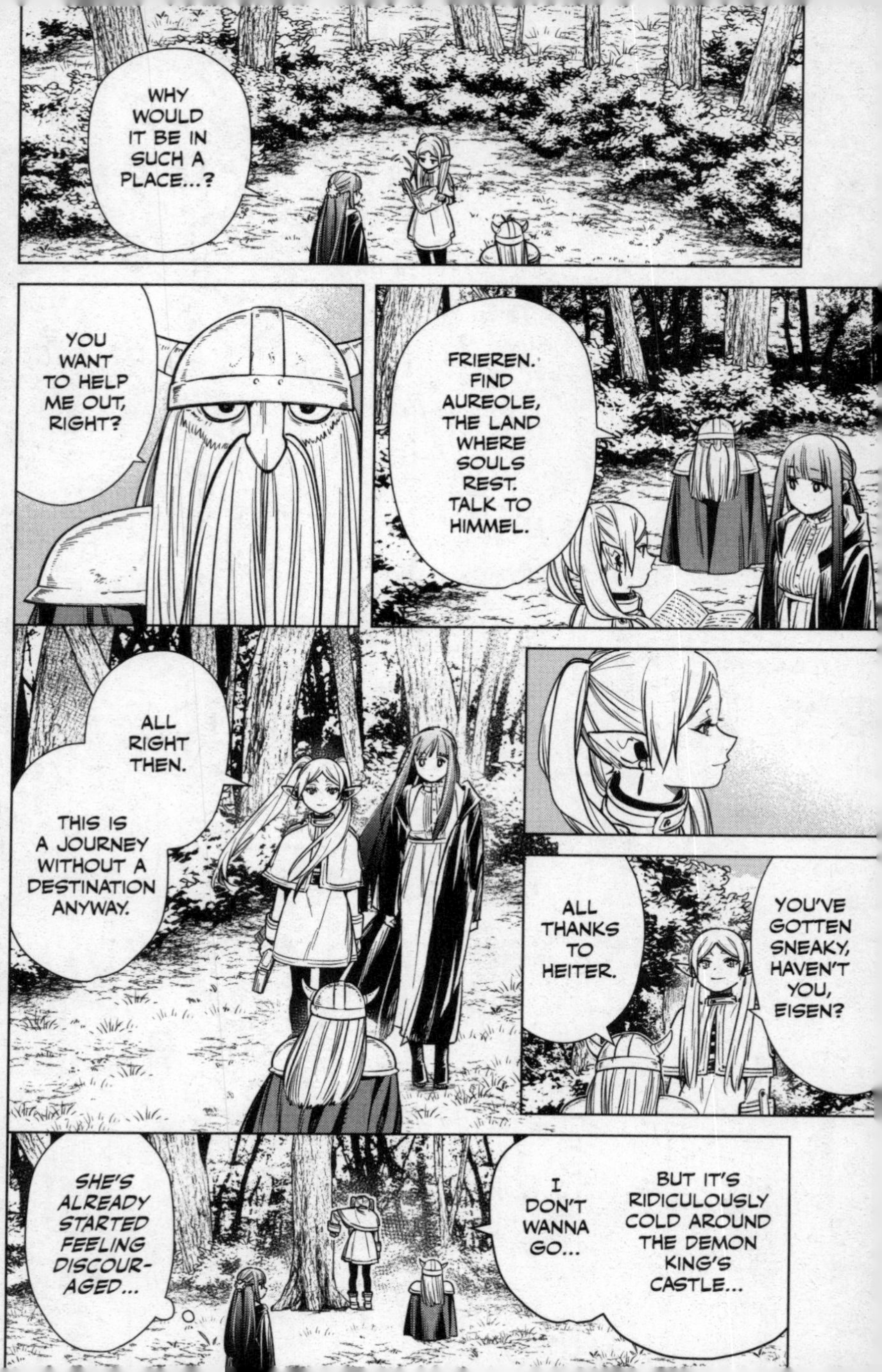
WHY WOULD IT BE IN SUCH A PLACE...?
FRIEREN. FIND AUREOLE, THE LAND WHERE SOULS REST. TALK TO HIMMEL.
YOU WANT TO HELP ME OUT, RIGHT?
YOU'VE GOTTEN SNEAKY, HAVEN'T YOU, EISEN?
ALL THANKS TO HEITER.
ALL RIGHT THEN.
THIS IS A JOURNEY WITHOUT A DESTINATION ANYWAY.
BUT IT'S RIDICULOUSLY COLD AROUND THE DEMON KING'S CASTLE...
I DON'T WANNA GO...
SHE'S ALREADY STARTED FEELING DISCOUR-AGED...

Frieren: Beyond the Journey's End – Vol 1 – End

# Frieren: Beyond Journey's End

VOLUME 1
Shonen Sunday Edition

STORY BY
**KANEHITO YAMADA**

ART BY
**TSUKASA ABE**

SOSO NO FRIEREN Vol. 1
Story by Kanehito YAMADA, Tsukasa ABE
© 2020 Kanehito YAMADA, Tsukasa ABE
All rights reserved.
Original Japanese edition published by SHOGAKUKAN.
English translation rights in the United States of America, Canada,
the United Kingdom, Ireland, Australia and New Zealand arranged
with SHOGAKUKAN.

Original Cover Design: Masato ISHIZAWA + Bay Bridge Studio

Translation/Misa 'Japanese Ammo'
Touch-up Art & Lettering/Annaliese 'Ace' Christman
Design/Yukiko Whitley
Editor/Mike Montesa

The stories, characters, and incidents mentioned in
this publication are entirely fictional.

Printed in the U.S.A.

Published by VIZ Media, LLC
P.O. Box 77010
San Francisco, CA 94107

10 9 8 7 6 5 4 3 2
First printing, November 2021
Second printing, December 2021

**PARENTAL ADVISORY**
FRIEREN: BEYOND JOURNEY'S END is rated
T for Teen and recommended for ages 13 and
up. This volume contains fantasy violence.

viz.com

shonensunday.com

**K**idnapped by the Demon King and imprisoned in his castle, Princess Syalis is...bored.

# SLEEPY PRINCESS IN THE DEMON CASTLE

**Story & Art by**
**KAGIJI KUMANOMATA**

**C**aptured princess Syalis decides to while away her hours in the Demon Castle by sleeping, but getting a good night's rest turns out to be a lot of work! She begins by fashioning a DIY pillow out of the fur of her Teddy Demon guards and an "air mattress" from the magical Shield of the Wind. Things go from bad to worse—for her captors—when some of Princess Syalis's schemes end in her untimely— if temporary—demise and she chooses the Forbidden Grimoire for her bedtime reading...

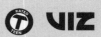